Walter Camp and the Creation of American Football

WALTER CAMP
and the Creation of American Football

ROGER R. TAMTE

UNIVERSITY OF
ILLINOIS PRESS
Urbana, Chicago, and Springfield

Manufactured in the United States of America

c 5 4 3 2 1
∞ This book is printed on acid-free paper.

Library of Congress Cataloging-in-Publication Data
Names: Tamte, Roger R., 1935– author.
Title: Walter Camp and the Creation of American Football / Roger R Tamte.
Description: [Urbana, Illinois] : University of Illinois Press, [2018] | Includes bibliographical references and index.
Identifiers: LCCN 2017042820 | ISBN 9780252041617 (hardback)
Subjects: LCSH: Camp, Walter, 1859–1925. | Football players—United States—Biography. | Football coaches—United States—Biography. | Sportswriters—United States—Biography. | BISAC: SPORTS & RECREATION / Football. | SPORTS & RECREATION / History. | BIOGRAPHY & AUTOBIOGRAPHY / Sports.
Classification: LCC GV939.C34 T36 2018 | DDC 796.332092 [B]—dc23
LC record available at https://lccn.loc.gov/2017042820

E-book ISBN 978-0-252-05027-5

For Gloria,
who makes all the difference

Contents

PART II: GETTING NOTICED

PART III: THE GAME ESTABLISHED

PART IV: WHOSE GAME NOW?

PART V: BIGGER AND . . . ?

Preface

Readers searching for the origins of American football in existing history texts soon come upon large gaps. One recent writer deals with beginnings briefly and colorfully by contending that the game "jumped up out of the mud," primitive and of uncertain origin. A different writer implies that a significant creation process must have occurred to produce American football's unique and superior features—"No other major sport . . . [involves such] complex and delicate strategy," requires of players such a "quick-witted body" and "wide . . . range of specialized functions," is "so American"—but doesn't delve into creation details. Still another observer recognizes invention in the process, marveling without elaboration that American football is "the best team game ever invented."[1]

Always the actual *how* of the creation process is largely missing. When, where, and why did it happen? Who was involved? What were their personal stories, their motivations, struggles, and achievements? Day by day, what steps led to creation—even to novel, nonobvious inventions, for inventions truly were required to bring this game into being.

Great stories await such examination, but most important and interesting is the story of Walter Camp, so clearly the primary actor and leader in American football's creation that his contemporaries called him "the father of American football." Camp was involved in American football from the beginning, starting as a student player in the game's early rugby stage and continuing for the rest of his life. He alone was continuously present in the early years of game development and rule making, loving the game, believing in its value, concerned for its continued existence. There were hurdles to overcome—keeping the game alive in spite of a constantly changing student population, protecting it from powerful critics who called it barbarous and tried to do away with it, overcoming crises by creating new and original game features. At a critical point, Camp accomplished invention, audacious, revolutionary, "game-making" invention, that dumbfounded and alarmed fellow rule makers but quickly became the game's saving foundation.

After college Camp went into business but continued to be involved in sports and football, energetic and almost restless in the multiplicity of his tasks—football rule maker, coach, creator of All-America teams, pioneering book author, prolific media writer (including a weekly sports column for *Collier's*), effective "athletics director" at Yale. All the while, he was rising as an executive at a large, worldwide New Haven clock-manufacturing company to serve for twenty years as the company's chief executive.

In the midst of such sustained activity and success, Camp had his first major football setback, arising from accusations the game was becoming too brutal and deadly. In response, Camp became more forceful and outspoken in advocating a rule change he had unsuccessfully proposed for several years; at the same time, he fought another change that fellow rule makers considered essential, but he feared was too drastic and disruptive of American football's essential character. A vigorous and public battle ensued, one that quickly included even President Theodore Roosevelt, Camp's friend but now convinced of Camp's error. Roosevelt tried to minimize the extent of his participation, almost hiding his role, but it surely was influential and perhaps decisive. In the end, Camp both won and lost: he got his change (today's "four downs to make ten yards"), and his opponents got their change (a start on forward passing). Changes in American football since that early 1900s crisis have been refinements rather than fundamental reconstructions.

Reflecting his personality, Camp remained at peace with his opponents throughout the crisis and continued as part of football's governing and rule-making hierarchy until he died. He continued to edit an annual football guide, name an annual All-America team, and occasionally write on football. The latter sometimes included sharp criticism of what he saw as distorted priorities developing in the college game—too commercialized, with enormous sums spent to develop a winning team and not enough attention given to the physical welfare of the larger student body. Mostly, Camp turned his attention to the physical welfare of the American population as a whole, catalyzed by the high rejection rate of American men as physically unfit for service in World War I. In the course of those efforts, he created a set of exercises he called the "Daily Dozen," popular enough to put *daily dozen* in the dictionary.

Watching his first rugby contest, Camp could not have imagined that a new, distinctively American game would develop and demand his attention, bring out his gifts, and depend on him, mixing his life story into the game's story so deeply that neither can be told apart from the other. Both stories need to be told, enjoyed, examined, and then pondered with a question too long forgotten: What would American football be—would there even be an American football as we know it—without Walter Camp?

Acknowledgments

Good fortune places me near both the University of Minnesota libraries, which became my basic place of research, and the Hennepin County Public Library system, which I also used extensively. Both libraries have broad collections and very helpful staffs, for which I am sincerely grateful.

The most indispensable library was the Yale University Library, Manuscripts and Archives, where the Walter Camp Papers are housed and which is very well staffed and hospitable to research. Over the years, many different staff members helped me, too many to accurately mention, but through the whole of those many years Michael Frost welcomed me, was always there, and went the extra mile many times. Also in New Haven is the Whitney Library of the New Haven Museum where papers of the New Haven Clock Company are stored as well as many other useful historical resources. Again the staff members were very helpful, but I especially relied on Frances Skelton, who had a special ability to locate materials and to respond to questions raised in the research.

I wish I could list all the other many libraries and librarians who helped in preparation of this book, but I would certainly overlook someone for whom I feel great appreciation. I hope all those who helped will consider their contributions to have been appropriately used and to have made a difference in telling this story of Walter Camp and his role in the creation of American football.

I also received important help and encouragement from history professors of the North American Society for Sport History, particularly Professors Ron Smith and John Watterson, who both reviewed some of my writing and sent helpful advice. The attention given the manuscript by the reviewers and editors of the University of Illinois Press, producing extensive and crucially important suggestions and corrections, was also very much appreciated.

The drawing of comparative game balls in chapter 4 was prepared by a longtime colleague, Paul Stenger.

Last, I want to publicly express my thankfulness to my wife, Gloria, who has supported me throughout this project. Though the project lasted much longer than expected, she graciously continued her support with only a few appropriate nudges toward the end that it was time to be done.

Walter Camp and the Creation of American Football

PART I

The Students' Game

Beginnings, Known and Unknown 1

He'd been waiting for weeks, and now the game was about to begin. The teams were lined up, facing each other on a field inside the oval of a harness-racing track in New Haven, Connecticut. Playing boundaries were marked with rough lines of chalk. Goals were formed by stretching ropes between poles. Still a crowd had gathered, undisturbed by field improvisations for this first-ever event. Harvard and Yale were about to compete in football for the first time, Saturday, November 13, 1875, playing Harvard's chosen game, rugby, seldom if ever seen in New Haven.[1]

Instead of rugby, Yale played soccer, the more common American choice of the two rival sports that had evolved side by side in England. Soccer was what he played—Walter Camp, sixteen years old, son of a New Haven elementary school principal, eager game player in an age of growing game enthusiasm. Rugby and soccer were part of that growing enthusiasm—in the past dozen years, rudimentary central organizations for each had developed in London and had promulgated rules, preparing both sports for an extended competition that now reached even into the United States. Just two years earlier, Yale and a few other colleges had formed a U.S. college soccer league with rules having a close kinship to the English game. About the same time, Walter and a few of his high school classmates had formed a student committee and started a school soccer team.[2]

But now came today's game, causing Walter and his friends to step back and wonder. Might Yale like rugby? Could rugby push soccer aside? What would happen to the college soccer league Yale had helped form—or to Walter's high school soccer team?[3]

Today's game was the result of a compromise. Yale had previously invited Harvard to join them in playing soccer, but Harvard's captain wrote a firm refusal, polite and correct, though perhaps a bit smug: Yale "must have seen" that Harvard had a *different* game that was incompatible with Yale's game. Among other differences, that game (developed on Boston sandlots and in preparatory schools) had some ball carrying and tackling.[4]

A year after refusing Yale, Harvard received a new invitation, coming cross-border from McGill College in Montreal. Ball carrying and tackling were included; this invitation was to play rugby brought to Canada a few years earlier by British immigrants and soldiers. Harvard accepted, played McGill, and, in a conversion momentous for American football, decided they liked the rugby game. The idea of a Harvard-Yale game was again raised, and Yale snapped at the opportunity—any chance to play their ancient rival as America's leading college.[5]

Two students from each college met "halfway," at Springfield, Massachusetts, and worked out game rules, which as a gesture to someone they called "Concessionary Rules." In fact, only minor concessions were made, such as using Yale's soccer-type round rubber ball instead of the watermelon-shaped rugby ball.[6]

Walter knew better than most how the game would be played. He was in his senior year at Hopkins Grammar School, adjacent the Yale campus, and occasionally stopped to watch as Yale's football team practiced on a vacant lot near campus. His older cousin was on the team, and other Yale players knew him. He had played several sports as he grew up, wrestling, sandlot baseball, and soccer, and now was playing more organized games at Hopkins—he was a stalwart on Hopkins's soccer team and pitcher on the baseball team. Youthful and lean, Walter was still tough enough for Yale players to invite him to join their practice on a scrub team that opposed the Yale varsity. As game day approached, he helped set up the field for the game.[7]

Now it was time for the game to begin. Of the approximately fifteen hundred gathered to watch, most were standing against ropes that surrounded the field, as close to the action as they could get. Just in front of them, a Yale player kicked off, and play began, with bodies banging, spinning, and rolling, the first time Harvard and Yale bodies had collided so forcefully. The heaving mass of a rugby scrum formed, a barely organized melee with two swarms of players engaging each other, grappling and panting, struggling to kick the ball and force it through the other side with brute strength. Then a wild scramble, sometimes close enough to touch, with players dashing to recover a ball banged out of the scrum, perhaps flinging themselves across the sideline and scattering spectators, other times grabbing the ball and running around scrum-bunched players until caught and thrown down by a defender. No padding was worn; the Yale players were in dark trousers, blue shirts, and yellow caps—ugly "yaller" things, according to the Yale student newspaper, tasseled and cone shaped like a nightcap; the Harvard players wore bright-crimson shirts and stockings with knee breeches.

Walter stood with the crowd, taller than average, slim, arms probably crossed, his longish face still smooth and by nature serious, hopeful for his Yale buddies. But Yale did not do well. Three weeks of practice had not prepared them, had not separated them sufficiently from their old soccer game. They knew they could handle and run with the ball, but their bodies reacted too slowly. Harvard ran away; well-timed laterals left the Yale players grasping. Sometimes Yale players stood and watched, too surprised or puzzled to act.

Within the first five minutes, Harvard kicked the ball across Yale's goal line, and Harvard's Leeds jumped on it for a touchdown by rugby's rules. Only a few minutes later, Seamans of Harvard got the ball in front of Yale's goal and drop-kicked between the posts and over the stretched rope. Yale improved, but by game's end Harvard was credited with four goals (three touchdowns counting as one goal) to none for Yale.[8]

Yet Yale's players and spectators were captivated. "Much more exciting than the old way of playing," exclaimed Yale's student newspaper. Harvard's earlier refusal of Yale's soccer invitation now seemed more understandable—the variety, vigor, and physical clashes of a ball-carrying rugby-type game that had resonated with Harvard players and fans now also resonated at Yale. The Concessionary Rules negotiators had labeled their rules a possible "standard for matches after this year," almost inviting continued rugby-based play. Now Yale at large was prepared to go along, set aside soccer, and give rugby a try.[9]

On such a decision, American football had its beginning. A long road was ahead, but it would lead to America's most popular team sport and, more than that, to profuse sidepieces—high school Fridays, college Saturdays, National Football League (NFL) Sundays . . . bowl games, playoffs, Super Bowls . . . homecoming, football bands, cheerleaders . . . life-changing opportunities, new careers, fulfillment . . . serious injuries, cries of player exploitation, monster commercialization . . . all, and more, the defining parts, delights, downsides, and challenges of a large slice of American life that traces its origin to November 13, 1875, and the events that began that day.[10]

2 Given a New Era

Walter Camp was born April 7, 1859, his father Leverett's thirtieth birthday. Fantastic change had marked Leverett's thirty years, producing a new era vastly different from the past—America's first public railroad was in operation a year after Leverett was born; Samuel Morse's telegraph was conceived two years after that. By the time Walter was born, travel and long-distance communication had been cut from days and weeks to minutes and hours, an incredible revolution among many revolutions bringing change greater than ever before experienced in human society.[1]

For Leverett, the new era brought enlarged career opportunities. Leverett had been born and grown up on farms north of New Haven, the fifth child of Elah and Orit Camp and the eighth generation after the family's American founder, Nicholas Camp, came with wife and child from a farm northeast of London; they had come early, less than twenty years after the Pilgrims. Their English farm was near the village of Nazing, where the earliest known Camp was a "Walter Campe," mentioned in records of the year 1277. In England Nicholas was a yeoman farmer, apparently substantial enough to be named trustee of a Puritan friend's estate with instructions to ensure an education of the friend's son at Cambridge. Nicholas left England not because of poverty, but with a Puritan spirit and expectation of even larger opportunity. By at least 1642, he had established a farm ten miles west of New Haven as part of a settlement that became Milford. From Nicholas on, essentially all successive generations in Leverett's line farmed in Connecticut.[2]

Leverett's opportunity away from the farm came in education. One of Leverett's grandfathers and both his parents had taught part-time in addition to farming, and Leverett's older brother David was teaching and attending teacher-training institutes. Leverett, the youngest child, was not eager to teach, but at age sixteen he was prevailed upon to teach for ten weeks at a small school near his home. The following fall, he taught at a larger school and continued there for three years.[3]

In 1850, when Leverett was twenty-one years old and had been teaching for a few years, a teacher-training "normal" school—only the fifth such school in the United States—opened in New Britain, about ten miles north of the Camp farm. Leverett's brother David became a teacher at the school. Leverett enrolled and continued to graduation in 1851.[4]

Before normal school, Leverett taught for twenty dollars per month plus board; after normal school he was hired by New London, Connecticut, at a salary of seven hundred dollars per year. That would support a wife, and Leverett had met the right girl—Ellen Sophia Cornwell, a fellow student at the normal school who had graduated with Leverett. Since graduation Ellen had taught in the New Britain high school; in a private school at Plymouth Hollow, Connecticut; and at a summertime grammar school in New Britain. She left the last job early for health reasons (ill health had also kept her from school for two years during adolescence). Ellen's father, Chauncey Cornwell, was a manufacturer of brass goods in New Britain and, like Leverett's father, Elah, was a "deacon" in the Congregational church, a formal named position by which each might be addressed in church and about town.[5]

Ellen and Leverett were married October 20, 1853, when Leverett was twenty-four and Ellen twenty. Leverett became principal of a grammar school in New London in 1857 and a year later in Norwalk, Connecticut, a growing town near New York City.[6]

Ellen had given up teaching and, about the time of their move to Norwalk, became pregnant with Walter. She decided to go home to New Britain for the delivery, and Walter Chauncey Camp was born there as spring began in 1859. He would be Leverett and Ellen's only child. His middle name, "Chauncey," the name of Ellen's father, was also the name of respected leaders in the early Puritan community.[7]

Leverett continued in Norwalk until August 1860, when he moved to Meriden, his hometown. The stated purpose was to farm, but there may also have been another purpose. Leverett's father, Elah, had made a shrewd investment in 1843 when he bought a farm adjacent to the town of Meriden and moved there with his family. By the 1860s, Meriden was growing, and Elah decided to sell portions of the farm as Meriden building lots. At least part of the property was apparently distributed among Elah's children, and real estate records show Leverett as selling some lots. By 1906 one-fifth of the town of Meriden was occupied by lots from Elah's farm.[8]

Leverett and family lived in Meriden for less than two years. In 1862 Leverett became a teacher at an elementary school in New Haven, a choice assignment in a leading city zealous for education. New Haven also illustrated the urbanization transforming America. From a population of ten thousand in 1830, the city had grown to forty thousand when Leverett and his family arrived in 1862. Numerous factories made New Haven a leader in carriage manufacture, springs, clocks, rubber boots, and hardware.[9]

In 1864 Leverett was promoted to principal of a newly built prime elementary school, Dwight School, named for a famous Yale president and within walking distance of the Yale campus.[10]

Leverett first rented a house away from central New Haven, but in 1866 he purchased closer to downtown, 595 Chapel Street, in an area of well-kept houses. The brother of the former governor of Connecticut lived a few doors around the corner, and the mansion of a New Haven entrepreneur was two doors away.[11]

The Camps' home was much more modest, a wood-frame building, but large enough to rent rooms to teachers from Leverett's Dwight School. More income came from a large duplex nearer Dwight School, which Leverett purchased with Timothy W. Stanley, husband of Jane Cornwell, Ellen's oldest sister. Stanley was prominent in the Stanley Rule and Measure Company of New Britain, a predecessor of today's Stanley Tools, and had enough money to help Leverett in a property investment that would produce rental income.[12]

Another sister of Ellen's, Elizabeth, lived in New Haven with her husband, Henry Peck. Henry Peck was from New Britain and with his father, Elnathan, had moved their fledgling plumbing-supply business to New Haven about the same time that Leverett, Ellen, and Walter moved there. Leverett helped the Peck business with a loan soon after their move. Apparently, in 1876 Leverett remodeled his house into a duplex, so Ellen's sister Elizabeth and Henry could move into half of the house; one wonders whether Ellen, with a history of sickness in earlier years, needed her sister nearby. In any event, Leverett and Ellen shared a duplex with Henry and Elizabeth the rest of Ellen's life, moving in 1882 to the larger duplex near Dwight School Leverett had earlier bought with Timothy Stanley, at the corner of Chapel and Gill.[13]

In the Pecks and Stanleys, Leverett was rubbing shoulders with quintessential Connecticut Yankee entrepreneurs, whom he emulated with real estate investments, room rentals, and later a side job as treasurer of a schoolbook publisher. Leverett's mix of scholarship and business interest seemed a family trait: his older brother David was both scholar (principal of the New Britain normal school and superintendent of education for Connecticut; author of articles and books, including a definitive history of New Britain; recipient of an honorary master's degree from Yale) and later a businessman (president of hardware and printing companies and director and vice president of the New Britain National Bank). Walter's older cousin Charles Camp, from the 1875

Walter Camp as an adolescent. (Walter Chauncey Camp Papers, 1870–1983 [inclusive], 1870–1925 [bulk], Manuscripts and Archives, Yale University)

Yale football team (son of Leverett's brother Alfred, who lived in Meriden), was another family scholar and would be valedictorian of his class at Yale.[14]

The Pecks, Stanleys, and Camps also had church associations. Chauncey Cornwell, father of Ellen Camp, Elizabeth Peck, and Jane Stanley, was deacon of the First Congregational Church of New Britain and led the formation of a daughter church, the "South Church," in which the Pecks and Stanleys participated. In 1873, when a new Congregational church was organized and built near Dwight School in New Haven, "the Dwight Place Church," Leverett Camp was named to a primary management committee of the church.[15]

Walter grew up in a house well populated with women: a young Irish maid, one or two female teachers from Dwight School boarding with the Camps, and his mother, Ellen ("a gentle soul," according to the editor of the local newspaper, from whom Walter "derived . . . patience and poise"). But boys' activities abounded outside the house, which was only half a block

David Nelson Camp, Walter Camp's uncle—scholar, writer, and businessman. In its first volume in 1904, a major Connecticut encyclopedia included biographical entries for both David and Walter. (*Men of Mark in Connecticut*, vol. 1, Minnesota Historical Society, St. Paul)

from a large tree-filled park and three blocks from the New Haven harbor: Walter later said that growing up, he was on the water every summer for a dozen years. There were other children in the neighborhood and a vacant lot here and there for games.[16]

Although other elementary schools were closer, Walter attended Dwight School, where his father was principal. A horsecar passed in front of the house bound in the direction of Dwight School, convenient for a group that might set out in the morning—Leverett, one or two teachers boarding at the Camps, Walter, and perhaps other students from the neighborhood. It could also be a cold and dangerous ride; one January morning, a New Haven horsecar driver who had been en route for some time got off to walk and warm his frozen feet; reaching a corner, he tried to guide the horse from the side, but slipped between the wheels and the track and was killed.[17]

The principal's son was a good and diligent student—seven years without an absence when he completed elementary school in 1870. For Walter's continued education, even public school administrators recommended a private high school such as the local Hopkins Grammar School, "well known to be one of the very best schools in the land" for college-bound students.[18]

Walter was bound for college, and the Camps chose Hopkins, a school that prided itself as among the educationally elite but also a school where

Walter would rub shoulders with an economic elite—his classmates would include the sons of New York merchants and a cofounder of Standard Oil. Leverett and Ellen were not in the economic class of many Hopkins parents, but in addition to income from his inherited Meriden real estate, Leverett's salary in 1870 was $2,000 (female teachers boarding with the Camps were paid about $650 per year, and the average annual earnings of a manufacturing worker in 1870 were $384). Leverett could well afford Hopkins's costs.[19]

While the new era brought Leverett expanded vocational opportunities, it brought Walter a steadily expanding world of athletic games, illustrated by two milestones that coincided in the year 1845: in 1845 the first known written rules for the game that would become American baseball were published by the Knickerbocker Club of New York, and in that same year the first known written rules for football were published in England by student leaders from the Rugby public school. Having evolved on Rugby School's playing fields, the game of rugby was now beginning to appear on other fields, facilitated by railroad service introduced to the town of Rugby in 1838.[20]

With kicking-only football games also developing in England, the conflict between rugby and kicking-only rules frustrated teams that wanted to play each other. In 1863 several rugby and kicking-only clubs formed a "Football Association" in London to merge their game rules, but the merger effort failed and the Football Association went on to focus on a kicking-only game that was soon called soccer. Formal organization came to rugby in 1871 with the Rugby Football Union (RFU), formed just four years before Harvard and Yale played their first rugby-based game.[21]

Both rugby and soccer spread out of England, mainly through emigration or the temporary residence in other countries of English businessmen or English troops. At the outbreak of the U.S. Civil War, Britain deployed additional troops to Canada, and games of rugby were played in Montreal between military garrisons and Montreal citizens, including at McGill College. From there, just a few years later, it would be a short journey to colleges in the United States.[22]

Baseball had been played at Hopkins Grammar School for a few years when Walter enrolled, but in 1873, when he was fourteen years old and in the ninth grade, it became more formally organized with uniforms and student financial support. Walter was eager to be involved and hung around the team, helping as a kind of ballboy.[23]

He dreamed of the day he could play, but as he looked in the mirror he saw an "under-muscled and gawky" body, which he set about to change. Physical training was increasing in America, partially in response to an increasingly desk-confined and sedentary lifestyle brought by urbanization. Colleges began building gymnasiums, and Yale built one in 1859.[24]

The Hopkins school was practically across the street from Yale, and Walter was occasionally given a ticket to enter the Yale gym. There he came upon what he later recalled as a "wonder world," where the Yale rowing crew, men who "seemed to be giants," practiced and built their bodies with weights hung over a pulley or suspended from a handlebar. Trapezes and climbing ropes hung from the twenty-five-foot ceiling, and climbing bars, buck horses, and springboards were distributed across the floor. Among these "giants," Walter found his heroes as he worked to improve his own body.[25]

In between his chances at the Yale gym, Walter worked out at home, where routines could include dumbbells, other small weights, and Indian clubs (beautifully decorated, elongated bowling-pin-shaped clubs originally brought from India and adapted for intricate swinging exercises that developed particular muscles). He was serious about building his body for athletics; he later argued that a boy's first admiration was physical prowess, more than mental expertise or moral commitment.[26]

Walter also played games. He was a leader in gathering friends and heading for a vacant lot to play baseball and the soccer-type football seen around New Haven. He thrived on the challenge of mastering a technique, of repeatedly working on a skill until he could do it well and succeed in competition. He owned a round black rubber ball, and after his playmates had gone home, he stayed to practice, learning to kick for distance and accuracy.[27]

His practice paid off. He was one of the best soccer players at Hopkins and the pitcher on the baseball team. Baseball rules still specified straight-armed pitching below the waist, but one local newspaper writer claimed Walter could "make a ball curve five times before reaching the striker." On occasion the team traveled out of town, giving Walter exposure to playing before a strange crowd.[28]

Walter participated in other activities at Hopkins, including writing for the student newspaper, the *Critic*, and serving on its editorial staff; if asked about a career, he would say he wanted to be a writer. An article undoubtedly written by Camp and published in the *Critic* early in his senior year elaborates on the "giant" theme discussed above that had come to him in the Yale gymnasium. But now there was a different perspective. Now Camp challenged himself and his fellow seniors to be giants—but not just physical giants: "Let us strive while we may, not only to preserve the ancient honor and glory of [Hopkins Grammar School], but also . . . so that those who succeed us, admiring our example and our achievements, shall exclaim: 'In those days there were giants.'" Serious words from a high school student conscious in some degree of social responsibility and mission. He was a good student, ranking seventh in a class of thirty-eight when he graduated in the spring of 1876.[29]

Officially Under Way 3

Tossing and turning the night of November 17, 1876, Walter Camp wondered if other players were having trouble sleeping. Harvard's football team was in town, ready for the next day's second-ever Harvard-Yale football game, and Walter would be playing. Having enrolled at Yale in the fall, he had been one of two freshmen chosen for the team. Walter couldn't help wondering how the game would go—how would Yale do; how would he do? When he did doze off, he dreamed the game was under way and he was struggling in "some impossible run or tackle."[1]

Walter's disturbed sleep was understandable, especially because Harvard and Yale had the oldest and foremost college rivalry in America, competing over how many college presidents they had produced, how many government notables, how many recognized scholars on their staffs, how big their libraries, now adding a major athletic competition to that rivalry. As to the next day's game, most Yale backers were worried, reconciled to a certain loss. Since soundly defeating Yale the previous fall, Harvard had won three additional games against Canadian teams: an all-Canada team of select players on the Harvard campus on May 8, 1876, and another all-Canada team as well as McGill College two weeks earlier in Canada. The *Yale Courant* summarized for the whole community, "We can scarcely hope that our players can make any respectable showing."[2]

Eugene Baker, a senior from Wilbraham, Massachusetts, had been elected Yale captain and had selected the players, mostly from Yale's rowing crew and baseball team. Walter Camp was an exception; Baker knew him from the previous year, liked his conscientious effort and running speed, and especially admired his careful, out-of-the-ordinary study of the rugby rules. In fact, Baker valued Walter's understanding of rugby rules enough to bring him along when he met with Harvard to negotiate the rules for this second game. In those negotiations, Baker successfully required eleven men per side in contrast to the fifteen of the last year's game. Playing on Yale's soccer team in 1873 against an Eton team, eleven men per side, Baker had liked the freedom and room for action that eleven allowed.[3]

Walter's cousin Charles Camp, a senior like Baker, was still on the team. Otherwise, Walter's friendships may have been somewhat limited in his first months at the school because he was living at home; a few freshmen lived on campus, but most rented rooms off campus, which the Camps apparently considered an unnecessary expense.[4]

Baker drove the team's training. Afternoons, they practiced on a vacant corner lot, narrow and bounded by a picket fence on one side and a cement curb on the other; Camp later claimed his body still had scars from that curb. Forty or fifty Yale students usually wandered over to watch and provide practice opposition. But afternoon practice was not enough for Baker. At nine the team ran three miles in the gymnasium; Baker's enthusiasm kept them at it. The Camp home was more than a mile from campus, so it was late when Walter reached home at night, where he "would drop down on the bed, kick off my shoes, pull a blanket over me and fall asleep, to know nothing until morning."[5]

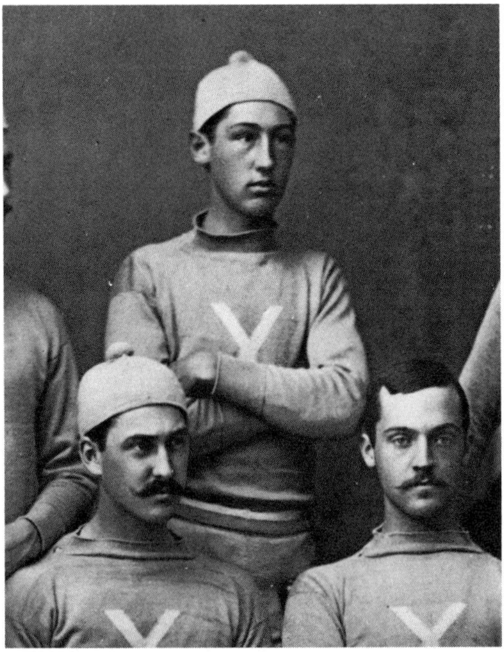

Walter Camp, freshman member of the 1876 Yale football team. (Yale athletics photographs, ca. 1850–2007 [inclusive], Manuscripts and Archives, Yale University)

A high wind and overcast sky threatened rain when Walter rose from his fitful pregame night and headed for school. But rain never came, and by two thirty nearly three thousand spectators were around the racing-track infield at Hamilton Park. The Yale team rode out in an open wagon, bumping and rattling along, quiet and pondering until they were near the gated park entrance. Then Baker began to encourage them. "Open up hard and we ought to win," he claimed.[6]

Having lost the toss, Baker kicked off, but the Harvard receiver had run only a few steps when he was hit hard by a Yale tackler. Yale stayed aggressive, and within ten minutes differences between the two teams were clear: Harvard, more systematic and skillful, passed the ball quickly to leave Yale players a step too late; Yale, harder tacklers, in better condition, were stiffer when the teams clashed in a scrum.[7]

During the first half, Harvard made two touchdowns, but under rugby rules a touchdown was simply the condition that allowed a try at a kicked goal; only a successful goal (kicked from a point in line with the spot the ball crossed the goal line) would count in determining the game's winner. For both Harvard touchdowns, Yale forced the Harvard runner to cross the goal line near the side of the field, and from that sharp angle the Harvard kicker missed the first kick and didn't even try the second. The half ended without a score.[8]

A while into the second half, after Yale had managed to force the ball toward Harvard's goal, Baker secretly signaled. As soon as possible, a Yale player kicked the ball toward Oliver Thompson, Yale's best athlete and probably the best athlete on the field. The ball bounded along, bouncing up nearly a foot off the ground when it reached Thompson. Striding forward, he kicked, hitting the ball squarely, but with his shin. Still the ball carried toward Harvard's goalposts, arching up before coming down as it neared the crossbar—and clearing it by a foot![9] The crowd rushed onto the field, cheering and yelling as if the game were over and won. Harvard tried to start playing, but the referee called them back for several minutes until the field was cleared.

Harvard was newly energized, again pushing the ball toward Yale's goal. Time had nearly expired when Harvard got the ball across for another touchdown. Hurriedly, they set up to kick a goal; time didn't stop for a kick, and the referee had warned that time was practically expired. Nervous and under pressure, the kick was missed. The game was over and Harvard defeated. What seemed impossible had happened.[10]

An early American football game, painted by famed western artist Frederic Remington, who played on Walter Camp's 1879 football team. (Yale athletics photographs, ca. 1850–2007 [inclusive], Manuscripts and Archives, Yale University)

It could be called a fluky win. Yet Yale's work of preparation, practicing day and night, had produced the stiff opposition that gave them their chance. The *Yale Courant* credited the win to captain Baker's "persistent efforts," studying the rules, and pushing the team in constant training. Years later, Yale mounted a plaque honoring Baker for his contributions.[11]

In the evening, Yale treated the Harvard players to dinner. Camp was impressed by the Harvard men, mature and engaging, singing songs and telling stories in spite of the disappointment of losing. Quietly, the young freshman pondered, could he someday become such a man?[12]

A week after willing Yale to victory, Eugene Baker showed another side to determination, a streak of independence—and conviction—at a historic conference, November 23, 1876, when American college students began an association to promote and manage rugby.

Whereas rugby in England had been primarily played and managed by athletic and social clubs outside the academic community, in the United States play and management arose within a unique college establishment. Unknown elsewhere in the world, this college establishment had its roots in American settlement, when colonists insisted that higher education be available in their newly colonized regions—Massachusetts's settlers founded Harvard within ten years after landing at Massachusetts Bay. By 1800 25 of today's U.S. colleges had been founded, and by 1860 there were 182. Critics might ask, where are colleges equal to "the most celebrated European universities"? But democratic, practical, and optimistic Americans thought it more important that a college had been made available "at every man's door."[13]

Colleges in new settlements meant colleges in small towns, with students often residing together in a dormitory and forming a tightly knit community. Those tightly knit communities, identified by scholars as the "outstanding peculiarity" of the early American college, transformed America's higher education system, leading to an on-campus college life that went beyond classes and studies, a beginning of the extracurriculum—student-organized debating or "literary" societies to hone skills and study matters not covered in the classical curriculum; fraternities, growing out of debating societies; student publications to practice journalism and communicate matters of student interest. Athletics followed naturally, irresistible in a close gathering of young men with time, energy, and an innate play motivation.[14]

The first athletic contest between U.S. colleges was a boat race. Rowing and regattas had grown popular in New York City in the early 1800s, and in 1843 a Yale student bought and brought to New Haven a used New York boat; Harvard students bought a boat the following year. Rowing clubs developed at the schools, and in 1852 a "commercial sponsor," a railroad manager who wanted to promote newly laid track to Lake Winnepesaukee in New Hampshire, persuaded the clubs to ship their boats to the lake and hold a race. Harvard and Yale were natural rivals—most prestigious and largest, though in 1852 they were really quite small: about 450 undergraduates at Yale and 350 at Harvard. Harvard-Yale boat races continued in subsequent years, and other colleges joined them. In addition, competition in other sports was gradually added—baseball in 1859 (a game between Amherst and Williams), a form of soccer in 1869 (between Princeton and Rutgers), and track and field about 1874.[15]

Students not only played these sports; they also formed organizations to manage their play. When Harvard and Yale were considering a second boat race in 1858, the editors of *Harvard Magazine* self-consciously made a proposal: "What say ye [college brothers], . . . shall we introduce a new institution to America?"

Students at several colleges responded and formed the "College Union Regatta" to plan and conduct future races. As other sports were added, further organizations were formed—a soccer association in 1873, track and field in 1875, baseball in 1879. Not only necessary for sport management, these organizations also had an educational function, teaching business and management skills, negotiation skills, political strategy, habits of discipline and effectiveness. Camp would later cite such educational values in defending student sport management against faculty efforts to take over.[16]

The November 23, 1876, conference to organize rugby-type intercollegiate football was initiated by Princeton. Harvard had sent a rugby challenge to Princeton in the fall of 1876, the same as they sent to Yale, but Princeton's leaders hesitated and made a counterproposal—before any game, a new association of colleges should first "adopt a uniform set of rules."[17]

The delay also allowed internal meetings about which sport Princeton wanted to play, rugby or the familiar soccer with which they had had good success. Rugby was finally chosen—to play with Harvard and Yale, there was no choice, and many at Princeton liked the idea of rugby—and it was decided to call a conference to establish a rule-making rugby association. At the time, nine or ten American colleges had competed in some type of football, but Princeton sent convention invitations to only three—Columbia, Harvard, and Yale, whom Princeton students considered their fellow leaders in the American college world. The student communities at all three accepted, and on November 23, 1876, each sent two delegates to the "halfway" point, Springfield, Massachusetts, to the Massasoit Hotel, named for the Indian chief who had reached out to the Pilgrims at Plymouth. The hotel, conveniently located just across the street from the train depot, would one day mount a plaque on its outside wall identifying it as the site where American football's first official intercollegiate organization was established.[18]

Camp waited at Yale with other Yale players and students as Eugene Baker and John Atwater, a nonplayer elected by Yale students, traveled to the convention as Yale delegates. At the convention, Baker was contrary from the start. When he was elected secretary of the meeting, Baker sensibly protested that he was a senior and much work would be required of the secretary the next year, after he graduated, but the delegates elected him anyway; the Princeton delegate, Phelps-Dodge heir W. Earl Dodge, was elected president.[19]

Then the delegates discussed whether to form an association, and again Baker and Atwater were opposed. They believed an association would limit

Yale too greatly in its choice of game opponents. The other colleges didn't agree and voted three to one to form an association, the "Intercollegiate Football Association" (IFA). Baker and Atwater refused to join, and the Yale student body later ratified their decision.[20]

To establish playing rules, the delegates adopted most of the rules of England's Rugby Football Union. But the subject of scoring brought a long and excited discussion. Harvard argued that the RFU's rules, which counted only kicked goals in the scoring, didn't sufficiently reward touchdowns; Columbia and Yale defended goals as demanding scientific execution. Finally, the delegates compromised: "Games shall be decided by touchdowns, [but] each goal shall count as four touchdowns."[21]

Then there was the issue of team size. Harvard, as customary in England, wanted fifteen. As discussed above, Baker believed the field was too crowded with fifteen and wanted eleven, a number perhaps first used in cricket.[22]

Princeton had been playing soccer-type football with twenty players per side; reducing to fifteen was enough change for them. Most delegates were satisfied with fifteen, and again the convention outvoted Baker.[23]

Yale's disagreements presented a challenge. Could a student association, already vulnerable because of the yearly change in student leadership, succeed with only three full members? In the end, Dodge led a compromise that allowed Yale to stay out of the association but still kept them involved. Yale would be allowed to attend conventions and participate in rule making, and Yale's games with other teams in the association would count toward the association championship. The delegates left Springfield still able to work together in an association.

Princeton and Yale had agreed even before the convention to play a game that year, and they chose an auspicious date, Thanksgiving Day. President Lincoln had declared Thanksgiving a national holiday in 1863. With six-day workweeks and only three other legal holidays (Christmas, Washington's Birthday, and Independence Day), many Americans frolicked on Thanksgiving. In addition to religious services, there were public parades and celebrations, bonfires and fireworks, theater and musical events—and sporting activities of every variety: horse racing, hunting and chasing the hounds, footraces, balloon rides, and baseball. In many small towns, a baseball game with a neighboring town was the principal outdoor activity on Thanksgiving Day. For Princeton and Yale, Thanksgiving weekend was open on the college calendar, making it easier for students to travel to a game.[24]

The 1876 Yale football team. (Yale athletics photographs, ca. 1850–2007 [inclusive], Manuscripts and Archives, Yale University)

Negotiating before the convention, Princeton had agreed to Baker's eleven-man team size. Columbia also had agreed to play Yale with eleven men. So despite the fifteen-man rule legislated by the 1876 convention, Baker and Yale in fact had their way on team size in all of Yale's 1876 games.

Yale defeated Princeton on November 30 and Columbia on December 9, with Camp playing halfback in both games. Yale had defeated all association members, and for their team photo Baker held a ball boldly painted "CHAMPION," even though they were not officially an association member. Camp stood in the back row, slender, young, arms folded as seemed a habit, a hint of uncertainty about him, three months into college with an unknown future for both him and the nascent rugby game that was no more than an experiment added to the college extracurriculum.

4 "You Must Do Something"

The introduction of rugby football on the Yale campus excited students as well as players. A visiting German professor later quoted by Camp said his "most important impression" on the Yale campus was "the feeling of fellowship and common interest of the entire student body . . . [extending to] the football field, . . . every individual . . . conscious of his part in the community life." Nonplaying students at Yale as well as other colleges supported their school's football by direct financial subscriptions as well as by attendance at practice and games. In the early years, when gate receipts were low, the players probably provided their own uniforms, but student subscriptions were needed to help with expenses like rent for a field, balls, traveling costs, and publicity. The players came from a student body that in the 1870s was still small and closely knit, and their fellow students wanted the players to succeed, both because the students cared about them and because they wanted their school to be a winner.[1]

To fellow students, Camp seemed "'in love' with the game, his main thought, as if he was born with a football in his hands." American football was played with a melon-shaped rugby football, twenty-seven inches around the middle, and Camp, as was standard for him, wanted to prepare: he held a rugby football while he studied, twisting and gripping it, to accustom his fingers to the feel and grip of the ball. "On campus, at Gym lot, [he was] always handling and passing." Camp had long, sinewy fingers and could carry the ball with one hand by gripping it at the end, with his palm wrapped around the end.[2]

Camp may have loved football most, but he also loved baseball. He probably wanted to play varsity baseball in his freshman year, but almost the whole varsity team returned. Instead of the varsity, he played for his class team, the "class of '80," 153 classmates who began together in fall 1876 and expected to graduate together in June 1880. Class units were the fundamental organization around which nineteenth-century college life was built: "Yale '80" was Camp's permanent and proud label for life. He was captain of the '80 baseball team and the '80 football team.[3]

There was plenty of time for sports. Few of the students had jobs; Walter Camp apparently never had a job while at Yale, during either the school year or the summer break.

Yale's school day began with a required chapel service at 8:10 a.m., preceded for many students by a hurried breakfast at an off-campus eating club—there was no on-campus cafeteria. With the chapel bell chiming steadily as 8:10 approached, students appeared in stages, a first group walking in suits and derbies, a second gently trotting, and a last group charging on a run, settling into their seats simultaneously with the final bell. In his second year, Camp still lived at home, so he had a long walk to chapel. The service generally lasted fifteen minutes and was largely accepted by students,

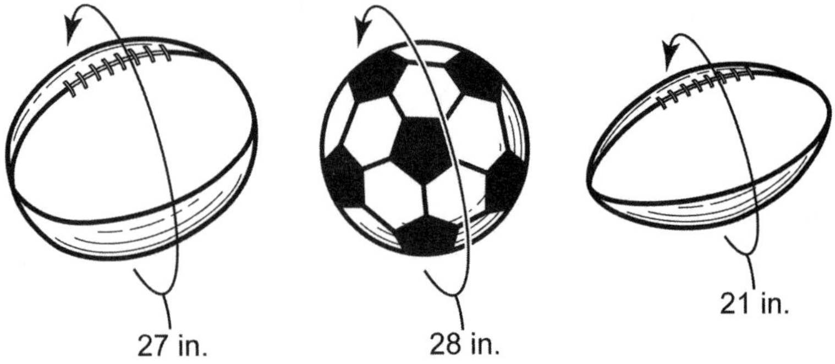

An 1870s rugby ball (left), today's soccer ball (center), today's U.S. football (right).

though some had a newspaper or textbook under cover. More than likely, the students came from religious homes where family prayers and blessings at the table were common.[4]

An hourlong class followed chapel, then another at 11:30 a.m., and a final one at 5:00 p.m., six days a week, except that the 5:00 p.m. class was omitted on Wednesdays and Saturdays. The curriculum was from the "classics"—Camp's classes in his sophomore year were Demosthenes (called the greatest orator from classical Greece), Horace (a Roman poet), Euripedes (Greek playwright), and trigonometry. Primarily classes were "recitations"; one student might be asked to read a short passage such as Greek lines from Demosthenes, another to translate the passage, and a third to answer questions about its construction. The class was divided into groups, each recitation having about forty students, seated alphabetically. Monitors checked attendance at classes as well as at chapel.[5]

Camp took his studies seriously enough; he was not in the top tier of students but high enough to expect some honors at graduation. The curriculum was standard for all students in the freshman and sophomore years, so it was not necessary yet to pick a career. But he likely pondered—should it be teaching like his school-principal father, his honored uncle David, and his just-graduated valedictorian cousin Charles Camp? The family standards were a bit intimidating.

Actually, if asked he probably said he wanted to be a writer, though he seemed not very specific as to the kind of writer. At Hopkins Grammar School, he had worked on the student newspaper; at Yale he worked on poetry, more literary but a familiar activity in everyday nineteenth-century

American life. Some said Camp's poetry was encouraged by his mother, Ellen, but he did enough of it to suggest he got personal satisfaction from bringing words together in efficient and evocative composition. A well-turned compact phrase caught his attention not only in poetry but also in aphorisms, terse and often ingenious in formulation; he collected hundreds over his lifetime.[6]

In the spring of his sophomore year, Camp submitted a poem to the *Yale Literary Magazine* (the *Lit*), a major early college publication produced by Yale undergraduates. Camp genuinely enjoyed writing poetry, but additional reasons might have encouraged his submission. Many years after he had graduated from Yale, Camp wrote of what had been expected of Yale students. Yale is "a great place, and there's the finest lot of fellows you ever saw." But those fellows are also measuring you: "Can you do anything? Work or play, studies, literary or dramatic work, musical work, athletics—surely there is a long enough list. But you must do something . . . and do it with all your might." Camp worked on poetry and submitted it for publication because he loved to write; in an environment of expectation, however, he likely also submitted it to show what he could do.[7]

Most pieces in the *Lit* were by members of the senior class, a few by juniors, one or two by sophomores and freshmen. Camp's poem was accepted, though it seems out of place from a teenage boy, perhaps an effort to follow classic models—writing about love for a girl instead of his true love, sports (first verse: "O stars that so softly are shining / O light that is tender and true / Look down on the face of my darling / Asleep, while I whisper to you").

Camp's life was not all seriousness. Though reserved and quiet (the most common adjective used about him), he was still friendly and active on campus; he loved whist and sometimes skipped class to finish a good game. A classmate wrote that although Camp was "an all-around athlete," he "was always ready for fun with his less ambitious friends"; the classmate had boxed with Camp, "played tennis and rowed in the same boat."[8]

Having graduated from Yale in the spring of 1877, Eugene Baker seemed gone, but in the fall he returned to enter Yale Law School and was again chosen football captain. Committed as ever to eleven-man teams, Baker began Yale's season with three teams agreeable to eleven-man play, Tufts, Trinity, and Stevens Institute. Yale won all three of these "practice" games.[9]

But Baker had difficulty scheduling games with teams of the Intercollegiate Football Association. Harvard informed Yale that this year's game must be played with fifteen men, as called for by IFA rules. Baker rejected that. Neither school backed down, and the result was no game; foremost rivals, Harvard and Yale in 1877 did not compete in football.[10]

Princeton was also adamant on fifteen. Negotiations continued almost up to Thanksgiving, the date scheduled for the game; at one point, Yale offered to play with thirteen, but Princeton was unbending. Two days before Thanksgiving, Yale capitulated and sent a telegram agreeing to play with fifteen. Too late for Thanksgiving, but Princeton (with Dodge as captain) agreed to play on December 8. They also agreed to decide the game with goals only—the same rule that had allowed Yale to win its 1876 game with Harvard.[11]

The Princeton game was a good one for Camp, who scored one of Yale's two touchdowns on a run down the sideline; meeting three Princeton players near the goal line, he smashed through and "scattered" them, according to a newspaper report, plunging across Princeton's goal line. Unfortunately, the rules negotiated for the game backfired on Yale; neither of Yale's touchdowns was followed by a successful kick. Yale and Princeton both were scoreless under the negotiated rules, and the game was a draw. No championship that year.[12]

In the spring of Camp's sophomore year, with days warming and minds dreaming, he was practicing one day with Yale's baseball team at Hamilton Park (he would play one varsity baseball game his sophomore year). During a lull, he wandered over to the harness-racing track, where Yale trackmen were practicing. W. C. Dole, owner of a New Haven sporting-goods store, was there as a volunteer, trying to strengthen track and field at Yale. Dole was offering prizes to promote an annual Yale intramural track event, and, knowing Camp's athletic skills, he encouraged Walter to enter. Stimulated at the thought of a new athletic challenge, Camp asked, "What event?" "Any event you like," Dole answered.[13]

Back at campus, Camp walked by the window of a tailor's shop where Dole's prizes were on display. A silver pitcher for the 120-yard hurdles seemed by far the best prize, and Camp decided to give that a try.

Here was what he loved, an athletic challenge he could work at mentally and physically—conceiving how to combine hurdling with running, then practicing to put his ideas and understanding in effect, and, finally, testing his preparation against a standard or competitor. Two years before, Yale's varsity hurdler W. J. Wakeman had learned to take a fixed number of steps between hurdles and had won at the intercollegiate track meet. Now Camp went to work to achieve the regularity in steps and the jumping required for successful hurdling. On May 29, he won and carried home the silver pitcher, the memento of a victory he always remembered.[14]

Making It Their Own 5

No report appeared in the newspaper. No panel of experts discussed it. But to any careful observer, it was obvious. Three years into playing the imported game of rugby, American college football players were messing with it, changing it enough to put a frown on the face of an English rugby player.

Camp said the change had begun on the practice field, spontaneous change that was more a reaction than a plan. The Americans tried to learn English rugby, to play by its rules and live up to what it required. Face-to-face, varsity against scrubs, pushing and kicking, they threw themselves into the rugby scrum, trying to blast the ball and themselves through the tangled, writhing mass.[1]

But rugby scrums between varsity and scrubs became one-sided. The varsity was heavier and stronger than the scrubs and too easily pushed through to move the ball downfield.

So the scrubs innovated, perhaps led by one or two creative individuals but soon joined by many. The scrubs' front line began to allow the ball to be intentionally kicked past them. They still kept in the way of the varsity players but allowed the ball to go by them, through the mass and out at the rear. Once the ball was out, one of the waiting scrub halfbacks picked it up and carried it, gaining by running around players still tied up in the scrum.[2]

The varsity quickly accepted and imitated the scrubs' technique, and that caused the scrubs to innovate again. Instead of depending on the varsity to kick the ball through the mass, the frontline scrubs did it themselves—*deliberately, they kicked the ball backward* to their waiting halfbacks.

True rugby players were disgusted. Forcing the ball through a scrimmage was at the heart of rugby, applauded in *Tom Brown's School Days*, an English novel describing rugby's early years at Rugby School: "Here come two of the bulldogs, in they go straight to the heart of the scrimmage, bent on driving the ball out on the opposite side." To an experienced rugby player, the American change—kicking backward—took away part of the manly contest of the game.[3]

But the randomness and uncertainty of England's rugby scrimmage went against the grain for Americans. *Practical efficiency* was Americans' watchword, purposeful, quick, effective. Balls bouncing out of a scrum with almost no predictability prevented purposeful effort.

Camp was present and necessarily participated as Americans made their initial modifications of rugby, changes in style at first but growing into more fundamental changes. The changes happened, Camp said, at more than one college, prompted by a general dislike for rugby's free-for-all scrimmage. And the changes began early, presumably in Harvard's practices for McGill or Harvard's and Yale's practices for their games. Gradually, beginning almost as soon as they took up rugby, Americans developed a kicking-back style of play—backward sounding but a fundamental forward step that set the stage for America's new football.[4]

This was the advance edge of America's rugby football in the fall of 1878 when the handful of participating American colleges on the East Coast began to put their teams together for a new season.

Eugene Baker had left Yale Law School to enter business, so Yale's football team had to elect a new captain. Their choice might have been a surprise—a junior, Walter Camp. Why not a senior such as Oliver Thompson, hero of the 1876 game with Harvard, the best player on the team, and, according to the *New York Times*, the best player in America?[5]

But Camp also was a strong player and was known as a student of the game and its rules; he had accompanied Baker to negotiate the rules with Harvard for the 1876 game. With increasing age and continuing exercise, his body was filling out; he looked like a football player. While Camp was routinely described as quiet and reserved, his actions did the talking and could set a standard by example. He was well respected aside from football—living this year in an on-campus Yale dormitory, he would soon be elected to a committee of juniors to plan the campus social event of the year, the Junior Promenade.[6]

As captain a first duty was to attend a convention called by the Intercollegiate Football Association, the second convention in the IFA's history. A convention had been omitted in 1877—perhaps because of Baker's intransigent insistence on eleven players—but a convention was now planned for October 9, 1878, in Springfield. Camp attended with the president of Yale's student football association, senior T. E. Rochfort; each of the IFA colleges had a student football association, generally headed by a nonplaying student, like Rochfort, to manage support for the team. Captains and football-association presidents from Harvard and Princeton also came to the convention. Columbia telegrammed that they would not attend; in a city location without a convenient playing field, they were having difficulty fielding a team.[7]

Six young men in their teens or early twenties sat down in a hotel parlor to consider rules for a game they had played for a couple of years, a game they still called rugby but one that they were steadily changing on the field. Camp and Rochfort continued Baker's advocacy of eleven-man teams, but they took a practical approach. They challenged Harvard and Princeton to games with eleven men; when neither school would budge from fifteen, however, they avoided direct confrontation: "We've heard your reasons and we'll present them to the Yale student body; if they agree, we'll play fifteen-man games." In another compromise, Yale now agreed to become an IFA member.[8]

The six youthful delegates made no major rule changes, but they did rewrite one rule (to halt certain developing playing practices) and in the process coincidentally offered hints as to how far the game had already been changed on the playing fields:

> 15. In a scrimmage it is not lawful *for the man who has the ball, nor the man opposite and opposed to him, to pick out* the ball with the hand under any circumstances whatever [the italicized words replaced the words *to touch* in the original rule, which had been retained from the RFU rules].

In a first hint, the two competing sides in an American football scrimmage seem already to be acquiring distinctive offensive and defensive roles; a "man who has the ball" and still "has" it as scrimmage action begins has a kind of "ownership" that could allow him to initiate offensive play. Also, there seems to be a pause, a time long enough for "picking out" to occur and perhaps a little thinking to occur, rather than immediately throwing the ball to the ground for a rugby scrum. Further, the amended rule recognizes that players were spreading out, with the two sides facing one another, so that there is a "man who has the ball" and another man "opposite and opposed to him." This spreading had begun early in the Americans' play, as indicated in the *Harvard Advocate* for a May 1876 game between Harvard and an all-Canada team: "The Canadians played the English style, or 'forward' game, which is to keep together, and force the ball ahead of them; while our men spread themselves over the field, and relied on 'passing' the ball." The American football defense had to spread out in response, to defend against outside passes or runs, and typically positioned a man "opposite and opposed to" the "man who has the ball."[9]

6 Captain

A single rugby football lay alone in the center of the room. Furniture was pushed back, making space for the Yale football team to sit in a rough circle, backs to the wall and facing the ball. Walter Camp, team captain, had invited them to his dormitory room to discuss football and game strategy. Though quiet and reserved, Camp now wanted discussion.[1]

As captain, Camp was almost czar, and he was busy. There was no football coach—not even a thought of obtaining a coach. The captain decided who would be on the team, what positions they would play, and who would play in games. He directed practices and shaped whatever strategy was possible. During a game, he organized players on the field and made any needed on-the-field decisions, all in addition to playing his own position.

But Camp's meeting allowed players to offer their ideas, to discuss, propose, agree, or disagree. One of the players at the meeting later wrote: "This conception of getting the men together to talk things over, to suggest, to listen and compare, Camp himself doing more listening by far than talking, was characteristic and natural to the man, although knowing most, willing and anxious to learn from any of them: gentlemanly, considerate, sympathetic of the lame spots and bruises."[2] It was a young team, three freshmen, four sophomores, three juniors, three seniors, one master's candidate, and one medical student. Here was no elite group of recruited athletes, just ordinary students attending Yale for an education but interested enough to practice and play. Most had played this young game hardly at all before arriving at Yale.[3]

The meeting supplemented on-the-field practice, giving opportunity to discuss, understand, contribute, and agree on playing plans and also bringing the players together in spirit. Camp believed football success came with team effort in which players "work together with mutual understanding." The Americans' changing style of play demanded planning. Once the ball was kicked back out of the scrimmage and into the hands of a halfback, there were choices: the halfback could run with the ball, punt or drop-kick, or pass laterally to other backs (forward passing was explicitly prohibited, a holdover from England's rugby rules). The correct choice depended on the circumstances, and the best choices needed to be considered and planned.[4]

On-field practice further developed the new scrimmage forms. From the early, primitive concept that forward players should take any available

Camp (center) with the 1878 Yale football team. (Yale athletics photographs, ca. 1850–2007 [inclusive], Manuscripts and Archives, Yale University)

opportunity to kick the ball backward in a rugby scrum, American players practiced for more regularity and reliability. The kickback became planned, the first act of a scrimmage, with a technique developed to reliably carry it out: foot on the ball, sudden downward pressure dragging the ball back, forceful enough to make the ball roll or bounce fast, far, and straight enough. Intended to be a sudden propulsion, the term *snap* apparently came to mind, and the kickback began to be called a "snapback."[5]

At first the ball was kicked back by anyone, whoever had the ball when it was downed and a new scrum begun. But some players kicked better than others, and soon the ball was routinely handed to or taken up by one of them; he might be called the "snapper-back" or simply "snapback," but he also became the "middle rusher," positioned in the center of the rush line where players beside him could "guard" against opposing linemen reaching the kicked-back ball.[6]

In addition, the practicing players began to move a halfback up closer to the line, five yards back and even closer, to quickly gather in the kicked-back ball before an opponent got to it. That player they began to call a "quarterback," distinguishing him from the "halfback" (about ten yards back) and "back" or "fullback" (fifteen yards back). The term *quarterback* had been used in England, but derisively—a shirker, someone not involved in the maelstrom of a scrum, lingering outside and waiting for others to do the dirty work. For Americans, the term *quarterback* was simply factual, a location-based description of a player who was becoming a necessity.[7]

Although exploration and development of new scrimmage forms were occurring at several schools, Yale was the leader. "In the majority of cases," Camp recalled in a retrospective on the game, "the first steps in advance toward the development of the [individual playing] positions or of a particular play apparently emanated from New Haven" and were then taken up elsewhere.[8]

Such leadership could have had several sources, but Camp's enthusiasm and study of the game were key—a player on the team later wrote that Camp's "knowledge of the game and his resourcefulness were so great that we were easily ahead of any other college." But Camp had a willing cast of partners—players eager to improve and build Yale's chances. Yale students were motivated—"something in you was driving you ahead," Camp later wrote, not specifically him alone but Yale students widely. A Harvard professor who visited Yale called it a "Yale Spirit," an active, enabling unity of purpose and effort that extended to athletics. A Yale professor spoke similarly of the student body's spirit or attitude toward athletics: collective aims prevailed over individual ones in Yale athletics—to be judged highly, a Yale athlete must be "working for the college" more than for himself.[9]

Innovation and development of the playing techniques described above probably started while Camp was simply a player. In an 1893 letter to Camp, Eugene Baker claimed that developments by the teams he captained during Camp's freshman and sophomore years "laid the foundation for the modern game." The 1878 Rule 15 amendment quoted above is consistent with development during Baker's 1876 and 1877 captaincy; Baker was honored in 1895 when his classmates mounted a tablet in the Yale trophy room recognizing his services to Yale football.[10]

But the limited language of the amended 1878 rule in contrast to the detailed language of upcoming 1879 and 1880 rules discussed hereafter suggests that a much larger development, producing more recognizable features of today's scrimmage, took place with Camp's 1878 and 1879 Yale teams.

As captain Camp remained committed to Baker's physical play. He had proudly endured and subscribed to the strenuosity of Baker's training regimen and now sought to make his own team physically well conditioned also. Although described above as "sympathetic" of lame spots and bruises, Camp did not shy away from physicality. As a freshman during the freshman-sophomore rush, he was tackled by a sophomore who soon found himself on the bottom of a scuffle, impressed enough to ask, "What is your name, freshman?" And in the last game of his freshman year against Columbia on a frozen field, Camp tackled a Columbia player forcefully against the frozen turf, knocking the player unconscious. Camp was quite relieved when the Columbia player got up and walked off the field.[11]

With Camp as captain, winning was to be pursued full-bore. One of the most important characteristics in choosing members of a team, Camp said, was "pluck" or "sand," an energy and commitment that would not break. Camp's guiding objective was to play by the rules, and as a gentleman, but with a commitment to winning, a never-give-up determination to end the game on top. Camp would say, "If you lose, put a good face on it; but go home and think out a way to win next time."[12]

Not everyone accepted the goal of winning with Camp's and Yale's commitment. Harvard students were publicly accused of, and some admitted to, an "indifference" to such mundane struggles:

> We deem it narrow-minded to excel.
> We call the man fanatic who applies
> His life to one grand purpose till he dies.
> Enthusiasm sees one side, one fact,
> We try to see all sides, but do not act.
> . . . We long to sit with newspapers unfurled,
> Indifferent spectators of the world.

Some at Harvard would suggest a different reason for downplaying winning: sport was for recreation more than victory—for fun, not with the grinding effort of work. Still others, admiring things British, thought a "gentleman's" standards—courtesy and respect for others—prohibited undue emphasis on winning.[13]

Yale students claimed their student body was more diverse geographically and economically than Harvard's and more accurately reflected America. Many students at Yale were sons of entrepreneurs for whom striving was a way of life. Others were middle class, striving at a different level to realize the American dream. Achievement was ingrained as a goal, starting with vocation but carrying over to leisure.[14]

Harvard indifference was overstated—they often won in rowing, track, and baseball—but perhaps it affected Harvard's football, the ultimate in a physically demanding game. In the fall of 1878, after Yale accepted play with teams of fifteen, a football game with Harvard was scheduled for November 23 at the Boston baseball grounds—the third-ever Harvard-Yale football game and the first since official formation of the Intercollegiate Football Association. The field was wet, with pools of water here and there, and a brisk wind blowing. Only about seven hundred were interested enough to attend.[15]

The Camp-led Yale team pressed hard through the first half, moving the ball close to Harvard's goal, but unable to score. Yet Harvard found it necessary to take ten "safety touch downs"—touching the ball down in Harvard's own goal area, which had no scoring consequence under the held-over rugby rules and allowed Harvard a free kick from their twenty-five-yard-line. After each safety and Harvard kick, Yale had to start over to move on Harvard's goal.

The only scoring came in the second half. With the game nearly over, Yale's Thompson got the ball in the Harvard end and coolly drop-kicked it twenty yards through the goal posts. Two Harvard games in a row, a kick by Thompson made Yale victorious.

During halftime a Boston schoolboy mingling with Harvard's players asked what they thought of the Yale team. Rubbing his arm, one player ruefully answered, "They're too damned rough." He wasn't alone in such thoughts, and in coming years there would be a number of complaints that Yale played too rough, "Yale-ism," it began to be called. To Camp such complaints came from people who didn't yet understand football; he happily acknowledged that Yale's teams would be known for toughness and forceful tackling.[16]

7 The Extracurriculum and Beyond

Some of New York's "best" citizens were in their coaches Thanksgiving Day morning, November 28, 1878, click-clacking over cobblestone streets toward the Hudson River. Down to the river and onto a ferry bound for Hoboken—horses, coaches, drivers, passengers, all.[1]

On the Jersey side, they trotted north along a riverside promenade bound for "Elysian Fields," a park established years before by a long-deceased entrepreneur, John Stevens, in wilderness he bought from a Tory after the Revolutionary War. Especially on weekends, city-dwelling New Yorkers crossed to Elysian Fields by the thousands for an escape into nature, initially to Stevens's benefit, coming on Stevens's ferry lines, renting some of his facilities, and purchasing land he developed in Hoboken.[2]

Playing grounds laid out many years before on level areas of Elysian Fields were rented to athletic clubs. On such a rented field, the pioneering Knickerbocker Base Ball Club and another team from New York in 1846 played America's "first game of baseball," so-called because today's American baseball grew most directly from that game and its Knickerbocker rules. Cricket was played on a different rented field by a club of Englishmen, the St. George's Cricket Club, who built a clubhouse and grandstand on their rented space.[3]

On this 1878 Thanksgiving Day morning, just five days after Yale had defeated Harvard, the carriages from New York were headed for St. George's grounds, which student managers from Princeton and Yale had rented for their football game. The clubhouse and grandstand on the grounds were now old and in disrepair, and residential and commercial developments were edging near. But a level playing field remained, surrounded by a decrepit fence and scattered trees.[4]

From the start, three years before, Princeton and Yale had brought their Thanksgiving Day football to Elysian Fields, conveniently located midway between Princeton and New Haven. Attendance had grown every year—eight hundred in 1876, two thousand in 1877, five thousand today, 1878. Five thousand! For a college extracurricular event three years old. What drew them? Family relationships with players? Thanksgiving? A location shrewdly chosen near a large potential audience?[5]

Yes, but also a special excitement arising out of the unique American college setting—residential colleges, closely knit student bodies, loyalties deep and continuing. Students and graduates were caught up in their college's games, ready to support their team and school. Even in the early days of college rowing, old graduates had gathered around telegraph receivers to follow a race's progress and check their college's performance.

The physicality of the contest was, of course, another important attraction. Until recently, colleges had an image of intellectualism, where the hero was apt to be "stooping, weak and sickly." Now robust athletes were engaged in strenuous physical contest, and loyal supporters were aroused to enthusiastic support.[6]

As with Yale, Princeton's players were committed to vigorous play. Just two months earlier, the editor of the *Princetonian* student newspaper, T. (Tommy) Woodrow Wilson, had written in defense of football: "Of course there is roughness . . ., but a man of moderate strength and common sense can take care of himself." As proof he cited the few serious injuries incurred "in our four principal" football-playing colleges (generously including Columbia with Harvard, Princeton, and Yale). He exhorted Princeton's students, "everyone who can play," to participate and promote success for Princeton.[7]

Although Princeton had roughly two-thirds Yale's undergraduate enrollment—about five hundred in 1878 versus Yale's eight hundred—they were a strong competitor. During the 1878 season, Princeton defeated the University of Pennsylvania twice, as well as Stevens Institute (a technical school founded by a son of John Stevens on a hill above Elysian Fields), Rutgers, and Harvard. Yale, in Walter Camp's first year of captaincy, had defeated Amherst, Trinity (of Hartford) twice, and Harvard. The championship of the Intercollegiate Football Association was hanging in the balance as the teams prepared to take the field for their 1878 Thanksgiving Day game.[8]

Arriving at St. George's grounds, the carriages from New York pulled into place behind already-standing spectators, who had crowded against a heavy rope that surrounded the playing field. More than fifty carriages plus hotel stagecoaches had come, with some of their occupants standing precariously on top for a better view. The *New York World* recognized "fashionable society"—businessmen graduated from one of the schools and women such as "Mrs. Dodge," whose son W. Earl Dodge Jr. was to be Princeton's umpire.[9]

The teams filed through the crowd and onto the field, Camp's Yale team and Princeton's team captained by Bland Ballard, a junior from Louisville. Each team was dressed in laced-up white canvas jackets and white knee breeches. Princeton had started wearing canvas jackets the previous year—they were durable, and their stiffness made tackling more difficult—and now other teams were also wearing them. Only the teams' caps and stockings were markedly different: Princeton's, orange and black; Yale's, blue. Princeton's team was older than Yale's, with no freshmen, in comparison to Yale's three.[10]

Yale began well, with Camp kicking off high and fairly deep. Several kicks were exchanged (both dropkicks and punts), but the ball was kept in Princeton's end. Yale pressed and Princeton escaped with a "safety touchdown," touching the ball down behind their goal line and then kicking the ball out of danger, with no scoring consequences under rugby rules. Yale kept pressing and blocked a kick by Princeton. Again Princeton took a safety. Throughout the first half, Yale pressed and Princeton took five safeties to none for Yale, all to Princeton's advantage with no gain for Yale.

Princeton played more aggressively in the second half and took advantage when Yale mishandled a Princeton dropkick in the Yale end; one report said "a famous back" (presumably Thompson or Camp) muffed his attempted catch of the large fluttering rugby ball, and a Princeton player recovered it a few yards from Yale's goal line.

Princeton had prepared a surprise and practiced it indoors in the gym. Play began in normal fashion from scrimmage, the forward lines facing each other, hands on knees and almost pressing against one another; no rule required separation of the lines. The Princeton snapback kicked the ball backward to Withington, a short, lightweight player who moved up closer to the line in "quarterback" position to quickly grab the ball. Picking up the bouncing ball from the ground, Withington lunged forward and vaulted into the air above Princeton's line; Princeton players caught him and catapulted him farther, up and over the Yale line. Yale's players must have watched like spectators: Withington landed on his shoulders, then somersaulted up and across the Yale goal line. Touchdown! Princeton's Theodore McNair successfully followed by placekicking the goal after the touchdown.[11]

Time was running out and Yale was desperate. They moved the ball toward the Princeton goal line, but Princeton again escaped with a safety. Once more Yale pressed, but Princeton successfully held. The game ended with Princeton the winner, one goal to none for Yale.

Princeton had won; there was no denying that. But in his heart, Camp was convinced that Princeton's several safeties without penalty had contributed to the result. Something would have to be done about safeties.

The college extracurriculum quickly moved to other activities. The Junior Promenade for which Camp was on the planning committee came in February. He later described some of the preparations:

> A surprise was planned for the Promenade girls when they arrived Monday, a sleigh ride after lunch. Then a couple of private teas, where the girls met here and there men who had requested a dance at the big event Wednesday night. Then back to the hotel and dinner, and in the evening a class german [dance]. On Tuesday the girls were escorted to morning chapel, and after that a walk about the campus.
>
> Wednesday was the grand event. After more teas and receptions, with a stolen hour or two for beauty sleep, the carriage came at nine o'clock, and off the girls went to the Armory.[12]

We don't know the name of Camp's date, but the next morning's *New Haven Journal-Courier* leaves a suggestion in a list of New Haven girls attending the event. Olivia English was on the list, Camp's back-fence neighbor through his growing-up years, one year older than he and a girl who never married; if she wasn't his date, he might have helped arrange her invitation.[13]

Entering the Armory, the couples found a room aglow with light from a huge central chandelier with many gas jets. The floor stretched out like a frosted lake, and overhead "Yale '80" shone from small gas jets. "Fine diamonds glistened in plenty," said the *Journal-Courier*, with silks and satins in pale blue, pink, cardinal, rich buff, or spotless white. Dancing began at ten o'clock, and there were fully 125 couples on the floor at one time, a "mass of whirling couples" continuing "well into Thursday morning." And then, Camp wrote, it was over, and for the men there was

> something somber about the thought . . . : the swish of the pretty gown, the bright smile, the color of the crushed flowers, were only memories, and the half-week's gayety, which had made such a pleasant break in the midwinter monotony of college life, had gone like a dream. But the touch of romance and sentiment the promenade had brought occasionally slipped in with a stray flower or two between the leaves of a book, whose perfume unexpectedly threw the chance reader into a reverie for many a day during the next few months, and accounted for some astonishingly poor recitation by even the best of students.[14]

In April 1879, Camp finally became a full-time member of Yale's varsity baseball team. Beginning April 11 and continuing through June 28, the team played twenty-four games, half with college teams and the rest with professional teams and athletic clubs. Yale won twelve games, of which eight were with college teams. In five games with Harvard, Yale won two. They played Princeton once, winning in New Haven 3–1.

Camp played in twenty-two of the twenty-four games, batting an even .300. He played left field and committed three errors among twenty-eight chances (fielding was still bare-handed), ranking him second among Yale's regular players in fielding average.[15]

On a Thursday night in late spring, just before school ended for the year, Camp was among the juniors who waited as messengers "tapped" students elected to Yale's secret societies. It was a major event, the campus crowded with students waiting for the selections to be revealed. In popular understanding, the selections were based on "scholarship, marked literary ability, social and athletic prominence, and family inheritance." Skull and Bones, it was said, "takes the clever men and Keys [Scroll and Keys] the good fellow." The crowd was noisy as first a Bones man appeared, stone-faced, making his way through the crowd, until he finally clapped on the shoulder a "young fellow whose face lights up with a perfectly happy grin as one might remember a lifetime."[16]

There probably was not much suspense as Camp waited; the growing popularity of athletics made him a big man on campus, and he was a likable, all-around student. Camp was one of fifteen tapped by the Skull and Bones society, Yale's oldest senior secret society, and he was undoubtedly happy for the honor. Yet in looking back several years later, he remembered the scene as "more sad than pleasant. . . . The value set upon an election to these societies cannot be entirely a fictitious one. [But] does the gain of the fifteen make amends for the loss whose existence is surely fact in the hearts of the many who miss it?"[17]

Fourth Year 8

Although it might have been uppermost in Walter Camp's mind as his senior year began, football in fact came second in Yale's 1879 sports year. Interclass baseball was first, a round of spirited contests between classes to get the school year under way with shared enthusiasm. Throughout September teams from each class year played the teams of other class years.[1]

Football was allowed two months—October, practice; November, games. Camp actually worried about football, in second place on the college calendar. Only a few colleges were playing, and he saw himself and other football leaders as "endeavoring against great odds to establish the sport." The worry led him to take on "the extremely unpleasant task of begging" for newspaper coverage of college football games. Although the Thanksgiving Day Princeton-Yale game had good coverage, other games, and especially games outside New York City, had lesser coverage and lesser attendance. And Camp wanted coverage by knowledgeable reporters instead of the drama critics more commonly used; he wanted a game to be occasionally "written up by an actual player."[2]

Camp was again elected football captain, and that meant attending another convention of the Intercollegiate Football Association. This year the convention almost shouted out Americans' departure from English rugby by eliminating, simply crossing out, a large portion of the scrimmage definition received from the Rugby Football Union: "A scrimmage takes place when the holder of the ball, being in the field of play, puts it down on the ground in front of him ~~and all who have closed around on their respective~~

~~sides endeavor to push their opponents back, and by kicking the ball, to drive it in the direction of the opposing goal line.~~"[3] The hints of playing-field change were now pushed even further: American players were not "driv[ing the ball] in the direction of the opposing goal line." (In fact, they were at least sometimes kicking the ball backward, though they apparently weren't ready to put that into words.)

The delegates also made a large rearrangement of the rules: definitions moved to the beginning of the rule book; plays having a categorical similarity were grouped together, all reflecting a decided departure from rugby and making the rule book more specific to Americans' new game.

Instead of changes made, newspapers were more interested in a change that wasn't made—team size. Camp didn't drop that issue, but presented it in a different manner; perhaps with tongue in cheek, he proposed that the playing area be enlarged by seventy feet in length and forty feet in width. This "reappearance of Yale's eleven men hobby," said the *Princetonian*, was "firmly opposed" by Harvard and Princeton. The 1879 season would again be played with fifteen to a side.[4]

Teddy Roosevelt and Walter Camp were both in their senior years in the fall of 1879, Roosevelt at Harvard, Camp at Yale. Roosevelt was on the editorial staff of the *Harvard Advocate*, one of Harvard's two student newspapers, and he apparently traveled to New Haven to write the paper's report of that fall's Harvard-Yale football game.

Limited to a November schedule, Yale's 1879 football season had five games, as did Harvard's. Harvard's season had begun with Canadian teams, a select team called "Britannia" in Boston on October 25 and again in Montreal on November 1, followed by McGill College in Montreal on November 3. Harvard won all three games. Yale's season began November 1 with an easy win over the University of Pennsylvania. Of the fifteen players on Camp's Yale team, five were new, including Frederic Remington, in his second year at Yale's School of Fine Arts, six feet plus, a "blonde Greek god" but rough looking, whom no one predicted for future artistic success.[5]

The undefeated Harvard and Yale teams were both hopeful as they took the field in New Haven on November 8, 1879—Harvard anxious to win after losing to Yale in 1876 and 1878 (1877 skipped because of disagreement on team size) and Yale eager to take the next step to claim the IFA championship after last year's miss.

Roosevelt's game report got to the bottom line in the first sentence: a "very unsatisfactory result." It was not that Harvard lost; the problem was neither team won. A draw was unacceptable to Roosevelt's—and Camp's—competitive perspective. At game's end, "Camp immediately challenged Harvard to another game at any time or place; but they refused."[6]

Skipping over most of the details, Roosevelt summarized, "Yale out-played us until the last half-hour." Harvard was compelled to take "several touch downs for safety," still of no consequence in scoring. Roosevelt thought Harvard became "rattled by the style of game Yale played," which he did not describe.

Yale came close to winning. "Camp made a drop kick from the field," a successful kick, except the referee said Harvard's Cushing touched the ball on the way; under the rules of the day, a kick had to cross the crossbar "without touching the . . . person of any player of either side."[7]

Harvard finally came to life in the last half hour, whereupon the ball was kept at Yale's end and Yale was forced to take two safeties before the game ended. The final tally on safeties was four for Harvard and two for Yale. But safeties gave no points, and neither side scored a goal or touchdown, so the game ended in a 0–0 tie. Not a happy result for Camp's final year and, irritatingly, another result influenced by the inadequate treatment of safeties in the rules.[8]

There was still Yale's "big" game—Princeton, Thanksgiving Day, Elysian Fields in Hoboken, the IFA championship on the line.

The week of the game was marred by an unpleasant incident. The team had agreed that for this week, they would stay on campus and be in bed by eleven. Johnny Moorhead, a good runner and member of the class of '80 with Camp, went to the theater and was caught by Camp past the deadline. Calling the team to his room, Camp quietly presented the issue and asked what should be done. Team members inclined toward a severe reprimand, which Camp considered a mere slap on the wrist. He announced he would resign as captain. That brought an uproar, players protesting and Moorhead announcing he would leave the team. Camp dismissed the meeting and the team dispersed. They never knew what happened next, but obviously Camp and Moorhead worked it out, because Camp remained as captain and Moorhead played against Princeton.[9]

The game drew an even bigger crowd than the previous year, six thousand, some standing twelve deep around the field. The *New York World*, intrigued by long dresses, bustles, and hats, noted that "many ladies had secured places in the rope-line and maintained them throughout the game." Under a pleasant sky, the players filed through the excited crowd onto the field, accompanied by honking coaches and rival cheers bouncing back and forth—Princeton, "Siss-Boom-Ah!"; Yale, "Rah! Rah! Rah!" Yale's cheers got a boost from an out-of-place cheerleader; each team had a student advocate on the field, an "umpire" to decide disputed questions under rugby's English-gentleman perspective, but Yale's was ready from the start to encourage his team and, dressed in suit, tie, and derby, waved his cane from the field to provoke cheers from Yale's student body.[10]

Princeton's captain thought the ball too soft, and with Camp's permission he uncovered the tubular inlet to the internal rubber bladder and blew into it forcefully. Finished, he handed the ball to Camp for a test punt; the ball "sailed out . . . like a shot from a mortar," and Camp agreed it was ready.[11]

With the game under way, Camp did his best, "doing wonders," said the *New York Times*; with a "splendid long kick," he pinned Princeton with the ball near their goal. At another point, he made a "fine dodging run" to move the ball in close to Princeton's goal line.[12]

But Camp also missed kicks on goal. Overall, the game's pattern was like last year's. Yale kept play in the Princeton end in the first half, getting close to the Princeton goal line several times. But Princeton successfully defended

Walter Camp, as captain of the 1879 Yale football team. (Walter Chauncey Camp Papers, 1870–1983 [inclusive], 1870–1925 [bulk], Manuscripts and Archives, Yale University)

with safeties. On the crowded field, with thirty players in total, Yale could not get through to score a touchdown.

The *World* reporter was conscious of a regularity in Yale's play. At times he heard Camp shouting above the din while waiting for the ball to be snapped back, something like, "Go through hard," apparently a word signal, though the reporter did not describe particular plays that followed. Camp later wrote that a first use of signals was simply to let rushers know whether a kick was planned, in which case they needed to protect the kicker and then move downfield as fast as possible.[13]

The second half was more even. Princeton forced the ball into Yale's end, but, the *Yale Courant* said, "Capt. Camp would not allow a safety touch-down to be made, but calling on his men to work steadily, gradually forced the ball the whole length of the field."[14] Later, Princeton just missed a dropkick on goal, and eventually Yale did take two safeties; for the whole game, Princeton took five safeties, Yale two. But no touchdowns or goals were scored by either team, and the game ended as a tie.

For a second year, Camp's team had been unable to defeat Princeton, and again safeties were an issue and irritant. To the *Courant*, Yale showed "superior ability and outplayed both" Princeton and Harvard. But both opponents had used safeties to divert Yale's effort, and the games ended as ties. The *Courant* concluded with a plea: "Is this just? . . . Why are goals and touchdowns counted in and 'safeties' counted out? . . . A 'safety' is a point gained over your opponents . . . and should be counted among the points that decide the game. This is a vital point and should be remedied."[15]

Camp's four years of football were over, and the record was good—in seventeen total games, Yale had lost only once, to Princeton in 1878; had beaten Harvard twice and Princeton once; and had tied Harvard once and Princeton twice. In one of the Princeton ties, in Camp's sophomore year, he scored a touchdown that would have won the game if touchdowns had counted in the scoring.

He had been a good player, even an outstanding one, according to newspaper accounts. As an early participant and convention delegate, he had assuredly helped American football out of the starting blocks. Though no major contribution by Camp may have appeared in the public record, he had made several quiet contributions—captaining the team that was leading the change from rugby's scrum to today's American football scrimmage, participating in rule legislation that reduced to writing the game's new methods, and seeking newspaper game coverage to support play among lesser colleges in what he saw as a struggle for the game's sustained existence. But others had also served as captain and rule legislator. Now someone else would need to step into the rule-writing club, because he was graduating.

Each graduating class at Yale made two prestigious awards—class orator, "the highest office that a class can confer," and class poet, "but little inferior to" orator. Scholastic honors were important to Camp, and he included them in his résumés: "First Division" in his freshman year, a "colloquy appointment" in his junior year. So election as class poet might have been on his mind.[16]

Camp seemed the most prolific poet in the class with three poems published his senior year in the *Yale Literary Magazine*—one addressing romance and another looking to the future, befitting an upcoming college graduate, with life portrayed through the metaphor of bubbles, "bright light bubbles of youth . . . drifting" away. The third poem was different, a narrative poem drawn from college life, more effortless, carrying the reader on naturally as a story unfolds. Unlike his other poems, this one was published over his initials, likely the winning poem in a contest.[17]

The vote for class orator and class poet came at a meeting during the winter. While published poetry seemed to make Camp the favorite, merit might not decide the issue. Even a candidate's membership in a senior society could work against him because of society rivalry or a desire to recognize nonsociety class members, "neutrals," who composed the largest part of a class.[18]

The vote for class orator was quick, Wm. Montague Hall named by acclamation. But a vote was needed for class poet, even though in the end the vote was far from close. The winner was William Hudson Harper, a neutral, chosen over Walter Camp, 66–15; Camp got the same number of votes as there were class members in the Skull and Bones society. In the class's eyes, Camp apparently didn't need more recognition. Or perhaps they sensed writing would be more important in Harper's career; he taught English upon graduation from Yale and within two years was working as a newspaper reporter. Camp was now thinking of medicine, which the class probably knew.[19]

On Presentation Day, June 29, 1880, Battell Chapel was filled as the class orator, Hall, and class poet, Harper, each made their presentations. However, the *Yale News* stepped in to report one other presentation, "The Parting Ode," by Walter Camp, calling it "more than usually poetical." Many years later, in a questionnaire for a biographical publication, Camp wrote that the poem had been chosen as the "class poem" *in sealed competition* (underlined by Camp). Camp's bonds to Yale seemed sincere, and six years later, at the Class of '80 Sexennial Reunion, Camp would be back, introduced now as the class poet and presenting another poetic and sentimental tribute to Yale.[20]

The day after Presentation Day, June 30, 1880, Camp was in Boston playing with Yale's baseball varsity against Harvard. Yale won, giving them three out of four against Harvard for the season. Camp was hitless but, according to the *New Haven Register*, "got in his usual fine work" and finished the game with a "splendid catch" in left field for Harvard's final out.[21]

Graduation exercises came the following day, July 1, with President Rutherford Hayes present to speak and receive an honorary doctor of laws degree. The 119 graduates marched to Center Church on the New Haven Green, and families, friends, and onlookers packed the building. Camp was honored with a "second colloquy," the lowest category; 58 of the 119 graduates in the class of '80 received academic honors higher than Camp's. Four hours of speeches filled the afternoon before the class of '80 was released to their future.[22]

Moving on, Ready or Not 9

On the train, Bob Watson could finally relax. As Yale football captain, he had just attended the 1880 convention of the Intercollegiate Football Association, and it had turned into a scramble. It lasted so long that he and the other Yale delegate had to skip supper and rush to the depot for their train.[1]

Now click-clacking and bobbing down the tracks in an 1880-era train perhaps warmed by a woodstove in the corner, Bob could settle back and get some perspective. He would have a lot to tell his good friend Walter Camp, Yale's former captain and delegate, who had moved on to medical school but still loved the game. This was certainly the most important convention since the IFA was organized in 1876.

The newspapers would probably focus on player numbers. After years of Yale's pushing, the rules had finally been changed to eleven players per side. Princeton had voted for eleven, overcoming Harvard's opposition.[2]

But there was more, much more. The delegates had gone through all the rules, one at a time. Bob read them out loud, and then they were discussed. All afternoon the delegates worked until it grew dark, when he would be required to read in the glow from gaslights on the walls or kerosene lamps on the tables.[3]

The most important change—ensuring bold letters for the year 1880 in football history books—was to put into words for the first time the essential events of a scrimmage, the central event of the new "American" football. Working with the original Rugby Football Union scrimmage definition, the delegates replaced the language removed at last year's convention with the following new (underlined) language:

> A scrimmage takes place when the holder of the ball, being in the field of play, puts it on the ground in front of him, <u>and puts it in play when on side by kicking or snapping it back. The man who first receives the ball from the snap-back shall be called a quarter back, and shall not then run forward with the ball, under penalty of a foul</u>.[4]

The new rule had developed in stages, last year deleting language everyone knew was no longer true, this year adding words to describe and give definition to the scrimmage that was becoming common in American play. Newly coined words were included that would become permanent—*snapping it back*, a backward kick intended to be a quick propulsion, and *quarterback*, italicized in the rule book to emphasize its newness and significance.

The changes were dramatic and fundamental, but, amazingly, 1880 reporters paid little attention. Only the *Harvard Crimson* even mentioned it, and they did not discuss its significance. To participants and observers alike, the new definition must simply have described what American teams in fact were already doing in practice.[5]

Actually, putting words to Americans' evolving on-the-field practices was more complicated than the rule's authors apparently understood. Important implications, both problematic and beneficial, were not fully appreciated until following years, such as potential allowance of ball possession without limit, creation of a framework for routine, and increased opportunity for planning.

Americans' rugby-based play was entering only its fifth year, but already it had changed in fundamental and crucial ways, giving it a beginning resemblance to today's American game. Yet big differences still existed:

1. Snap-back with the foot, not the hands

Incredible, even humorous as it may seem today, the snapback of 1880 was done with the foot, not the hands. Having evolved from a backward kick, the snapback procedure continued to use the foot in 1880 and for several years afterward.[6]

2. No time limits and no huddle

When one play ended and players were back on their feet, sideline observers could hear captains calling out, "Line up, Yale," "Line up, Princeton." Players did not first gather into a huddle to decide a strategy. In the early years, strategy was limited, but the captain sometimes gestured or spoke a signal describing what players were to do.

The "snapback" was primarily initiated at the offensive team's timing. No time was specified for the possessing team to make the snapback, thus allowing play to be slow or faster at the offensive team's option.

3. No forward passing

Americans' 1880 rules were verbatim with English rugby rules on the subject of "passing." A player could throw the ball to another player "who is at the time behind him," but could not throw the ball "in the direction of the opponents' goal line." Thus, the quarterback could throw the ball sideways or backward, that is, "lateral" it, to a back or sometimes a lineman who moved behind him, but he could not throw the ball forward toward the opponents' goal.[7]

American football scrimmage as first defined in an 1880 rule amendment, with a kickback from the center to the quarterback. (Yale athletics photographs, ca. 1850–2007 [inclusive], Manuscripts and Archives, Yale University)

Historians have commonly, and incorrectly, listed Camp as a delegate to the October 1880 convention that enacted the new scrimmage definition; some have even contended he imagined and created the new scrimmage procedure and presented it at the convention. The assertion of his attendance is certainly not correct; contemporaneous reports confirm Camp was not a convention delegate.[8]

More important, neither Camp nor any other single individual "created" the 1880 American football scrimmage. This essential feature developed on the field, a trial-and-error, gradual effort. It involved acts of significant creation, but by multiple players in combination, reflecting a shared dislike of rugby's unpredictability.[9]

The Americans' gradual change from rugby's scrum to America's scrimmage was mostly unreported in American newspapers, but signs could be found. One such sign surprisingly appeared in the *Toronto Mail*, reporting an 1879 game between the Universities of Michigan and Toronto. Michigan was a new entrant to American football, a public university with a supportive legislature and progressive leadership; since its 1837 founding, it had grown to an 1879 enrollment of about five hundred undergraduates, with more in the medical and law schools, large enough to be Harvard's and Yale's primary rival in size. The informative *Toronto Mail* article was reporting Michigan's second intercollegiate football game, played in Detroit in November 1879 against the University of Toronto (the first had been in May 1879 in Chicago against Wisconsin's Racine College). The *Mail* reporter was struck by Michigan's style of play: "The first scrimmage showed that Michigan intended playing the open or Harvard formation. Instead of the forwards . . . forming a regular scrimmage, they simply line out while one of their number passes the ball out at the side or behind to some one of the second line."[10] Here are the essentials of the new scrimmage being developed by America's players: "forwards" who "line out," a "second line" (backfield) located "behind" the forwards, and a player who "passes the ball out," possibly the snapper-back but more likely a quarterback because of the term *passes* rather than *kicks* (the snapback was a kick, not a "pass") and because the passing can be in multiple directions—"to the side" or "behind" (the snapback was straight back to reach the quarterback as soon as possible).

The *Toronto Mail* report shows how developed Americans' new style of play was in 1879 and how far across the country it had moved, a year before the 1880 convention, sometimes alleged to be the first appearance of the procedure. The *Mail*'s reference to a "Harvard formation" suggests the Canadian reporter had seen Harvard use it during games in Canada. But it was more than Harvard's style. Princeton and Yale had also used it, as indicated in the *New York Times* report of the 1879 Princeton-Yale game, where after a ball carrier was downed, "the rushers lined" to resume play.[11]

The aim of delegates at the 1880 convention was not to create a new style of play, but to reduce to words practices already occurring on the field and to standardize play by incorporating those words in the rule book. Words in the rule book also ended pretense, giving official sanction to the "heeling out" developed through originally surreptitious or rebellious evasions of rugby's traditions and practices.

Although Camp did not create America's new football scrimmage, it would not be surprising to find he was involved in developing or writing the rule book's new scrimmage definition. The primary early historian of American football, Parke Davis, contended Camp wrote the definition, but neither Davis nor anyone else provided supporting evidence.[12]

Involvement by Camp would be consistent with other known facts. Bob Watson, Yale's 1880 captain who succeeded Camp as a delegate to the 1880 convention, would certainly have discussed the upcoming convention issues with him; in fact, he said he depended on Camp's counsel—his "knowledge of the game . . . [was] so great." As discussed earlier in chapter 6, at least some details of the new scrimmage formation had likely been developed at Yale while Camp was captain. Further, "snapping back" was explicitly identified on the agenda of a student-body meeting held at Yale on October 4, 1880, to instruct the school's delegates for the 1880 convention. Such a preparatory discussion, with Camp likely present, could have produced suggested wording for a new snapping-back scrimmage definition.[13]

Yet Camp never claimed to be the author of the scrimmage definition, possibly because the definition involved joint effort, at either Yale or the convention or both. Also, it was quickly apparent the definition was not a finished work justifying an authorship claim, for the attempt to put the critical scrimmage feature of American football into words had left serious problems soon revealed on the next year's playing fields.

By the fall of 1880, Camp had moved home and enrolled at Yale Medical School, aiming to become a surgeon. Along with two-thirds of his fellow '80 Yale graduates, Walter Camp decided to attend professional school.[14]

Good reasons supported his choice. He had been interested in the human body and its physical development since boyhood when he visited the Yale gymnasium, and that interest continued while he was football captain with training programs for himself and members of his teams. Additionally, there was a practical encouragement: a surgeon friend had a place for him in his practice. A writing career was unlikely to match that financial security.[15]

Another reason, perhaps unstated but likely more than incidental: continuing at Yale kept him connected to Yale athletics. He could remain on Yale's football and baseball teams; no rule barred any student in any department of a college from playing on the college's teams. More than that, he could continue on two groundbreaking committees formed in his senior year to promote and manage Yale's athletic program, one to find and develop a Yale playing field to replace the rented field at Hamilton Park and another to receive input from Yale alumni seeking to ensure strong Yale athletic teams; Yale's students had accepted the alumni initiative but insisted that the committee include students and be only "advisory" in nature. As Yale football captain, Camp had been a member of both committees.[16]

During Camp's first year in medical school, the two committees were consolidated, and he was added to the consolidated committee, a clear recognition of his reputation among students and alumni. The one other addition was a prominent Yale professor, Theodore S. Woolsey, professor of international law, son of an earlier Yale president, and an ardent sportsman and supporter of Yale's athletic teams. The combined committee comprised seven undergraduates, one graduate school student (Camp), four alumni,

Walter Camp's 1880 Yale College graduation picture. (Images of Yale individuals, ca. 1750–2001 [inclusive], Manuscripts and Archives, Yale University)

and two professors. In the world of college athletics, this student-alumni-faculty committee was an innovation.[17]

Camp's deep continued interest and involvement in football even though he had moved on to medical school is evidenced by a document tucked into a present-day Yale archives folder. The folder is a repository for early American football rules, and the tucked-in document is an early rule book that is curious as well as noteworthy.[18]

Curious because, though apparently intended as the official 1880 rule book—commercially printed and with an official-looking blue cover like others in the folder—the rules in the book are a mess, incredibly incomplete and garbled, impossible to use. Printer's error? Confusing print instructions by a less-than-businesslike student scribe? Was a replacement published? No other rule book for 1880 has been found.[19]

Noteworthy because this flawed document includes the first-known instruction manual for American football players, an eleven-page section written by "Walter C. Camp, '80," entitled "Hints for Practice." In this messed-up, impossible-to-use 1880 rule book appears Camp's first public writing on football.

Buried in a useless rule book, Camp's instruction manual was nevertheless a milestone: it provided some record of American football's 1880 nature and status, it testified to Camp's continued love for the game and sense of ownership and responsibility, and it demonstrated that his participation was deep, sufficient to write a detailed discussion of the game with instructions for its play. Some initiative was still moving Camp, some wish to make the game better, and some confidence he had something to say. His own playing days were limited, yet Camp wanted to build football and in some way make it more fulfilling and enjoyable not only for himself but for all players and other interested parties.

The instructions were of a practical nature and provide insight as to the nature of the game in 1880:

> DIVISION OF PLAYERS.
>
> There are three principal divisions of players—"backs," "half-backs" and "rushers," [and] also four individual positions—"middle rusher," "quarterback," "goal kicker" and "placer."[20]

Although a "middle rusher" had been established, located centrally and performing the snapback, other rushers had no set positions and no titles—no "guards," "tackles," or "ends." From his 1880 perspective, Camp regarded "middle rusher" as "the most prominent and important" position:

> You must follow the ball wherever it goes, be with it always, and never be satisfied unless your own side has possession of it. . . . When the ball is down by one of your side he gives it into your hands. When your rushers are in line, your half-backs in position, and your quarterback ready, you place the ball on the ground, being careful not to let go of it, put your foot on it and snap it back by a downward and backward pressure to your quarter-back.[21]

And the quarterback? He is "the middle rusher's assistant"—*assistant!* He must make up his mind "to many hard knocks," for the opposing rushers will frequently be

> upon you before you have time to pass the ball, and you must never lose it. . . . Always make up your mind what you are going to do with the ball before you give the signal to snap it back. . . . If the ball does not come to you accurately from the middle rusher [as it rolls or bounces along the ground], don't try to pass it, but throw yourself upon it and have it "down"; don't stoop over and try to pick it up, but fall on it, thus making sure of it.[22]

The two other positions that Camp identified and discussed were a "goal kicker" and "placer":

> When you are to kick select a good spot; your placer drops on the ground with the ball, careful not to let it touch the ground . . . ; you stand over him, and direct the change of [the ball's] position until the seam points over the middle of the goal; tell when it suits you, then watch and the instant he places it on the ground, step and kick.[23]

Having written carefully, striving to advance football and perhaps his own reputation, imagine the shock and dismay Camp felt when he first paged through the finished printed document that now resides in the Yale archives. Revolting, laughable, sad—unusable as a rule book, a likely candidate for the trash can.

10 Still under Construction

Two months—that's all it took to learn that the new scrimmage definition of the 1880 convention had a fatal flaw. And who should make it obvious—demonstrate it in public for all to see—but Frank Loney, Princeton's football captain and chair of the 1880 convention that enacted the new rule.

Loney faced a challenge on Thanksgiving Day 1880. Princeton and Yale were again playing for the college football championship. Yale had a veteran team, agile and big, much bigger than Princeton's. Camp was included, still playing in his first year of medical school, physically mature and experienced (but his presence was no different from last year when Princeton's Theodore McNair, one of Princeton's best athletes ever, played in his first year of seminary and helped Princeton hold the Camp-captained Yale team to a tie). Arriving at the game, Yale's fans were waving cash and offering two-to-one odds.[1]

Facing the Yale juggernaut, Loney came up with a defensive strategy based on past championships: Princeton claimed to be the defending IFA champion; if they could simply avoid losing to Yale, get at least a tie, they could maintain they still were champions, never having been dethroned. Pressed to the wall before the day was over, Loney retreated to a loophole in the new scrimmage definition that could keep Princeton from losing.

The game was played on new grounds in New York City. James Gordon Bennett Jr.—sportsman-playboy, having succeeded his father as publisher of the *New York Herald*—owned a field north of Central Park that he had converted into a playing ground for polo. Bennett's "Polo Grounds" attracted others: a new professional baseball team had obtained a lease to play baseball there, upgraded the field, and built a grandstand.[2]

College football players immediately recognized the benefits of the new grounds and grandstand. Also, two nearby elevated-train stations made transportation easier and faster than to the Elysian Fields in Hoboken. Princeton and Yale got permission to play their 1880 Thanksgiving Day championship game at the Polo Grounds.

Thanksgiving Day was preceded by a snowstorm, and when the Princeton and Yale teams arrived at the grounds, a small army of workmen was still shoveling the field, working in a stiff breeze. Even in the storm, four thousand people had gathered, half standing in snow and the rest divided between the setback grandstand and the tops of carriages and hotel coaches.

Princeton won the toss and, with the breeze at their backs, started play aggressively. Before long Yale was in trouble, with snow blowing in their faces and Princeton pushing them back to their goal. Yale was forced to touch the ball down behind the goal line—to take a safety, costing nothing but pride and allowing Yale to kick out of immediate danger. With that help, they managed to push Princeton back. For the rest of the first half, the game was fairly even and no one scored.

Sides were changed to start the second half. The field had become slick, and it was difficult for a kicker to keep his balance. Few kicks were attempted, and the players limited themselves to running.

Yale gradually forced the ball near Princeton's goal, but Princeton got possession on a turnover. Facing the wind and unable to advance the ball, Princeton took a safety. Yale's superiority began to show, and they continued pressing toward Princeton's goal. Within a fifteen-minute span, Princeton took five more safeties—they would end the game with eleven safeties that cost them nothing in the game scoring.

Princeton's safeties were merely a prelude to their final effort, Loney's loophole in the new rules. With Princeton still under pressure in their own end of the field, Loney directed his men to neither kick nor pass the ball after a snapback, but simply run forward into the Yale line. Princeton achieved no cumulative forward progress and could not win by their strategy, but they succeeded at keep-away, holding onto the ball. Spectators loudly disapproved, hissing as Princeton held the ball until the end of the game—twenty minutes without Yale ever having a chance for an offensive play.[3]

Early American football game as drawn by A. B. Frost and published in the November 5, 1881, *Harper's Weekly*, with the crowd apparently of as much interest to the artist as the players. (The Lost Century of Sports Collection, LostCentury.com)

When time ran out, Loney ran off the field, triumphantly waving his cap. Camp was so frustrated at the rules gone awry that on the spot, he challenged Princeton to name the time and place for another game; Yale's Hill and Watson promptly formalized the challenge in a letter to Princeton's football officers. Princeton refused, claiming they were still champions: they were the last team to win the championship, and until defeated they continued as champions. Princeton's claim was hollow, and the IFA, with Harvard, Princeton, and Yale the only active members, awarded no championship in 1880.[4]

The players and fans had a name for Princeton's strategy, the "block" game: it blocked play and prevented an accurate conclusion on the field. The block-game strategy was made possible by the possession feature of the American game inherent in the new scrimmage definition just enacted at the 1880 IFA convention. Princeton had legitimately gotten ball possession, and unless they fumbled or intentionally kicked the ball away, they could legitimately keep possession. Possession in hand, Princeton made no attempt to win, simply to avoid what otherwise would likely be a loss. This was a consequence legislators at the 1880 convention had not foreseen, and thoughtful players and observers knew the rules had to be changed.

Shortly after the Princeton game, Camp became ill with typhoid fever, fairly common at the time and dangerous. In 1880 New Haven County had forty-seven deaths attributed to typhoid, and that was a typical year.[5] Camp had moved back home for medical school, so he had a place to rest and be cared for. His first year in medical school was seriously interrupted, yet the illness did not get in the way of sports. He had played football for the Yale varsity in the fall before he became ill, and by spring he was ready for Yale baseball. The next fall, he was again ready for football.[6]

He was also ready for rule making. Even though he had graduated from Yale College and was now in medical school, he joined Yale's two regular undergraduate delegates (the 1881 captain and the president of the Yale Football Association) at a critical rule-making convention on Saturday, October 8, 1881. Delegates had come from all four member colleges to take up the "block" games that threatened American football (Columbia had been reinstated after promising to field a team). Newspapers reported that Yale was aiming for "radical" change, and Camp's senior status and unique experience might help achieve that.[7] He fitted in comfortably, not loud or aggressive and with a respected background. In fact, the delegates elected him secretary of the meeting. Perhaps he could help avoid a rule-printing mess like last year's and get the rules published correctly.[8]

Yet there was tension in the room. Princeton saw their strategy last Thanksgiving as skillful defensive play. Yale saw it as an evasion, a distortion from what was intended and denying a legitimate win for the stronger team. Yale wanted the rules changed to prevent such an event from happening again.[9]

The delegates readily agreed on one change: if games ended in a tie, two fifteen-minute periods would be added at the end, like mini-halves of a standard game, giving an added chance for one team to achieve a tiebreaking score.[10]

But that avoided the real problems. For one, safety touchdowns should count against the team making them. Princeton and Yale had officially played to a draw in Camp's last season as captain, but Yale was stronger and Princeton even then had used safeties to escape Yale's pressure and a possible Yale score. The previous year's convention had tried to make safeties count but without success. Now Yale renewed the effort, and they were helped by the eleven safeties Princeton took in the past Thanksgiving game, which further dramatized the problem. Neither players nor spectators wanted a game not decided by true football skills.[11]

But Princeton resisted. Only after extended discussion and negotiation in which Harvard sided with Yale could the convention compromise on a new rule: "A side which makes four or more safety touch-downs less than their opponents shall win the game in case nothing else is obtained."[12]

This compromise-weakened language did not directly address the whole block-game problem. Perhaps the delegates counted on a stronger team forcing four or more safeties from an opponent playing a block game. A standard of "four" would have given Yale the win against Princeton both in 1879 and in 1880. Although the new rule still allowed too much freedom for a weaker team, it was a start and better than no rule at all.

This year, with Camp as secretary, the rules did get published—at least twice. One set was published October 29, 1881, as a supplement to the *Yale Courant*; another set was published as a separate rules booklet by "Princeton College." The Yale set, presumably prepared for publication by Camp, included section headings that introduced the theme of the rule or rules that followed.

The big test for the new rules came in the Princeton-Yale game, again the last game of the year on Thanksgiving at New York's Polo Grounds. Princ-

The 1881 Yale football team; Walter Camp is to the captain's left, legs stretched straight forward. (Yale athletics photographs, ca. 1850–2007 [inclusive], Manuscripts and Archives, Yale University)

eton had tied, and Yale defeated, Harvard; whoever won today would be IFA champion. The day was raw and chilly, with a strong northwest wind, but no snow. Nearly ten thousand spectators showed up, by far the largest crowd yet to watch an American football game.[13]

Early in the game, with the ball at midfield, Princeton fumbled and Yale recovered. Camp was again playing, and, with the wind at his back, he launched a strong kick out-of-bounds in the corner near Princeton's goal. Princeton would have to put the ball in play dangerously near its own goal line. But their best option for doing that, a kick, was out of the question: it would be foolhardy to kick into the strong wind from a point so near their own goal line. And taking a safety to avoid a dangerous kick could also be costly under the new safety rule.

Now came the most ingenious method yet to block play and escape a loss. The teams lined up, and the ball was successfully snapped back to Princeton's quarterback, who turned and threw to a Princeton halfback oddly waiting in what was called "touch-in-goal"—the portion of the field behind the goal line and outside the sideline. Touch-in-goal had its own rule: a ball that "goes into touch in goal . . . is at once dead and out of the game." Princeton's halfback touched the ball down in touch-in-goal, and Princeton claimed the ball was dead, giving them the right to put the ball in play from the twenty-five-yard line.[14]

Yale immediately appealed to the referee, Billy Manning, a senior and captain of Harvard's football team. Each side made their case while fans waited in their seats, increasingly impatient. Yale argued that the touch-in-goal section of the field was behind the goal line, and in at least the spirit of the rule passed at the just-completed convention, a ball touched down anywhere behind the goal line was a safety to be counted against Princeton.

Princeton answered simply: the words of the rules explicitly contradicted Yale's argument. A ball touched down in touch-in-goal was dead and could have no effect in the scoring. Manning pondered and then decided for Princeton—the rule's words were clear and controlling. Princeton's play had not produced a safety, and Princeton could take the ball to the twenty-five-yard line and put the ball in play from there.

Throughout the first half, Princeton held onto the ball as long as possible, throwing into touch-in-goal when the pressure grew too great and then kicking from the twenty-five. During the whole half, they gained only ten yards. Before the half was over, Princeton had downed the ball in touch-in-goal four times, enough, if they were safeties, to make a score for Yale. But under Manning's ruling, they were of no effect in scoring.[15]

In the second half, it was Yale's turn to face the stiff wind. Camp was serving as captain because of an injury to Eaton. Yale needed only a tie. They had defeated Harvard; Princeton had only tied Harvard. If the present game ended in a tie, Yale would be ahead in the standings and should be awarded the championship. So in the second half, now facing the wind, Yale made its own effort to hold onto the ball. They were never forced to take a safety or down the ball in touch-in-goal but managed to hold the ball throughout the second half. Princeton never had an offensive play.[16]

Disgust settled over American football. Football's student legislators still had not solved their possession problem. The game was still in danger, even more than before.

Englishmen were appalled at what had happened to their rugby game. Writing to the *New York Herald,* "A Resident Englishman" decried the woeful game he had gone to see: too slow; ball kicked backward, not forward, as proper in a manly game; players sparring with one another all over the field, whether the ball was between them or not; long delays over disputes about rules. Bottom line: Americans, return to real rugby before it's too late![17]

But it was not just the English. During the winter and spring, American students and players debated in person and in the college press. Something was missing; play had become negative, a game of keep-away rather than determined effort to advance and win. Camp was especially worried. He had been struggling to strengthen football and to obtain newspaper coverage to build up the game. The last two games between Princeton and Yale were ugly and impossible to sell to players or the public. And they were counter to what he had known and appreciated about football, where striving, determination, battling were of the essence. Somehow he and other leaders of the six-year-old game had to get it back on track.[18]

The Main Invention 11

Billy Manning, Harvard football captain and president of the Intercollegiate Football Association, listened as contentious voices struggled to agree on an answer. Twelve students from the four colleges of the IFA were debating football rules at an emergency convention in April 1882—no waiting for the regular convention in October. Two seasons now had passed with no solution to the block-game problem, and alarm was growing. How much longer would it be until the few colleges involved in American football lost interest and the game faded away?[1]

Yet there was no simple answer. Walter Camp had recently warned in the *Yale Courant* that some publicly advocated solutions would remake American football into primarily a kicking game, taking away the running, ball possession, and quarterback play that made the game appealing. Earlier rule making had involved known options: How long should the game be—ninety minutes or sixty? Relative to touchdowns, what scoring value should a kicked goal from the field have—four to one or three to one? No such options were available today. Today something more like a miracle was needed, a solution where there was no apparent answer.[2]

Each member school—Columbia, Harvard, Princeton, and Yale—had responded to Manning's call and sent three delegates. Of all the conventions since the IFA's founding six years ago, this was the largest. The delegates had first taken up a fervent wish still pressed by concerned Englishmen: solve the block-game problem by returning to real rugby. On that a no vote was immediate and unanimous! No discarding the snapback that had given American football an exciting new mechanism and pattern of play.[3]

Still, what would they do? As Manning listened, the discussion moved to a new idea Camp had brought to the convention, a revolutionary new rule he proposed to add to the rule book: "If in three consecutive downs a team does not advance the ball at least five yards, they must give up the ball to the opposite side on the spot of the last down." The idea had met with skepticism, and Camp was its only defender. All the others, including Manning, had doubts.[4]

Admittedly, the idea was radical. A ball possession that was limited but potentially extendible was a completely new idea. Making an advance of a specified number of yards the condition for continued possession was further new. In fact, just measuring the yards of ball movement along the length of a rugby football field was new—unprecedented and irrelevant to rugby's wild physical whirl. The earlier development of American scrimmage procedures—organized, intentional, planned—had injected a dose of modern order into primitive rugby, but now Camp was proposing even more alteration, inserting a kind of technology, crucial physical measurements where they had never existed, definite locations to be pinpointed on a 110-yard expanse of mostly unmarked green.

Camp's proposal seemed variously to amuse, offend, or dismay convention delegates. His seniority—twenty-three years old and in medical school, secretary of the IFA, longest American football experience—didn't stop the laughing, the pooh-poohing. Princeton was the leading doubter, and Princeton's strapping captain, "Ned" Peace, was boisterous and irreverent. Delegates threw many questions and doubts at Camp, predictions of impossibility for the single referee in charge of the games:

- How could the referee measure whether five yards had been gained?
- He would have to sight, perhaps across the whole field, and pretend to know whether the ball had been advanced five yards forward from its original spot.
- He could easily forget the exact spot from which five yards must be gained.
- The game would be repeatedly delayed to measure and argue the distance gained.

At one point, Camp responded, "The field can be marked with lines five yards apart to assist the referee." More laughter! "It would look like a gridiron!"[5]

Princeton had its own proposals. Defeat the possession problem by limiting possession to four consecutive downs. Camp had publicly warned about that idea. Four downs would hardly ever allow a team to gain the whole distance needed for a touchdown. After three downs, the incentive would be to kick the ball downfield, to move play away from the kicker's goal toward the opponent's goal. Running would be minimized; the game would become mainly a kicking game.[6]

Though partly parallel to Princeton's proposal, Camp's idea was vastly different in concept and effect. Allowing a team to continue offensive play by satisfying a condition, specifically a measured advance of five yards in three downs, was not suggested by any other relevant games or prior writings or teachings, a true out-of-the-blue invention. A century-plus of play may have obscured the boldness and innovation of the idea, made it seem natural and necessary. But at the time, it was not at all natural. Introduction of critical numerical distance measurements into a still primitive game that previously had no hint of such measurements and no methodology for making them went beyond nonobvious—more like impossible! And reconstructing the basic method of play in reliance on a steady repetition of such measurements was a further reach. Camp's fellow delegates generally considered the idea crazy and unworkable.

Princeton had another proposal based on positioning players on the field. Each team would be required to have exactly six men on the rush line, and the offensive team's halfbacks would be required to be at least ten yards behind their rush line. Such an arrangement, requiring the halfbacks to receive the ball many yards behind the line of scrimmage, apparently was expected to force a run forward and attempt to advance the ball; playing a block-game strategy (that is, continuing to hold the ball irrespective of the position on the field) would risk too great a loss.[7]

Again Camp could doubt: Wouldn't such a change introduce artificial and rigid requirements? America's game had a desirable simplicity, an openness to strategic imagination by quarterbacks and captains; do we want to limit that?

On the discussion went, with scant support for Camp's proposal. Columbia was siding with Princeton. Manning himself, at a meeting a few weeks earlier where the British Football Club again advocated a return to rugby, had spoken in favor of Princeton's proposal to keep halfbacks ten yards back.[8]

But today, at this special meeting searching for some new break with the past, Manning held back. A natural leader (president of the Harvard senior class and soon to be chief marshal at Harvard's graduation ceremony), he tried to impartially gauge the merits of the conflicting arguments. Manning and Camp had worked together as IFA president and secretary, and Manning knew Camp as a serious student of the game. Camp came to rules meetings with pages of analysis—summaries of how referees had interpreted particular rules in previous game situations, historical explanations of when and why a previous rule had been changed or omitted, interpretations of rules, and studies of their consequences. One observer called Camp a "plodder," not characterized by quick, brilliant insights. A better description would be "deliberate" or "prepared," one who reached decisions after careful study and consideration. Camp's notes[9] reveal a thorough and energetic mind, searching, gathering, and recording numerous and varied items of data and then assembling and working with that data to think out an issue, arrive at a decision, and develop an argument to explain and defend the decision. No one else studied rules as Camp did; no one else gave as much thought to rule-making issues.[10]

Certainly, Camp had discussed his three-down, five-yard idea with Manning before the meeting, probably even before Manning called the meeting; Camp had sketched the idea in a *Yale Courant* article a few months earlier. Now at the meeting, Camp could press his idea verbally, offering reasons calmly and respectfully, "like a clergyman," not loud, but with conviction showing in "a pair of exceptional, keen, piercing brown eyes that were always talking." Then he would wait, dependent on other delegates to see the advantages of the proposed rule. He respected the democratic process; this was his fourth convention, but he had still been welcomed and even given the secretary's job.[11]

Finally, Manning decided he trusted Camp enough to take a chance. He stated a tentative approval of the Camp proposal: "Let's give it a try." When some delegates resisted, he added: "If it doesn't work, we can try something else." Grudgingly, the convention accepted that outcome, but not before extracting a condition: the rule would be reevaluated early in the coming fall and if ineffective put away before the important championship games.[12]

Princeton still doubted, and a long article in the May 12, 1882, *Princetonian* set forth their doubts, emphasizing a perceived difficulty in measuring forward progress: "To make the rule practicable, a surveyor . . . should be on the grounds . . . to drive a stake . . . and measure with chain and pegs." In addition:

> The sport will become unintelligible to the average spectator.
>
> The referee will be given superior powers and yet faced with impossible decisions.
>
> Constant delays will surely occur.

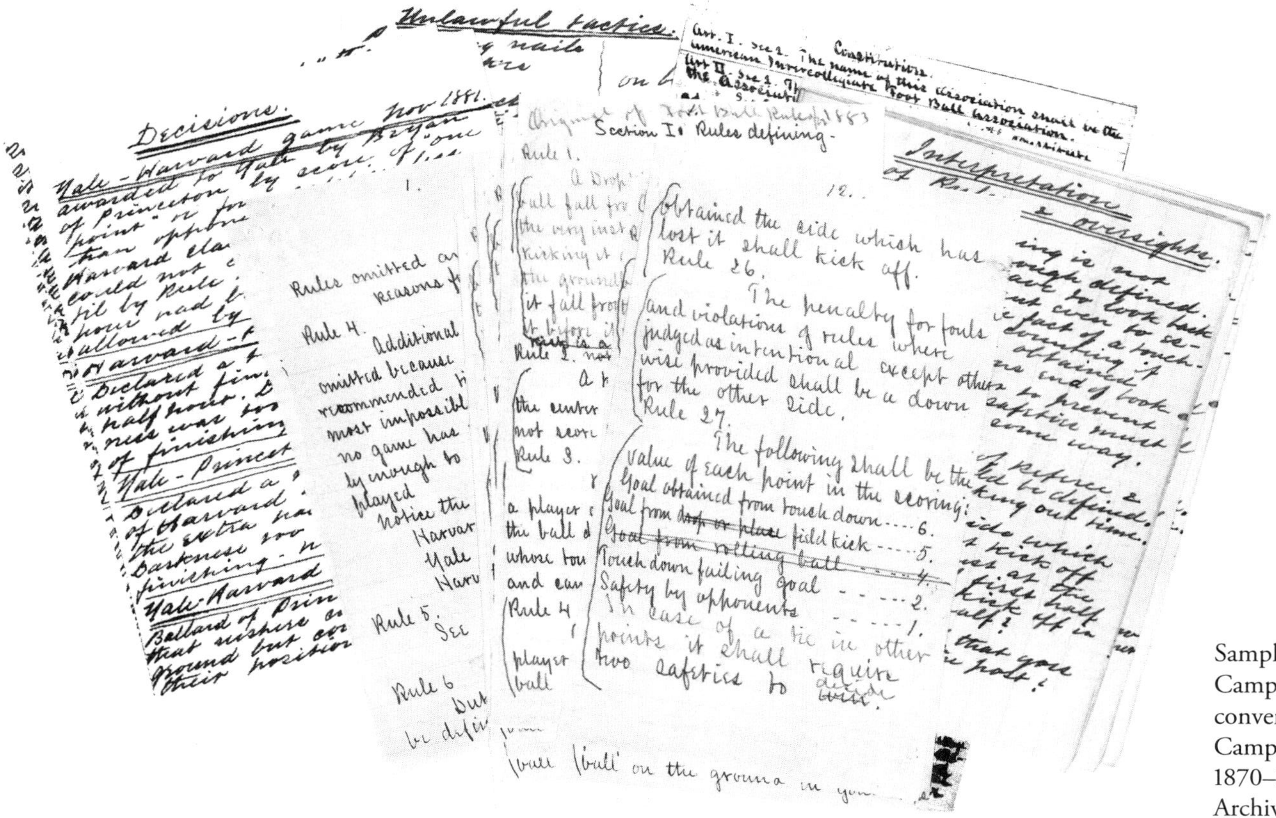

Sample of notes made by Walter Camp in preparation for rules conventions. (Walter Chauncey Camp Papers, 1870–1983 [inclusive], 1870–1925 [bulk], Manuscripts and Archives, Yale University)

> The new rule should be tested before the fall so a change may yet be made before competition begins.

Despite Princeton's doubts, the rule had passed, a tentative experiment to be tested in the fall games. Camp was always thankful to Manning, crediting him as the key to the rule's passage.[13]

The April 1882 convention was good news with its qualified approval of his "downs-and-distance" or "five-yard" rule; Camp soon got bad news, however. Two months after the convention, at the end of the school year and in the midst of playing Yale varsity baseball, he took the final tests for his second year in medical school. The results were a status report, a wake-up call: out of ten subjects, he failed five. Anatomy and surgery, major subjects critical for an aspiring surgeon, were among those failed. Was he putting in the effort needed to be a doctor? Did he have the kind of memory required for a course like anatomy? In any event, in the upcoming year, scheduled to be his final year, he would need to catch up on the five failed subjects, as well as undertake new subjects. Not unheard of, but he had a lot of work to do.[14]

Camp's medical-school setbacks didn't keep him from football. In the fall of 1882, just four months after the failed courses, Camp was again working with the varsity football team. But one day in practice, he dislodged cartilage in a knee, a worse injury than he'd ever experienced before. The leg was put in a cast; he would not play football for Yale this year.[15]

However, he kept involved with the team, involved enough to be later described as helping coach the team. Camp was early in a custom that would become common at Yale and other colleges: graduates attended practice to teach and offer suggestions from their experience. Sometimes he offered correction ("Kick high so your rushers can get to the ball when it comes down"), sometimes encouragement ("Nice tackle, Deacon"), sometimes a yank on a player's dislocated finger to get it back in place.[16]

One day Yale's football captain and two of his players made their way over to see Camp at home. The Camps, with Walter, had moved west across town to the corner of Chapel and Gill Streets, to a duplex closer to Dwight School that Leverett had purchased many years before. Leverett, Ellen, and Walter lived in half of the duplex; Uncle Henry and Aunt Elizabeth Peck had purchased and occupied the other half.

Camp welcomed the visitors, husky young men who could enliven a nineteenth-century parlor. Game strategy was the subject of discussion. The new five-yard rule would make planning even more important, giving new reward for coordinating team effort to advance the ball. But how would the captain communicate the play to the rest of the team? (Huddles were unknown.) That led to a discussion of signals—a spoken word or words with a secret meaning that would tell the whole team the planned play.

Signals had been used in limited ways, but at this meeting more elaborate and extensive signals were discussed. Before the conversation was over, Camp wrote out a set of signals to be distributed to Yale players, the first-known written set of football signals. The signal "Play up sharp, Charlie" meant that when quarterback Twombley received the snapback, he would pass it to the end Wyllys for a sideline run. Five different signals were on the list, each of which had several variations through removing words.[17]

The signals were a step of preparation, getting Yale more ready for the 1882 season, when the new five-yard rule would get its test. No longer playing, Camp was still helping, still part of the team's preparation.

The 1882 American intercollegiate football season was the longest yet, a confirmation that students still wanted football. Harvard, Princeton, and Yale each scheduled eight intercollegiate games that year instead of last year's six and the previous year's five. Beginning in early October, Yale played Wesleyan, Rutgers (twice), the (Massachusetts) Institute of Technology, Amherst, and Columbia, all easy wins. Yale's first serious challenge came against Harvard at Cambridge, but Yale continued its winning pattern, scoring one goal and three touchdowns to none for Harvard.

Again the season would close on Thanksgiving Day, with Princeton against Yale at New York's Polo Grounds. Now April's rule-making rivals could together test the new five-yard rule. October had already passed with no effort made to cancel the rule, but since block games had unexpectedly afflicted the last two Princeton-Yale games, uncertainty was necessarily present as the teams lined up to play.

With a bigger line than Princeton's, Yale began the game by pushing the ball downfield. Then, in a coordinated play begun by Captain Tompkins's signal, "Quick Deac," Twombley got through the line to Princeton's fifteen-yard line. Two plays later, with Yale's halfback Eugene Richards having dropped noticeably back, apparently to try a dropkick, Tompkins signaled "Cheese it." At snapback Princeton's rushers barreled toward Richards, ready to block his kick when he got the expected lateral from quarterback Twombley. But Yale's tackle C. S. Beck had drifted casually back on the opposite side of Twombley from Richards; instead of Richards, Twombley turned and threw laterally to Beck, left alone and open to run for a touchdown. Richards kicked the goal, Yale's first against Princeton since 1876.[18]

Princeton did score a goal, but in the second half Yale managed another touchdown followed by a goal. The game ended with Yale in front two goals to one.

How had the new five-yard rule worked? The *Princetonian*'s game report gave a direct answer: "The new five-yard rule worked well in this game, and no attempt was made by either side to play any sort of block game. The result was as fine an exhibition of foot ball as has been seen for some years."[19] That's what others thought, too. A transformation had occurred, so clear and definite that it was immediately recognized. Camp later claimed that no rule ever obtained such "an immediate and satisfactory reform as did this five-yard rule."

12 Birth Year

The year 1882 should be celebrated in American football—the closest the game has to a "birth" year. Camp's April 1882 five-yard rule reworked the game, establishing a new content of play based on new playing goals—for the offense, sufficient advances to maintain ball possession; for the defense, limitation of advances sufficient to take away ball possession. Constant and imperative, these goals built structure, order, and regularity into the game, providing a backbone, a mechanism that dictated playing procedure from beginning to end.

Just as important, the new rule infused the game with tension and interest. Each play became important, a limited opportunity to advance toward the needed five yards and contribute to game success. Careful planning became a must, an occasion for study, innovation, and practice. Because each play had a specific and identifiable objective—a needed yardage gain—viewers watched with greater awareness as well as suspense. Knowing the goal, they waited eagerly for the outcome. Each play told a story, with winners, losers, and sometimes heroics.

At the end of the 1882 football season, America's football community was satisfied to know that the five-yard rule had pushed aside the threat posed by block games. But passing years and accumulating games brought recognition of a greater accomplishment. The time came when Camp inserted a credential in his published résumé: "author of the five-yard rule." And eventually, he became bold enough to write matter-of-factly as part of a different discussion, not boastfully but truthfully, "[The five-yard rule] has done more to make the game satisfactory than all of the rest of the legislation combined."[1] Huge changes were yet to come in American football, but none of them would alter the essential character impressed on the game by the five-yard rule and its eventual ten-yard replacement. Play was still primitive in 1882, with linemen facing each other in a standing posture while the center's kick rolled the ball on the ground backward to the quarterback. Yet basic mechanisms were in place to carry the game into the future. Besides laying a foundation on which American football could grow, Camp's downs-and-distance rule had provided a defining, recognizable, never-changing face for the game.

In an unprecedented flurry, the Intercollegiate Football Association held two more conventions that further marked 1882 as a birth year, with Camp critical to both. The most dramatic, though at the time receiving little media coverage, was a convention in late November or early December, where change began with acceptance finally of a penalty for safeties. The just-completed 1882 Harvard-Princeton game, in which Princeton had taken two safeties and Harvard none, had convinced the *Harvard Crimson*: "This kind of game . . . must be ruled out by next fall. . . . The five-yards rule has worked well and should be continued, so the only way to make the desired reform is to affix some penalty to safety touchdowns."[2] With time so ripe, leaders of the IFA met and, though working in a "decidedly hurried" manner, accomplished major change, reported in the December 23, 1882, *Spirit of the Times*:

> At a recent meeting, the Inter-Collegiate Foot Ball Association made some necessary changes . . . [that] . . . bid fair to abolish the "block" or "baby" game. . . .
>
> Hereafter the safety touchdown will be the unit of scoring. A touchdown equals 2 safeties, a goal kicked from the field equals 5 safeties, and a goal kicked from a touchdown equals 6 safeties.[3]

The last phrase contained an error, undoubtedly arising from the writer's background in rugby, where scores came only from a kicked goal and a touchdown had value only because it gave the right to try a goal kick. By contrast, in the IFA's new rules of November or December 1882, a touchdown was worth points; a goal following touchdown was worth more points, and in combination they totaled six "safeties," as shown in the following schedule:

Safety	1
Touchdown	2
Goal following touchdown	4
Goal from field	5

Roundabout, American football had come to a point system of scoring. No longer would telling a game's result require a complex sentence listing each team's number of touchdowns, goals after touchdown, goals from the field, and safeties. All of a team's scores could be summed up in a single point total.

Not stopping with safeties and a point system of scoring, the meeting also began a wholesale revision of the rules, cutting them from sixty-four to thirty-eight and rearranging their order. The old rules, built on an English rugby rule book, had become too cumbersome and obsolete. Camp almost certainly was a leader in the changes—he came to the convention with a handwritten draft of proposed rule revisions (including the point system of scoring) and with a copy of the April 1882 rule book profusely annotated with analysis and history as background for the desired cutting back of rules.[4]

Camp's work was recognized by his rule-making colleagues in their issuance of the 1883 rule book with a cover that read, "Revised by Walter Chauncey Camp. Authorized and Adopted by the American Intercollegiate Association." He in fact had been the rule reviser, and that is what the booklet's cover said.[5]

The 1883 rulebook was published by a Boston sporting-goods store, Wright and Ditson, beginning a new era of rules publication. The previous six years of rule books (1876 and 1878–82) had been published by local printers or college newspapers. Now, certainly with involvement by the rule reviser Camp, publication was being moved to a nonpartisan commercial enterprise having a dependable organization and broader geographic reach, allowing wider and surer circulation and saving publication costs for the IFA.

The third convention of 1882, the regular October convention, adopted a constitution that gave the six-year-old, four-member IFA a stronger foundation. Camp was again a prime mover, bringing a handwritten draft to the convention. The nuts and bolts of organization were set out—procedures for choosing officers, holding meetings, voting on business; rules for deciding where games would be played, for dividing gate receipts, for determining a champion.[6]

Camp's proposed constitution was accepted, except the delegates added two articles, the first of which applied directly to Camp: "No man shall

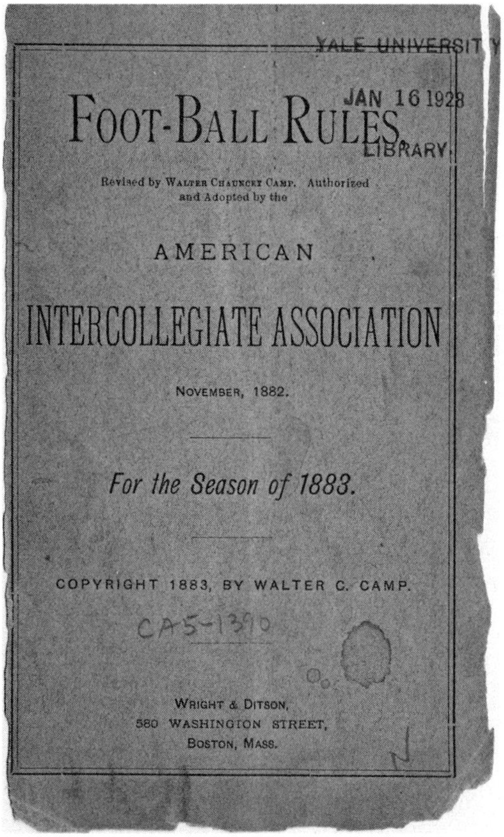
FOOT-BALL RULES.

Revised by Walter Chauncey Camp. Authorized and Adopted by the

AMERICAN

INTERCOLLEGIATE ASSOCIATION

November, 1882.

For the Season of 1883.

COPYRIGHT 1883, BY WALTER C. CAMP.

Wright & Ditson,
580 Washington Street,
Boston, Mass.

American football rule book for 1883. (Walter Chauncey Camp Papers, 1870–1983 [inclusive], 1870–1925 [bulk], Manuscripts and Archives, Yale University)

play in championship games for more than five seasons." Certainly, it was known that Camp had practiced with the Yale football team. Now, his college football playing days were definitely over. In fact, under the added article, he would have been ineligible in 1881, when he helped push Princeton into the block-game tactics that fortuitously led to the new five-yard rule.[7]

The second added article reflected the importance of a championship in the student mind. Each member of the IFA was required to contribute fifteen dollars for the purchase of a pennant to be awarded the IFA's season champion. These American schoolboys placed a high value on winning; championships were a prime achievement to be honored and displayed, not simply hidden away in record books.

Besides being a birth year for American football, 1882 was a year of beginnings for Camp—new commitments and participation, possibly even new life directions. Student populations had constantly changed since he became a rule maker in 1878, but he had been essentially a continuous presence, the one constant among those planning and administering American football. In 1882 his role became even larger—prominent in the installation of a constitution for the IFA; helping overhaul football's rules in three separate conventions, including extensive preparations before and persuasive leadership during the conventions; and, most important, contributing a new rule that remade the game.

On top of that, in 1882 Camp undertook to promote the new game. As the year ended, he wrote an article for the *Yale Courant*, an answer to British critics but also a tribute to American football. As a major theme, he asserted that American football had moved beyond British rugby to greater order and science: "Instead of a mass of men with no definite positions, kicking indiscriminately at the ball and their opponents [as in rugby], we have a game perfectly systematized. A position for every player and a duty for every position. We have two *end rushers* and two *next-the-end*. We have a *snapper-back* and his *right* and *left guard*. We have two *half backs*, one *quarter back* and one *back*."[8] Camp's own understanding of the game had advanced from 1880, when his abortive instructional text, "Hints for Practice," referred to the quarterback as the middle rusher's "assistant." Now further practice and play had developed the quarterback position: "The quarter back play which the Britishers so much despise is the key to the whole game. That whole game is one system and the whole team a machine which depends on the slightest move of that one man." The scrimmage organization with its quarterback position had given American football a distinct and original character recognized in Camp's "machine" metaphor, which was especially timely for late-nineteenth-century Americans. Six years earlier, machines had been the central theme at the 1876 centennial world's fair in Philadelphia, which was ceremonially opened by simultaneously starting a huge multistory steam engine and hundreds of adjacent machines in "Machinery Hall." For a society increasingly permeated by machines and science, Americans were building an ordered game in which players worked together like parts of a machine.[9]

The machine metaphor carried over to Camp's new five-yard rule, which produced increments of play repeating with machinelike regularity—line up, snapback, play, pause; line up, snapback, play, pause—steady, ongoing, certain as a pulsating piston. As a modernizing feature, the routine of the new rule brought organized efficiency, in which planned play increments proceeded steadily according to an established schedule. With that established regularity and planning came productivity, each play converted into a meaningful event with a consequential outcome. Players' time and energy were applied in goal-oriented, coordinated effort, attracting viewers' full and constant attention.

In contrast to the minimally structured and random play of English rugby and soccer, American football required study and planning, innovation, teaching, repeated practice. Increasingly, Americans would call American football scientific, as play became more studied and creative. And the distinctively American quarterback position—no other sport has a position like it—would increasingly become a central organizing feature.

At the time Camp wrote his 1882 article, he could only glimpse the benefits provided by the five-yard rule. Yet he was certain that American football was much better to watch and play than rugby, requiring greater skill and training. He boasted in his article that if the British were to play their best players against America's best—one game under their rules, one under America's, total score to decide—Americans would win two to one.

America still looked up to Britain in 1882, the leading country in the world industrially and politically and the source of many of America's sports. But now Camp was convinced Americans had created a quality institution of their own, and he seemed eager to proclaim and describe what had happened. Despite recent travails personally and in football, the twenty-three-year-old medical student was increasingly confident of a promising future for the new game he and his fellow students had presented to the modern American sports world.

PART II

Getting Noticed

Impossible to Ignore 13

Harvard president Charles W. Eliot came to his office in September 1882 with plans that would mark a new era in college sports. Eliot perceived a problem, a problem best illustrated by Yale athletic teams: Yale players were too focused on "winning"! They put too much time and effort into sports, distracting them from a college's primary educational mission.[1]

Eliot was a recognized leader among college presidents. In thirteen years since becoming Harvard president at age thirty-five, he had reformed the school: students had been freed to move from ancient required classics to a broad range of electives, Harvard's medical and law schools had been overhauled to greatly raise the stature of professional education, and the college's faculty had been enlarged and strengthened and its administration modernized and firmly controlled. Harvard was pulling away from Yale, with 887 undergraduates in the 1881–82 school year to Yale's 786; plus Harvard had another 400 students in its well-regarded medical and law schools, compared to Yale's 90.[2]

Crossing the campus to his office that late-summer morning, Eliot typically would have been aloof and somber. A large liver-colored birthmark covered much of the right side of his face, which he tried to minimize with full sideburns stretching halfway to his mouth and down under his chin—even then, he always posed for pictures with only his left side showing, a handsome profile, the dignified son of an old Boston family. He seemed not to notice students as he passed them, and it was claimed they didn't like him.[3]

He walked vigorously. Many years before, as a twenty-four-year-old Harvard instructor, he had been recruited onto the Harvard crew, and when they defeated local Boston crews, he exulted in a note to his fiancée, Ellen,

"Hurra! Hurra!! Hurra!!! We've beaten the entire crowd—and made the quickest time ever made round the course." Now twenty-four years later, he was still physically active—tall, erect, a walker, bicyclist, and excellent horseman who summered outdoors on the Maine coastline, swimming, camping, and yachting.[4]

He was also an alert and energetic administrator, a new breed of college president, who studied the business of college presidency as "no President ever did before." "Wherever any of the business of Harvard went on, he looked in."[5]

For such an administrator, the growth of sports on campus was impossible to ignore. Eliot had no doubt that athletics and physical exercise were good for college students. In his detailed, erudite annual reports, he touched several times on athletics. For the school year 1881–82, he wrote: "The increased attention given to physical education and athletic sports within the past twenty-five years, has been . . . of great advantage to the University . . . [with] the average physique . . . improved . . . [and] discipline . . . made easier." The ideal student, Eliot said, had been transformed from "stooping and weak" to "robust and healthy."[6]

But college sports were becoming more and more prominent on the campus, demanding more time and effort of players, and moving toward what Eliot considered an academically unhealthy standard of professional excellence: "College sports cannot approach the professional standard of excellence without claiming the almost exclusive attention of the players, and becoming too severe, monotonous, and exacting to be thoroughly enjoyable. . . . Moreover, a high standard of excellence tends to make the number of persons who actually take part in athletic sports very small." College athletics, he said, should involve "amateurs who are amusing themselves," not demand the effort of professionals "who are earning a living."[7]

To counter the perceived unhealthy move toward professional standards, Eliot was planning a letter to other college presidents, asking cooperation initially as to games between college and professional baseball teams. With limited opponents available, college baseball teams sometimes played half their games with professional teams, promoting the professional effort Eliot rejected. Eliot also worried about the influence of wise-to-the-world professional players, whom he disdained with almost a class-like dislike: students should not associate, he said, with the "class of persons who make their living practicing or exhibiting" in athletic sports.[8]

Eliot wanted two actions from his fellow presidents: first, bar their college baseball team from playing with professional teams; second, limit the number of games their baseball team played. He sent the letter to the presidents of Amherst, Brown, Dartmouth, Princeton, and Yale.[9]

At Yale Eliot's letter was received by seventy-two-year-old Noah Porter, a president quite different from Eliot. Porter's reputation came as a scholar and former pastor, not an administrator. He had written several textbooks (his *The Human Intellect* was reissued several times and received international recognition; it is said to have introduced the term *psychology* into American academics), and despite his Yale presidency he continued as principal editor of *Webster's* English dictionaries.[10]

Under Porter, Yale had a narrow curriculum holding to the past, in sharp contrast to Harvard's broad freedom. Yale had more required courses than electives, and the focus was on classical languages and literature. For Porter, "language is the chief instrument of intelligence" and "the study of language the most efficient instrument of discipline." "Disciplined study of the classics will best prepare the mind for future challenges."[11]

The differences went beyond curriculum. A Yale professor was expected to mentor by example and moral leadership. Chapel was mandatory. The educational aim was student self-development, producing a "whole" man having moral and religious development as well as intellectual development. The epigraph for a Porter book on American colleges quoted Rugby School's headmaster Thomas Arnold: "It is not necessary that this should be a school of three hundred . . ., but it is necessary that it should be a school of Christian gentlemen."[12]

As an administrator, Porter was "hands-off"—some would even say lax. Kant's philosophy was his interest, not a Yale financial statement. Yale historians would say Porter's inattention to administrative matters and fund-raising set back Yale's development as a university.[13]

Whether it was Porter's administration or something else, Yale's attitude toward athletics was different from Harvard's. Influential professors at Yale empathized with students and their sports and saw them as educational, building character and promoting development of business and management skills. So far student management at Yale had caused no serious problems; Yale students had recently welcomed alumni and professors onto a committee advising students on athletics, the first college committee overseeing sports with such a mix of students, alumni, and faculty.

As to Eliot's initiative, neither Yale's students nor the Yale faculty saw danger in playing games with professional baseball teams. Camp may have participated in considering Eliot's letter: he was a member of the athletic advisory committee with professors who surely made their ideas known to the larger faculty. Camp would point out that members of the Yale baseball team had no contact with their professional opponents before or after the game. Only the managers met, and that was merely for business arrangements.

The Yale faculty formally considered Eliot's letter, but voted against participation in Eliot's plan. Eliot claimed Yale was the only college to reject his appeal for cooperation. But with the exception of a short-term ban by one other school (discussed in the next chapter), Eliot's effort achieved no lasting prohibition on play with professional teams.[14]

Although Eliot had many insights that echo through college sports even today, he also had distastes and misunderstandings not widely shared by others. He called baseball a "wretched game, with only two active players, pitcher and catcher." Curving a baseball was an unfair deception, devoid of the straightforward manliness of a rowing contest.[15]

He also lacked an appreciation for athletic competition and couldn't understand some team's driving push to win. A *New York World* reporter said that in conversation with Eliot and the director of Harvard's gymnasium, he was told, "Social pressure at that college [Yale] urges the men to play a 'winning' game."[16]

The rejections by Yale and other colleges did not deter Eliot; Harvard proceeded alone with steps important for the future of American sports. A three-member Harvard faculty committee was appointed to regulate athletic sports. The new committee imposed the limits Eliot was seeking, forbidding Harvard from playing professional teams, reducing the number of matches of the Harvard baseball team, and limiting them to Saturdays. The committee also required physical examinations for college athletes: no student could engage in an athletic contest until he had been examined and pronounced fit by Harvard's director of the gymnasium. Here was a committee that would make itself known in the college sports world.[17]

14 Besides Medical School

President Eliot's interventions into student sports diverted Walter Camp from medical school, but he had other distractions also, one of which was a girl named Alice. Alice Sumner was the half sister of a much older Yale professor, the imposing William Graham Sumner, a pioneer in sociology and political science still read and studied today. Students judged Sumner "the foremost man on the faculty"; without a class from "Billy Sumner," proud graduates claimed, you really had no degree from Yale.[1]

Alice and her professor half brother were children of an English immigrant, Thomas Sumner, who worked as a machinist in Hartford, Connecticut's railroad shops. Thomas Sumner's first wife—William Graham Sumner's mother, Sarah Graham—died when William was eight, whereupon Thomas married Eliza Van Alstein, who raised William but died the year William left for college. Thomas married still again, this time to Catherine (Kate) Mix, and two children quickly followed: a boy, Henry, and, when Thomas was fifty-three years old, Sarah Alice Sumner.[2]

Professor Sumner had a high regard for his father, self-educated with the "best possible" principles and habits of life. But a few years after Alice was born, Thomas was blinded in one eye by a shop accident, and later he was lamed by a fall. He left the railroad shops to manage property owned by his first wife's brothers; he also tried investing in property himself, but ended up losing money. Increasingly sensitive about his appearance, he mingled with people as little as possible and even declined to attend William's marriage in 1871. He died in 1881, when Alice was twenty, with the family impoverished.[3]

As a young girl, Alice wrote to her older half brother, William ("Dear Brother Will"), thirty miles south in New Haven. She gushed about his position and accomplishments and apologized about her own deficiencies. When she invited him to her high school graduation in Hartford, she cautioned she "won't be on the stage"; unfortunately, he, William, got "all the brilliance" in the family.[4]

Though much older, William—Professor Sumner—responded to Alice. In addition to genuine caring, he may have sensed an obligation, having emphasized in his writing that family sentiments, more than any other force, "tend to hold the individual up to the virtues which make the sound man and the valuable member of society." Alice came to live in New Haven with Professor Sumner and his wife, Jeannie, at least by 1880, when Alice was nineteen, a year before her father died. Sumner was scary in the classroom, a virile, massive personality given to bold and controversial assertions. But Alice was comfortable in the household and became a well-accepted family member. For a few years, Alice occupied herself with Professor Sumner's family, helping care for his and Jeannie Sumner's two young sons, Eliot and Graham (Grae).[5]

It is not known exactly when, but at some point Walter met Alice at Professor Sumner's home. Yale professors commonly had open houses for students at their homes, and Walter could have met Alice at such an occasion in his senior college year when he would have taken a class from Sumner. A high-spirited and attractive girl, she apparently caught the eye of the quiet and reserved Walter.[6]

They continued to see each other, how often we don't know, but two summertime occasions in 1880–82 are discussed in Alice's correspondence with Professor Sumner. With Alice staying home to care for the children during a vacation by Professor Sumner and his wife, Jeannie, Alice sent a report about events at home, including some shoreline outings: "Mr Camp walked out with Eliot and me one day and became so interested in Eliot's boats that he came and took us to Whitneyville one day and made E. some very nice flat-bottom sail boats that went beautifully. When we came home he had to make one for Grae too." In a second letter, "Eliot says to tell you he has a nice row-boat that Mr Camp made him and Grae a canoe—that you won't know how nice they are till you come and see them. I've my doubts as to whether they will last till you get home." The letters are undated, but Alice addressed them "Dear Brother Will" and wrote in a large hand, suggesting they were written between 1880 and 1882, when she was nineteen to twenty-one and Walter was in medical school. By at least 1883, after she had lived longer with the Sumners in New Haven, Alice began to address Sumner as "Dear Graham," and her handwriting had become smaller."[7]

In 1884 Alice enrolled in a teacher-training program at Welch Training School in New Haven, where aspiring elementary teachers learned by practice teaching under the direction of experienced teachers. Her decision to enroll could have been influenced by William, who was involved in public education enough to be made a member of Connecticut's state board of education in 1883. Alice must have learned well because by 1885 she herself was a teacher at the Welch Training School.[8]

Meanwhile, Walter and other student athletic leaders were facing a new attack by a different college president, Princeton's James McCosh. McCosh was a Scotsman who served first as a Presbyterian pastor in Scotland and then as a college professor in Ireland, where he built a scholar's reputation, writing five major works reprinted in several editions. His reputation reached the United States, and in 1868 at age fifty-seven he was recruited to Princeton's presidency.[9]

Princeton was at low ebb when McCosh arrived, with a declining enrollment scavenged further by the Civil War's removal of southern students. McCosh proved an effective and energetic leader. Large in stature with "a splendid head" covered with white curly hair and a pronounced Scottish brogue, McCosh was ready even in his sixties and seventies to travel the country to find students and build support for Princeton. When he retired in 1888, Princeton's enrollment had increased to more than 600 from the 280 when he came, and the school had a strong faculty, the second-largest college library in the country, an engineering school, three new dormitories, and other new facilities on a beautified campus.[10]

McCosh had his disagreements with Harvard's President Eliot, sometimes expressed in public debates (defending a balanced classics-based education against Eliot's "overly broad" allowance of electives and also arguing for keeping religion central in college life). But McCosh welcomed Eliot's initiative on college sports. Several years before, he had voiced his own concern that college authorities lacked sufficient control over athletic competition between colleges.[11]

A few months after Yale rejected Eliot's initiative, McCosh received a convenient invitation from Robert Bonner, an Irish immigrant who was publisher of the largest-circulation magazine in America, the *New York Ledger*. In his inaugural address at Princeton, McCosh had appealed for a gymnasium, and Bonner provided part of the funding. Now, noting criticisms by McCosh of college athletics, Bonner requested an article reconciling those criticisms with McCosh's request for the gymnasium Bonner had helped fund. McCosh accepted and took it as an opportunity.[12]

His article began by recognizing a need for physical exercise; all Princeton students were required to exercise at the gymnasium. McCosh's problem was not gymnasium exercises, but the competitive intercollegiate contests to which he believed a number of students devoted too much time. "The enthusiasm of the college is visibly in favor, not of literature or science, . . . [or] . . . great political and national questions, but of muscles and bones. . . . [T]he idlest fellow in his studies becomes the hero of his class . . . [and] the fine scholar is not appreciated." To solve the problem, McCosh said, would require "a combination of parties": "Harvard has taken the lead . . . and I am glad it has done so." Then, in a barb clearly directed at Yale: "Most of the colleges seem prepared to do their duty in this matter. . . . [I]f there be any colleges refusing to . . . [forbid play with professionals] to gain popularity among a certain class of young men, let parents combine to keep them from gaining their end."[13]

A response to McCosh came quickly, not from Yale's president or faculty member, but from a rising student sports leader, none other than the medical-school senior Walter Camp. Having seen football resuscitated by the five-yard rule, Camp now was sensitive to a new threat, disruption by college administrations. He did not hesitate but quickly wrote a letter that the *New York Tribune* agreed to publish.

Camp's letter, published April 9, 1883, two days after his twenty-fourth birthday, filled most of one column. Initial parts of the letter seem awkward and not very effective, less than thorough comments apparently made in an attempt to touch on all of McCosh's points before getting to those Camp wished to make most forcefully. At times he seems condescending, perhaps encouraged by stories of McCosh idiosyncrasies—Woodrow Wilson remembered the Scottish-brogued McCosh as a man "you could laugh at every day, and yet never for a moment despise."[14]

Camp's most effective argument, made on "behalf of all college athletes," was an answer to McCosh's assertion that in athletic events, "the idlest fellow in his class gets the honors." The "idlest fellow" cannot be successful in athletics, argued Camp, because athletics require hard work. Then Camp marshaled facts, listing year by year for the past seven years the academic achievements of Yale athletes. In 1876 graduation honors went to "one baseball man, four foot ball men, . . . one of the crew, [and] the winners of four out of five events of the spring track and field event." In addition, a prize for composition was awarded to two football men and one member of the crew, and a prize for scholarship in the law school was taken by a member of the crew. Similar facts were presented for each year through 1882.

Camp was apparently alone in responding to McCosh, but his letter made an impression on fellow students, a kind of rallying cry that was remembered for years. Whether the letter helped or not, the Princeton faculty in fact changed its decision after a few weeks, first supporting McCosh and Eliot by prohibiting play with professional teams, but quickly rescinding the ban.[15]

15 Career Realities

What was he doing there—on a tennis court in Hartford, Connecticut, playing doubles for Yale in a first-ever tennis match with Harvard? Football, baseball, now tennis. When did Walter Camp study medicine?

One reason for being there: Yale was short of tennis players. The lawn tennis being played was new, invented in England and brought to the United

States less than ten years before. Yale had refused a match the previous fall for lack of an adequate doubles team.[1]

Now, the first tournament of the Intercollegiate Lawn Tennis Association was being held, June 6, 1883, at an unlikely site, the Retreat for the Insane in Hartford—unlikely except for the well-made tennis courts on beautiful grounds designed by noted landscape architect Frederick L. Olmsted. The ILTA had been formed two months earlier in Hartford by hometown Trinity, joined by Amherst, Brown, Yale, and later Harvard. Having just helped form the Tennis Association, Yale needed to present both a singles and a doubles team in the tournament.[2]

And Camp was good enough to be there—a sports lover challenged by a new sport, playing enough (with his summers free), and being athletic, diligent, and competitive enough to be a decent player. He was paired with a much better player, Henry Slocum Jr., a Yale senior who would progress to become American singles champion in 1888 and 1889. Slocum played a safe and sure game, staying in the backcourt most of the time. He took great pride in his physical condition, making Camp a good match; neither he nor Camp would seem to tire or become discouraged.[3]

Camp and Slocum were facing Harvard's Joseph Clark and H. A. Taylor; Clark was a very good player who had learned tennis in Philadelphia on a court laid out on his family's estate; he would win the singles phase of the tournament, and he and Taylor would win the doubles phase. They easily defeated Camp and Slocum. But later in the day, Camp and Slocum beat the doubles team from Trinity. The next day, they lost to Brown but defeated Amherst, giving them a third-place finish in the tournament.[4]

Despite Camp's willingness to help Yale compete in tennis, a huge question still begs for an answer: Why wasn't he home studying? In just a few days, he would sit for his final exams in medical school.

What had first claim on Camp? Medical school? Or was it football, baseball, and now tennis? He had played varsity football and baseball his first and second years in medical school and helped coach Yale's football team in the third. He had participated in football rule drafting, edited the published rule book, written informative football pamphlets, and defended the game against college presidents; it was just two months since his written response to President McCosh. On April 28, a few weeks before the tennis tournament, Camp was a baseball umpire in a game between Yale and a Providence professional team.

Although he had continued in medical school despite failing several exams at the end of his second year, he must have experienced some self-questioning.

Anatomy was still a major obstacle, and that was not uncommon—"Hatred of this essential but dull, difficult, and exhausting business," one observer wrote, "is the biggest single reason why medical students give up or fail their course." Either Camp hated Anatomy, or he had trouble with it, or both.[5]

A poem he wrote and got published in the April 7, 1883, *Yale Courant* student newspaper is interesting in the context of his possible struggle and self-examination. Titled "Kismet" (Turkish for "fate"), the poem began with a "smoky Turk" sitting "in regal ease" and dreaming, "Dreamy days without a care," as if life moves on independent of anything he can do:

> Rise Life—Rise Death—what matters all
> And what's the use of praying?

The author (Camp) also dreams, though his dream seems to seek material success:

> Now when *I* sit in regal ease
> And dream thro' smoke-rings breaking,
> My kismet is a coach in four,
> My fortune is some millions more, . . .

But then he awakens,

> With ragged jacket smoke-perfumed,
> With tattered slippers mating,
> With kismet—doubtful—twenty cents,
> While trust in fate is flying hence
> And creditors are waiting.

Had Camp's entry into medical school been an unrealistic dream from which he was now awaking? Presumably he had worked at his Anatomy class. But could he have tried harder? Or was his mind simply not adapted to the somewhat rote memorization and detail of anatomy? He would later say he lost interest because a surgeon he intended to practice with had died. And it was suggested that his bout with typhoid in the foundational first year of medical school had set him back. To his old friend Walter Jennings he joked, "I couldn't stand the sight of blood."[6]

Whatever doubts Camp had, he did take the medical school exams a few days after the tennis tournament. And many years later, when a questionnaire asked which profession he would choose if he could live his life over, he replied, "Corrective and preventive medicine or the science that will develop from this."[7]

Any thoughts Camp had of a medical career ended when the results of the exams were announced. In courses dealing with general principles, he did well; he made the highest score of all those tested in Theory and Practice. But Anatomy and Surgery got him again. He had failed; his three years invested in medical school and his dreams of a professional career were gone; he would not be graduating.[8]

What now? Signs are that friends came to his aid as he searched for an alternative career, with the first assist being a job at the just-formed Manhattan Watch Company (MWC) in New York City. The choice of a watch business is not so surprising—Connecticut was at the center of the U.S. clock and watch business. But the choice of MWC requires a little guesswork, though there is a likely explanation. The president of the start-up MWC was Arthur O. Jennings, first cousin of Walter Jennings, Camp's good friend and classmate. After it was clear he was done with medical school, Camp happened to meet Walter Jennings in New York, where Jennings was in business. Camp explained about medical school (the apocryphal "I can't stand the sight of blood") and then offered that he was "looking for a chance in business." Walter Jennings must have been aware of his cousin's New York business initiative and could very well have suggested it to Camp.[9]

Whatever route Camp took to MWC, he did not stay long, perhaps a month or two in the summer of 1883. The quick exit may have come because the company was so new; they didn't have a product ready for sale and wouldn't for many months. But the exit may also have been due to the efforts of another friend working to find an opportunity for Camp. George A. Adee, an 1867 Yale graduate and now a New York lawyer and leader among alumni on Yale athletics, had been a founding member in 1879 of a Yale student-alumni-faculty sports advisory committee and in 1880 of an advisory committee assisting in purchase of a new Yale athletic grounds. Camp had worked with Adee on both. It was Adee who had helped persuade New York newspapers to publish Camp's letters on sports matters.

On July 8, 1883, Camp wrote Adee about Yale rowing. As a member with Adee on Yale's advisory athletic committee, Camp should be interested in rowing—the annual Harvard-Yale race at New London was still the big event in the American college sports world. But Camp's letter to Adee went beyond general interest. Yale's performance at the just-past race on June 28, 1883, had been abysmal, with Harvard winning by a large margin. The Yale crew had been directed by a professional rower with novel ideas—an unusually high stroke rate and strenuous practice to the day of the race. Some of Yale's rowers were said to have been exhausted before the race began.[10]

Camp's letter apparently proposed changes such as use of a graduate coach instead of the professional coach. One possibility was to persuade Robert J. Cook, an old Yale rower and coach, to again coach or advise the Yale crew. Camp offered to go to Philadelphia, where Cook lived and worked. Camp's letter may simply have reflected the interest of a concerned committee member. But it might also have demonstrated Camp's own desire, perhaps even his response to others' encouragement, to stay involved in Yale athletics.

Adee responded to Camp with two letters. First was an eighteen-page letter on July 18, mainly agreeing with Camp's ideas and offering to go with him to Philadelphia. The second letter, two days after the first, is especially interesting in view of subsequent events. Adee invited Camp and the next year's Yale crew captain, H. R. Flanders, to spend a day or two with Adee at his home in Westchester County, north of Manhattan. There they could get started on crew plans for the next year. But there was something more: "It is important that you and Flanders should come here. Graduates here make a practical offer which you ought to hear at once."[11]

A "practical offer" by graduates became public in early October when the *Yale News* reported that Walter Camp had been hired for a job at Yale. If he was still employed by MWC, Camp now left to take the job at Yale that seemed more in line with his lifelong interests. The Yale job was without parallel at any other college—"general supervisor of all athletic interests of the college," somewhat grandiose in title but reflecting the breadth of student and graduate involvement in Yale athletics. The *Yale News* said the idea had come from "influential graduates" involved in Yale's "new Athletic Field," in other words from some of Camp's colleagues on the field-oversight committee, one of whom was Adee. These graduates, said the paper, wanted Camp to superintend the new field when it was ready to open. To cover the time before the field was ready, the graduates proposed that Camp take charge of the various athletic teams at Yale. The graduates offered to pay three hundred dollars as their share of Camp's salary, and the football, baseball and athletic associations agreed individually to pay four, three, and two hundred dollars, respectively, making a total salary of twelve hundred dollars.[12]

Not everyone was happy about Camp's new job. The front page of the October 16 *Yale News* printed a letter at the top of the first column, claiming that Yale's students were amazed by Camp's arrangement. According to the letter, the students wondered: "When and where did we [the students] consider and vote on the election?" "By what authority" was he appointed?

But defenders far outnumbered the questioners. Alongside the questioning letter was a reply from R. W. Hammill, president of the Yale University Foot Ball Club. First, Hammill stated, the hiring was decided by managers of the various student athletic associations, who "have full control" of their designated associations. As for reasons for the hiring, beginning with the spring of 1880 (when Camp captained the baseball team against Harvard due to the illness of the regular captain), Yale's football and baseball teams had experienced "a continuous succession of victories, and Yale has had the foot-ball and base-ball championship flags ever since." This success, Hammill argued, was due "in great part to Mr. Camp's own influence and executive ability."

Ironically, just ten days before Camp's hiring was announced, the *Yale News* carried an appeal from Hammill asking Yale students for subscriptions to help underwrite football's costs. But the newspaper itself editorially supported Camp's hiring, stating that anyone "at all acquainted with the work he has done" for Yale athletics could not doubt the wisdom of the hiring.[13]

Camp's competence and acceptance of responsibility were already well demonstrated: two years as varsity football captain, interim service as football and baseball captain in the absence of the regular captain, diligent and inventive football rule maker, writer of football instructions, and member for several years of Yale's athletic advisory committee. Influential members of the alumni, student body, and faculty were persuaded that he could benefit Yale's athletic program; they wanted Camp's involvement and were ready to help him as he explored a new career.

The job should not be overrated—not a faculty job, a one-year commitment, underwritten by alumni and students. It could end as a stopgap measure, tiding Camp over for one year while he looked for something else. But Camp's acceptance of the job demonstrated a continuing and growing interest in sports and sports administration and also a happiness to work at Yale, to promote the school's athletics.

Other opportunities for a career in sports also came to him. In the middle of the 1883 professional baseball season, the National League of Professional Baseball Clubs offered him appointment as an umpire, salary two hundred dollars per month and necessary expenses. He was obviously seen as having the knowledge as well as the impartiality and temperament to be an umpire. No evidence that Camp accepted the offer has been found, though such an appointment was again offered in November 1883 for the full 1884 season at a salary of one thousand dollars plus expenses.[14]

16 Not So Easy After All

Harvard football players and fans had been waiting a long time, but in 1883 it was finally their turn for the big game in New York. Harvard and Yale had finished the 1882 season with the two best won-lost records, requiring under the Intercollegiate Football Association constitution that they play their following year's game "in New York on Thanksgiving." That was no burden. The New York Thanksgiving Day game was a celebration, the climactic football game of the year, attended by many thousands in holiday mood, a game to aspire for.

But Harvard's newly established faculty athletic committee had a different idea. One week before Thanksgiving, the committee announced that Harvard could not play. The chairman of the committee, Charles Eliot Norton, professor of fine arts with a reputation as "the most cultured man in America" (and also President Eliot's cousin), explained that football had "begun to degenerate from a manly, if rough, sport into brutal and dangerous contests. . . . [T]he Harvard eleven can not be allowed to take part in any further intercollegiate match games until substantial changes in the rules have been made."[1]

The new Harvard committee had taken their job seriously and met often, but they had little experience with football and could hardly have appreciated what they were doing by issuing a ban on a week's notice. The *Yale News* listed some economic consequences: first, a claim by the Polo Grounds for damages from breach of contract and, second, the loss by the Yale students of fifteen hundred dollars, "realized for several years past at the Thanksgiving game, upon which we have been relying to meet our financial agreements." Harvard students complained of the dishonor imposed on them, "obliging our eleven to break its agreement."[2]

Harvard's football captain urgently appealed to the committee, which agreed to meet the next day. Finally recognizing an impossible situation, the committee accepted a face-saving compromise. Harvard's student managers promised changes in the referee: the referee would be "a graduate of either Harvard, Yale, Princeton or Columbia" and would have "absolute power" to disqualify a player not obeying the rules. Yale's football captain formally agreed by letter, and with that the committee allowed the game.[3]

On Thanksgiving Day, "all the good places at the Polo Grounds were gone hours before the game," and Professor Norton was reported to be at the game, watching "over his 'lambs' from the grandstand." But according to the *New York World*, "not the slightest change [was] made in the character of the play." Yale won easily, 23–2.[4]

Fulfilling their promise to Harvard's committee, IFA delegates convened in New York a week after Thanksgiving, December 5, 1883, and wrote rules making promised changes in the selection and duties of referees (particularly requiring that the referee be "an alumnus").[5]

The 1883 Thanksgiving game was barely over when Harvard's faculty made the next move, proposing a conference of colleges to discuss common intercollegiate athletic problems. In a not too subtle effort to get their fellow academic leader involved, they asked Yale to convene the conference.[6]

Yale immediately declined (Eliot complained Yale responded to his suggestions like "a porcupine on the defensive"), whereupon Harvard convened the conference itself, in New York, on December 28, 1883. Yale, represented by mathematics professor Eugene L. Richards, did attend with six other colleges—Columbia, Pennsylvania, Princeton, Trinity, Wesleyan, and Williams. The conference appointed a committee of five persons, with Richards as chair, to prepare a plan for the colleges to cooperatively control and administer intercollegiate sports.[7]

Richards soon had second thoughts. He was not really aligned with this effort and could not support the goals some delegates might pursue. Richards withdrew as chairman, and Yale withdrew from the conference.[8]

The public soon heard what the conference was planning. On February 14, 1884, a new chair, Professor William Milligan Sloane of Princeton, announced the committee had agreed on eight resolutions. The resolutions had been sent to twenty-one colleges and would become binding when adopted by five.[9]

The resolutions would definitely alter the college sports scene. A new multicollege committee, with one faculty member from each participating college, would take charge of college sports. More than that, the committee would "*approve all rules* and regulations under which such contests may be held."

Three resolutions would govern who and where college teams played:

- Play only with other college teams
- Play only with colleges agreeing to these same regulations
- Play only on the grounds of one of the competing college teams

Another resolution limited an individual college student's play to no more than four years. Still another, if not aimed at Walter Camp, certainly covered him:

"Every director or instructor in physical exercises or athletic sports must be appointed by the College authorities, and announced as such in the catalogue."

In yet one more resolution, the committee applied themselves to decide a contestant's allowable effort: "Rowing contests were to be limited to no more than three miles."

Harvard and Yale had opposite views about the resolutions. Harvard's were influenced by President Eliot's wish to reduce the effort demanded in college sports, to avoid what he called a "professional" effort. In his 1882–83 annual report, Eliot confronted those who disagreed: "The opposite view is that all games should be played to win, and that whatever promotes winning should be done,—that the best trainers should be employed, and the most expert professional [baseball] clubs be hired to play with college clubs, and to meet these expenses that the largest amount of gate-money . . . should be sought for in a business-like way." For Eliot, there seemed "no tenable middle ground" between confining intercollegiate athletics to the "amusement of amateurs," on the one hand, and an utmost effort "to win," on the other hand. "Whoever tries to occupy a middle position soon finds himself pushed to one extreme or the other." Eliot favored amateur contests, and the multicollege supervisory organization proposed by the Harvard convention would be expected to make rules to ensure such contests.[10]

Yale's Professor Richards offered another view. Forty-five years old, Richards espoused physical exercise, though he had injured his back while wrestling and never totally recovered. Yet he was himself a hiker and as a student had rowed on Yale's crew. His son, Eugene Jr., had been playing football for Yale since 1881 and would be Yale's varsity football captain in the fall.[11]

Professor Richards wrote a defense of college sports as a two-part series in the March and April 1884 issues of *Popular Science Monthly*, a then-scholarly magazine in which his arguments would reach opinion leaders. Richards didn't concern himself with Eliot's attacks on "professionalism," but he listed several contributions he asserted were made by college athletics:

1. Develops qualities not otherwise developed by the college curriculum—"courage, resolution, and perseverance," and a "faculty for organization, executive power, the qualities which enable men to control and lead other men."
2. Provides a positive outlet for the "superabundant animal life" that in the past led to disturbances on campuses.
3. Promotes attention to exercise and thus leads to a general improvement in the physical condition of the students.
4. Provides an opportunity for faculty-student interaction outside the classroom.

5. Awakens enthusiasm among students (avoiding "dry intellectualism") and develops a "warm interest" among a college's alumni.
6. Exposes students to a wider world.[12]

Instead of the multicollege supervisory committee proposed by the Harvard-initiated Sloane committee, Richards favored a laissez-faire approach. The students created the existing system and maintained it without major fault that Richards could see. The existing system, with the benefits he had listed, should not be disrupted by a new faculty-based superorganization. The existing system is like a "little republic of young men," student "presidents, captains and commodores" to whom authority has been delegated. "Is it not worth maintaining as a means of preparation for the responsibilities of life in the larger republic outside the campus?"

One more Yale representative also undertook to speak in the public debate—Walter Camp, Yale's new twenty-five-year-old unofficial sports supervisor, whose responsibilities as delegated by fellow students would apparently be regulated by the proposed new multicollege committee. On February 25, 1884, in *Outing*, a new monthly magazine of recreation and sports, Camp wrote to defend student management of college sports, arguing, "Business principles and self-reliance can be learned in no better way than by actual business transactions." Colleges should restrict themselves to maintaining requirements for work and attendance and allow student management of athletic organizations.[13]

Camp also explained the value of intercollegiate competition and championships: "Championships are invitations to physical culture. Without the sport there would be little interest, and without the rivalry there would be no training." Training was one of Camp's regular themes: training means "temperance, restraint, and exercise," resulting in better physical condition as well as moral health.

Besides the *Outing* article, Camp also wrote letters of similar content that George Adee got published simultaneously on February 27, 1884, in the *New York Tribune*, *Times*, and *World*.

With the draft resolutions distributed to twenty-one colleges, Professor Sloane's committee awaited the responses.

Harvard and Yale responded quickly: Harvard, for; Yale, against. Two other colleges, Princeton and Cornell, joined Harvard in a quick approval.[14]

Three down, two more needed to establish an operative set of rules and organization. Who would they be?

As it turned out, nobody. Amherst, Brown, Dartmouth, and Pennsylvania soon joined Yale in voting no. The committee waited in vain for two more votes.[15]

Reflection would have revealed obvious problems in the resolutions.

- As to the first resolution, creating a multicollege supervisory committee, the resolution proposed to give the committee authority to "approve" game playing rules. But could nonplaying professors better decide appropriate playing rules than actual players?
- As to the resolution limiting the length of races, what experience allowed professors to establish that rowers could safely row three miles but not four?

Even Eliot later admitted that the draft resolutions were "in some particulars not well considered."[16]

Harvard's students were also unpersuaded. They held their largest mass meeting ever on athletic issues and, with but one dissenting vote, asked for revocation of the faculty's acceptance of the conference resolutions. They warned they would not "co-operate with the Faculty in effecting these changes."[17]

On March 11, 1884, less than four weeks after publication of the resolutions, the conference committee capitulated. Meeting at Columbia University in New York, they announced that, while sensing general support for the "principles" of the resolution, there had been "such diversity of opinion in regard to the details" that the committee was now informing the various colleges that "no further joint action is proposed."[18]

So now Harvard had initiated three faculty efforts to take control of college sports, none of which had produced the desired result or effective support from other colleges. Camp and Yale must have wondered whether and when Harvard would try again.

17 Writer, Teacher . . . Director?

A new subject was on the agenda when delegates met for the October 1883 convention of the Intercollegiate Football Association. Walter Camp wanted approval for a new kind of book—a nuts-and-bolts book that he called the "Referee's Book on Football Rules." Brief, one- or two-sentence interpretations of each rule were provided to aid referees in on-the-field decisions. Camp had been a referee and worked with other referees and knew rule interpretations would be welcomed. Moreover, a central set of interpretations would make refereeing more sound and consistent.

Camp's participation in the convention a month after he began his job supervising Yale athletic interests stretched even further the convention's attendance criteria—he was not a student as always before but in fact a paid sports administrator, and he was in his fifth year attending conventions. Never mind; he and his contributions were welcome. The delegates promptly approved his referee's book.[1]

Camp must have come to the convention with the book already written, because it was published almost immediately with an October date on the cover. In twenty-one four-by-six-inch pages, each rule was concisely discussed:

> Rule 13 - The snapper-back is entitled to but half the ball. May use his hand, but must have his foot on the ball.
>
> . . .
>
> Rule 16 - In blocking it is allowable to stand in any position with arms extended, but not locked with the next man. After the ball is snapped no man can change his position for the sake of blocking his adversary.
>
> . . .
>
> Rule 20 - The field should be marked with transverse lines every five yards.

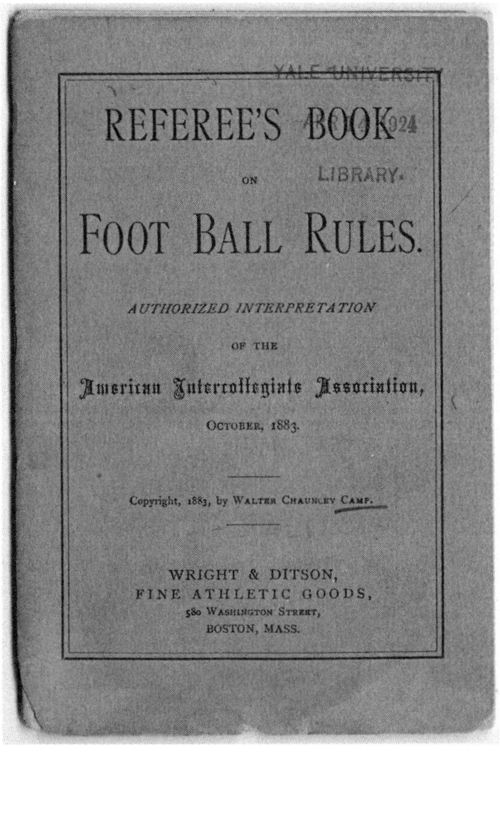

The 1883 booklet for referees authored by Walter Camp. (Walter Chauncey Camp Papers, 1870–1983 [inclusive], 1870–1925 [bulk], Manuscripts and Archives, Yale University)

Camp's innovation didn't stop with the referee's book. In just a few months, as soon as the 1883 football season was over, he assembled and published another booklet through Wright and Ditson, the *Foot Ball Record of American Teams*, with forty-four pages of compiled information. First came a list of existing football teams—twenty-three, comprising fourteen colleges, six academy and high school teams, and three club teams. Addresses and the name of a manager or captain were provided for each team—data Camp must have dug to obtain and assemble.[2]

Next was a section specific to "association" (IFA) teams—Harvard, Princeton, and Yale (Columbia had withdrawn by forfeiture of games). All players for Harvard, Princeton, and Yale in the eight years since introduction of the "Rugby Game" in 1876 were listed, followed by the scores of those schools' games with one another. Nonassociation teams were also represented with a list of players and results. Then came a list of referees who had served in the various games, a convenient roster for choosing referees for future games. The book made several contributions to the world of American football, gathering and preserving statistical and historical data, providing information to help arrange future games, and promoting football's presence in American life to attract other participants.

Both books were further instances of Camp initiative—new and novel undertakings to develop and enhance the game. It was as if he were an entrepreneur, alert to opportunities and eager to build his business. The books actually continued a surge begun with the April 1882 convention and its five-yards-in-three-downs rule, continuing with the two additional conventions of 1882 that pared rules from sixty-four to thirty-eight and installed a point system of scoring and now including two further booklets that would strengthen American football. This new sport rising among a few colleges in the East had a distinctive leader, continuing to put in time to make the game succeed. And perhaps his contributions would help convince relevant parties that he could perform a useful role at Yale.

Still one more book was in Camp's bag in late 1883, a new rule book for the 1884 season, authorized by the December convention held by the IFA as promised after reinstatement of the 1883 Harvard-Yale Thanksgiving game. The convention made further amendments besides those promised Harvard's athletic committee and then went on to again "award" Camp the "privilege of copyrighting and printing the rules." Entitled *Foot-Ball Rules and Referee's Book*, the book was also published by Wright and Ditson, with "Revised by Walter Chauncey Camp" prominent on the cover. The combination of

Camp with Wright and Ditson had successfully published four books in a row, in contrast to the hit-or-miss publishing schedule of previous years.[3]

The book was ready for publication May 1884, well before the 1884 season. Besides rules and rule interpretations (the latter were basically the same as those in Camp's 1883 *Referee's Book*), the book also included further aids such as record sheets on which a referee could enter information to manage and document a game—time when play began, time-outs taken, goals kicked, touchdowns scored, number of warnings given to a particular player, and so forth.[4]

Two of the convention's rule changes were of special significance:

- The penalty for a safety was increased to two points, still its value today, reflecting increased acceptance by 1883 players that safeties should not be a routine tool in a team's strategy.
- The value of a touchdown was increased to four points and a successful kick-after-touchdown reduced to two points. The total from a touchdown and successful kick remained six points, but the four-two ratio, touchdown-to-kick (reversing the previous two-four ratio), recognized the greater effort required for a touchdown.

No change in point value was made for a kicked goal from the field; at five points, it continued to be the most valuable single scoring play.

With the book publications of 1883 added to that of 1882, each with his name on the front cover, Camp was making himself known. Repeatedly, Camp was described as quiet, reticent to reveal personal feelings, someone who preferred to stay in the background. But these booklets, with his name on the cover, truthfully reflecting his authorship and the leadership he brought to football, would give him prominence within the football community and beyond.[5]

Aside from IFA rule making and booklet preparation, Camp went about teaching and coaching at Yale. He encouraged athletic participation by all students, not just intercollegiate athletic teams, and he posted hours when he was available for advice, training, and practice. He also helped outside Yale, traveling in the fall of 1883 to Wesleyan College, twenty miles north in Middletown, Connecticut, to assist in coaching the Wesleyan football team.[6]

Sensing the possibility of a permanent position at Yale, Camp wrote to an athletics supporter on the Yale faculty, history professor A. M. Wheeler, who replied December 21, 1883, with some encouraging thoughts. Wheeler had conferred with several other members of the Yale faculty and had learned (his "personal opinion only") that "there will be no difficulty in securing for you a permanent appointment . . ., *provided* a sufficient endowment can be raised for a professorship in athletics." Wheeler went on to explain that funds for the college are already "strained to the utmost," but he was going to Chicago and "will do what I can to further your interests" and suggested that Camp do what he could "through your friends."[7]

Teaching was in Camp's genes, and he liked the academic atmosphere; perhaps he would be an academic himself, a student of history. About this time, he began a scholarly research project, a study of America's early sports; he wrote to men "well along in years to learn what the games of their youth had been," information he might be able to put together in a book. The academic atmosphere also encouraged poetry, and in December he had a Christmas poem published in the *Yale Courant*."[8]

Camp's coaching efforts were publicly praised. On May 31, 1884, the *New York Times* headlined that Princeton's baseball team had experienced its "Waterloo," beaten badly by Yale, which "showed by their skill in the field the result of hard training under their veteran and most skillful coach, Walter Camp." Yale's team had batted "like professionals" and run the bases "in a daring manner."[9]

As for football, a just-graduated Harvard football player, a lineman disappointed in the play of Harvard's backfield players and wanting better training for them, wrote to the *Harvard Advocate*: "These very points [improved techniques for halfbacks] you will find Yale's fatherly Genius in Football, now a director-in-chief of Yale athletics, installing daily into the New Haven half-backs, and the sooner Harvard learns the lesson the better."[10] Not too early, apparently, to be called "fatherly" in connection with football.

With his twenty-fifth birthday approaching in April 1884 and his one-year arrangement with Yale students and alumni coming to a close, Camp got an attempted assist from Yale's Professor Richards. In the second installment of his *Popular Science Monthly* articles defending intercollegiate sports, Richards got to the question of "professional trainers" (meaning coaches) for teams. Richards saw little danger from such trainers, but he offered an alternative, a "better idea": hire someone who is a graduate of the college, is himself an athlete, and has been "educated as a physician" to serve as a "general advisor and guardian of athletic interests."[11]

What could be more clear? Yale had such a person; Walter Camp was already serving as such an "advisor and guardian" and satisfied Richards's carefully worded criterion, "educated as a physician." Instead of his current sponsorship by students and alumni, under Richards's proposal, he would move to Yale's official staff with a "salaried appointment."

However, Richards's, Wheeler's, and Camp's efforts did not produce a job, most likely because an endowment was not raised. The idea also undoubtedly received no support from Yale's President Porter. A few years earlier, a Yale Medical School graduate who had worked as an instructor in the Yale gym sought appointment to a Yale faculty position in physical education. Porter declined and let the graduate know he thought such a job was unworthy of college-educated men.[12]

Throughout the 1883–84 school year, no problems arose in Yale's athletic matters. The baseball team lost only twice in thirteen games against college opponents, and the football team won all eight of its games. The biggest win of the year came when the Yale crew beat Harvard at New London with a new stroke practiced diligently in private. When the crew arrived home, they were brought to the "fence" and a huge bonfire lit with tar barrels. Chimes rang both from Battell Chapel and nearby churches. Students marched wildly around campus to loud drumbeats.[13]

Yet Yale took no step to give Camp a permanent staff job. As the 1883–84 school year approached its close, Camp understood he was waiting for something that wasn't going to happen. It was time for a change. He had to find something else.

"Having Waited in Vain" 18

On a summer day in 1884, Walter Camp traveled across town to a new job at the New Haven Clock Company, seemingly continuing the course he began with the previous year's brief fling at the Manhattan Watch Company. But now he was joining a company at a different level, a large, long-established maker of timepieces. This job could be permanent: instead of a college campus or a doctor's office, Camp's work site might be a clock manufacturing company.[1]

After a hands-on introduction to the company's clocks in the factory, Camp was scheduled to sell clocks at NHCC's store in New York City. He had a lot to learn, with more than two hundred pages of clocks in the company's catalog—shelf clocks, wall clocks, tall clocks; one-day, thirty-hour, eight-day, thirty-day movements; spring driven, double-spring driven, weight driven; myriad case sizes and constructions. The line was almost all in clocks; watches were a small part of NHCC's business.

NHCC had grown from an early pioneering business of a Connecticut entrepreneur named Chauncey Jerome who had used breakthrough New England machining technology and Connecticut brass sheet to make clocks that could be sold for $1.50, an astounding price that would make clocks a common household item. Jerome's nephew Hiram Camp (no relation to Walter) founded the New Haven Clock Company to manufacture parts for Jerome and eventually took over his uncle's manufacture and marketing of clocks. When Walter Camp came to work in 1884, NHCC was one of the United States' largest clock manufacturers and a leading New Haven employer, with 460 men, 52 women, and 88 children. Business was flourishing, and there had been a recent (1880) large addition to the factory.[2]

As the twenty-five-year-old Walter set out for NHCC that summer day in 1884, he could have been discouraged, forced from a preferred academic world and relegated to a business office. Just as likely, there was excitement, the challenge of stepping into the mushrooming world of U.S. business with a clock-industry leader. In his family, he was surrounded by entrepreneurs, next-door Uncle Henry Peck growing his plumbing-supply business into a national company, Uncle David and Uncle Timothy Stanley with responsible New Britain business participation, even his father, Leverett, with real estate investments.

Leverett and Uncle Henry certainly knew Hiram Camp and may have helped Walter's approach to NHCC. Besides that, there was a connection through Mrs. John English, the Camps' longtime backyard neighbor and mother of Olivia English. Mrs. English certainly knew of Walter Camp's situation—failure in medical school, brief experience at MWC, expiration of his Yale employment—and could have sought ideas from James English, her deceased husband's brother living nearby, who was prominent in New Haven business and a principal investor in NHCC.

After a summer of factory work, Camp moved to New York City to clerk in the company's store. The *New York Times* took note, identifying Camp as "the moving spirit" of Yale athletics for several years. "Having waited in vain for a professorship in physical culture" at Yale, he was now moving on. Yale students and alumni wondered how Yale would do without him, but he had promised to come back when possible to help coach Yale's football team.[3]

In New York, Camp at some point rented a room on West Thirty-Fourth Street between Eighth and Ninth Avenues in a brownstone owned by seventy-two-year-old Louis Mealia. It was a good-size house with twelve occupants, at least eight of whom were members of the Mealia family. A half block away, on Ninth Avenue, was the station for an elevated train on which Camp could travel downtown, pulled by a coal-fired steam engine puffing and whistling to within two blocks of the New Haven Clock Company's store in Lower Manhattan. The store was near city hall and only a few blocks from the law office of his friend and fellow Yale sports committeeman George Adee.[4]

Little is known about Camp's private life in New York. He was honored to be chosen as first president when a group of Yale alumni organized an athletic club, the Crescent Athletic Club, in Brooklyn, in January 1886, to play football and other sports—another indication of the regard in which friends and acquaintances held him. Camp seems to have been more a club official and occasional referee than a player for club games. Camp also maintained contact with Yale, often serving as a referee for intramural games on the Yale campus as well as periodically coaching football.[5]

Camp's dating interests apparently broadened in New York. The *New York Times* called him "popular with the ladies," and it is known he dated a girl named Sallie Barnes from Paterson, New Jersey. He also vacationed on Martha's Vineyard, where, the *Times* said, "his word was law" among the ladies. Alice Sumner remained an interest, though she also had other suitors, as shown by her correspondence files.[6]

For several summers beginning about 1883, Alice took the Sumner boys, Eliot and Graham, to vacation on the northern coast of Maine, at Northeast Harbor, on wooded, glacier-sculpted Mount Desert Island, now Acadia National Park. Northeast Harbor had just been discovered by outdoor-loving college professors and city elites (President Eliot was one of the earliest to build a residence there). Upon first arriving in 1883, Alice found a dozen or so scattered houses and, in a large clearing, two wood-frame hotels barely more than boardinghouses; cottages were adjacent to one of the hotels. Activities were centered outdoors—rowing, sailing, hiking in the island's mountains. After rowing along the coast, a party might come to shore for a picnic supper.[7]

Life outdoors on the Maine coastline appealed to Walter Camp, and he is known to have visited Alice in Northeast Harbor. At Northeast Harbor, he could happily enter into the outdoor life. Alice was a take-charge person who would have made plans; Walter and she presumably took the Sumner boys, Eliot, twelve in 1885, and Graham, six, picnicking, hiking, and boating. The well-conditioned Walter must have handled the oars of a rowboat well and could also handle sailing if that was available. Perhaps later in the day, there was time for a stroll after the boys were in bed. Or perhaps one of Alice's friends watched the boys while Walter and Alice took their own private row, hike, or picnic.

A move to New York might have been the time for Camp to get less involved in football, but that didn't happen. Shortly after his move, he got an article published in a highly regarded academic journal, the *New Englander and Yale Review*, in which he presented a philosophical rationale for college sports and a literate but rousing defense against "uninformed" faculty intervention.[8]

Camp argued that intercollegiate competitive athletics drew students into productive exercise, which college faculties hindered by intervening without adequate knowledge. Students had established and developed competitive college athletics with care. Did faculties understand that students managed their sports through organizations having "constitutions and printed rules, legislated upon annually"? Before faculties attempted to intervene, it was their "duty" to "study" the constitutions and rules established by the students. "If the critics who call . . . [football] brutal and dangerous could be persuaded to spend the necessary time in learning the game, they would change their opinion. . . . All the college athletes ask is fairness. . . . They ask interest from the Faculties, not interference without knowledge. Justice [requires that a party seeking to judge have] knowledge of the subject before criticism." Camp also addressed parents. When parents sent a young man to college, they should urge him "not only to study hard, but also to play hard and be athletic." That was undoubtedly a new thought for many Americans as to the purpose and benefits of college education.

Instead of the reasoned, academic air of his *New Englander* article, Walter Camp showed emotion a month later in a letter to the *Yale News*. Harvard's faculty committee on athletics was in action again, this time to issue a *total ban* on intercollegiate football at Harvard. Now Camp seemed in pain, trying to reach the unaware faculty members with no appreciation of the joy football players had in their game. "There is no game better loved than football. There is about the sport a fascination that none but players know, but which is far beyond that of any other sport. . . . When recounting bygone games, telling over again of the magnificent runs, the beautiful drop—how the game was lost and won—enthusiasm grows strong, and the time slips away, and the true football lore obliterates for the time all antagonisms and rivalry."[9]

Before recommending the ban, the committee had left Harvard students one tiny sliver of hope, an offer to listen to students' opinions and arguments at a meeting in the Harvard gymnasium. Convening on December 1, 1884, the committee (with two members changed from the 1883 committee) spoke first—William E. Byerly (mathematics), John W. White (Greek), and Dudley A. Sargent (director of the gymnasium), professors confident of their facts and logic. They had attended four games, and in each game, "brutality had been exhibited. Blows were struck and men were knocked down. . . . Men were obliged to leave the field because of their injuries." Dangerous and demoralizing, football should be banned until corrected.[10]

Both Byerly and White openly admitted they lacked football knowledge. Another professor later claimed that "blows" such as apparently perceived by the professors were actually vigorous hand slaps as players tried to move one another aside; the smack of hands against players' canvas jackets reverberated across the field as the sound of blows.[11]

But the committee's admitted lack of knowledge was unlikely to matter; Harvard's faculty would readily agree to a ban. President Eliot would also; last year's players had promised to reform the game to gain permission to play Yale, but Eliot's current annual report called the game "essentially unchanged." Actually, Eliot's true feelings were becoming ever more clear: to him it was "very improbable that a game which involves violent personal collision between opposing players can ever be made a good inter-collegiate game."[12]

When the committee invited students to speak, Harvard's football captain, M. M. Kimball, tried an idea one step better than surrender. Let a student committee meet with the Harvard faculty committee and together draw up playing rules for a game the committee considered unobjectionable. Other colleges would be advised that Harvard could play only under the new rules.

Kimball's idea was quickly dismissed—"unrealistic," "will not be effective," other colleges would not abide by the game Harvard's committee would accept. Professor Byerly pointed to Yale: "No Yale man" known to him "saw anything objectionable in the present rules." Yale would not agree to the rules Harvard would accept.[13]

A Harvard Law School student, Mr. Curtis, had a more novel idea. A game should have three referees, each assigned to watch a specific portion of the play. Alert observation by three different referees would minimize violation of the rules.[14]

None of the students' arguments moved the professors from their plan. On January 6, 1885, Harvard's faculty banned Harvard students from further participation in intercollegiate football.[15]

Camp's response to the Harvard action, including the impassioned defense of football quoted above, was published in the February 5, 1885, *Yale News*. He began by explaining in measured tones the years of effort by college students to develop American football, of the step-by-step development that had been required to achieve a workable and pleasing game. Now, Camp said, faculties were intervening but not on the basis of sound information. As an example, he cited an amendment required the previous year to get permission from Harvard for the 1883 Thanksgiving game. The required amendment specified that the referee of an association football game be an "alumnus of an Association school." "Alumnus" was not the proper criterion for choosing a referee, Camp said; the proper criterion was "an experienced player, known to be firm and decided."

The Harvard decision was especially disturbing because the decision makers "were not experts; in fact, they were barely acquainted with the rules in print [and not] at all in their application." By the end, Camp had worked up to despair and accusation. Harvard's ban was based on "unfair methods" and "concealed motives," producing an "underhand stabbing of a sport that deserves better treatment."

More than emotional hurt, the Harvard ban imposed a practical problem. Princeton and Yale were now the only two active members of the IFA (Columbia was still unable to field a team). A two-member IFA was not workable.

Camp had laid the groundwork for a partial solution a year earlier in his January 1884 *Football Record* book, where he encouraged three additional colleges to apply for membership in the IFA. "The energy of their manager, the merit of their players, or the success of their team," he said, demonstrated their qualification for membership.

Within a month after Harvard's ban, on February 7, 1885, the IFA scheduled a convention in New York. From New York, Camp had even less direct connection to Yale, but Yale's students named him a delegate. The other Yale delegates were Eugene L. Richards Jr. (senior halfback, 1884 team captain, son of Professor Richards) and F. G. Peters (captain-elect of the 1885 team).[16]

Two of the three colleges Camp had encouraged in his *Football Record* book sent representatives to the IFA convention. First was Wesleyan, a Methodist-sponsored college of about two hundred students in Middletown, Connecticut, twenty miles north of New Haven. Relations between Wesleyan and Yale were good, and Camp had helped coach Wesleyan's football team. Wesleyan was not in the same football category as Yale or Princeton, but they were a good second-tier team. And Yale's closeness to Wesleyan might help politically in the IFA.[17]

Second was the University of Pennsylvania, an old university that had lagged in growth and development but was now surging under the leadership of two back-to-back energetic provosts, Charles J. Stille (1866–80) and William Pepper (in office since 1880). The school had moved to a new campus in West Philadelphia in 1873 and instituted new programs, among them the Towne Science School in 1872 and the Wharton School of Finance in 1881. Undergraduate enrollment was still fewer than four hundred, and no dormitories were on campus, leaving students scattered about Philadelphia. Pennsylvania's first football game had been nine years earlier against Princeton, and the two schools had played every year since then; Pennsylvania had never won. In 1879 and 1880, Pennsylvania had played and lost to Yale and in 1881 and 1883 lost to Harvard. Their biggest win had been a defeat of Harvard the previous fall.[18]

Wesleyan and Pennsylvania would be smaller members, not on the level of the Harvard-Princeton-Yale "Big Three," but the IFA needed them to continue. And broadening out could be healthy. The convention voted to admit the two additional colleges, accomplishing the first major enlargement in American football rule-making organization.

Even with two new members, delegates at the 1885 IFA convention continued to reshape the game and separate it from English rugby. They decided that a touchdown would be scored simply by crossing the goal line with the ball, thus eliminating rugby's held-over "maul-in-goal," under which the defense continued to battle a ball carrier who had crossed the goal line, trying to take the ball away from him before he could down it. Advancing the ball down the field and across the goal line with well-thought-out and well-executed plays was the important accomplishment these American rule makers thought should be emphasized, not a battle on the other side of the goal line. Also, at this convention, the referee's position was strengthened: there would be "one referee, and he absolute." No delay from any cause whatever was to last more than five minutes. A team refusing to play after being ordered to do so by the referee would forfeit the game.[19]

As the most experienced rule legislator, Camp presumably was influential in the changes. Yet the convention did not approve another change he proposed, that opposing rush lines in a scrimmage be separated a specified distance, thus establishing a "no-man's-zone" between them to minimize pre-snap skirmishing. It would be twenty years before that concept became reality.[20]

Camp was again appointed to publish the rules and constitution. Beginning with the rule book he prepared for the 1883 season, this would be Camp's third official rule book.

The last football repair of the year came from Harvard itself. Despite their dramatic football ban in early 1885, Harvard's faculty committee reached out to the student body over the remainder of the school year. They offered weekly sessions at which any officer or member of any athletic organization at Harvard could meet with them. One result was a changed perspective by the committee, a confidence that Harvard students sincerely sought reasonable athletic policies. The committee suggested its own replacement by a committee of radically different composition: one, the director of the Harvard gymnasium (the only faculty member); two, a physician residing in Boston or Cambridge; three, a graduate of Harvard College interested in athletic sports; and four and five, two Harvard undergraduates chosen from among the leaders in athletic sports. The committee was to be appointed by the president of the university for a term of one year.[21]

The suggestion was accepted, and by the fall of 1885 a new committee had been appointed. The graduate named to the committee was J. J. Storrow, who had just graduated from the undergraduate college in June 1885 and was now enrolled in Harvard Law School. Storrow had captained Harvard's crew and was knowledgeable and sympathetic to college sports. President Eliot professed satisfaction with the new committee, reporting in his next annual report that they "commanded the respect alike of the Faculty and of the students."

On January 5, 1886, the new committee reported they had found the "game of football has been much improved during the past season." Thereupon, the faculty voted to rescind their ban.

Though he approved the committee, President Eliot did not share their optimism: in his 1885–86 annual report, he stated that football had been reinstated at Harvard in "the hope that the prohibition of the game for a year would serve to check for the future the brutal and dishonorable practices which had become part of it," but he immediately added, "The experience of the present [1886] season affords little reason to believe that this hope will be realized."[22]

Perhaps Eliot's energy on the issue was waning, though. Politically, this was Eliot's most vulnerable time at Harvard; a majority of Harvard's constituency was opposed to his radical expansion of electives at the school, and that included opposition among the corporation and overseers. Alumni support for football was growing. Although Eliot certainly didn't change his opinion about football and continued to openly criticize it, Harvard as a whole seemed more ready to accept the game.[23]

Father of Football 19

Outing magazine gave Camp an unofficial title when they introduced him in their April 1886 edition: "Walter C. Camp, *the father of foot-ball in American colleges*, and for many years head of the Yale team, has, we are happy to say, joined our staff." Camp was barely twenty-seven years old, but his résumé could support the introduction: contributor of the foundational five-yard rule, participant and leader for the last eight years in guiding game changes or making rules, author of letters and articles defending and promoting the game, and originator and dependable producer of an annual rule book and referee's guidebook. Even today, more than ninety years after he died, students of the game recognize Camp as the "father of American football."[1]

Outing, in its fourth year and still losing money, had been purchased by the modestly wealthy Poultney Bigelow, a Yale graduate one year ahead of Camp, who called on Yale friends and acquaintances for help. With the magazine struggling to survive, working up to a circulation of about twenty thousand, Bigelow drew no salary and the magazine's staff worked "on a practically honorary basis." By day Camp was a seller of clocks. But now, without leaving clock selling, he had added a writing assignment on the staff of a commercial magazine.[2]

Outing was happy to add Camp's football expertise because American football was growing and spreading farther into the country, as illustrated for 1886, the year Camp joined *Outing*, by events in Indiana. Intercollegiate football had been first played in Indiana in 1884 as a kind of hybrid of soccer and rugby. But according to an Indiana observer, American football

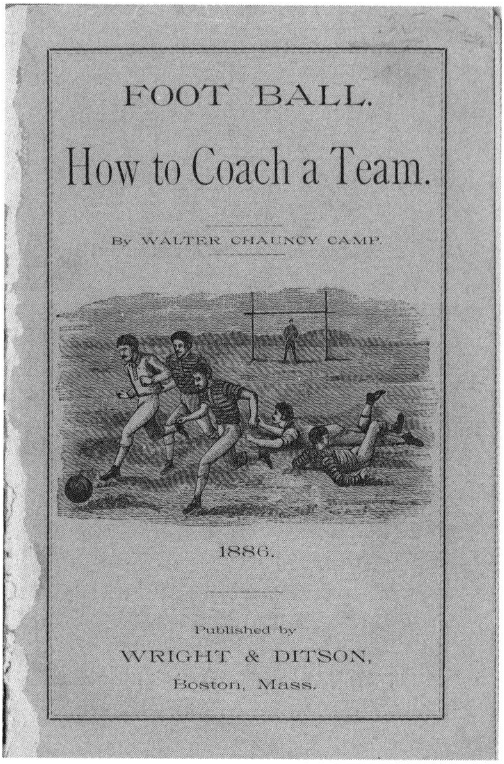

The 1886 booklet by Walter Camp to help American football captains prepare for coaching. (Courtesy of Springfield College, Babson Library, Archives and Special Collections, Springfield, Mass.)

"was introduced at most of the Indiana colleges in the fall of 1886, under the auspices of the Indianapolis Athletic Association, organized about this time by resident graduates of eastern colleges. This new force . . . was able to secure the formation of a college league."[3]

Overall, in 1886 about fifteen major American colleges and universities, including such midwestern universities as Minnesota and Northwestern and in the Far West the University of California, were playing America's form of rugby football; eighteen smaller colleges were also playing.[4] Camp reviewed the season of 1886 in his first bylined *Outing* article, and the article was successful enough to become a future Camp staple. *Outing* also published an "Events of the Month" section that included schedules, scores, and game summaries, likely with input from Camp.[5]

Camp's most significant 1886 football project was a new instructional text, a "guide to assist captains" titled *Foot Ball: How to Coach a Team*, thirty-five pages in eight chapters (with ads for publisher Wright and Ditson's products). The audience for such a booklet was small, with only fifteen major colleges playing; there is no evidence Camp was paid for writing it. But the booklet could improve the ten-year-old game, and despite clock-selling work in New York, Camp was still football's main champion, seeking to develop and strengthen the game.[6]

Besides being the most detailed teaching yet about American football, the booklet also revealed some Camp insights:

- Primary in choosing players, even more than individual talent, should be the individual's ability to work as part of a team.
- Disagreeing with the common wisdom that "beef" wins games, Camp argued for "trained weight": "Brains will beat brute force . . . every time."
- Quarterback was "the most responsible position on the field." "The coaching of a quarter is entirely different from that of the rest of the team, for he must be praised or blamed—as the case may be—for *results*. If he follows out the signal and executes his part of the play and the rest of it fails, he must receive the blame. It is only by this almost unfair treatment that he can be taught to exercise the very best judgment on all occasions."[7]

At summer's end, 1886, Walter Camp mailed a short letter from Northeast Harbor, Maine, where Alice Sumner was caring for the children of her brother Professor Sumner. In careful, uniformly lined, left-slanting handwriting, Camp wrote:

> North East Harbor
> Aug. 30th 86
>
> Prof. W.G. Sumner
> New Haven Conn.
> Dear Sir,
>
> I write, with the consent of your sister, to ask your permission to marry her as my position will warrant. I intend coming to New Haven the end of this week and will at once call upon you and put you in possession of the facts upon which rests the possibility of my supporting and making her happy. I do not imagine you need the assurance that I love her.
>
> Very truly yours,
> Walter C. Camp[8]

Two years into employment at the New Haven Clock Company, Camp did not consider himself ready to support Alice and thought he needed to lay out the details for Professor Sumner, the remaining father figure in Alice's life, while seeking Sumner's blessing on the marriage.

Alice sent her own letter the next day, with a caution as to timing:

Dear Graham,

You have heard from Mr. Camp, I trust, to the effect that with your consent, I will engage myself to marry him some time. It cannot be for a long time yet, as a sufficient income is first necessary.

I have never cared for any other man. I am very sure of my affection for him and I am glad to go on with my school work until that time comes when I may become his wife.

Yours affectionately,
Alice[9]

Alice soon returned to New Haven and began to tell her friends of her engagement, whereupon Walter received a letter from an old friend, a neighborhood girl, Eliza C. Hotchkiss, who had watched him through adolescence and young manhood and his first dating interests. She wanted "to be among the first to offer you my heartiest congratulations. I don't pretend to be surprised, but I am delighted that everything has turned out so nicely, and you both must know that you have my very best wishes."[10]

Life returned to a regular routine for a while—Walter in New York, Alice in New Haven—but only for a while. On Saturday, March 5, 1887, two New York City police detectives greeted Walter as he arrived at the New Haven

Walter Camp and Alice Sumner about the time of their engagement to marry. (Walter Chauncey Camp Papers, 1870–1983 [inclusive], 1870–1925 [bulk], Manuscripts and Archives, Yale University)

Clock Company store in Manhattan. Camp had planned only a brief stop on his way to New Haven, where he was to referee Yale intramural games that evening. But there were the detectives, with their shocking words—impossible, laughable words, except how can you laugh when told you are a suspect in attempted murder?[11]

Two days earlier, Thursday, March 3, 1887, at one in the morning, a young man named George Condit Smith had been shot in Madison Square, a parklike space across the street from Madison Square Garden and the Fifth Avenue Hotel. Smith had been lured to the square by a note, unsigned but apparently from a rival suitor for Sallie Barnes of Paterson, New Jersey. Smith was in the hospital, able to speak, and had named Camp as one potential rival. Camp fitted the description given by Smith of his assailant.

Camp first told the detectives he had not seen Sallie Barnes for at least a year; then he remembered seeing her briefly five weeks earlier at a reception in her honor at the Murray Hill Hotel, where Camp's parents were staying during a visit to the city. But the crucial fact, Camp told the police, was that he had been in New Haven on Wednesday and had not returned to New York until after one in the morning on Thursday, when the shooting was said to have occurred.

Despite Camp's contentions, the detectives continued to probe. How well did he know Sallie Barnes? He was asked to describe more specifically his last meeting with her. Camp refused to answer—he had explained to the detectives why he could not be involved; under those circumstances, the questions were not pertinent or anyone else's business. And he had no lawyer present.

Explaining that he needed to get to New Haven to fulfill his scheduled refereeing obligations, Camp excused himself and walked to the elevated-train station at the end of the block. If he looked back as he climbed the stairs to the station platform, he might have seen the detectives following him, up the steps and onto his train. Before the train reached the Eighth Street station, they approached and placed him under arrest!

Arriving at the police station, Camp asked permission to notify friends. Soon a representative from the clock company and a lawyer arrived. Captain Williams of the New York police was persuaded to bring Camp to the hospital for identification by Smith. Camp walked back and forth in front of Smith, who assured the police that Camp was not the individual who shot him. A handwriting test also showed that Camp had not written the letter that lured Smith to Madison Square. Back at the police station, it was confirmed that Camp had been on a trip to New Haven at the time of the attack.

Released, Camp proceeded to New Haven. News of his arrest had preceded him; he was well-enough known that involvement in a shooting was first- or second-page news in the *New York Times* for four days running. Unbelievable! Could it be true? What about Alice Sumner? What would she and Professor Sumner do?

Now, with Camp back in town in the flesh and clearly unconcerned, there was relief. Actually, it was a simple story, a simple case of misidentity. A momentary hint of scandal, an entertaining story on the front page of the *New York Times* for a few days, but quickly put aside.

Smith recovered, and later that fall he and Sallie Barnes were married. Even then no assailant had been identified, and there were hints the wound had been self-inflicted.

Real news came later that summer of 1887, when Camp was promoted by NHCC and moved back to New Haven. He had performed a variety of jobs for NHCC in New York: work in NHCC's New York office his first year, traveling salesman the next year, supervision of the sales force out of New York City his last three years. He had worked alongside others who had closer and earlier connections to NHCC—for example, George Stevens, manager of NHCC's New York store, was a grandson of the early clock pioneer Chauncey Jerome and the son of Edward Stevens, who had been a prominent officer and investor in NHCC. But now Camp seemingly was being promoted over George Stevens to a higher job in the company, to "superintendent of the order department," a job that a later officer of the company suggested might more currently be called "general sales manager." Camp also became a formal stockholder, owner of ten shares, valued at $250.[12]

A few months after returning, Camp attended his first stockholder meeting, January 25, 1888, together with Hiram Camp, age seventy-six; James English, age seventy-five; F. J. Stevens, another son of the deceased Edward Stevens; and F. E. Morgan, himself a son-in-law of Edward Stevens and now secretary of the company.[13]

The company was facing difficulties; business had slowed in 1886 and was still slow, raising several questions that might be discussed at the stockholder meeting or simply wondered at: How could business be improved? How would the twenty-eight-year-old Walter Camp, "superintendent of sales," work with Hiram Camp, the seventy-six-year-old company president? And how long would Hiram Camp remain active in the company?

Such questions could also have been part of any conversation Walter Camp had with Professor Sumner to present "the facts upon which rest the possibility" of supporting Alice. A superintendent of sales should have an adequate income, but the outlook for the company was not clear. Uncertainty at NHCC perhaps set the background for other questions Sumner might have asked—about the time and effort Walter Camp devoted to football and how that fitted with his NHCC job. Yet the fact was, so far, Camp had successfully carried on football and writing jobs while growing into and being promoted to an important full-time job at NHCC.

Actually, Camp's life seemed to be moving along with more order: engagement to Alice, promotion to a meaningful and important job, accepted leader of the ever more popular American football. Management of the clock company had promoted him, while surely knowing he would continue as football rule maker, writer, advocate, even a kind of organizational center for the game—increasingly the "father of American football."

PART III

The Game Established

An "American" Game of Football 20

Student management of American football was in jeopardy by the end of the Princeton-Yale game of 1886. Trouble had begun a year earlier, when the McCosh-led Princeton faculty had refused another Thanksgiving game in New York City, and unhappy Yale student officers responded by insisting that in that case the game be played in New Haven. Now, one year later, Princeton wanted its turn, a game in Princeton. But Yale's student officers still wanted New York with its big income-producing audiences to bolster their athletic bank account. And so did Princeton's graduate advisory committee. Better a game in New York on the Saturday before or after Thanksgiving Day than a game in Princeton where, the fact was, the facilities couldn't handle the large crowds that now attended Princeton-Yale games. But Princeton's students and football captain were insistent. Yale had required New Haven last year; Princeton was now due a game in their town.[1]

Yale finally agreed, but game day brought its own crises. The flood of people entering Princeton overwhelmed the small town's food services, and rain intruded, a daylong, soaking rain. Worst of all, at the scheduled 2:30 game time, the teams were still arguing about the game referee. Princeton said the agreed-upon referee refused to perform and proposed a different Princeton graduate. That Yale refused. Finally, the agreed-upon referee appeared, and play began at 3:30, one hour late.[2]

Yale managed to take a lead, but for the second time in three years, daylight failed before the game was over. With about fifteen minutes of game time remaining, both sides agreed playing conditions were hopeless, and the game was stopped. Once more Yale got a shock. The referee refused to declare Yale the winner because the game had not been played to the finish. Just like two years earlier, Yale was winning but could not claim a victory—or the IFA championship. This wasn't the way the system was supposed to work.

But this time, discontent reached beyond Yale students. A Princeton professor writing in the *New York Evening Post* turned advocate: Get "older men" involved in managing football games and championships. We need "less jockeying and more football." Actually, students also were ready for a change. Two weeks after the game, the *Yale News*, published by students at a school that was a bastion for student management, went on record for game planning by graduates "unaffected by undergraduate hotheadedness."[3]

It turned out many people were ready to help with a change—players, students, and alumni, even college officials—wanting to preserve football but give it better management. A plan was developed that soon unfolded in apparently orchestrated steps.

First, a sympathetic student-run IFA convention in May 1887 appointed a three-student constitution-revision committee chaired by Yale's captain-elect, Harry Beecher.[4]

As if on cue, Beecher's committee immediately delegated the drafting of a revised IFA constitution to Walter Camp. The choice of Camp—the foremost public figure in football—may not have been surprising, but it was still revealing. Students trusted him, ready to place in his hands a revision of the constitution that would certainly lessen their power and prerogatives.[5]

And it wasn't only students; within three weeks, Camp met with a multicollege committee having an amazing membership: seven representatives from Harvard, *including two professors*; three representatives from Princeton, *including two professors*; five representatives from Yale, *including one professor*; and one representative each from Pennsylvania and Wesleyan. Camp would look back on the committee's involvement as transformational—multicollege and extending across faculty, students, and graduates. College authorities, including professors from Harvard, were now ready to support football and place it on a more sustainable course. The twenty-eight-year-old Camp was accepted and trusted with leadership of this broad-based committee, and it was to this committee that Camp brought the draft of an amended constitution. On June 11, 1887, at a New York hotel, Camp and the diverse committee met, and the draft constitution was approved. The next day, Beecher's student committee added their approval, and in October, after students had returned to college, a full convention of the IFA ratified it.[6]

First and foremost, the revised constitution established a new five-member "Graduate Advisory Committee" (GAC), one graduate from each college of the IFA. The individual committee members were to be elected by "the Alumni, or appointed by the Faculty" of the college they represented.[7]

The new committee had several tasks and a timetable. As a main task, they were to meet each year in March to "propose" rule changes for consideration by a May IFA student convention. The committee's proposed rules would take effect once approved by the convention. But *even without approval by the student convention*, a proposed rule would become effective if four members of the advisory committee voted for it. The committee was called "Advisory," but it could do more than advise if it wanted to.[8]

This was revolution, not evolution. Theoretically, students still had a role in writing playing rules—they were to review the rules recommended by the Graduate Advisory Committee. But even if they disapproved of a proposed rule, the committee could overrule their decision. Theoretically, also, the students could retrieve their authority by again redrafting the constitution. But that seemed unlikely.

Besides essentially transferring rule making to the Graduate Advisory Committee, the revised 1887 Camp-drafted IFA constitution made other core changes:

- Two officials, a referee and an umpire, would supervise each game.
- All referees and umpires were to be "permanently elected or assigned on or before October 15 of each year."
- The GAC would act as a "committee on appeals." No longer would students make the final judgment about the outcome of games and the award of a championship.
- IFA members were to play one game each year with every college in the IFA, and the "two leading colleges of the preceding year" were to play their game the succeeding season "in or near New York."
- The "printing of the rules and constitution shall be given to Mr. Walter C. Camp." No diminished role for Camp, and now embedded in the IFA constitution! Not just a kudo, this could be a useful source of future leverage.[9]

American football had taken a major turn, with the previous all-student management supplemented and in effect overseen by a committee of graduates.

At their first rule-making meeting on March 3, 1888, the new Graduate Advisory Committee of twentysomething elder statesmen made two rule amendments that would fundamentally change American football:

Tackling. Incredible as it now seems, American football's early rules barred tackling "below the hips." In 1888, wanting to make tackling more effective, the new GAC amended the rules to permit tackling down to the knees.[10]

Importantly, the amendment not only advanced tackling but also prepared the way for a major change in football strategy. Above-the-hips tackling had allowed ball carriers to more easily escape a tackle, encouraging an "open" game with spread-out formations, open-field running, and long laterals. With tackling made more effective by the down-to-the-knees rule, offenses gradually changed their attack to use more runs into the line. New player deployments were invented, moving linemen into the backfield to bring additional blocking at the point of attack. Such massed blocking and straight-ahead plunges became a timely fit for Camp's six-year-old downs-and-distance rule, because even short advances often accumulated five yards in three downs and extended the offense's ball possession.

Interference. Interference, which Camp would one day call a "keynote" of American football and which was the next important game development after the downs-and-distance rule, had developed only minimally by 1888, limited by rugby's offside rules. Under rugby rules, players were "offside" when "in front of the ball," as when a runner carrying the ball was behind them. An offside player could not "in any way interrupt or obstruct" opposing players.[11]

Even though Americans still sometimes called their game "rugby," they increasingly closed their eyes to rugby's offside rules. A first evasion came of necessity when Americans developed the snapback procedure, because the snapback automatically put offensive rush-line players in front of the ball and thus offside. To permit development of American football's snapback, referees necessarily ignored this literal offside obstruction by offensive rush-line players.

Gradually, American players pushed matters further—extending their arms to widen their "passive" obstruction, then beginning to grab and hold opponent rushers, and then, with greater sophistication, coordinating efforts with a ball carrier, running alongside to complicate tackling and sometimes pushing ahead. By the mid-1880s, some teams were shielding ball carriers inside V-shaped player combinations, "wedges" that clearly violated the rules but that, Camp said, umpires "too carelessly" allowed.[12]

The issue generated a long discussion at the March 1888 GAC meeting, but in the end Camp and the committee used only a few words to change the rule and thereby fundamentally alter American football. To the existing rule that prohibited an offside player from "obstructing" his opponent, the committee added the limiting statement "with his hands or arms." A necessary implication was that obstruction with the body was allowed. An offensive player ahead of the ball carrier could interfere with his opponent if he did it with his body only.[13]

Even more than the tackling amendment, the interference amendment opened the way to major new playing procedures. Ball carrying had begun primitively in rugby with the solo, extemporaneous running of a ball bounced out of a scrum. Now running would become a coordinated team action, preplanned, practiced, and orchestrated by spoken signals, becoming a central feature of American football. To defend against interference-aided running and other play, the defense would be assisted by a consciously different rule, a "privilege" Camp said, permission for the defense to continue using their hands and arms, thus enabling them to more easily "break through and get at the runner."[14]

To Camp, the new interference and tackling rules together produced a "structure of attack and defense" that made the game more "scientific." A "complicated system of signals and attack" developed, balanced by "a defense that must be planned and thought out with equal care." Overall, a new cycle of offensive development and defensive response would get under way, part of continual change that Americans accepted as valid and admirable.[15]

While the above changes were happening, Camp said, the American football player began to feel a "sense of responsibility for the development of his own American game." Changes had accumulated gradually, but now in the mid-1880s players were recognizing that a line had been crossed. Their game was no longer rugby, but a fundamentally new and distinctive "American rugby" or "American football."[16]

Camp marked the arrival of this new understanding with an October 1887 article in *Outing* titled "The Game and Laws of American Football." He described the history of the game, including its development from rugby, and then analyzed in detail American football's rules compared with those of rugby. The "original" rugby rules from which Americans began play in 1876 were appended to the article, as were the American football rules for 1887. For the growing sport-focused audience of the five-year-old *Outing* magazine, here was a serious and historical introduction to the new game.[17]

One year later, Camp introduced American football to a different set of readers with an evocative article in *Harper's Weekly*, America's leading general-audience newsweekly. Titled "The American Game of Football," this article took a broader look, discussing not only the sport but also the larger event growing around it. Camp seemed in genuine awe: "And the audience! Never until the advent of this sport has anything like it been assembled. Ten thousand people, the bulk of them flying college colors, would make a grand sight anywhere." This audience was "surging up against the ropes," rising in the grandstands as "waves of humanity," and cheering even before the players were on the field. Camp marveled not only that the new game held such fascination for its viewers, but that it had all developed in "not more than a dozen years." The American scrimmage and the downs-and-distance rule had been created within six years after American college students started playing rugby. Now, six additional years had brought the next big change, an organized, soon-to-be-elaborated running attack.[18]

In addition to development of a more workable and playable game, more colleges were now participating. About eleven major colleges had been playing in 1882 when Camp's downs-and-distance rule was enacted, but by 1888 the number had grown to twenty-six major colleges. And with interference now enacted and a full-fledged running attack thus encouraged, even greater growth might be expected.[19]

The 1887 *Outing* and 1888 *Harper's Weekly* articles not only expanded Camp's public image as a spokesman for American football, but also signaled new writing opportunities. The *New York Times* on October 12, 1888, included a long article that was essentially a quotation of Camp's remarks and opened with the lines: "Walter C. Camp, the great football authority says . . ." In 1889 the *New York Evening Post* presented several signed articles by Camp—November 13, 22, and 27, discussing and predicting the outcome of upcoming games. On November 16, 1889, the morning of the Harvard-Princeton game, the *New York World*'s headline read, "Walter Camp Names Princeton"; the *Times*' headline was, "Princeton Will Win Today, So Says the Football Expert Walter C. Camp."

An even bigger writing opportunity came in the fall of 1889—a series of articles by Camp in *St. Nicholas*, a high-quality monthly young people's magazine. In ten monthly issues, *St. Nicholas* published, first, a continuing series by Camp on football and after a two-month break a Camp series on baseball. In total, the articles filled sixty-three pages, providing detailed "how-to-play" descriptions of features, rules, and methods. With a teacher's enthusiasm, Camp explained the facts of the games, including practical descriptions showing how to set up a field, equipment to use, and rules to learn, as well as playing techniques and strategies. The articles illustrated that Camp was not fixed on football but cared about, and wanted to teach and promote, other sports; he also wrote articles for *St. Nicholas* on college rowing and track and field. *St. Nicholas* prominently cited the football-baseball series in large newspaper ads promoting the magazine.[20]

Camp had been writing about football at least since his 1880 "Hints for Practice," but those earlier writings had been directed to players and other participants. With his articles in *Outing*, *Harper's Weekly*, *St. Nicholas*, and newspapers, Camp was now reaching a broader audience and laying the groundwork for a new career. An outlet was growing for the writing ambition that had pulled at him from an early age, as well as a source of added income—helpful because the time had arrived for important new personal responsibilities.

Headquarters on Gill Street 21

By three thirty, June 30, 1888, guests were arriving at Trinity Episcopal Church on the New Haven Green, coming on foot, by public horsecar, or in horse and buggy down Temple Street. The church fronted on Temple Street, a narrow lane passing through the center of the green and lined on both sides with majestic elm trees. On this day, a walkway extended out to the street from the church entrance, with awning above and carpet below for guests in Sunday finery to proceed into the church. They quickly filled the sanctuary—family, friends, and a large majority of Yale's faculty, come to watch the marriage of Walter Camp to Alice Sumner, Professor Sumner's young sister.[1]

Alice entered the long sanctuary at four o'clock with the organ playing Lohengrin's wedding march, escorted by Professor Sumner and followed by her maid of honor (Amy Sharpe, resident of Providence, Rhode Island, and friend from Northeast Harbor) and five bridesmaids. She wore plain white silk; the maid of honor and bridesmaids each wore silk mull over silk, two in pink, two in white, and two in yellow, each carrying large bouquets the color of their dresses.

Walter met Alice at the chancel gate together with his best man, Edward Bailey, a Yale graduate from Harrisburg, Pennsylvania. Five ushers were also in the wedding party, all Yale graduates and generally involved in athletics as players or Yale athletic club officers; among them were Bob Watson, 1880 captain of Yale's football team, and Walter Jennings, who had attended both Yale and Hopkins Grammar School with Camp.

Trinity was Professor Sumner's church, and Trinity's pastor, Dr. Edwin Harford, was Sumner's old friend. Harford was assisted by Rev. Charles Camp, Walter's cousin and former football teammate, now a pastor both in Westville, Connecticut, and in New Haven's All Saints Mission.[2]

After a wedding tea at Professor Sumner's home, Walter and Alice left to spend a few weeks at a "leading summer resort."

When they returned from their honeymoon, Walter and Alice came home to a cottage-size house on Gill Street directly in back of Walter's parents' home on Chapel, a few blocks from Dwight School, where Leverett was principal. Leverett and Ellen occupied one half of a large white wood-sided duplex facing Chapel (1303 Chapel), and Uncle Henry and Aunt Elizabeth owned and occupied the other half (1305 Chapel). Walter and Alice's house, owned by his parents and at the edge of their backyard, faced Gill (12 Gill Street), a one-and-a-half-story gingerbread-style cottage with vertical siding and filigreed edges on dormer roofs.[3]

The combined buildings formed a miniature family compound at the corner of Chapel and Gill—Walter and Alice, Leverett and Ellen, Uncle Henry and Aunt Elizabeth—a close family group in which Walter had lived many years and Alice would now join.

Besides getting comfortable with the new family group, Alice would need to get comfortable with football. An early visitor to Walter and Alice's Gill Street cottage was William H. (Pa) Corbin, captain of the 1888 Yale football team, who had asked Walter to coach the team.[4]

Coaching in American football had been mainly in the hands of the team captain, sporadically assisted by graduated players such as Camp. Corbin now had in mind more than sporadic help; Camp was "placed in entire charge," Corbin later said. Before school was dismissed for the 1888 summer vacation, Corbin called the team together and had Camp speak to them, giving him an opportunity to describe the training the players should do during the summer and recent changes in the tackling and interference rules. As was then the pattern for graduate coaching, Camp was unpaid for this work.[5]

Walter and Alice had barely gotten settled when football practice began in late September. Players gathered at "the fence" on campus at two o'clock every afternoon and boarded horse-drawn coaches for the half-hour ride out

The home of Walter and Alice Camp during the first ten years of their marriage. (Pictures of buildings, grounds, and landmarks in New Haven, 1653–1970 [inclusive], Manuscripts and Archives, Yale University)

to Yale Field (purchased through the efforts of the Field Committee of which Camp had been a part while in medical school). They traveled through a district under development with empty lots here and there on every side, then across a bridge into a pleasant rural scene and up a slope to the level top of a wide plateau with a baseball grandstand and two football fields; varsity and scrub players practiced at one of the fields and freshmen and other players at the other. Nearly two hundred spectators clustered around the ropes around the first field, where there was commonly a practice game between the varsity and scrubs.[6]

Camp liked to make practice vigorous, no rest or respite allowed. Such relentless effort, he argued, contributed to Yale's unmatched record—*only two losses* since adoption of the rugby game in 1876! Standing beside the field as play progressed, "Pa" Corbin and he called out instructions and comments. Corbin was tall, with a large-jawed face and a drooping handlebar mustache that brought a look of maturity to match his nickname. As captain Corbin was in charge; he knew football, having been varsity center since he was a sophomore, but he also sought advice from Camp.[7]

A new challenge was to take advantage of the new rule that allowed tackling to the knees. As Camp and Corbin stood on the sideline, they repeatedly called, "Tackle low," trying to develop the habit of tackling at a runner's thighs. Through the next several years, the admonition to "tackle low" would be heard often on the practice field, with parallel admonitions for runners to "stay low" and "lower your head" to shoot through or under the arms of a would-be tackler.

When work kept Camp from practice, another former player might take his place, but the enthusiastically helpful Alice also came, walking the sidelines and taking notes, watching together with Corbin, students, and others. Players began to refer to her as "Mrs. Walter," and Corbin later honored her and Walter at a dinner as "co-coaches."[8]

In the evening, Corbin often came to the Camps' home to review and make plans, sometimes bringing some of the players or other graduates who were assisting in coaching. Corbin had a varied and active life—he sang in the chapel choir and Yale Glee Club and was a leader in the Young Men's Christian Association (YMCA). He liked people; when he visited, there were fun conversations. Alice also participated, a "generalissimo of high spirits," one observer later recalled, paired with her quiet and insightful husband who had studied and been involved in the game for its full American life. In the modest home on Gill Street, preparations were made for the upcoming 1888 season, perhaps around a lit fireplace in a scene of lively congeniality and camaraderie but with serious and thorough discussion of the events of the day, consideration of strengths and needs, formation of plans, and suggestions for the next day's practice.[9]

The new interference rules provided new opportunities for tactics and strategy. With Camp as coach, Yale began in 1888 to develop interference-escorted running plays around end that Camp later wrote about: "The principal study of the play is directed toward the proper timing of it. . . . It is necessary to form a protection for a space of perhaps five yards, and the protection must move as fast as the runner behind it. [An object] . . . is to move the play quickly [outside] . . . where the [opponent's] heavy centre and guard cannot assist . . . and to allow the runner to get his full speed on." "A great deal of labor," he added, "was involved in teaching" the blockers to stay together, to form a continuous and impregnable phalanx running ahead of the ball carrier.[10]

End run of a Yale team coached by Walter Camp. (*Harper's Weekly*, November 26, 1892, 1148, courtesy of the University of Minnesota Library)

The 1888 Yale team working under Camp and Corbin's direction brought together a unique collection of players who would have a long and important influence on football.

The team's right guard, George Washington Woodruff, could tell of an 1865 pioneer migration to Nebraska that went awry, leaving him and a younger brother orphaned and raised back in Pennsylvania by their grandparents. George arrived at Yale in the fall of 1885 at age twenty-one, a self-described "green farmer boy"—a square-faced block of a man, one of the strongest on campus. He was said to have never heard of college football but arrived at practice one day in an undershirt, long trousers, full black beard, and straw hat. Almost immediately, he was placed on the varsity at right guard; by 1888 he was a three-year veteran. He also participated in track and crew while maintaining a good scholastic standing, on schedule to graduate with a Phi Beta Kappa.[11]

At left guard, two spots from Woodruff, was a freshman from Minnesota—Walter Heffelfinger. Walter was overweight as an adolescent, with the nickname "Pudge," but grew tall and athletic, an unusual physical specimen. Becoming interested in football, he hung around the University of Minnesota, which had begun playing football with local colleges and secondary schools in 1882; on occasion Heffelfinger filled in when the university team was short a player. He played well enough to draw attention from a recent Yale graduate, who persuaded him to attend Yale.[12]

The October 22, 1888, *Princetonian* had learned of Heffelfinger and was impressed: "Heffelfinger, the new right guard of the Yale foot ball team, is an athlete of much promise. He is six feet, two inches in height, weighs two hundred pounds and is a remarkably swift runner for a man of his weight." The new interference rules were made to order for Heffelfinger, who could

Walter (Pudge) Heffelfinger leading a run for a Yale team coached by Walter Camp.

swing out of the line and lead a ball carrier around end, a model for future teams.

The right halfback, (Thomas) Lee McClung, was another freshman and a southerner of deep roots: his Scotch-Irish great-grandfather Charles came to eastern Tennessee in 1788 and three years later surveyed and helped lay out Knoxville.[13]

Lee's mother apparently contracted tuberculosis and died when Lee was eleven, and after a few years his father decided to send three of his sons to boarding schools—Lee and an older brother to Phillips Exeter and the third to Phillips Andover. Lee was fourteen and short and stocky when he entered Exeter, but he attracted athletic notice in the spring of his first year, when he was the only Exeter student who could catch a wild-throwing pitcher. He was the baseball catcher all four years at Exeter and in his last two years became the regular right halfback in football.[14]

His oldest brother, Calvin, had graduated from Yale in 1876, so it was no surprise when Lee entered Yale in the fall of 1888, with a slight southern drawl and southern gentleman's manners.

The oldest and financially most needy player on the 1888 Yale team, Amos Alonzo Stagg came by a long and roundabout route. Born in West Orange, New Jersey, son of a shoe cobbler and general workman, "Lonzo" attended public school but proceeded slowly because of work with his father—he was eighteen before he entered tenth grade.[15]

Upon graduation from high school, Stagg aspired to the ministry and wanted to attend Yale, but could not pass Yale's entrance exam. A high school classmate and friend, also unable to pass Yale's exam, persuaded Stagg to join him for makeup work at Phillips Exeter. Stagg lived cheaply, found jobs, and studied the Latin, Greek, and mathematics needed for Yale admission.

Stagg was twenty-two when he entered Yale in 1884. He found a job waiting tables in a student dining club, but made time for other activities (first tenor in the Yale Glee Club, financial manager of the *Yale News*, and active work at the Yale YMCA). At 5'3¾", Stagg was Yale's ace baseball pitcher, a muscular 150 pounds and natural athlete who struck out twenty Princeton batters in a May 1888 game. The *New York Herald* claimed "no man is better known in baseball circles" than Stagg; after graduation in the spring of 1888, he reportedly turned down a professional contract to enroll in Yale Divinity School and prepare for the ministry. He worked as student director of the YMCA and at age twenty-six decided to try for the Yale football team.[16]

Pa Corbin was one of the team's New Englanders, from Connecticut, where his father was a merchant and manufacturer. Another New Englander, sophomore William P. Graves, whose father taught at Andover and later at Amherst, was the left halfback. Fullback and preferred goal kicker was William Tillinghast Bull, from Newport, Rhode Island, where his father was in the insurance business and president of the gaslight company. The twenty-one-year-old Bull had graduated from Yale's Sheffield Scientific School in the spring of 1888, but was unsure of future goals. He enrolled in one of Professor Sumner's classes in the fall and played football, his fourth year of varsity play.

The fruits of Camp and Corbin's coaching began to appear September 30, 1888, when Yale defeated Wesleyan, 76–0. Next came Rutgers, 65–0 for Yale. The game with the University of Pennsylvania was closer but another win, 34–0. Throughout the first twelve games of the season, there were big scores for Yale and no points for the opposition. The most difficult game was against Princeton at the Polo Grounds, the Saturday before Thanksgiving. With fifteen thousand watching, Princeton and Yale had a tough battle that Yale won 10–0 on two memorable goals by Bull.

To one observer, the "modern Yale game may be said to have been started in this year." Yale won the IFA championship and finished the season with a never-before-achieved 698 points for Yale and no points for the opponents. Camp's first year of serious coaching had produced a shining and long-remembered year.

22 Rivalry Demands Rules

It had come down to one man. Four of the five members of the IFA's two-year-old Graduate Advisory Committee were obviously deadlocked, two to two. The fifth delegate would have to decide this angry and unprecedented dispute—yes or no, were all players on Princeton's football team eligible to play Saturday against Harvard?

Winning had gotten new priority at Harvard with the election of Arthur Cumnock as football captain. The blond, wavy-haired Cumnock had played varsity end at Harvard since he was a freshman, a solid, well-built, and determined athlete. When Cumnock became captain, he got the expected 1889 players to begin gymnasium practice in January and to practice again outdoors in the spring, a novel and significant departure from alleged "Harvard indifference."[1]

Harvard had grown tired of losing to Princeton—in twelve games, Harvard had three wins, one tie, and eight losses, and the losses were coming faster, four out of the last five games. Harvard's emotions went up another notch when they heard about Princeton's 1889 football team. Bowled over by the last year's undefeated, unscored-upon Yale juggernaut, Princeton had brought together its own team that couldn't be beat, an unusual group of players. W. J. (Bill) George, Princeton's outstanding varsity center the past three years, who had graduated and was teaching at a nearby private high school, had recently entered Princeton Theological Seminary and joined the team; he was still teaching part-time at the high school and had entered the seminary late but in time to play Harvard. Another seminarian, the fierce and tough tackle Hector Cowan, was in his fifth year of varsity play.[2]

Then there were two "traveling athletes," also late arrivals—Benjamin (Sport) Donnelly, on the team about mid-October, who reportedly boxed professionally in Chicago, the hometown of Princeton's elected captain, K. L. Ames, and Walter (Monte) Cash, last year playing for the University of Pennsylvania, this year joining the Princeton team in November from his home in Wyoming. In addition, E. O. Wagenhurst, a graduated former Princeton football captain, out of school for more than a year, had returned for "graduate" work and joined the team in mid-October.[3]

A Harvard alumnus had seen Princeton play and wrote Cumnock: "Princeton hasn't a doubt that she has the best team that ever walked the face of the earth," and she had "reason for confidence": they "blocked beautifully," and their line "was impregnable . . . the strongest I've seen."[4]

Walter Camp had a mischievous, tongue-in-cheek response to Princeton's 1889 team. When Yale played a certain-win "practice" game with Stevens Institute on October 31, 1889, three former Yale players no longer enrolled at Yale suddenly appeared and played in the game—Pa Corbin, last year's captain; Harry Beecher, 1888 graduate and former quarterback and captain; and Wyllys Terry, 1885 graduate and outstanding former halfback. Two days later, the *New York Times* got an explanation from Camp. "As the rules now stand," Camp said, "these veteran players can join the Yale team even if they do not re-enter college until the day before" they play. But according to Camp, no such move would be made by Yale unless it "is forced to . . . by the action of Princeton and Harvard in taking back their old players." Princeton's Wagenhurst was cited as one such graduated player now playing for Princeton. Yale hoped, Camp reportedly said, that it would not be forced to use graduated players by the actions of Princeton or Harvard and instead could use "only the men who are pursuing a regular course" at Yale.[5]

In other words, Camp seemed to be saying, two could play the Princeton game. If Princeton continued with the team they had organized, Yale was apparently prepared to include graduates on its team. Time would tell whether Camp and Yale were simply calling attention to Princeton's actions or were seriously prepared to add graduated players to their team. However, the fact was, under existing rules, a case of legitimacy could be made for Princeton's players—all were enrolled in established Princeton academic programs.

But Harvard thought another issue might dislodge some Princeton players, namely, some who were said to have received money for playing baseball in the summer. To Harvard's football leaders, those Princeton players were "professionals"—not football "professionals," but "professionals" nevertheless. Players paid to play any sport had no place on a college team.

The issue of professionalism versus amateurism was quite alive in the sports world. One year earlier, disputes about definitions of amateurism versus professionalism had led to the formation of the Amateur Athletic Union. Camp had strong feelings about professionalism. College teams could play professional teams without danger, he had written, but professionalism within a college team was intolerable. Usually Camp was cool, focused on practical considerations, but now he told a reporter: before "we teach students that the ultimate end is not victory or success, but money, let us break our oars and boats and plow up our fields."[6]

Harvard wanted action, but there was a problem: the IFA had never made any rules on player eligibility; no regulation of the IFA even discussed "professionals." So Harvard got a special meeting of the IFA Graduate Advisory Committee called, convening November 4, 1889, only twelve days before the scheduled Harvard-Princeton game. When the meeting got under way, Camp quickly proposed an amendment to the IFA constitution, specifying: "No professional athlete shall take part in any contest of the Association, nor shall any player be paid for playing in an Association game." Players alleged to have violated the rule would be required to file an affidavit showing they were not in violation; if the sufficiency of the affidavit was challenged, they were "to submit on two days' notice to an oral examination before the committee."[7]

Princeton objected that the proposed regulation extended to actions unrelated to football. They urged that players be barred from college football only if they had been paid to play football. Also, they noted the new regulation would be retroactive, outlawing payments after they had already been made.

Princeton also went on the attack, proposing to bar graduate students from college football teams. Princeton claimed that Billy Bull, the Yale player who kicked two field goals to beat them in 1888, had come back to Yale after graduation only to play football. After the season, they said, he dropped out of the single class he was taking from Professor Sumner and went back to New York. If we're instituting eligibility rules, let's deal with this abuse as well, they said.[8]

Harvard and Yale had three graduate schools (law, medicine, and theology) versus only one (theology) at Princeton. Since 1877 Harvard had played twenty graduate players, Princeton eight. If Princeton's proposed regulation against graduate students were enacted, it would hurt Princeton by removing a couple of players from this year's team, but it would hurt Harvard worse.[9]

The University of Pennsylvania offered a still different proposal, a more basic attempt to decide who should be eligible for intercollegiate competition:

> Players in Association games must be bona fide students in a course requiring attendance at at least five lectures or recitations a week. If a particular player is challenged, he shall furnish a) a certificate signed by three members of the faculty establishing that he is a bona fide student, and b) an affidavit by himself to the

same effect, which also states it is his intention to continue in the stated courses until the end of the current college year.[10]

All the proposals were discussed, and then the delegates voted:

- Pennsylvania joined its neighbor Princeton, voting no on Camp and Harvard's "professional" regulation.
- Wesleyan joined its neighbor Yale and, with Harvard, voted yes.

Harvard had its desired regulation. Pennsylvania's regulation on bona fide students also passed, but Princeton withdrew its proposed regulation on graduate players.[11]

Harvard expected the new "professional" regulation to target primarily two Princeton players, the first being E. O. Wagenhurst, former captain (in 1887) of Princeton's football team, alleged to have played professional baseball on an openly professional baseball team after graduation. Under scrutiny, and with the new regulation in place, Wagenhurst withdrew and never again played for Princeton.[12]

That left Knowlton B. Ames, probably the main object of Harvard's attack from the beginning. Ames was one of the dominant players then playing college football, given the nickname "Snake" because he could twist and slide through the opposition. Camp's newspaper analyses of the upcoming Harvard-Princeton game described Ames as "unquestionably the best back in the Association . . . a wonderful runner and kicker . . . [with an unusual] . . . gift of dexterity." Harvard claimed Ames was a professional, paid to play summer baseball in Illinois, a charge disputed by Ames and Princeton.[13]

At Harvard's request, the Graduate Advisory Committee convened again, November 14, ten days after the first meeting and just two days before the scheduled Harvard-Princeton game. Each IFA member sent a representative, young New York lawyers and businessmen, meeting in a room of the Fifth Avenue Hotel while a horde of interested students and reporters gathered in the hall outside. Walter Camp was not there, apparently away on clock-company business; in his place was twenty-six-year-old Eugene L. (Gene) Richards Jr., a four-year Yale halfback and 1884 football captain, now a lawyer in New York. Richards would chair the meeting.[14]

One can imagine the tension and the scene in the room as this first "legal" confrontation between IFA schools began—delegates pulling their chairs around a table and facing each other in high-buttoned suits, starched collars, and tied bows of the day. Harvard's representative was the oldest delegate, Herbert C. Leeds, an 1877 graduate who scored the first touchdown in the 1875 Harvard-Yale football game and was Harvard's varsity shortstop four years. Leeds presented two main items of evidence:

1. An affidavit of Paul Buckley, a Chicagoan, who swore that
   a) in the just-passed summer he directly paid Ames for Ames's services in a baseball game, and
   b) on another occasion, he saw a member of the baseball team from Joliet, Illinois, deliver money to Ames, who later told Buckley the money was payment for playing for the Joliet nine.
2. A note that Ames himself wrote to a baseball manager in Chicago, reading: "The manager of West Ends owes me for pitching that last game against Whitings. See him."[15]

Princeton's representative was Duncan Edwards, a tall, trim, neatly groomed New York lawyer (Columbia Law School), who had played varsity football as an undergraduate at Princeton. Edwards answered first that the money paid Ames was for expenses. But more important, he relied on the just-passed regulation that gave Ames the opportunity to present an affidavit and, if there was any question, an opportunity to be examined after two days' notice. Princeton moved that Harvard's motion to bar Ames be tabled until the regulation's requirements were fulfilled.[16] Of course, any delay to allow time for an Ames affidavit was unacceptable to Harvard, because the game was less than two days away.

Richards asked for discussion, and for two hours they battled back and forth. The discussion clearly revealed two positions: N. B. Young, representing the University of Pennsylvania, would vote with Edwards to table. Richards would join Leeds against the motion to table. That left the deciding vote to Frank D. Beattys, an 1885 graduate of Wesleyan who was now manager of a school-textbook publisher in New York.[17]

Beattys thought long and hard. Together, he and Leeds left the meeting room and reviewed Harvard's evidence. He pondered the requirements of the regulation enacted just ten days earlier. With the crowd waiting outside, he internally debated, back and forth, until he could put off a decision no longer.

Later he explained his decision in a letter to the *New York Sun*, "Wesleyan refused to vote with Harvard to cripple Princeton's team within forty-eight hours of their championship game, when by so doing it would have been in direct opposition to the constitution [requiring two days' notice before oral examination]." Immediately after the meeting, Beattys returned to his office and wrote Camp to explain and justify his vote. He noted that Harvard had their evidence for some time; why did they delay offering it until shortly before the game, thus limiting Ames's opportunity to respond?[18]

Though not taking Ames out of the Harvard-Princeton game two days thence, the flurry of meetings had produced the IFA's first eligibility standards. The constitution now included the following:

- A bar on "professional" ball players, though that category was not defined in detail
- A requirement that players be full-time bona fide students
- Procedures for enforcing the new regulations

The final act of the Harvard-Princeton dispute took place Saturday, November 16, before seven thousand who had crowded around Jarvis Field on the Harvard campus. As the competing elevens came out of the nearby gymnasium and trotted through an opening in the rows of spectators, the strength and athletic ability of Princeton's team stood out; Camp regarded five Princeton players as the best in college football at their positions.[19]

But Harvard had come ready for battle, inspired by the eligibility controversy and well trained by Cumnock. At the end of the first half, Harvard was ahead, 15–10. But in the second half, the roof fell in, with Ames, Harvard's nemesis and the focus of their anger, leading the way. Twisting and sliding past tacklers, he ran thirty yards for a touchdown. More long Ames runs followed, and by game's end Princeton had won, 41–15.

Four days later, on November 20, 1889, Harvard students held a meeting with upwards of fifteen hundred students and graduates attending, the "largest mass-meeting ever held in any college in the United States" to that date and including "men of prominence in Boston professional circles."[20]

Cumnock opened by reading a letter from a member of Harvard's Board of Overseers, advocating that Harvard "take a stand against professionalism" by withdrawing from the "present Intercollegiate League of foot-ball." Instead of that league, a different league was proposed—a "dual league" limited to just Harvard and Yale. Telegrams were read "from prominent Yale graduates and foot-ball men" to the effect that Yale would join with Harvard in such a dual league.

The *New York Evening Post* contended that discussions had taken place between Harvard and Yale for some time: "For years there have been groups in each college among undergraduates and alumni who have favored the withdrawal of Yale and Harvard from all sports with other colleges. They have said frankly that Yale-Harvard contests were all they cared for. Oxford only cared to row with Cambridge, and why should not Yale and Harvard follow similar lines?" Yale's Professor Richards, Gene Richards's father, was also quoted: "The formation of a dual league will result in the improvement of athletics generally. It will do away with the practice of winning games after they are played, and will enable us to make stringent rules in regard to the eligibility of players. We have never been able to get a single rule passed without a strong fight against it from Princeton, and we do not want to have that college join the minor colleges and leave us in a minority in an association."[21]

A dilemma seemed to confront Walter Camp. On the one hand, important Yale supporters such as Professor Richards were calling for a dual league that restricted Yale's play to Harvard only. On the other hand, Camp was deeply involved in managing and building American football through the IFA. A dual league limited to Harvard would require Yale to withdraw from the IFA. It was difficult to imagine the IFA without Yale and Camp.

Meetings about a dual league began after the football season ended, but the Harvard and Yale negotiators came to these meetings with different perspectives. Within Harvard there was significant sentiment for a rigorous dual-league network, limiting Harvard's intercollegiate competition to Yale. They visualized Harvard and Yale would have multiple contests each year—four baseball games and two football games.

On the other hand, according to a summary of the talks later coauthored by Camp and a Yale undergraduate, Yale looked "with decided disfavor" at a plan for two football games between the schools per year. The two sides were also reported to have disagreed about eligibility rules: Harvard wanted "special" students to play; Yale did not. Yale's negotiators made counterproposals to Harvard's positions but were advised that the Harvard position had been decided by Harvard's athletic committee and that the Harvard negotiators were not free to make changes. Negotiations got nowhere.[22]

Within a few months, the impetus for a dual league dissipated, and the subject faded away. Whatever views Camp might have had as to a dual league, nothing had happened to indicate Camp would ever support Yale's withdrawal from the IFA.

Harvard withdrew from the IFA, but Yale did not. Once again the IFA consisted only of Pennsylvania, Princeton, Wesleyan, and Yale. Harvard was out on a limb by itself again, the outlier among major football teams and out of the IFA.

Harvard's students and alumni soon got a boost, as well as an exhortation, from a beloved Boston citizen. Henry Lee Higginson was a Harvard dropout who had moved to Europe to study music. Unable to make a career in music, he returned to the United States shortly before the Civil War and was among the first to enlist in the Union army. During a battle in 1862, he was severely wounded and invalided out of the army.[23]

After the war, he joined a family firm of investment bankers and became prominent in the firm's success. Public spirited, he gave generously to various causes and persuaded others to give. In 1881 he founded the Boston Symphony Orchestra and for several years was essentially its only support.[24]

By the late 1880s, he wanted to make a gift to Harvard, believing "the hope of a nation is in its young men." He liked sports, especially football and rowing, and sometimes went to watch at Holmes and Jarvis Fields on the Harvard campus. Foreseeing that these playing fields would be taken for school buildings, he determined to give land for a new sports field. He found and purchased land across the Charles River from the Harvard campus, adjacent to a parcel given earlier by former Harvard professor Henry W. Longfellow and friends.[25]

On June 5, 1890, Higginson transferred what he had purchased—twenty-one acres of upland pasture and ten acres of marsh. He asked that it be called "Soldiers' Field" to honor six of his friends who had died during the Civil War.

At the formal gift-giving ceremony, the fifty-five-year-old Higginson eloquently explained his motivation, speaking first about his friends being honored—"men of mark," who at the first call left friends, parents, and sweethearts and "went at once, gladly, eagerly, to the front and stayed there." The gift of a sports field was appropriate, Higginson said, because these men delighted in athletic games and would have used this field. More than that, the new field had present-day educational value, as Higginson explained to his student-listeners: "My chief hope is that it will help make you full-grown, well-developed men, able and ready to do good work of all kinds—steadfastly, devotedly, thoughtfully."[26]

Higginson closed with a flourish, an exhortation possibly born as he watched the Harvard-Princeton controversy unfold during the past year. He began with a story, an experience while traveling with a southern former artillery officer.

"I asked him of his family, and he said: 'I've just sent a boy to Yale, after teaching him all in my power. I told him to go away, and not to return with any provincial notions. Remember,' I said, 'there is no Kentucky, no Virginia, no Massachusetts, but one great country.'" And then Higginson said: "Mates, the Princeton and the Yale fellows are our brothers. Let us beat them fairly if we can, and believe that they will play the game just as we do." Such magnanimity, caring, and respect could hardly provide a better basis for sportsmanship; yet, after 1889, America's football leaders understood that detailed, enforceable, written rules were also required to help sportsmen meet their intended goals.[27]

23 Why American Football Grew

Alert pedestrians strolling on New York City's Fifth Avenue on Thanksgiving Day afternoon, November 28, 1889, could hardly miss the horse-drawn enclosed wagon with high sidewalls as it passed by. Painted on the sidewalls were a Geneva cross and in a half-circle around the cross "The World's Football Ambulance." As the ambulance continued by, strollers could see someone lying inside.[1]

Anyone acquainted with the *New York World* newspaper could not have been too surprised: one more promotion by the legendary Joseph Pulitzer—recruited from Hungary as a seventeen-year-old to fight in the U.S. Civil War, moving on after the war to build a newspaper in St. Louis, coming to New York in 1883 with capital from his St. Louis success to purchase the *World*. In New York, he carried on a newspaper revolution, transforming the *World* with increased illustration, innovative page composition, not-to-be-dismissed editorial quality, and abundant human-interest stories (mostly crime, sex, and tragedy). Besides changing the newspaper itself, Pulitzer also surrounded the newspaper enterprise with promotions—crusades (collecting funds for a mounting platform for the Statue of Liberty) and "stunts" (sponsoring a trip around the world for Nellie Bly). The whole effort produced amazing circulation leadership—from an average daily circulation of 15,000 when Pulitzer purchased the paper in 1883 to 342,206 in October 1889, a far larger circulation than any other U.S. newspaper.[2]

Eighteen days after purchasing the *World*, Pulitzer announced editorially that sports coverage would be emphasized: "In the matter of turf and sporting news the World is without equal in daily journalism." Pulitzer wanted to reach new readers, including the working classes of New York, and he was sure sports news would help. Editorially, he explained, "Our people run to athletic sports. Why? Because they enjoy the contest of strength against strength." To support increased sports coverage, Pulitzer is said to have established a separate sports department and appointed the first sports editor of a U.S. daily newspaper, H. G. Crickmore, an authority on horse racing.[3]

At first Pulitzer's *World* emphasized horse racing and boxing, but football grew on him as a news event and a tool to build circulation. By 1889, when Princeton and Yale played their first New York Thanksgiving game since 1884, he was ready to break new ground. Readers opening the *World* newspaper the morning after Thanksgiving found half of page 1 and all of page 3 devoted to the Princeton-Yale game. Of the paper's twelve pages, one and a half were devoted to that one game. Given the *World*'s circulation of about 350,000 and the front-page prominence given the game, not many New York newspaper readers could miss the fact that an exciting football event had taken place in the city on Thanksgiving Day.[4]

To draw even more attention, the *World* sent ambulances to the game, another advertising promotion, though the *World* cast it differently: "The World, as usual, had prepared for all emergencies. . . . Five minutes before the game was [to start] two ambulances drove into the Oval and took a position behind the grand stand. . . . The ambulances were brand new and . . . were greeted with a storm of cheers . . . by those who understood the dangers of the game. . . . 'What a wonderful newspaper' came from all parts of the grand stand."[5]

The game had been a battle, scoreless through the first half and well into the second. Princeton was loaded with the players who had infuriated and defeated Harvard just a week earlier. But that controversy had been set aside, and neither Camp nor anyone else at Yale challenged any Princeton players.

In the second half, Princeton's Ames missed a field-goal attempt, but the ball rolled over Yale's goal line, where it was still alive. Yale's McClung, McBride, and Morrison urgently gave chase, and McBride jumped on the ball—but it bounced away. Princeton's Warren, coming downfield "like a race horse," dove over McBride's shoulders and grabbed for the ball, followed by McClung and Morrison. The teams crowded around, and the umpire "peered deep into the tangle." Suddenly, Princeton's players threw their caps in the air, and the umpire confirmed: Warren had the ball and had downed it for a touchdown. Ames kicked the goal, giving Princeton the lead, 6–0.

On almost the last play of the game, Princeton scored again and won, 10–0. For the first time since 1881, Yale had failed to score in a football game.

During the game, Princeton's big center, W. J. (Bill) George, the part-time high school teacher, part-time theology student, and committed football player, suffered a severely sprained ankle. He was carried off the field and into an adjacent clubhouse, where a *World*-supplied surgeon, having "long experience in the medical corps of the Austrian army," attended him. George declined a dose of brandy. After the doctor determined no bones were broken, he bandaged the foot and injected morphine above the site of the sprain.[6]

When the game was nearly finished and George was confident Princeton would win, he consented—conveniently for the *World*—to ride back to his hotel in the *World* ambulance. The wagon-ambulance was outfitted with a rubber bed, soft blankets, and pillows, allowing George comfort and style as he traveled to his room at the Murray Hill Hotel near Grand Central Station.[7]

Pulitzer's expanded football coverage came at an opportune time, when rules had been put in place—Camp's downs-for-distance rule (seven years old) and expanded interference and tackling rules (one year old)—that gave American football a new workability and appeal. The game was ready to grow, and Pulitzer's coverage would help it grow. Other newspapers joined the *World* in increased football coverage, and in a few years a fierce new competitor—thirty-two-year-old William Randolph Hearst, fresh from building the *San Francisco Examiner*, given him by his mining-entrepreneur father—added a new dimension.

Hearst purchased the *New York Journal* in 1895 and immediately took aim at Pulitzer by raising "human-interest" journalism to an even higher pitch. Sports news was part of the plan, and in carrying out that plan Hearst pioneered a new presentation of sports news. More pages were devoted to sports, and they were made more graphic and dramatic—more headlines, more drawings, more photos, and bigger type. Soon a heading, "In the World of Sports," was at the top of the sports news, a few columns wide on weekdays and across the full page on Sundays. Camp himself got headline treatment when Hearst introduced a Camp article with a cross-the-page headline, "Walter Camp on the Football Outlook for the Season of '96"; below that was a three-line subheadline stretched across extra-wide columns, "The Famous Coach and 'Father of American Football' Analyses [*sic*] the College Teams and Their Strengths and Weaknesses." Pulitzer had flirted with headlines but then seemed to discard them; his paper's makeup was dense, despite an increased use of pictures. Hearst gave the sports page greater identity and visually opened it up: in physical makeup, Hearst's late 1890s *New York Journal* gives the first glimpse of today's sports page.[8]

Newspaper coverage undoubtedly helped American football grow, but there were other growth drivers also—most important, the game itself. Walter

Camp once tried to summarize what made the game appealing, listing some reasons as the following:

- The fact that the game is constantly developing and admits of new combinations, strategies and surprises.
- The very seriousness of the struggle, the determination with which men go into it, the long period of training and work, the self-denial and subjugation.
- To those who have formerly played, the added element of interest for there is no sport that holds men so closely together.
- No sport that offers such opportunity for the development of unselfishness and needed self-control.
- No sport where the premium placed upon brains and cool courage is so high.[9]

Though seldom discussed and never adequately recognized, Camp's own downs-and-distance rule is fundamental and critical to the game's popularity—"more important than all the other rules combined," Camp eventually asserted. The importance of the rule, of course, begins with game methodology; the rule is at the heart of how the game is played. But its importance goes far beyond methodology in ways not even Camp could have foreseen. By the downs-and-distance rule, the game is subdivided into what becomes a steady stream of compelling narratives. Each played-out down presents a contest that to some degree is challenging and balanced, accompanied by tension, suspense, coordinated action, and often triumphant athletic displays. "From the moment the ball is kicked off," Camp came to realize, "the game goes rapidly on," packed throughout with excitement and meaning.[10]

Another unforeseen downs-and-distance benefit is that each down's contest is uniquely suitable for study, planning, innovation, and practice. The specific, limited nature of the yardage goal of an American football down (in contrast with the diffuse aims of an open-ended rugby down) narrows and focuses the range of actions useful for achieving or defending against the goal. Each side knows at least broadly what it needs to do and can prepare accordingly, creating an opportunity for forethought, study, trial, planning, and practice; it also leads to a contest that is in greater balance as a result of informed preparation by each side. Variety, possibility, innovation do remain, sufficiently intriguing that under the challenge of competition, the study, planning, and development become year-round and lifelong, and the game is enriched with new playing ideas, approaches, and actions. Parke Davis, American football's first early historian, testified to the prime importance of the downs-and-distance rule by asserting that the rule gives American football "its pre-eminent characteristic over all other games of strategy and pre-arranged tactics." Football becomes "scientific" as well as orderly, appreciated by a society that aims to conduct its affairs with logic and planning.[11]

Some contributions of the downs-and-distance rule are only partially sensed or known, as illustrated by a perceived relation between American football and a human territorial instinct. Teams battle for territory in American football, and Camp's downs-and-distance rule enhances those battles—each down involves a fight for a specific, identified piece of territory; all eyes focus on that territory, and all efforts are directed to conquering or defending it. Similarly, watching a football game is like watching a military campaign, with movement of the sticks and chain confirming a successful territorial advance. According to one writer, American football becomes "par excellence the game of instinctual satisfactions, especially among Americans, who are notorious as violent patriots and instinctive defenders of private property."[12]

Americans do delight in American football. About three years after Pulitzer began his expanded newspaper coverage, the president of the Massachusetts Institute of Technology (MIT) commented that the rapid spread of football "shows how eagerly it is welcomed as a relief to the monotony of life," giving the community "not merely two hours, now and then, of intense excitement, but something to look forward to and to look back upon, for weeks and for months, with pleasure." That is as true today as it was then, about many sports, of course, but Americans receive football in a unique way. At a football game, spectators are often on their feet, passionate about what is happening—they yell a college cheer, wear a college color, sing a college hymn. Somehow they sense they are participating. Football games come to represent more than just a contest between "two sets of young men but rather as a giant and abstract manifestation of two contesting wills," the embodied pride of a school, geographic locale, or social group.[13]

The American delight in American football was and is primarily responsible for the growth of the game. Newspaper coverage is important to that growth, even vital, but it is secondary, a tool that reveals and capitalizes on the game's inherent appeal. At an American football game, viewers sit at the edge of their chairs not because of newspaper reports but because the game triggers responses ingrained in them. It is love of the game that causes fans to spend hours engrossed in game reports and analyses and in discussions around the water cooler.

One more growth driver for American football should be acknowledged, operating even in the absence of newspaper promotion or spectator interest, namely, the efforts of committed educators who believed in the game's educational value. In 1891 George Petrie returned to Auburn University (then

The 1891 Thanksgiving Day game in New York as drawn by W. T. Smedley and published in the November 28, 1891, *Harper's Weekly*. (The Lost Century of Sports Collection, LostCentury.com)

Alabama Polytechnic Institute) with a Ph.D. from Johns Hopkins University, where he had been inspired by eastern college athletics and football. He immediately set out to create a gymnasium. Funds were scarce, but he raised money from private parties. He also set about teaching students the new game of football, and in 1892 he arranged a game against a University of Georgia team coached by Charles Herty, a contemporaneous Johns Hopkins Ph.D. graduate who was working to promote athletics at Georgia. Interest in football grew at both schools, and within three years an Auburn student manager persuaded John Heisman to coach Auburn and Georgia found and hired Glenn Warner, and both schools became prominent in the football world.[14]

In 1889, the year Pulitzer expanded his paper's football coverage, most southern and West Coast colleges, some of today's big names—Alabama, Florida, Louisiana, Mississippi, Texas, Oregon, Oregon State, and Washington in addition to Auburn and Georgia—had yet to compete in intercollegiate football. But that would soon change, whether it was the work of educators like Herty and Petrie, or of local residents' exposure to the game through newspapers and other media, or of migration or a growth in population and college enrollment, or any of a variety of many other reasons, all underlaid and energized by the inherent popularity of the game. Within ten years, at the turn of the century, all the named schools would be playing. The game that had begun in 1876, less than twenty-five years earlier, and for many years was limited to the East Coast, had spread and become well established across the whole breadth of the country's college campuses.[15]

24 All-Americans

Twenty-seven years old in the summer of 1889 and newly married, Caspar Whitney had a dream. He wanted to start a magazine about sports—not all sports, but "amateur" sports, especially those played at colleges. Not ready to financially support a new magazine himself, Whitney had a backer—James M. Waterbury, an 1873 Columbia graduate and successor in his father's successful cordage business; James Waterbury was a noted personage among New York sportsmen and among the founders of the New York Yacht Club.[1]

Somewhere Whitney had connected with Walter Camp, and Camp agreed to supply reports for the new magazine, incognito. Camp's other newspaper and magazine writing paid better. Yet Camp must have believed in Whitney's project, with its focus on the amateur and college sports that Camp had also been trying to defend and promote. A regular weekly publication devoted to amateur and college sports could further support and strengthen those sports, including football.[2]

Whitney got the magazine started in August 1889 as the *Week's Sport*, with a motto under the title "In the Highest Interests of the Amateur." It was a small magazine, almost a newsletter, no illustrations and no bylines, paragraph-long newsy reports with an air of informed comment, including information direct from college campuses.[3]

Although Camp was older than Whitney and had his own résumé of published writing, Whitney still tried to guide him to insightful and exciting comment that would attract readers; Whitney wanted Camp to make his paragraphs "bristle with comment and caustic criticism." Camp's approach was more fact based and neutral, but Whitney wanted controversy as well as depth, seeking to offer the most insightful account yet about college sports, stories deeper than the surface reports appearing in the daily newspapers.[4]

A few months into publication, the *Week's Sport* made its most lasting contribution, presentation of the first-ever "All-America" football team—a hypothetical team existing only on paper, playing no games, with players selected to the team simply to recognize and honor them.

The selections appeared in the December 18, 1889, issue, in the second installment of an analysis of the just-completed season. Without promotion or fanfare, in a matter-of-fact tone, this second installment continued a discussion of the Intercollegiate Football Association:

> To return to the Association, taking the players on a rating based upon their actual work in games, the All-America team would be composed of the following players.
>
> 1. Cumnock [Harvard]
> 2. Cowan [Princeton]
> 3. Cranston [Harvard]
> 4. George [Princeton]
> 5. Heffelfinger [Yale]
> 6. Gill [Yale]
> 7. Stagg [Yale]
> 8. Poe [Princeton]
> 9. Channing [Princeton]
> 10. Lee [Harvard]
> 11. Ames [Princeton]
>
> . . . I have no doubt that this team could go to England and, after watching the English style of play for one week, enter into matches to be played, one under the English interpretation and one under American interpretation of Rugby Rules, without the slightest discredit to themselves or the sport.

Camp said he wrote the article and selected the team. Some have argued Whitney had some role in creation of the team, but authoritative evidence of that is lacking (see chapter 37, note 8). Whitney himself said he didn't remember.[5]

What prompted the naming of an All-America team is not known. Some have suggested Camp saw the All-America team as a useful promotion for football. He worked in sales at the New Haven Clock Company, so selling of football—a "product" near and dear to him—would be natural. He has been called a football "entrepreneur," someone who "aggressively created and introduced a new game form, resulting in a product that was attractive and profitable." But the 1889 All-America team was presented in the *Week's Sport* with no buildup or promotion and in barest detail. There seems no anticipation of the promotional impact All-America teams would ultimately develop and exhibit today.[6]

Probably there was not much enterprise-style calculation in the naming of the All-America team. Camp's season-end analyses for other magazines and newspapers had included player evaluations; some players made enough difference to influence a big game or even a season, and gathering them on a hypothetical team was a novel way of identifying and writing about them. Also, fans discussed players with praise or criticism, and as an insider Camp might have wanted to offer his own evaluation. Actual teams calling themselves All-America and playing real games had been formed; Camp could have been expressing an opinion about who really belonged on such a proudly representative team.

The selections give insight into Camp's personality and approach—an attempt at objectivity and perhaps political diplomacy. Although he had just helped the IFA enact a "professionalism" regulation triggered by allegations against K. L. Ames, Camp included Ames on the team. On football merit, Ames deserved to be on the team, and no official judgment had declared him ineligible. Similarly, although Princeton had made accusations against Harvard's Cranston—alleging he was at the school on a scholarship (true) to play football (vehemently denied)—Camp also included Cranston on the team.

Selecting players only from Harvard, Princeton, and Yale might seem biased, but those schools routinely and easily defeated other schools. Even though Camp was coaching at Yale, the choices reflected Princeton's superiority on the field, with five Princeton players to three each from the Harvard and Yale teams that Princeton had defeated.

No special note of the team was taken by publications other than the *Week's Sport*, but Camp and Whitney were encouraged enough to name another team in 1890.[7]

By September 1890, Whitney's letters to Camp were hinting of problems at the *Week's Sport*. He admitted "the babies are not crying for the paper," but also contended that "circulation is steadily increasing."[8]

In November Camp wrote to Whitney, noting that his last check was overdue and then adding: "For your own satisfaction, add up everything you have paid me from Sept 1st to date and compare that with the sum I can get from any of the dailies or weeklies for a single article. See if I have not demonstrated my promise of seeing you through."[9] The increases in circulation claimed by Whitney were not enough to achieve financial success. In December 1890,

Waterbury sold the magazine, ending Whitney's attempt to create a new sports publication directed toward amateur sports. The magazine had lasted less than a year and a half, and only traces remain today. But it had given Whitney a start in the magazine world and brought him a friend and kindred spirit in Camp. And an All-America team was here to stay.[10]

When advising Camp of the sale of the *Week's Sport*, Whitney also reported confidentially that he had an offer to write a new sports column for *Harper's Weekly*. Although *Harper's Weekly* was still a leading magazine—with prominent authors and an effective editorial voice, lavishly illustrated with large pen-and-ink drawings and photos on calendered paper—the magazine had lost circulation and needed a jolt.[11]

Wanting to appeal to younger readers, the magazine hired a young managing editor, Richard Harding Davis, twenty-six years old and a flamboyant name-reporter for the *New York Sun*, who possibly had been a sportswriting friend of Whitney's. Davis began at *Harper's Weekly* in February 1891 and brought in young friends who could "write on topics that interested young men." In a nice coincidence, friend Whitney's own magazine was just coming to a halt.[12]

In February 1891, when Davis began to edit *Harper's Weekly*, Whitney began a weekly column called "Amateur Sport," a new initiative presenting weekly sports news in a major magazine. The column at least initially contained much the same information as had been presented in the *Week's Sport*, but in a more popular and respected media vehicle and to a much larger circulation. It appeared as the closing feature of each issue—usually two or three pages, part of which was advertising. Suffering no lack of confidence or opinions, Whitney boldly offered his views. He was a gifted writer, and his column, together with the growing appeal of sports, broadened the magazine's appeal. There were few knowledgeable authorities in sportswriting, and copies of *Harper's Weekly* began to be "absorbed in large numbers" in college dormitories.[13]

Camp continued to provide copy ("I have had a talk with Mr. Harper," Whitney wrote, "and he has agreed to allow me to pay you $25 monthly" [roughly five hundred dollars in today's currency]). Camp and Whitney had a frank relationship, and Whitney's letters held nothing back:

> Of course I want what you have written up about the men coming back. You don't mean to tell me that you are going to give that to some newspaper, we don't want any newspaper to get the same stuff that we get, if they do where is our supremacy.

> This season [we will] make "Harper's Weekly" known as the only exception on foot-ball, in other words, I want every man in the United States who reads football matter and who is interested in such stuff, and who wants to know anything about the game, to pick up "Harper's Weekly." I don't want any other paper in it at all.[14]

At the end of the 1891 football season, Camp sent Whitney the selections and text for naming an 1891 All-America team, as he had done the two previous years. But this submission was in a different form, ready for printing as a separate stand-alone article. Presumably, Camp expected and planned that it would be published in *Harper's Weekly* under Camp's byline and that he would be paid for a separate article apart from his regular monthly arrangement with Whitney. The interest shown in the previous two All-America teams could have justified in Camp's mind a separate article for the naming of a team for 1891.[15]

Whitney objected. He wanted a continuation of the previous arrangement, with features that had appeared in the *Week's Sport* to appear in his *Harper's Weekly* column. Camp was being paid monthly for submissions to "Amateur Sport"; that meant, thought Whitney, that Camp's submissions should be in Whitney's column.

Camp quickly accepted Whitney's request in a handwritten note: "Of course you want the rating of the players under the department. . . . I ought not to have suggested it as a special article." A pattern had been established: Camp's incognito reports in the *Week's Sport* had established All-America teams as coming from Whitney, and Whitney wanted that to continue in his new column. Camp said he would cut the article to a form for inclusion in Whitney's column and send it that night. The material was published in Whitney's column and apparently came from Whitney, but Camp was the author, just as he had been in the past.[16]

After accepting Whitney's wish about inclusion of the All-America team in Whitney's column, Camp made a salesman's shift to a lighter and more agreeable subject, Yale's performance in the 1891 Thanksgiving game with Princeton: "What did you think of that little team from Yale upon the whole? Rather clever, were they not?"

Whitney returned Camp's note with his own note in the margin: "Clever!!—well rather! . . . [T]hat head of yours is a long one—the team that downs Yale must do so either by a fluke or phenomenal work."

Camp was pleased and proud of the Yale team he was coaching, and here was a knowledgeable friend with whom he could exchange banter and get a pat on the back.

Author for an Expanding Game 25

Walter Camp had more important business with Caspar Whitney in the fall of 1891 than where the All-America team would appear in *Harper's Weekly*. Camp had written a book that Whitney took up in an August letter:

> My Dear Mr. Camp:—
> Mr. Harper having returned from Europe, and the matter of the proposed foot-ball book having been thoroughly discussed, I am prepared at Mr. Harper's directions to make you the following proposition:- We will accept your manuscript, and will publish the book in corrected form, paying you 10 percent royalty on its sales, and $300 in cash on advance . . . on the day of publication.
>
> Caspar W. Whitney

This was not a pamphlet-like book as Camp had written before, but 175 pages of text for a hardback book, the first such book on American football.[1]

Once again, Camp could see both need and opportunity. The upcoming 1891 season would be the tenth under the five-yard rule that had dramatically changed the game and empowered its spread across the country; football's growth needed the support of knowledgeable teaching and explanation. And Camp had just finished his third year of serious coaching at Yale, giving him additional teaching insights.

Also, there was now a baby at home, Walter Camp Jr., born February 12, 1891; the "co-coach" had been pregnant as she walked the sidelines during the 1890 season when Yale went 13-1, losing only to Harvard. A baby probably would make added income welcome and meant more evenings and weekends at home, possibly with quiet times available for a motivated writer. So, besides work at the clock company—not to mention coaching, rule-making meetings, and newspaper and magazine writing—Camp had written a book.

Whitney had been assigned to edit the book by Harper's and did not like Camp's suggested title, "Some Chapters on American Rugby Football." Whitney sent proofs September 10 and added that Camp's title "would be entirely too much. I don't think 'American Football' as a title can be improved upon." The "intercollegiate game" of the book, Whitney said, is the only serious football in America. Yes, he admitted, the game was "derived" from rugby, but changes have made it something else, a distinctively "American football"; that name would exactly describe what the book is about.[2]

Whitney stated he was reluctantly agreeing to Camp's request that Camp's photograph be omitted from the book. His picture unquestionably should be published, "as one who is more closely identified with Foot Ball, and who has done more for the game than anyone in this country."

Friendliness and bantering aside, Camp wanted quick action, and on October 12 he wrote Whitney: "I dislike extremely to bother you, but really it is getting very late in the season, and that foot ball book ought to be on the market. At any rate the advertisements for it should be out." The book actually came to market the first week in November: *American Football*, as Whitney wanted, about five by seven inches, with a blue-cloth hardback cover with title and Camp's name in gold print. An embossed design that Whitney said was "drawn from suggestions I made" was above the title—an iconic American shield covered half with a field of stars on a blue background and half with red and white vertical stripes, with the shield surmounted by two opposite-facing winged, fire-breathing dragons, each clutching a football in their claws to symbolize that an essential and mighty American spirit is embodied in American football.[3]

First book-length text on American football, by Walter Camp, published in 1891.

As with Camp's earlier football texts, *American Football* was mostly a practical guide of instruction, organized by playing position. "End rusher" was first, with a discussion that began by emphasizing the superior conditioning needed by that player to support aggressive defense as well as repeated races downfield to cover the kicks that were a common part of 1891 rugby-derived American football. On defense an end should not simply wait for a runner's approach, but should get up "as far and fast as he dares" and stay alert to the right moment when he can "shoot in at his man" through the practiced mass of interference that is certainly coming. Even after a runner has passed by, the end should follow to possibly catch up and get the tackle.[4]

The end should position himself on end runs to always "force the runner in," where the tackle and guard can help contain the runner, and the end is responsible for defending the edge of the field during throw-ins from the sideline after the ball has gone out-of-bounds. Altogether, seventeen pages were devoted to ends.

The second player discussed had previously been called the "next-to-the-end," but in 1891 Camp called him a "tackle," a name he said probably came simply because that player did more tackling than other players. Defensive techniques were addressed first, including reference to the tackle's coordination with what Camp called a "line halfback," who comes up to the line and performs the duties of a rusher: if the tackle edges out toward the end, the opposing tackle is likely to move out also to maintain blocking position; when the ball is snapped back, the defending tackle should immediately engage the opposing tackle to keep him occupied and help open a path for the "line halfback" to rush through into the opponent's backfield. On opponent's running plays, the tackle should drive forward quickly but with eyes open and alert to a possible lateral pass in the backfield.[5]

On offense the tackle "has the most responsible work of any man along the line, having more openings to make." Also, he must protect against breakthroughs by defensive rushers; more than two-thirds of breaking through by the defense comes between the end and the guard.

A good opponent cannot be blocked every time in the same way; sometimes the blocker should dash violently at his opponent, sometimes shoulder him as he tries to go past, sometimes fall down in front of him. In a kicking situation, the tackle on the kicker's side should block long and hard to prevent the opponent from getting through to block the kick, but opposite the kicker's side the tackle should release earlier to get downfield to cover the kick.[6]

Separate chapters were titled "The Guard," "The Centre, or Snap-Back," "The Quarterback," "The Half-back and Back," "Signals" and "Training."

The "Signals" chapter illustrated the game's increasing complexity. Teams of 1891 came into a championship game, Camp wrote, with "at least twenty-five different plays, each of which is called for by a distinct signal of its own," communicated in the open since player-huddles were still for the future. The source for signals—quarterback or captain—was still a matter of debate, but Camp reported quarterback was becoming "better practice." Instead of manual or word signals such as had been previously used, teams now used "numerical combinations," aiming to "never confuse their own men and yet completely mystify the opponents." One possibility was number combinations that a player added up as he listened—for example, any combination that totaled twenty-four ("10-8-6," "12-3-9," . . .) might signify a dropkick by the left halfback.[7]

The timing of plays was under the control of the offensive team. When a play had ended and the ball was down, the center went to the ball, and the quarterback needed to be "figuratively tied to the center's jacket tails. As soon as the center reaches the ball, he should know that the quarter is with him." A silent signal, separate from that informing the whole team of the selected play, was used to tell the center when to snap the ball; for example, the quarter might put his hand on the center and pinch or remove his hand when he wanted the ball snapped.[8]

The "Training" chapter, in addition to text, included nine pages of tables describing model training systems—diets, activity schedules, exercise plans, bath and massage recommendations—apparently taken from training regimens developed mostly in England such as the following one for rowers:[9]

THE CAMBRIDGE SYSTEM. SUMMER RACES (1866).

Rise at 7 A.M.	
Exercise	Run 100 or 200 yards as fast as possible.
Breakfast, 8:30	Meat, beef or mutton.
	Toast, dry. Tea, two cups. Watercresses occasionally.
Dinner about 2 P.M.	Meat, beef or mutton.
	Bread.
	Vegetables—potatoes, greens
	Beer, one pint.
	Dessert—oranges, or biscuits, or figs; wine two glasses.
Exercise	About 5:30 start for river and row to the starting post and back.
Supper about 8:30 or 9.	Meat, cold.
	Bread.
	Vegetables, lettuce or watercresses.
	Beer, one pint.
Bed at 10.	

Thirty-one "portraits"—photos—of individual players were included to connect readers with well-publicized players of present and past. As a pioneering, insightful description of American football, Camp's book became a kind of classic, and in 1974 it was republished as part of a series called Popular Culture in America.

While Camp's well received book was a sign of football's growing popularity, a more dramatic sign was New York City's annual Thanksgiving Day game. Camp wrote about the game in a *St. Nicholas* article and began by describing the festive procession down Fifth Avenue that preceded it. The game was usually between Princeton and Yale, and the procession began at Yale headquarters, the Fifth Avenue Hotel. A few hours before the game, a coach typically drew up outside the hotel, pulled by a team of perhaps four prancing horses. From a waiting crowd of Yale fans, young men clambered onto the coach, topcoats tightly buttoned and derbies precariously balanced, shouting and laughing as they climbed higher, using footholds to reach the top, where they waved and found seats among rows of chairs on the coach roof.[10]

Soon other vehicles arrived, some draped with blue cloths printed "YALE" in large letters; they were quickly boarded by more passengers, including young women wearing something blue, who climbed inside or were hoisted to the top, laughing and buoyant in the commotion.

Gradually, the vehicles departed in a parade-like procession up Fifth Avenue, bound for the ballpark several miles away. A few blocks uptown, orange-and-black-decorated vehicles filled with celebrants from Princeton's headquarters at the Murray Hill hotel joined the procession. Spectators lined the street, in some places three or four deep, as the parade of coaches trotted by. Vendors ranged along the sidewalks, selling banners, flags, and artificial flowers of Princeton and Yale colors. Pictures of Princeton and Yale players were displayed in shop windows along the avenue, and here and there a home was flying a banner marked with a large *P* or *Y*. It was a day of jubilation for players, students, alumni, and a larger public, unmistakably demonstrating the acceptance and popularity of American football and the events that surrounded it.

The players left the hotel later than the parading coaches, after they had eaten lunch, though Camp wrote they probably were too nervous to eat much. After lunch they went to their rooms to put on playing uniforms and then gathered in the captain's room, where the captain said "a few words of caution or encouragement, as he thinks best. He is evidently in dead earnest, and so are they, for you might hear a pin drop as he talks in a low voice of the necessity of each man rendering a good account of

Yale partisans beginning annual coach ride up Fifth Avenue to the Princeton-Yale football game. (Reprinted from William H. Edwards, *Football Days*, facing page 1)

Additional coaches join the Fifth Avenue procession to the Princeton-Yale game.

himself."[11] Putting on their topcoats, they filed out, down the stairs to a side entrance, and boarded their waiting coach, most climbing to chairs on the top. At first there was some excited chatter, but "hardly a word is spoken after the first few moments. . . . Every man has his own thoughts and keeps them to himself. . . . Each man has made a mental comparison between himself and the man he has to face, until there is little left to say." Upon reaching the grounds, they entered dressing rooms, removed their topcoats, and then waited until a signal came that they were to take the field. Coming out, "they approach the great black mass of people and carriages surrounding the ground . . . and their hearts begin to swell within them as they really scent the battle." Arriving at the field, it seemed "too small," surrounded by a three-to-four-foot wooden fence with spectators surging against it and more spectators behind, in the grandstands, rising as great waves of humanity. As the players broke through the crowd and into the open field, kicking a ball ahead of them, a tremendous cheer went up, soon replaced by the ringing slogan of Princeton and the rattling cheer of Yale. All was ready for two old college rivals to begin another Thanksgiving Day battle, what many called America's premier sporting event of the year.[12]

Camp would be there also, walking with the players as they headed for the field, part of an entourage of coaches and trainers. But according to Caspar Whitney in *Harper's Weekly*, Camp stayed in the background, modest and "an inconspicuous figure on Thanksgiving day." While the "faces of seven out of ten occupying a similar position [as Camp] would be familiar to newspaper readers from Maine to California," Camp was "a stranger to the forty thousand spectators that have come to give homage to the game his skill has popularized."[13]

Second Most Important Man in New Haven? 26

As festivities began, the toastmaster loftily summarized: we are here to honor a quiet gentleman from New Haven, a gentleman "who has created the game that has more interest and excites greater enthusiasm than any other yet brought before the American people." The toastmaster had no doubt—the quiet gentleman from New Haven had "created" American football, and American football already excited "greater enthusiasm than any other" American sport. The crowd applauded, four hundred guests at a meeting room in Madison Square Garden, February 26, 1892, come to honor Walter Camp.[1]

The toastmaster's words would not have been Camp's words. "Created the game?" No! Creation was the effort of many persons. He had worked hard, had led several times, yet he was just one among many. Further, creation was not complete; American football was constantly changing, and more changes were needed—Camp was sure of that.

But historical precision was of little interest to this joyous gathering still exhilarated by Yale's 1891 football season. For the second time in four years, Yale was undefeated, untied, and unscored upon. In those four years, there were only two losses, one each to Harvard and Princeton, outbalanced by three wins over Princeton and two over Harvard.

The banquet's sponsors—primarily Yale alumni in New York City—had a sincere sense of obligation, going back even more than four years. A pamphlet on each dinner table listed Yale's record since 1879, Camp's second year as football captain and the year Yale's athletic advisory committee had been formed with Camp on the committee. At first there were losses: Harvard defeated Yale in rowing and baseball in each of the three years ending with 1879. Only a couple of Yale football wins avoided complete domination.

But in the twelve years since Camp graduated from college and took a growing role in Yale's athletic management, Yale had dramatically turned the tables: in head-to-head competition during those twelve years, Yale had won two baseball games to every one for Harvard, two rowing races to every one for Harvard, and ten football games to Harvard's one. Yale's success was trumpeted by the media; to a growing world of sports lovers, there was no doubt which school was dominant in college sports.

Camp did protest—not "Absolutely no; this is not the way it happened at all" but instead simply, "You are giving me too much credit." He accepted a heavy silver loving cup contoured as a large open-ended half-football supported by three sculpted football players.[2]

Camp's acceptance speech demonstrated the quiet man's ability as an after-dinner speaker, perhaps the growing skill of a sales executive. Tall, trim, thirty-two years old, he told many stories and produced many laughs, including one built on Yale's joy at beating Harvard. "I am like the man in the gallery at the time when his old enemy was being immersed by the Baptist preacher. He sat quietly until the elder lifted the man from the water, and then in an ecstasy of glee, cried out, 'Souse him again, Elder! Souse him again! He's a dirty dog.'" Many spoke, and a triple quartet from the Yale Glee Club led the singing of old college songs.[3]

Walter Camp in about 1892, as drawn in *Harper's Weekly*, March 5, 1892, 226.

Loving cup presented to Walter Camp at 1892 Madison Square Garden dinner in his honor. (Images of Yale individuals, ca. 1750–2001 [inclusive], Manuscripts and Archives, Yale University)

When Walter Camp joined the New Haven Clock Company in 1884, it was apparent the company would soon need a new president. Hiram Camp, the company's president for more than thirty years (no relation to Walter), was then seventy-three years old.[4]

Six years later, when Walter attended his third annual shareholder's meeting on January 29, 1890, the need was more pressing. Hiram Camp was still president, and business had declined, with no dividend paid since 1885.[5]

The company's ownership was already changing. A major stockholder, Harmanus M. Welch (cofounder in 1853 with Hiram Camp and James

English), had died the previous year and been succeeded by his son. Thirty-eight-year-old Pierce N. Welch was attending his first shareholder meeting in January 1890, and the meeting elected him a director.[6]

Less than two months later, as if planned on high, James English suddenly died, and his forty-eight-year-old son, Henry F. English, was promptly elected a director of the company. The new owners went into action two weeks after Henry English joined the board, naming themselves and L.W. Bristol (an attorney representing the estate of Edward J. Stevens, who had died in 1884 as the third largest stockholder in NHCC) as a three-man committee to develop a new plan for the company. By May they had already implemented a big part of the plan, a cash infusion, increasing capitalization from two to five hundred thousand. The largest portion of the additional capital undoubtedly came from English and Welch; they weren't ready to give up on the company yet.[7]

But they were ready to change management. Eleven days after deciding on a capital infusion, the English-Welch-Bristol committee became an executive committee—without the aging president, Hiram Camp—to handle "all matters of importance in the management and direction of the business."[8]

Since joining the company, Walter Camp had moved up and was in effect sales manager. He was still young, just turned thirty-two in May 1891, and not even a member of the board of directors. But according to a then popular novel, this was a "young man's epoch: a man feels a failure nowadays if he hasn't distinguished himself before thirty." Camp had certainly distinguished himself in athletics and football. Now, as the company's second-ranking officer, he logically could be in line for a larger role in company management.[9]

It soon became apparent the company was looking outside. On June 9, 1891, forty-five-year-old Samuel A. Galpin joined the company as assistant treasurer. A lawyer, Galpin had been an executive at a local business, the E. S. Wheeler Company. When that company foundered, he became a trustee-receiver, working to put the company on its feet—Galpin thus had experience with companies struggling to survive. Not just coincidentally, Mrs. E. S. Wheeler was Pierce Welch's sister.[10]

In September 1891, with business still faltering, Hiram Camp resigned. It took the company several months, until January 28, 1892, to name a successor. Even then the process was strange: the board first chose Pierce Welch to be president (an attempt to put off Galpin's succession?). But Welch immediately declined to serve. At that point, Galpin was elected president and treasurer of the company. Camp was elected assistant treasurer, the position Galpin was surrendering.[11]

The Madison Square Garden event honoring Camp was held almost exactly a month after Galpin was elected president of the New Haven Clock Company. If Camp needed it, the dinner might have offered consolation: with the forty-five-year-old Galpin in place as president, the top job at the clock company might never be Camp's.

A few months after the Camp dinner, newspapers announced a new organization at Yale. Yale's four student athletic associations had formed the "Financial Union of Yale University Athletics," with an objective "to take charge of the investment and expenditure of all moneys earned, collected and used by the athletic organizations of Yale University." College sports were continuing to grow, to become more established, to incur greater expense and produce more income, raising greater strains on student management.[12]

The *New York Times* speculated about the new organization while reviewing a treasurer's report of the Yale Football Association. The report showed significant receipts—$10,000 from the Princeton-Yale game, $6,750 from the Harvard-Yale game, and $5,000 from other games. But it was the expenditures that really caught their eye, including "$2000 for trophies and gifts to coaches." "A little more economy," they concluded, "is likely to result from the new arrangement for centralized finances." The new organization would include a *graduate* treasurer plus the presidents of the four student athletic associations, who would annually appoint the graduate treasurer. This effort to manage Yale's sports income very likely was the brainchild of the businessman Camp, and he was immediately named the first graduate treasurer.[13]

Several years later, Camp acknowledged that despite Yale's unique emphasis on student management, he in fact was the person most in charge, not just in finances but of the whole athletic program, including most specifically the football team and its play. It was of vital importance to the success of Yale's program, Camp wrote, that a single person was in charge—"the czar principle, if it might so be called." Yale athletics was run with organization, like a business, and in this case the leader was passionate in his love for the activity he managed. However, Camp realized his success depended more on loyalty than organizational authority:

> When there has been an explanation [for] a result, that explanation has not been given to the public, but has been . . . made the means to further triumphs. . . .
>
> By means of this loyalty men have been brought back to coach; through this loyalty they respected the policy that might be mapped out, and relying on this

> loyalty the . . . [czar] . . . was always able to see that his tenets were upheld and his plan carried through.[14]

Despite his dominance and influence, Camp still remained modest, according to Caspar Whitney in *Harper's Weekly*, known more by name than by appearance. Undoubtedly, this modesty and quiet nature, free of "wild gesticulations and Fourth-of-July oratory," helped Camp continue in his many roles without raising apparent jealousy or rancor.[15]

But people in New Haven knew Camp and his reputation. *Harper's Weekly*'s young editor Richard Harding Davis visited Yale for a *Harper's* article and wrote a startling, if a bit dramatic, impression: "There is only one man in New Haven of more importance than Walter Camp, and I have forgotten his name. I think he is the president of the university."[16] Then Davis told a story apparently making the rounds in New Haven. For Yale football games in New Haven, the Camps often entertained friends at their Gill Street bungalow. Before a recent game, a streetcar conductor came to the Camps' door to report that he had a streetcar waiting one block away for the Camps and their guests. It took the guests "some time to find their gloves and veils and overcoats, and so, ten minutes later, the car conductor arrived again, and with apologetic mien asked if Mr. Camp's 'party' would keep him much longer, as there were at the time six cars blocked, and each car loaded to the roof with students and towns-people going to the game." To Davis the conductor's actions were a "specimen of public veneration . . . worth much more than a bronze statue." Camp was still subordinate at the New Haven Clock Company, but in this city where he had grown up, played, and led Hopkins and Yale sports, and was prominent in building the game of football, his name and role dwarfed even that of the company president.

PART IV

Whose Game Now?

27 It's Official: We Want to Win

Amos Alonzo Stagg, from the Camp-coached 1888 and 1889 Yale teams, had changed career plans. His dream of Christian ministry, pursued sacrificially since high school days, was out. He had come to realize—even overheard others say—that his public speaking was not good enough to be an effective minister.[1]

Now he was into something new, a school recently opened in Springfield, Massachusetts, to train physical directors for YMCA gymnasiums. An inspiring teacher at the new school had persuaded Stagg that the YMCA could provide a different ministry career, ministering to young men at YMCA gymnasiums, where they were increasingly gathering for physical exercise.[2]

Stagg left Yale in the fall of 1890 and enrolled at Springfield. Already at the school was James Naismith, a Canadian recently graduated from a Presbyterian seminary in Montreal; Naismith had been influenced by the same Springfield teacher to choose work as a YMCA physical director over pastoral ministry. Stagg and Naismith became friends with several things in common—former seminarians, continued commitment to ministry, older age (Naismith, twenty-nine; Stagg, twenty-eight). Naismith and other students had begun a Christian support and prayer group, the "Ahikamin Circle," that Stagg also joined.[3]

Enthused by football after two years of play at Yale under Camp, Stagg formed and coached a football team at Springfield. From fifty-seven students at the school, most of whom had never played the game, Stagg fielded a team that achieved a winning record, five wins and two losses, playing several nearby colleges and high schools. The short, stocky Naismith, full black mustache projecting fiercely from his upper lip, was an important part of the team, running nearly the full length of the field in one game to score an important touchdown. The following year, when both Stagg and Naismith were teachers at the school, Naismith would invent basketball for use in a class he was teaching.[4]

Stagg arrived at Springfield aiming to be a YMCA physical director, but within a month he was offered a different option. The offer came as a surprise during breakfast with a Yale Divinity School professor, William Rainey Harper. Stagg knew the professor well—he had taken a class from him at Yale and had worked under him as athletic director when Harper directed the Chautauqua Institute in New York. At thirty-four years, Harper was not much older than Stagg.[5]

Though short and a bit pudgy, Harper was in other ways a giant, a prodigious bundle of intellect, energy, personality, and entrepreneurial drive—teenage Ph.D., admired professor, director of Chautauqua Institutes, creator of a successful side business in which he taught Hebrew through institutes and correspondence courses. He now had a unique assignment—to build a new university in Chicago—invited personally by John D. Rockefeller, the oil magnate and Baptist layman who was the principal benefactor behind the new school. Harper and Rockefeller's vision was a great university—a distinguished faculty and a distinguished program, with a graduate school to advance research and scholarship.[6]

But a school needed students, and Harper was practical and gifted enough to find and attract them. Football could help: students were excited about football, and nowadays football could get a school on the front page of the newspapers. Actually, football was becoming a regular activity at most northern major colleges; by 1890 football was being played at all nine of the major colleges near Harper's new university.

As they met at breakfast, Harper proposed that Stagg coach football at the new Chicago university. Mostly listening as Harper talked, Stagg tried to consider the implications of Harper's proposal. What he seemed to hear was revolutionary—a coach hired not by students or alumni but by the school administration, paid by the school, and acting as part of the school's permanent staff.[7]

In addition, Harper wanted Stagg to direct physical education, involving all the undergraduates. Several colleges had physical education programs, and Harper wanted one; he visualized Stagg handling both physical education and coaching, a logical but novel combination.[8]

Stagg gave no definite answer at the breakfast meeting, but after a month of internal debate he wrote Harper and accepted the offer. Football was moving west, Stagg was moving with it, and, through Stagg, Camp would be connected to this western outpost.

Stagg's paid and official position on the college staff wasn't all that was different about athletics at Chicago—President Harper's athletic goals were also different, at least in their expression. In a letter home to his mother and sisters in New Jersey, Stagg excitedly reported a recent conversation in which Harper told him, "I am most heartily in favor of [intercollegiate athletics]. I want you to develop teams which we can send around the country and knock out all the colleges."[9]

There was purpose in Harper's instructions to Stagg. The proliferating American colleges were in competition, searching for funds, students, faculty, and prestige. As one step in such pursuits, Chicago had pioneered college advertising, a new sophisticated campaign for students.[10]

Football could be another useful tool. Once the simple extracurricular possession of students, football now had a divided "ownership," shared at least between students and university administration. And to really benefit the university, Harper knew Chicago needed to have a winning team. He was open with Stagg, revealing his understanding and acceptance of the stake Chicago (and other universities) had in the game they had once only passively accepted.

Football was front and center at another new college in 1892, Stanford, opened in 1891, a year earlier than Chicago, with 559 students. Another project of a major benefactor, Stanford had been founded by Leland Stanford (railroad entrepreneur, California governor, and U.S. senator) together with his wife as a memorial to their deceased son, Leland Stanford Jr.

Stanford's students got a football team together even in the school's opening year, playing their first game on March 19, 1892, and unexpectedly defeating the University of California, 14–10. For the second year, the student manager, a "Mr. Champlin," wanted progress taken to a new level. With a bit of boldness, he wrote to the most familiar name he knew, Walter Camp, and asked for suggestions of a coach for Stanford. Camp replied that all men he could suggest were already coaching at other schools, but then he offered a surprising and tantalizing hint; if Stanford had obtained no one by Thanksgiving, Camp might come himself.[11]

Thanksgiving would be soon enough for Champlin; Stanford was to play the University of California on December 17, and that was the game they most wanted to win. Champlin so notified Camp, and on November 10, 1892, Camp telegrammed Champlin that he would come, a message that was quickly relayed to the *Daily Palo Alto*, Stanford's student newspaper, and trumpeted in a front-page article headlined simply, "WALTER CAMP": "No one who is up on the great game needs to be informed who Walter Camp is. The mere mention of his name to a football man is sufficient to awaken football enthusiasm." Camp would remain with the Yale team until their last game, November 24 with Princeton, and then come to Palo Alto.[12]

Camp was not coming alone. Lee McClung, the just-graduated star and captain of the 1891 Yale team, was coming also to coach California's team, probably the result of a Camp initiative. McClung and Camp had a warm relationship. Considerate and stylish, a southern gentleman, McClung occasionally sent flowers to "Mrs. Walter," appreciated by both Alice and Walter. Stanford and California each wanted to win, and so did their coaches, but it would be a friendly rivalry. McClung was reportedly being paid for coaching California, but there is no indication Camp was paid other than, perhaps, expenses.[13]

Mountain storms slowed Camp and McClung's train, and it was November 30 before they actually reached San Francisco. Alice Camp was not along, staying home to be with her ill mother and one-and-a-half-year-old Walter Jr. This was apparently Camp's first trip to the West Coast, and besides allowing him to teach and promote American football in a new location, it would provide several other opportunities—surveying California athletics for a possible article (such an article was published in *Harper's Weekly* a few months after his return), vacation and relaxation in sunny California, and a visit to the New Haven Clock Company's sales office in San Francisco, where Camp could develop a firsthand connection and help look for more business in a state growing by about a thousand persons a day.[14]

Camp and McClung began practice with their teams on December 1. Temperatures had cooled, and Camp came to the first practice in a long dress coat and fashion-forward contoured cap, dapper with a groomed, handlebar mustache. His manner surprised a newspaper reporter: "He could not have been heard twenty-five feet away, and he seemed more like a clergyman who was there to protest than like a professor of the rugged art." However, Camp warned the players they could expect "sharp rebukes"; a coach should correct errors "in a manner to leave an impression."[15]

He began practice by having each man take a turn at punting and catching. Then he watched as a practice game was played. Later, at the training table, each man was told of faults Camp had seen. A blackboard was set up, on which Camp could diagram plays.

Camp and McClung each wrote articles in the *San Francisco Examiner* describing their players and the state of preparations. Camp's comments about individual players generally included both praise and criticism. With his Yale experience as background, he wrote that the Stanford team seemed "lacking in that intensity of desire to win that would lead them to the hardest work"; they had not learned the "everyday constant effort made for weeks" that was required to reach a fully competitive level.[16]

December 17 was clear and cold, ideal for football, and fans were waiting at the gates when they opened. By game time, at least fifteen thousand were inside the enclosed grounds, with another two or three thousand on hills overlooking the field. Such numbers required the presence of more than students—aficionados who had seen football elsewhere or the curious who had simply read about the game and its growing presence.[17]

Camp and McClung were on the field, but as referee and umpire. Their two weeks of coaching were over. The game was now in the hands of captains and players to put into action strategies that had been planned and practiced.

Stanford, with smaller but faster men, would try to run off tackle and around end. Midway through the first half, helped by a quick double pass in the backfield and organized interference, Stanford got captain Cleamons free around the right end for a forty-yard run to California's ten-yard line. From there Walton twisted over the goal line and touched the ball down between the goal posts. Kennedy kicked the goal-after.

California's heavier team relied on short line plunges and began to have success in the second half over Stanford's small center. Holding the ball twenty-one consecutive plays, California moved eighty-seven yards for a touchdown. However, they missed the goal-after, leaving Stanford ahead, 6–4.

Stanford responded by again putting together long runs and a touchdown, but the kick-after just missed, leaving them ahead 10–4. Then it was California's turn, steadily marching upfield with short smashes into the line. Shortly before the game ended, California scored a touchdown and successfully kicked the goal, producing a tie score, 10–10.

That was how the game ended, perhaps more satisfying for the two coaching friends from the East than for the rival teams and their fans.

The year 1892 was also when the University of Pennsylvania went looking for a coach and turned to another former Yale player—George Woodruff from the 1888 Camp-coached team.

Pennsylvania had some handicaps. Having moved to its present site in "West Philadelphia" only in 1872, the school had no campus football field until 1885 and would have no campus dormitory until 1896. Still, Philadelphians were determined that their historic school with roots back to Benjamin Franklin achieve parity with the "Big Three" of Harvard, Princeton, and Yale—athletic parity as well as academic parity. Athletic parity would require a lot of improvement: in twenty-five football games over sixteen years, Pennsylvania had never defeated their neighbor and natural rival, Princeton.[18]

After graduating from Yale, Woodruff returned to Pennsylvania, his home state, to both teach and coach at prominent secondary schools: a year at the Hill School in Pottstown, northwest of Philadelphia, and then two years at William Penn Charter School in Philadelphia. His football teams at both schools impressed a prominent Pennsylvania alumnus and Philadelphia attorney, John C. Bell, chair of Pennsylvania's Athletic Association and Pennsylvania's representative on the Graduate Advisory Committee of the IFA. Bell persuaded Woodruff to attend Pennsylvania's law school and at the same time coach Pennsylvania's football team and rowing crew. In exchange, Woodruff received free tuition and a thirteen-hundred-dollar salary.[19]

Woodruff had immediate success at Pennsylvania, starting the 1892 season with twelve straight wins (including Penn State, Virginia, Navy, Williams, Lafayette, Lehigh, and the Chicago Athletic Club). Hopes were soaring as November 5 and the annual game with Princeton approached. Princeton came to Philadelphia—"Manheim," the grounds of Germantown's popular cricket club—and brought a crowd: total attendance was at least eighteen thousand.

It was a very windy day, and when Pennsylvania won the toss, they elected to have the wind behind them for the first half. With the wind's assistance, they gained ground on punt exchanges. Also, their running was aided by a new version of the wedge Woodruff had developed, the "plough," with several players arrayed across the front. Pennsylvania drove in for a touchdown before the first half ended and successfully kicked the goal: six points.[20]

With the wind in their favor in the second half, Princeton also managed a touchdown, but they missed the kick-after, leaving them with only four points. That was all the scoring. Pennsylvania won 6–4, their first win ever over Princeton.

Princeton was in shock, not just students but fans and school administrators, too. Ellen Wilson, whose husband, Woodrow, had returned to Princeton as a professor, wrote to a friend two weeks after the game, thankful for the consolation of Grover Cleveland's presidential election: "We needed something as great as [Cleveland's] victory to endure the overwhelming football calamity, and defeat by the U. of Pa. . . . Really, I think Woodrow would have had some sort of collapse if we had lost in politics too!"[21]

"A Chief Charm of the Game" 28

On the train west to Stanford in late 1892, Walter Camp had something new to think about—a new line of play just seen in the Harvard-Yale game that could add a new dimension to American football. The play was the brainchild of a Boston engineer, Lorin Deland, fascinated by football even though he had never played it. Newspapers grandly reported that Deland's study of tactics from chess to Napoleon had led to his play, the "flying wedge."

The basic novelty in Deland's new play was to place some offensive players in forward motion before the ball was put in play, which in the recent Harvard-Yale game took form as a kickoff play. As the play began, most of Harvard's team was several yards behind the Harvard kicker (captain Bernie Trafford) and divided into two groups, one on each side of Trafford. At the referee's signal to begin, the divided groups began to move forward, aiming to converge in front of the ball. When they reached Trafford, he touched the ball with his foot (the "kickoff"), picked it up as allowed by the rules of the day, and passed it to a halfback waiting behind him. The players on Trafford's left and right merged to become a V-shaped "flying wedge," with Trafford and the ball carrier close behind and within the wedge. The whole group bore down on Yale's stretched-out line of players ten yards away, aiming at a single point, Yale's right tackle. Yale was unable to stop the Harvard runner until he reached Yale's twenty-five-yard line.[1]

Whatever apologies may be owed to Napoleon, Deland's play mainly arose from the 1888 rule amendments that expanded interference and allowed blockers to precede a runner. Those amendments had already led to "mass play," offensive players bunched and pushing forward in a coordinated effort, such as the wedges used by Princeton, Yale, and Pennsylvania. Deland added a new aspect to mass play, with almost the whole team in motion before play began. Momentum was coupled with mass, creating a new category, "mass-momentum" plays that increased the offense's power. Mass-momentum plays could originate from scrimmage as well as from kickoff, putting a phalanx of players in motion behind the line of scrimmage before the ball was snapped, aiming to overpower the defense waiting at the scrimmage line.[2]

Mass play had critics, beginning with a concern for injury from force applied massively at a narrow point of the defense. Momentum now added to those concerns, enhancing mass with a running head start.

Camp pondered the broad subject of mass play (with or without momentum) on his trip, discussed it with others, and was stimulated to write an article that he submitted while still out west. Published in *Harper's Weekly*, January 21, 1893, as "A Plea for the Wedge in Football," the article focused on mass plays from scrimmage without momentum. Admitting mass play's dangers, Camp nevertheless contended that wedges and other forms of mass play should only be limited, not prohibited; the wedge was a useful option, allowing variation in play. We should, he said, give captains all the chance we can to exercise strategic imagination, to plan, place men, and carry out the plan, because that *exercise of imagination "is one of the chief charms of the game."*[3]

Mass play was, of course, a form of team play, in which the actions of a number of players were coordinated toward a desired result. Planning and developing strategies was a major delight for Camp and growing larger with every year the game was played. A year earlier, he had written about planning in *Harper's Weekly* in an article titled "Team Play in Football":

> Team play is the road to victory, and the only one in these days of football, when captains and coaches spend far more time and thought over the conduct of the campaign than over individual work. Not only is the general dependence of one man upon another brought out and made a feature of the work, but the general movement of the struggle, the point of pressure, and the lines of resistance—all are become an interesting study for those who mean to win.[4]

Camp's 1891 book, *American Football*, had mostly focused on individual playing positions. In this late 1891 article, Camp took up the coordination of individuals, the tactics and strategy of a team as a whole. In an article longer than usual for Camp—almost two full folio-size magazine pages of dense copy—he dug into several parts of team play, the wedge, "bucking the line," end runs, and punts (punts were a prime weapon of nineteenth-century American football used often in a kind of territorial battle). These four plays, Camp said—wedge, run through the line, end run, and kick—are a "framework upon which a coach may build up an almost endless variety of movements."

Camp's use of the term *coach* in the preceding sentence showed something new. His own intensified coaching role at Yale in 1888 and the following years had anticipated a trend. In American football's early years, captains were in charge of developing team play and strategies. But with the development of new plays such as Deland's mass-momentum plays and more sophisticated team play, tactics, and strategy, captains' efforts were no longer enough. Coaches, Camp now believed, were the main force in developing American football. In an 1891 article, Camp pushed the use of coaches. "During the last year or two, most of the teams have learned the absolute necessity of having an efficient coach for the men. . . . From the time that a team begins regular practice they should never be without a coach, . . . and the general direction should be in the hands of one thoroughly experienced coach." He emphasized the need for coaching again in a November 1891 article in *Outing*, calling the coaching benefits seen in actual play on the field really "remarkable."[5]

Coaches were in fact spreading across the country in parallel with the expanding number of teams. The October 20, 1892, *Yale News* reported that twenty-one former Yale players were in place around the country, coaching a variety of teams. And Camp had concluded that a team serious about competing "should never be without a coach" from the time the team began regular practice.[6]

However, captains were still in charge. Almost all 1892 coaches worked for a captain, the local student football association, or both. And once the game began, captains made the decisions—deciding in the midst of a contest out on the field what plays should be used. That was the way it should be in Camp's mind: football was educational, and the captain's experience on the playing field, making on-field decisions under contest pressure, would educate and strengthen him. Coaching came during the week and in pregame planning; once the game was under way, coaches were banned.

"What Does Walter Think?" 29

By the 1890s, Walter Camp had become as "official" as could be found in American football, his name published on the cover of every American football rule book after 1883. The rule book became more visible about

1890 when publication officially shifted from Wright and Ditson to the mushrooming sporting-goods enterprise of the former baseball star A. G. Spalding. Spalding created a new rules-containing booklet, *Spalding's Official Foot Ball Guide* (paralleling the pioneering fourteen-year-old *Spalding's Official Base Ball Guide*) and made the reviser's name "Walter Camp" on the cover nearly as large as "Spalding"; Camp's name apparently brought salable authenticity—the recognizable name of a prominent spokesman and commentator on football.[1]

Besides benefiting Spalding's business, a football-based *Spalding Guide* would also benefit American football because of Spalding's greater reach and distribution, including a greater nationwide distribution. For the initial football rule book published in 1890, Camp added something new, an introductory section with seven-plus pages that briefly discussed the game's history and rules and also touted its qualities and growing popularity. Though the new section was primarily an advertisement for American football, Camp apparently also saw it as a personal opportunity, which he emphasized by adding his signature at the end. At the same time, he adopted a less formal tone—through 1888 his name on the rule-book cover was "Walter Chauncey Camp," and in 1889 it was "Walter C. Camp." Now, in 1890, it was simply "Walter Camp," and the signature was plain, essentially vertical and casual, in comparison to the formal Palmer style he had used with his full name. Through regular publication in the *Spalding Guide* and other writings, the plain upright signature "Walter Camp" developed a kind of trademark significance, common and recognizable enough that Camp later used it even in ads for New Haven Clock Company products.[2]

Appropriate to his official status, Camp seemed to avoid provocative public positions. Perhaps he consciously sought to be recognized as objective and fair, or perhaps it was natural, part of his personality: quiet, reserved, fact based, analytic. A February 1892 drawing in *Harper's Weekly* pictured him with a professorial image—Van Dyke beard and mustache, plus thinning hair and lengthening forehead, a pleasant- and mature-looking thirty-four-year-old.[3]

But controversy would soon reach Camp and American football, foreseen in a late 1892 letter to Camp from Vance McCormick, Yale's football captain. McCormick and Camp had worked closely during the just-past 1892 season to lead Yale to another undefeated, untied, unscored-upon season—the third year for such a record since Corbin asked Camp to coach five years earlier.

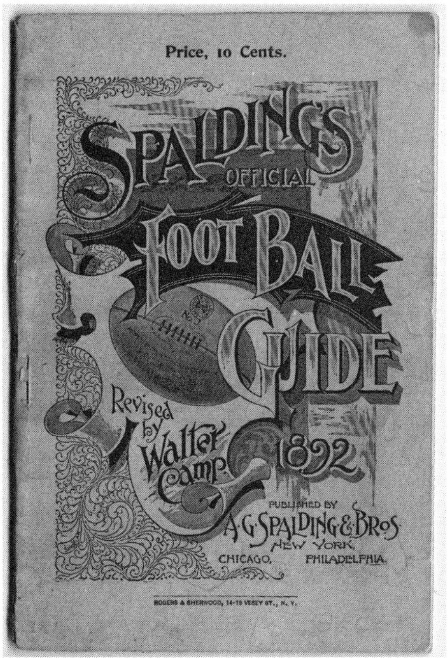

The 1892 edition of *Spalding's Official Foot Ball Guide.* Camp edited this guide annually until his death. (Walter Chauncey Camp Papers, 1870–1983 [inclusive], 1870–1925 [bulk], Manuscripts and Archives, Yale University)

McCormick wrote Camp after the 1892 Yale season was completed and less than a week after Camp got to California to coach Stanford. After some gracious preliminaries (he visited "Mrs. Walter yesterday," and both she and "young Walter are looking exceptionally well"), McCormick got to his problem, which ironically centered on the growing strength of the Pennsylvania football team led by former Yale stalwart George Woodruff. The most serious problem arose from Pennsylvania's graduate and professional schools, home to three-fourths of Pennsylvania's students as well as to several Pennsylvania football players. Graduate and professional school players were considered unfair by some in the football community—older, bigger, more experienced, sometimes with skills acquired through extensive play at other colleges.[4]

Yale alumni were some of the most upset by Pennsylvania's graduate players. To the public, they called the Pennsylvania players a threat to amateur standards; inwardly, they surely sensed a threat to Yale's football dominance. Bring back the old days, the alumni argued, when undergraduate players fought on behalf of a college central in their lives from freshman year on, when play was not only for themselves but also on behalf of classmates and alma mater. The upset alumni pressured the Intercollegiate Football Association to enact eligibility standards, limiting play to undergraduates.[5]

As president of the IFA, McCormick was at the center of this new eligibility crisis. But there was a lot to consider—the desire of alumni and students to maintain Yale's success counterbalanced by the desire of graduate and professional school students to play. McCormick had met with a group of Yale alumni on the issues but wasn't satisfied. More than once, McCormick said, someone in the group would say, "If only Walter were here." McCormick closed by asking if Camp could write his views, "or do you think you had better wait until you return?" Then, "we miss you awfully, and I wish to goodness you were here now."

Although Camp may have publicly steered clear of controversy, McCormick's letter is evidence that Camp's associates sought his views and expected them to be sound and helpful. Camp must have responded to McCormick, but the existing correspondence files don't reveal what he said; he surely could not have recommended what McCormick actually did.

About six weeks after he wrote Camp, on January 14, 1893, McCormick convened a special meeting of IFA delegates. Presiding as chair, McCormick proposed that the IFA's rules be amended to allow only undergraduates to play football for IFA teams.[6]

Pennsylvania was a clear target of such a rule, and they tried to change the delegates' minds, arguing that all students of a university, no matter the field of their study, should have an equal right to play football for that university. Pennsylvania didn't change minds, but they managed delay; the IFA meeting dismissed without a decision, giving everyone time "to think the matter over."

McCormick had the delegates back in session within a week, January 21, 1893, and proposed the following amendment of the IFA constitution: "No member of a graduate department or a special student shall be eligible to the football teams of colleges in the association, nor any graduate who has registered or attended lectures or recitations at any other university or college." Despite a vigorous argument by Pennsylvania, the amendment was adopted, with Princeton and Yale strongly in favor and Wesleyan, according to the *New York Times*, "falling in line" (as discussed earlier, Harvard was not in the IFA at this time).[7]

Critics of the new rule quickly went on attack, revealing substantial discord even within Yale's student body. Yale law students objected first, dismayed at their threatened loss of eligibility. But objections quickly spread throughout the larger student body. Yale had become a "university" in 1887, shortly after President Porter's retirement, and objectors argued that the new undergraduate rule would contradict that effort. Yale's aim as a university was for its multiple colleges to be unified; barring graduate and professional school students from Yale's football team conflicted with that, keeping them from full membership in the whole university.[8]

Yale student leaders decided to call a meeting to attempt to resolve the divisions. Camp had just returned from California and understandably felt obligated to support McCormick. A letter from Camp was published in the *Yale News* the day of the scheduled Yale meeting, February 1, 1893, appealing for support for McCormick's actions. The focus of Camp's appeal was narrow: when Yale sent representatives to a convention, those representatives should not have their actions repudiated when they returned home. Refusal by Yale students to ratify the undergraduate rule, Camp said, would be the first-ever repudiation of Yale delegates. For the sake of effective action by future delegates, Camp begged for no repudiation; it would "only do ourselves an injury." If this was a bad regulation, there would be opportunity to modify it soon enough, when new representatives were chosen the next year.

Yet Camp's defense was muted because tucked sideways into his letter was an indication he would have sought a different rule, something he contended would have been "more stringent" than McCormick's undergraduate rule. Camp's different rule brought a new idea into the discussion, a one-year-residency requirement for students new to a university. Such students, either undergraduates or graduates, would be barred from playing football during their first year at the school, thus discouraging attendance simply to play football.[9]

By calling his one-year-residency proposal "more stringent," Camp perhaps sought to avoid undercutting McCormick. Or perhaps he was trying to tread a narrow line—lend support to his friends and allies yet move the discussion to a different point of view. Most of his letter argued against repudiation of McCormick; his alternative one-year-residency requirement was inserted indirectly as background. But to alert and motivated readers—including agitated Yale students—Camp's alternative seemed in line with their objections to the undergraduate rule. Graduates could play under Camp's proposal, assuming they met the one-year-residency requirement.

A huge attendance at the Yale meeting on February 1—more than two thousand, including alumni from all parts of New England—demonstrated the great interest in the undergraduate rule. Only students voted, and the vote was close: 502 to 440 against ratifying the actions of Yale's delegates. For once Camp had been unpersuasive at Yale. The undergraduate rule was in limbo, since the students at the college leading its enactment had voted against it.[10]

Rumors circulated during the summer of 1893 that Princeton was switching to Pennsylvania's side and would vote to rescind the undergraduate rule at the next IFA convention.[11]

The previous year's Princeton quarterback, short, sturdy All-American Phil King, had graduated but was returning for graduate school. And last year's Princeton center, D. M. Balliet, another All-American-caliber player, was already in graduate school. Both players would greatly help Princeton's team, but were prohibited under January's undergraduate rule, officially still part of the IFA constitution. The most obvious solution was to explicitly vote the undergraduate rule off the books.

Another ally also stepped up for Pennsylvania. Harvard and Pennsylvania had not competed in football since 1889, when Pennsylvania sided against Harvard's allegation of Princeton "professionals," but now that past was put aside and Harvard and Pennsylvania worked out a significant new partnership. Not only would they play, but they would play on Thanksgiving, the domain of Princeton and Yale. This year there would be two major games on Thanksgiving, one in New York between Princeton and Yale and one in Cambridge between Harvard and Pennsylvania.[12]

In making arrangements with Harvard, Pennsylvania agreed to accept new eligibility rules recently developed by Harvard; these rules were the most thorough and carefully drafted rules yet, *but* they were protective of graduate players. Both Harvard and Pennsylvania had an interest to protect. More than a third of Harvard's students, and as noted above three-fourths of Pennsylvania's students, were graduate or professional school students.[13]

Use of graduate school as a facade for recruiting football players was not addressed, but such abuse might be limited by thoroughness in enforcing the rule requiring that a player be a bona fide student "throughout the college year."

With player eligibility such a live topic, many wanted to know what football's senior rule-making group, the IFA's Graduate Advisory Committee, led by Walter Camp, would do. What did they think about the undergraduate rule? When would they take up the issue?

A newspaper reporter finally learned the committee would meet October 21, 1893, at some unknown New York hotel. Searching from hotel to hotel, reporters found the committee at the bar of the Fifth Avenue Hotel discussing matters in "an undertone." Both Pennsylvania's John Bell and Camp were there, "victim" and "aggressor," perhaps causing the reporters to wonder what answer these senior advisers would provide for the undergraduate issue.[14]

As the reporters watched from a distance, the meeting seemed peaceable and united, but the reporters ached to ask more questions: Did Camp and other committee members assure Bell that their committee would not act against Pennsylvania's graduate players? Or did they all agree to abstain, to let the student bodies involved proceed with democratic processes, faulty or not? Or did Camp have some vision of a way out, some way to bypass the present conflict?

At meeting's end, the committee addressed the reporters but made no comment on the undergraduate question. Camp simply named the umpires the committee had chosen for fall IFA games.

Not satisfied, reporters asked directly, "What is the committee's position on the undergraduate rule?" Answer: that subject was outside the committee's jurisdiction; the committee was offering no suggestion to IFA student delegates.[15]

That was too much for the *New York Times* reporter, who ended his story with an alleged final inquiry:

> "Mr. Camp," . . ."Did you take this off," pointing to Camp's chin, where he formerly sported a Van Dyke beard, "to throw us off the scent?"
>
> "Sir!" and Mr. Camp was lost in the army of politicians in the corridor of the hotel.
>
> If he had remained a few seconds longer he would have learned what newspaper men think of the Graduate Advisory Committee and its methods of conducting affairs.[16]

Personal invasion? Public condemnation? A reaction to Camp's long presence and possible domination of the committee? Not Camp's normal experience. But once again, from the public's perspective, he would seem neutral on a controversial issue.

Inaction by the Graduate Advisory Committee left the undergraduate rule for students to handle. A meeting of the IFA was called for October 27, with delegates present from each member school, Pennsylvania, Princeton, Wesleyan, and Yale. The graduated McCormick was replaced by Yale's new captain, Frank Hinkey.

On a three-to-one vote, the delegates enacted new eligibility rules. Mostly, the new rules were not controversial. On the graduate-student controversy, there was some moderation, but in practice the new rules continued to strike at Pennsylvania: a transfer student entering a college of the IFA from a different college could not play "until he has spent one year of resident study in the college, and has passed a satisfactory examination upon a full year's work." Here was the one-year-residency requirement Camp had advocated in February, applied without distinction between undergraduates and graduates: none of the large number of students in Pennsylvania's graduate and professional schools who had transferred from another college could play until they had spent one year at Pennsylvania.[17]

But still there was a question. To apply the rule immediately would be retroactive—barring Pennsylvania players who had entered Pennsylvania before the rule was enacted. Some thought that unfair. Pennsylvania asked for a year's delay in application of the rule, but that too was rejected.

Leaving the meeting, Pennsylvania's captain, Mackey, was in distress: "It is plainly evident that all of the big colleges are afraid of our team. Yale, Wesleyan, and Princeton can use every man at the training table, but my college will have to drop the nucleus of the team."[18]

After the meeting, Princeton's football captain immediately announced that Princeton would not insist that the new transfer rule be observed when Pennsylvania and Princeton played November 4, eight days thence. Princeton thus avoided any retroactive application of the rule. Just as last year, the game was played at the Manheim cricket field in Philadelphia, and again it was a close and fierce battle, but this time Princeton prevailed, 4–0.[19]

Contrary to Princeton, Yale did not waive application of the new residency rule. First announcing they would not play a Pennsylvania team having students prohibited by the new rule, Yale then became more "compromising" and offered alternatives: Pennsylvania could abide by the rule, that is, drop offending players from the team, or resign from the IFA. Either alternative upheld respect for the new rule and its standard for player eligibility.[20]

The Pennsylvania-Yale game was scheduled for November 11, only two weeks after the IFA meeting, so Pennsylvania didn't have long to decide. And it didn't take long. On November 6, 1893, Pennsylvania tendered its resignation from the IFA.[21]

Wesleyan had also resigned, two days before Pennsylvania, giving the reason that severe injuries prevented them from fielding a competitive team (before the season began, they had only four returning players). So now the IFA was down to two members, Princeton and Yale. The organization that had managed American football since the start in 1876 was coming apart.[22]

The End of Student Rule Making 30

With rule making paralyzed by disruption of the Intercollegiate Football Association, Walter Camp found help from an old friend, George Adee, who was president of the University Athletic Club of New York City, a new club founded in response to the growing interest by graduates in their college's athletics. Besides club activities, the UAC had taken on operational roles such as managing the 1892 Thanksgiving Day game in New York for Princeton and Yale. Caspar Whitney was impressed with the club and had written that it could be a force for moderation in American football.[1]

Rule-making thoughts were percolating among UAC leaders almost immediately after the 1893 football season ended, likely with Camp encouragement. On December 21, 1893, only two months after the *New York Times* had criticized Camp for the allegedly do-nothing Graduate Advisory Committee, Camp and representatives from Harvard and Princeton met with Adee and others at the UAC to discuss the future of football management.[2]

It was the first meeting in four years bringing together football representatives from the "Big Three," Harvard, Princeton, and Yale. Discussions continued after the holidays and through January. James Barr Ames, Harvard Law School professor and chair of Harvard's athletic committee, took an active role and made insistent demands: in case Yale thought differently, Harvard would require that Pennsylvania be included in any new rule-making body. Princeton and Yale probably already accepted that; Pennsylvania had moved into the top rank; perhaps now there would be a "Big Four" instead of a "Big Three." But Ames wanted to stop with four members, while the other delegates wanted a fifth to avoid ties. Letters and telegrams from the Harvard constituency were required before Ames would agree to five members.[3]

On February 6, 1894, the UAC announced formation of a new football rule-making committee to operate under its auspices. Harvard, Pennsylvania, Princeton, and Yale each had a member on the committee, and the fifth member was Paul Dashiell, a twenty-six-year-old professor of chemistry at the Naval Academy. Born in Annapolis, Dashiell had studied chemistry at Johns Hopkins University both as an undergraduate (1884–87) and as a graduate (1887–91). In the midst of his Johns Hopkins graduate work (1889–90) and again after receiving his Ph.D. (1891–92), he had taught at Lehigh University. In 1892 he joined the Naval Academy staff.[4]

Dashiell was not only a scholar but also a gifted athlete. He played football at Johns Hopkins and was captain for two years; he also played for Lehigh the two years he was there.

After his playing days, Dashiell became a referee, highly regarded and often selected to referee major games—the previous year, 1893, he refereed both Princeton-Pennsylvania and Princeton-Yale. He had also helped coach the Naval Academy team in 1893 with Yale-graduate and Camp-recommended Josh Hartwell. Though Dashiell had a relationship with Camp and others on the committee, he had no real partisan commitment to any of the Big Four teams; as a fifth member, he could break any tie among the rest of the committee.[5]

All the committee members were several years removed from college, with significant practical experience: Pennsylvania's John C. Bell, a practicing attorney; Harvard's W. A. Brooks, a practicing physician and teacher at Harvard Medical School; Yale's Camp, business executive with long experience in football rule making; Princeton's Alex Moffat, an electrical contractor in New York; and Dashiell, college professor.

With Moffat elected chairman and Camp secretary, the committee began to meet and within two months, on May 8, 1894, announced significant rule changes:

- Some "momentum-mass plays" were barred, defined as plays "in which more than three start before the ball is in play." Nor could more than three players group together more than five yards back from where the ball was to be put in play. (For Camp, this was a start but not enough; within two years, he would lead a total removal of momentum-mass plays. But there was a limit on the rapidity of change, especially when some leading teams, such as Pennsylvania with its "flying interference," had made momentum-mass plays an important part of their current playing strategy. Camp wrote that the rule-making committee had a kind of gracious unwritten rule not to change a rule suddenly so as "to cripple the known play of one of the big teams"; it was not "necessary to go so fast . . . as to force a team to lose a play that they have perfected" and were depending on.)
- Another game official was added to the existing referee and umpire, a "linesman," to mark under direction of the referee the gain or loss during a play and also to "give testimony to the referee" as to a rule violation, such as unnecessary roughness, offsides, or holding.
- New rule language gave a referee authority to decide when a play was over, irrespective of whether the runner had cried "down": "As soon as a runner

attempting to go through is tackled and goes down, the referee shall blow his whistle and the ball shall be considered down at that spot."

- Any piling up on a man after the whistle was blown was to be punished by a fifteen-yard penalty.
- In making a fair catch, a player was to hold up his hand, whereupon the opposing team could not interfere or tackle him (penalty fifteen yards). The receiver could not run with the ball after signaling for a fair catch.
- The time of play was reduced, changing from forty-five-minute to thirty-five-minute halves (actual playing time was perhaps not shortened because time limits had been imposed on delays, and time-outs now were taken while a team was bringing the ball out for a kick after touchdown).
- Teams were given a new option, to refuse a penalty against the opponents and instead take yardage gained during the play, up to a maximum of fifteen yards.

The new committee of "old men," Camp being oldest at thirty-five, had made an extensive and promising start.[6]

Besides responding to disruption of the IFA, the new rules committee of more experienced men was a timely response to recent explosive growth in American football. In the eleven years since Camp's 1882 five-yard, downs-and-distance rule transformed the game, colleges competing in football had grown from about 15 to more than 150. Six thousand attended the New York Thanksgiving Day game in 1882; thirty to forty thousand attended in 1893. Newspaper coverage of football was mostly local in 1882 but had become national by 1893, often on the front page for major games. A corps of coaches with accumulated experience and skills was developing and ready to make coaching a profession, and college administrators were becoming eager to use football for their own purposes.[7]

The game had become too big for oversight by partisan student bodies, which changed personnel each year. In presenting the rules in *Spalding's Official Football Guide* for 1894, Camp made an effort to tie the new UAC committee of seasoned graduates to the old student-originated IFA through a kind of devolution of authority. The guide reported that Camp and Moffat, representatives of the two remaining members of the IFA, had concluded "that this year was a crucial one for the game, and that a general committee of experts ought to be appointed to consider alterations in the rules. At the same time the University Athletic Club, at the invitation of several of the prominent colleges, took steps toward the formation of such a committee. . . . The suggestions of this committee, approved by the U.A.C., have been adopted by the Advisory Committee, and also ratified by the . . . Association."

The reference to the "association" kept a flavor of student participation, but actually the IFA was now an inactive shell. Student rule making was at an end. From now on, American football rules would be written by persons several years removed from college, for whom student interests might be only one of several considerations.[8]

31 New Voices

Henry L. (Harry) Williams didn't lay out all the details when he discussed his 1893 book plans with Walter Camp. Perhaps he couldn't foresee dangers the book would raise for Camp.

Williams was an 1891 Yale graduate and an athlete—not only starting left halfback on Yale's 1890 Camp-coached football team but also the "world record holder" in the 120-yard high hurdles. The fall after graduation from Yale, Williams taught at a preparatory school in New York close to the West Point academy and at the request of the academy football team coached and helped them defeat Navy at Annapolis, 32–16, avenging Army's loss the year before in the first-ever Army-Navy game. Camp's end-of-season survey in *Outing* credited Williams's coaching for the victory.[1]

After just a year in New York, Williams moved to Pennsylvania, where he coached at William Penn Charter School and attended Pennsylvania Medical School; given those tasks, he didn't play football at Pennsylvania. Yet Williams wanted to write a book about football and agreed to do that with Alonzo Stagg, whom he had known at Yale. The increasing complexity of football, the spread of the game, and the growing use of coaching might support a market for a new instructional book.[2]

With football books the domain of Camp, their Yale mentor, Williams apparently went to Camp to discuss the planned book, and from Williams's description Camp must have had no objection. Together Stagg and Williams went to work; Stagg wrote his Ahikamin Circle friends on September 17, 1893, that he and Williams had been working "10 hrs a day for a month" to finish a book, and Stagg hoped to be able to send each of them a copy in a "little over a month."[3]

But when Williams sent Camp proofs of the book, Camp got worried. Instructions about playing positions, team play, tactics, and signals were no concern, but the book contained sixty-nine play diagrams, each accompanied by a half page of detailed discussion that Camp thought in some cases included Yale proprietary information. In Camp's wide writing, he had never considered it necessary to reveal details of Yale's plays. After receiving the proofs, Camp quickly wrote to Williams, asking that he delay publication and send copies to "Pa" Corbin, Josh Hartwell, and Frank Hinkey, present Yale football captain, to consider whether the book's disclosures would endanger Yale's football success.[4]

Williams was working hard to get the book ready for publication early in the upcoming football season, and he apparently didn't get around to Camp's request. Camp wrote again, with specific objections, such as the inclusion of a defensive play he considered private to Yale.

Williams now responded, deferential, but refusing to change: "I sent all your correspondence and Hartwell's letters to Lonnie and he agreed with me entirely that it could not be said in any way that the diagrams revealed any of the Yale tactics." Further, Williams contended, the diagrammed defense was played by Yale in the big games, and the coaches of Harvard and Princeton could not have failed to notice it. Williams also noted that the book did not identify the play as a Yale formation, and nothing was said to emphasize the "vital point" Camp made about it. He concluded, "I am very sorry indeed to go against your wishes in the matter."[5]

Stagg and Williams proceeded to have the book published, but instead of the October release date Stagg had predicted to his Ahikamin friends, the book came out the week of December 18, 1893. Perhaps Stagg and Williams didn't finish the book on time; more likely, they couldn't find a publisher. The book turned out to be self-published, printed by a firm in Williams's hometown of Hartford, Connecticut.[6]

Another football book was also published in fall 1893, *University Football*, edited by James R. Church and published by Charles Scribner's Sons. In subject matter and organization, the book was similar to Camp's 1891 book, *American Football*. Each chapter dealt with a specific player position or subject (such as training) and was written by a different author, a former football player who in most cases had played the position he wrote about. Church was a Princeton graduate and former Princeton player, and five of the other writers were also former Princeton football players; two each were from Harvard and Yale. Several, like Church, had graduated in 1888, the rest more recently.[7] Here was no problem for Camp, an instructional book that would build football but not reveal proprietary knowledge.

Still one more sports book was coming to market in 1893—*Walter Camp's Book of College Sports*, by the leading college-sports author himself, destined for the largest sales and greatest impact in this breakout year of multiple publications. This was Camp's second major book, but it consisted of earlier writings, verbatim reprintings of articles Camp had written for *St. Nicholas* magazine, plus chapters on rowing and track.[8]

Though the book capitalized on writing already done, a reviewer from the *Nation* praised it as a "handsome volume," providing a full account of the sports covered plus a wealth of anecdotes that made the book "a new departure and . . . sure to delight [Camp's] readers." Admittedly, the reviewer said, the discussion of football was "somewhat barren of novelty," given that Camp had already "covered the same ground" in an earlier book. But as to baseball, Camp had "left nothing needful unsaid" on the theory and practice of the game. And the reviewer welcomed the encouragement given young readers to participate.[9]

The reviewer's principal criticisms were outside the book. With some sense that Camp was too dominant in American football, the reviewer contended that more opinions were needed: "Hearty praise is certainly due Mr. Walter Camp for the interest he has shown in football and the care and study he has bestowed upon it; but it is not good for such a game to owe too much to any one man. . . . Mr. Camp would probably be the first to welcome the suggestions and advice of [graduate opinion]."

Despite having self-published in December 1893, Stagg and Williams eventually found a commercial publisher, D. Appleton and Company of New York, which agreed to publish their book before the 1894 season. By that time, another, allegedly competitive, book was also going on sale. J. E. Sullivan, president of Spalding's publishing arm, American Sports Publishing, had written Camp on July 27, 1894, with a surprising suggestion: "I talked to Mr. Curtiss today and do you not think you could get up for us at once a book say of 50 pages for our Library How to Play Football, something cheap we could sell for 10 cents. . . . My idea would be to have this book come out in Sept. and to a certain extent kill the sales of this book of Stagg and Williams, for I believe it would have a great sale."[10] Obviously, Sullivan and Julian Curtiss—the latter being Camp's old Hopkins and Yale schoolmate and a Spalding vice president to whom Sullivan reported—knew Camp was unhappy about the Stagg and Williams book. Now they thought they saw an opportunity to enhance Spalding's business, help their old friend, and perhaps limit dissemination of Yale's football secrets.

Camp accepted Sullivan's suggestion but only in part. He prepared the requested pamphlet, *How to Play Football*, but contrary to the protectionist sentiment behind Sullivan's suggestion, he invited other writers to join him.

Only fifteen pages were written by Camp, and the rest comprised articles by Phil King, the former Princeton quarterback, and L. T. Bliss from Yale. Camp's invitation to other writers may have had some political benefits and marketing benefits, but it also reflected a native charitableness. Grantland Rice called Camp "one of the most attractive personalities that sport has known," with "a kindness and a gentleness and charm of manner which made friends from one coast to another." The *How to Play Football* booklet was successful, and revised editions were published yearly under the same title for many years. Camp was always a major author, but he was joined by several different additional authors. Similarly, Camp invited other writers to prepare sections for *Spalding's Official Foot Ball Guide*.[11]

Whatever Camp may have thought about the Stagg-Williams book, he did understand that American football had become too big to be one person's domain and that others needed to participate in governing and writing about the game. He had been a singular figure, a recognized authority, the "father of American football." Now others were ready to do some of the things he had done. And he would have limited control over what those others did; he had been unable to stop dissemination of what he considered valuable Yale trade secrets. If ever he had controlled American football, he knew that the game now was moving outside his control.

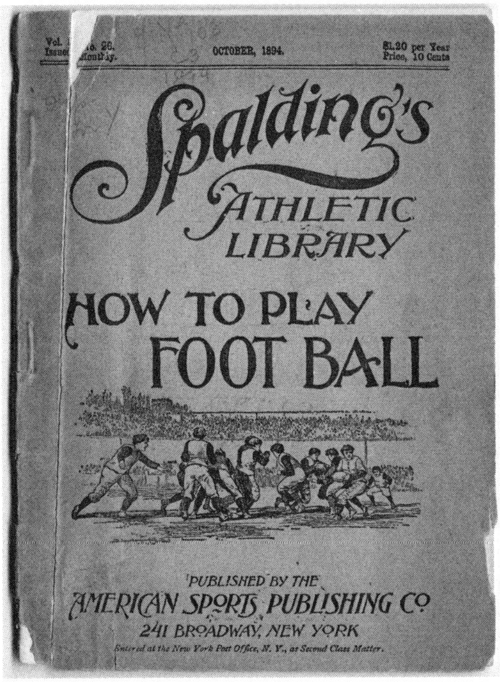

How to Play Foot Ball booklet, begun in 1894 and annually written in part and edited by Camp. (Walter Chauncey Camp Papers, 1870–1983 [inclusive], 1870–1925 [bulk], Manuscripts and Archives, Yale University)

PART V

Bigger and . . . ?

Critics and Defenders 32

"College football is fast becoming a national calamity."[1] E. L. Godkin, editor of both the *New York Evening Post* newspaper and the *Nation* magazine, took to a new field in the fall of 1893, away from his usual focus on political, international, and economic issues. Godkin was now seized by a new phenomenon irrepressibly advancing in American life, the college sport of football, which he addressed with definite opinions: football was "brutal," "one degree removed from prizefighting," a distraction from the educational mission of a university—"Who in any college is the better [from] it?"

Despite dogmatic assertions, Godkin knew little about football or its appeal. To him, college football players were "gladiators . . . trained to scuffle, scratch, cuff, push and pull for the amusement of an immense crowd." As to injured players, they "got into this condition . . . largely for the amusement of other people." It was beyond Godkin that athletes played football because they chose to, wanted to, loved to.

Godkin's reporters were more fact seeking than he was. One from the *Evening Post* visited Yale, where almost every faculty member interviewed "referred him to Walter Camp, 'the man who makes football.'" To the reporter, Camp offered diplomacy: "I have noted the *Evening Post's* attitude toward football and am interested in it." He distinguished different kinds of rough play, criticizing "severe play," such as "the concentration of eleven men upon one with the idea of putting him out of the way," and he predicted that rules would be drafted to eliminate that kind of roughness.[2]

Beneath his diplomatic posture, Camp had strong opinions about allegations of football "brutality." Those alleging brutality, he said, needed to learn more about the game, to understand better what risks of injury were actually present and how players regarded those risks. To Yale's Professor Richards, "In the eyes of timid people any collisions between young men" seem brutal, while "the average school boy" considers them "tame." Camp seldom wrote about football's "manliness" in terms of physical dangers; instead, he praised football for such traits as "self-denial, discipline, obedience, unmurmuring pluck, and a good deal of patience." Camp knew that in 1893, trained college players experienced few serious injuries. Players didn't have the speed, size, and momentum of today's players, and the style of play, often with open-field tackling around the waist or shoulders, was less conducive to injury. The starting eleven many times played a complete game, and they might have one game on Wednesday and another on Saturday.[3]

Caspar Whitney was not so diplomatic as Camp. In his *Harper's Weekly* column on December 16, 1893, he assailed the "futile crusade against football the editor of the *New York Evening Post* has recently flung himself with well-developed hysteria." Whitney was ready with facts, gathered from "trustworthy and painstaking" correspondents around the United States. From the University of Michigan: "We have had no serious accidents here this fall. Several men have suffered bruises and sprains at various times, but all are nearly well now, and there is not one of them who will not be perfectly sound in a few weeks." Nineteen correspondents reported similarly, and Whitney concluded: "Here is a fact for Mr. Godkin and other uninformed carpers to bear in mind: Looking back over ten years of football, we find the hardest games of the year—those between Harvard, Yale, Princeton—to have recorded the least injury to players."[4]

One of football's defenders was a doctor, William Conant, writing in October 1894 in a leading scholarly journal, the *Boston Medical and Surgical Journal.* Conant proposed that college athletics "be divided into different grades, some of which are harmful to certain men, but not harmful to the right men." For severe and arduous sports such as football, the doctor wrote, an examination of a man's physical condition was absolutely necessary before allowing him to take part.[5]

Conant worked with the Harvard football team, and he listed all the injuries that Harvard football players, both varsity and intramural, had experienced during four years, 1890–93. Harvard had grown large—3,160 in the whole university in the 1893–94 school year, with 2,000 undergraduates—and hundreds of students were involved in intramural and varsity programs. There were several injuries, especially among the many intramural players: each year, on average, at least four broken noses, ten knee injuries, nine ankle sprains, two broken leg bones, four shoulder injuries, and three scalp wounds. But Conant said there had been very few severe injuries to the well-trained men of the varsity, and he suggested that intramural programs be better supervised and players provided with better training.

That is not to say there were no serious injuries on the football field—in fact, there were deaths. The *New York Times* listed football injuries at the end of the 1893 season, including two deaths. A player of the Farmington Athletic Club fell on a loose ball and was then fallen on by two opponents, causing his neck to be twisted and spine badly injured. Paralyzed, he lived for eleven days and died on November 29. In another case, a player for the City College of New York fell during a game, apparently without contact, and died; his neck was said to be "broken by the fall."[6]

Football's defenders, including Camp, replied that serious injuries and deaths primarily occurred when players were inadequately trained or not in proper condition or were playing without proper supervision. Any physical activity entails risks; death occurs in yachting, but no one argues yachting must go; in fact, they said, death even occurs in the national game of baseball.

To Dr. Conant, football was worth the risk of injury. He asked college leaders to "inform themselves upon the value of athletics." "Many a man feels that his success in after life is due in a great measure to the excellent condition of his mind and body brought about to a large extent by athletics which he followed when in college."

The most wide-ranging factual defense of football got under way in November 1893, with a visit by Robert Bacon to Walter Camp. Bacon was an investment banker of growing responsibility and prominence—he would soon assist J. P. Morgan in bailing out the nearly bankrupt U.S. Treasury, and he later served briefly as U.S. secretary of state—but he still found time to work on behalf of football. At Harvard Bacon had played football and baseball, run track, rowed crew, and boxed, a "blond giant, handsome as Adonis," according to Camp. He and Camp were well acquainted, rival football captains in the fall of 1879 when their two teams played to a scoreless draw.[7]

Now in his midthirties, Bacon had been recently elected to the Harvard Board of Overseers and was a member of an overseer subcommittee appointed to investigate football's alleged "brutality." He came to Camp with an idea: they should conduct a survey of past players to learn their injury experience from playing and the consequences of any injury both at the time of playing and later in life. It was now eighteen years since American-style football began. How did players from past years, looking back from today's perspective, evaluate their football participation? (Camp had already participated in a similar survey distributed in July 1893 by John E. Loveland, a doctor in Middletown, Connecticut, as will be subsequently discussed in this chapter.)

Bacon proposed that Camp chair a committee to develop and conduct the planned survey. Camp agreed, and a distinguished six-person committee was assembled with representatives from Harvard, Princeton, and Yale, as well as the headmaster of a private secondary school. Dr. William Pepper, president of the University of Pennsylvania, was invited but declined because of work conflicts.[8]

Early in March 1894, Camp mailed letters on behalf of the committee to three different groups: all Harvard, Princeton, and Yale football players from 1876 to the present; the 1893 players at all other football-playing colleges; and administrative heads of every secondary school having a football team. Appealing to the players as having "always stood together in defense of their sport," Camp wrote:

> In order to arrive at conclusions regarding American intercollegiate football, will you kindly mail answers to the following questions? Will you add also as much of a statement as you feel disposed to make and have time to give as to your present occupation and your opinion of the good and bad effects traceable to the sport, both in your own case and in that of others whom you know?
>
> How many years did you play?
> What was the most serious injury you received?
> Was that injury permanent?
> Was it received in a match or in practice?
> Had you been properly trained?

The letters brought a prompt and widespread response, nearly one thousand answers by April 10, which Camp analyzed, presumably reviewed with the committee, and presented as the findings of the committee in a report or book published by Harper and Brothers in November 1894, *Football Facts and Figures*.[9]

The responses were grouped—Harvard, Princeton, and Yale players from the past eighteen years in one group, players from 1893 teams of other colleges in a second group. As to overall physical effects:[10]

Harvard, Princeton, and Yale players (337 responses)	
Number who considered themselves benefited	328
Number said to be permanently injured	3
Number who failed to answer	2
Number who considered football had no effect	4
Other college players (359 responses)	
Number who considered themselves benefited	357
Number said to be permanently injured	1
Number who considered football had no effect	1

Because permanent injury was a special concern, Camp stated in *Football Facts and Figures* that the report included "the exact words of every man who replied otherwise than 'No' to the question of permanency of any injury received." Twenty-three such cases were among the Harvard, Princeton, and Yale responses, including:

No. 680. Played 11 years. Broken nose, affected one nostril, but bored out.
No. 636. Played 3 years. Broken ligament in knee. Knee occasionally slips.
No. 163. Played 3 years. Never lost a day to injury. Left knee a little weak.
No. 891. Played 3 years. Sprained knee, think the weakness permanent.
No. 923. Played 6 years. Injured knee; still affects me.[11]

Although not part of his survey, Camp did include in *Football Facts and Figures* a summary by Dr. Loveland of the results of Loveland's survey. Loveland's conclusions were somewhat different from Camp's. For example, Loveland concluded that 20 percent reported "some permanent injury," but Loveland included a swollen knuckle and the like in calculating that percentage. Camp appears to have contemplated removing parts of Loveland's statement and crossed them out in a draft of *Football Facts and Figures* retained in the Camp Papers. This crossing-out has led some scholars to believe Camp excised unfavorable results from his text. Camp likely tried to dissuade Loveland from certain comments, but in the end Camp did include Loveland's complete statement at pages 40–47 of *Football Facts and Figures*, including the supposedly excised statement.

The book also reported on football players' academic performance:[12]

Princeton men from 1874 onward who played in games with association teams:	
First honor men, that is, first in class	1
High (above 95 per cent.)	23
Second (above 90 per cent.)	31
Good (above 75 per cent.)	29

Low (50 per cent.)	37
Failed	8
Yale (in decades)	Average score; scale of 4
1869–78	2.508
1878–88	2.677

In addition to survey results, the book also included more than fifty pages of considered statements by established academics and doctors. For example, Harvard's law professor James Barr Ames, chair of Harvard's athletic committee and future dean of the Harvard Law School, wrote:

> The successful football player must possess strength and endurance; he must think and act quickly; he must be brave; he must control his temper in the face of strong temptation and be always ready to subordinate his individual action to the interest of the team as a whole.
>
> The merits of a game demanding these qualities will be obvious to everyone. Are they outweighed by the objections most frequently urged against the game, namely that it is physically dangerous and that it interferes too seriously with the scholarship of the players? I think they are not.[13]

Camp added a few comments that seemed elementary but undoubtedly would provide practical improvement, such as that some person at a college should be made accountable for maintaining the college's playing fields in good condition, because playing fields in poor condition contribute to injuries.[14]

Out of one thousand replies, there was an occasional critic, and there were nonplayers such as preparatory school headmasters who came to the study already critical of the game. Overall, the book achieved what the survey's originators hoped for and expected—a persuasive case that the vast majority of past players did not consider football brutal, had not been permanently handicapped, and were happy they had played.

The most scholarly 1893 defense of football was presented by Francis A. Walker, president of the Massachusetts Institute of Technology. Since becoming president in 1881, Walker had led MIT from an enrollment of 302 and precarious financial condition to an enrollment of more than 1,000, with a strong faculty and sound financial condition. Cordial, dynamic, perceptive, Walker was an entertaining and sought-after speaker.[15]

Asked to speak at a dinner honoring scholars, Harvard's Phi Beta Kappa graduates, Walker's choice of subject—*athletics!*—perhaps surprised his audience. But he contended that no other subject was of "greater consequence to the colleges and universities of our land." There was a "rising passion for athletics [that] has carried all before it. . . . Honors in football, in baseball, and in rowing have come to be esteemed of equal value with honors in the classics, in philosophy, or in mathematics." Looking on, "some applaud, some doubt, some disapprove." But he believed most college presidents "see some good in the new movement and sympathize largely with the enthusiasm of their pupils."[16]

As an introductory premise for his remarks, Walker called attention to a basic shift in Americans' "religious" outlook: people in America now thought not only about how they should die, but also about how they should live. "To a perfectly sane man, physically, life itself becomes a joy." Paralleling this change was a change in what Americans admired. In the past, Americans admired "the speechmaker and the fine writer." Now they saw "how much nobler are strength of will, firmness of purpose, resolution to endure, and capacity for action."[17]

The task of education should be aligned with this change in values, Walker said, and competitive college athletics should support that alignment. They taught "courage, coolness, steadiness of nerve, quickness of apprehension, resourcefulness, self-knowledge, self-reliance." They demanded that the contestants learn to work with one another and subordinate personal desires to a common end. "Any profession" would benefit from such personal qualities and character; athletics helped prepare college students for useful careers.[18]

Walker also saw other benefits from college athletics: "In the competitive contests of our colleges, something akin to patriotism and public spirit is developed." When not carried too far, such participation and public spirit were good, "as counteracting the selfish individualistic tendencies of the age and [whereby] the body of students should now and then be stirred to the very depths of their souls, . . . should have something outside themselves to care for, . . . should learn to love passionately, . . . should at times palpitate with hope and fear and anxiety for objects that bring them personally neither gain nor loss."[19] Here was another college president praising football, apparently with no gain for himself or MIT—MIT didn't depend on football for students or prestige. Instead, Walker spoke as an informed and thoughtful leader of America and its colleges, and he saw value in football, a reason for it to continue, an important and growing part of American life.

33 Breakup

A crime! What else could you call it? One player intentionally injured another. That essentially was the accusation, publicly asserted and greeted with an uproar, a day after the Harvard-Yale game of 1894. And just that quickly, the six-month-old UAC football-rule-making committee, with its fresh and reinvigorated approach, was in trouble.

Though rarely played on Thanksgiving Day, the Harvard-Yale game was still a major celebration, a day "when all Harvard and all Yale, past, present, and to come, assemble in one intense crowd." Over the past six years, the game had grown into a major extravaganza for the host town of Springfield, which welcomed the event with banners over city streets, displays in storefronts, and a festive ball. Special trains came the morning of the game, six trains alone from New York City chugging in with five thousand passengers. Smooth scheduling and routing were required to unload those five thousand and other arrivals into the stream heading to Hampden Park a few blocks away. With a thrill of anticipation and excited greetings, the crowd filled the grandstands built around the field—twenty-five thousand in all for the 1894 game, the largest crowd yet for a Harvard-Yale game.[1]

Harvard had won only one of the six games at Springfield, and the 1894 team was determined to break that trend. All season they talked of "the last Saturday in November" and practiced "until the moon was out." Some players were injured, but they scrambled for substitutes—most important, a new quarterback. Robert Wrenn was chosen, a great athlete, the reigning U.S. singles tennis champion, though with limited play on Harvard's varsity football team.[2]

When the game got under way, Harvard got a quick shock. Stillman, Yale's center, broke through Harvard's front line, blocked a punt across Harvard's goal line, and fell on the ball for a touchdown. The try-at-goal was successful, and Yale quickly led 6–0.[3]

Fighting back, Harvard drove well into Yale territory before being stopped on Yale's thirty-yard line. Quarterback Wrenn sent a beautiful lateral to Harvard's J. C. Fairchild, who stepped into a dropkick, on target in a long crowd-hushing arc toward the goal. "Thud!" Inches too short, the ball hit the crossbar and bounced back.

Still Harvard pressed on, clearly outplaying Yale. Finally came a breakthrough: a well-executed reverse from a double pass in the backfield brought a long gain to near Yale's goal line, and from there Harvard punched in for a

American football scrimmage as drawn by T. Dart Walker for a 1900 *Collier's Weekly*. (The Lost Century of Sports Collection, LostCentury.com)

touchdown. The try-at-goal failed when Wrenn mishandled the ball, leaving the score 6–4 for Yale.

Then Stillman struck again, once more breaking through Harvard's line to block a punt, this time out-of-bounds on Harvard's six-yard line. Yale got the ball and in three plays plunged into the end zone and kicked goal, making the score 12–4 for Yale.

Play became more physical and intense, as a frustrated Harvard battled to score and Yale struggled to resist. Two players were ejected for "slugging," and players were often slow getting up after a down. Each team had several players injured badly enough to leave the field. Charlie Brewer, Harvard's left halfback, was helped off the field with a bad ankle sprain. Harvard's end Hallowell broke his nose and bled so badly that he left the field, "looking a sorry sight." Yale's tackle Murphy was knocked out and carried from the field on a stretcher and brought to the hospital.

Disputes were common, as Harvard complained that the referee, Princeton's Alex Moffat, was favoring Yale. On one drive, as Harvard neared Yale's goal, Moffat called an offside on Harvard, requiring a critical transfer of the ball to Yale. Another time Moffat ruled Harvard was stopped at the one-foot line, while Harvard claimed they scored.

The "crime" came in the second half when Harvard's right halfback, Edgar Wrightington, ran forward to receive a punt, allegedly without signaling for a fair catch and with a plan to run with the ball. The *World* reported, "The

Harvard interference was very bad, and [Yale's] Capt. Hinkey was on top of Wrightington when he caught the ball. In making the tackle Hinkey's knees struck the Harvard man's neck with terrific force. When he was able to arise it was necessary to take him off the field . . . with a broken collarbone." There was no more scoring in the game. Harvard had lost again. They were sure they had played the better game, but help from the official and dirty play had allowed Yale to outscore them.

Dr. W. A. Brooks, Harvard's coach and representative on the new UAC rule-making committee, was certain that Wrightington was already down when Hinkey jumped on him—so certain and angry that he wrote a public letter accusing Hinkey. He withdrew from his scheduled assignment to referee next week's Princeton-Yale game, saying he feared he would be prejudiced against Yale.[4]

William Conant, physician for the Harvard team, quickly tried to calm the waters. Reports of injuries, he said, were greatly exaggerated. Although there were several injuries, none was more serious than happened occasionally in practice. Even Wrightington's injury was not so serious as reported; his collarbone was not broken, only slightly dislocated. Conant also knew that none of the Yale players was seriously injured; Murphy, who had been rumored near death in the hospital, was already released and expected to play against Princeton on Saturday.[5]

But the next day, a former Harvard football captain blunted Conant's efforts by again publicly accusing Hinkey of jumping on Wrightington with his knees when Wrightington was already down. All the "unusual and uncalled-for roughness" of the game was begun, he claimed, by Hinkey's unlawful and outrageous tackle of Wrightington.[6]

Yale had been quiet but now moved to respond by forming an investigating committee comprising "men of recognized experience in football matters." The committee obtained statements from officials supervising the game: the referee, linesman, and assistant linesman all stated that Wrightington's injury was pure accident with no unnecessary roughness and that Hinkey was no rougher than any other player.[7]

The Yale investigation seemed high road, but Yale's student and alumni response was more gut level. Harvard was untruthfully blackening both Hinkey's and Yale's names! Yale should play no football game with Harvard until Harvard sent a "satisfactory reparation," something to maintain "the honor and self respect of the University, Captain Hinkey and the team."[8]

Yale partisans must have been dreaming. Harvard alumni were just as adamant that Yale players had caused the problem. A "reparation" to Yale was inconceivable.

Passions were also rising at another address in football's hierarchy. Two weeks before the disputed Harvard-Yale game, Princeton played Pennsylvania at the state fairgrounds in Trenton, a site near Princeton with capacity for a large crowd. Special trains came directly to the fairgrounds. Semaphores from the field signaled the game's progress to downtown fans.[9]

Both Pennsylvania and Princeton had strong, unbeaten teams—Princeton with four members from the previous year's All-America team, Pennsylvania with seven returnees from last year.

George Woodruff had devised a new formation, "guard's back," in which Pennsylvania's two large and athletic guards—George's brother, Wylie (205 pounds), and another medical student, Charles (Buck) Wharton (212 pounds)—moved into the backfield, one behind the other, making six in the backfield to assist runners with interference in front and pushing from the back. As an option, if Princeton backs moved up close to the line to help defend against the guards-back play, Woodruff had installed a quarterback kick as an offensive play, a short kick forward and to a side of the field where a Pennsylvania back—behind the kicker when the latter kicked the ball and therefore "onside" under held-over rugby rules and eligible to catch or recover the ball—might reach the ball faster than a drawn-in Princeton back.[10] Woodruff also innovated on defense, positioning his guards to pull back slightly, free to cover more ground laterally, while the ends crashed in.[11]

When the game got under way, Pennsylvania's defense dominated Princeton's offense, keeping them well away from the Pennsylvania goal line. But Princeton also put up a strong defense, and the game was scoreless through the first half. A break came in the second half when Pennsylvania partially blocked a punt and Pennsylvania's Carl Williams, a dental school student who had previously played football as an undergraduate at Oberlin, scooped up the ball and ran for a touchdown. Pennsylvania later scored again on a novel reverse-style double pass; "Win" Osgood, in his second graduate year at Pennsylvania after a full career at Cornell, took the second pass as a reverse and ran in. The game ended with Pennsylvania the winner, 12–0.[12]

Pennsylvania had turned the corner, established as a major competitor. This was their second defeat of Princeton in three years, and Princeton had had enough of Pennsylvania and their graduate school players. Within months they decided to remove Pennsylvania from their schedule. The two schools had played every year since 1876, twenty-five games in nineteen years, but that streak was over. Pennsylvania and Princeton would not compete in football again for more than forty years.

While Walter Camp surveyed the troubles between Harvard and Yale and between Princeton and Pennsylvania, he was also experiencing a personal sadness. He had missed the Harvard-Yale game and Wrightington's injury, taking another trip west to coach Stanford. When he returned, both his parents were ill with typhoid fever. His mother, Ellen, vulnerable to serious illness more than once in the past, was unable to fight off the attack and died on January 24, 1895, a month short of her sixty-second birthday.[13]

34 Failure Achieved

As the time approached for 1895 rule making, Walter Camp knew he was facing a challenge. The logical first step would be to reconvene the rules committee formed so successfully last year through the University Athletic Club. But Yale's own Josh Hartwell had twice called George Adee, president of the UAC, protesting that no Yale representative should participate in a rule-making convention with W. A. Brooks, last year's Harvard representative and now Hinkey's public accuser.[1]

Despite what anybody else thought, Camp wanted the UAC to help with the rules review. On February 21, he wrote Adee, noting a "strong personal desire to get all of the suggestions we can" on rule revision and asking, "If the University Athletic Club does not care to call together the Rules Committee," perhaps they could still "obtain suggestions" from the committee as to any rule improvements they would recommend.[2]

Adee undoubtedly wanted to help, but influential club members wanted to stay clear of the Harvard-Yale dispute. The club had gotten a rules committee going last year, and now it was up to that committee to initiate its meetings. In letters on March 1 and 3, 1895, Adee tried to gently inform Camp that the UAC would not be an aid to rules revision.

So if Camp wanted work on rules, it would be his problem to solve. American football rules had been reviewed and amended every year except one since the game's inauguration, and they needed it again this year. Important issues needed to be considered: Did the fair-catch rule have any part in

Wrightington's injury? Did Harvard's charge of bias against Moffat suggest some needed change in choosing officials for a game? Should the rule on momentum plays—which now allowed three players in motion before the snapback—be further restricted? How could he get the rules committee to meet and rule on these questions?

Camp's first idea appears to have been a resurrection of the nearly defunct Intercollegiate Football Association. With only Princeton and Yale remaining as IFA members, Camp got help from Princeton's Moffat; despite occasional disputes, Princeton and Yale seemed to avoid any real blowup in their relationship.

On March 6, 1895, Camp and Moffat convened an official meeting of the Graduate Advisory Committee of the IFA. Stating a need to make "vigorous changes" in football rules, they invited captains of several football teams to meet with them in two weeks to discuss rules revision. Camp had already managed to obtain rule suggestions from several football captains—not only from Princeton and Yale but also from *Harvard* and *Pennsylvania*!—and he incorporated those suggestions into a printed flyer accompanying the letter of invitation. Perhaps by developing momentum through the football captains, he could do an end run around the Harvard-Yale blowup and get rule amendments written through the IFA.[3]

Harvard quickly vetoed Camp's plan and did it through Camp's friend George Adee. Adee wrote, "For the first time on record," James Barr Ames, chair of Harvard's Athletic Committee, came to visit. Ames, who had written a section in Camp's *Facts and Figures* book just a few months earlier, was a top lawyer and had adeptly devised rebuffs clearly intended to be sent to Camp:

- First, a direct message: since Harvard was not a member of the IFA, Harvard would not participate in Camp's efforts to develop new rules through the IFA's Graduate Advisory Committee. (In other words, whatever help Camp had previously obtained from Harvard's captain, that was now ended.)
- Second, Harvard had "only the most friendly feelings toward Yale" and thought that Yale, "as the leading Football Institution," should call a convention of a number of colleges. (That sounded democratic, but what of the rules committee just created last year? The committee had worked well; why discard it and undertake the task of developing rules in a new large convention?)
- Third, although Ames was in New York and would travel through New Haven on his homeward trip to Boston, he "could not stop in New Haven" to see Camp. But if Camp wanted to see or speak with Ames, Ames was staying at

the Windsor Hotel in New York until Wednesday night. (If Yale wanted Harvard's cooperation, they would have to solicit it on Harvard's terms: no retraction and no apologies for accusations against Hinkey.)

- Fourth, Ames voiced a not too hidden threat, involving the University of Pennsylvania. Pennsylvania, Ames advised, had not called a meeting to counter Yale's efforts at rule revision. And if Yale called the broad-based convention of several colleges as Ames proposed, Pennsylvania would respect that call. ("Had not called" obviously suggested "*would* call" if Yale refused Ames's suggestion of a broad-based convention. A separate set of rules would surely result from Pennsylvania's separate meeting. Two sets of rules would be divisive, taking away the unity needed to administer and promote the game.)[4]

With such an unambiguous full rejection by Harvard's chief athletic official, Camp knew he needed to find a different middle ground. Noting the call by Harvard and the University of Pennsylvania for a general conference, Camp again turned to the UAC. He announced to the media that he and Moffat, in the name of the Graduate Advisory Committee of the IFA, had sent an urgent communication to the UAC requesting that they call a rule-making conference. As a sweetener, he cited the praise received by "the University Athletic Club last year in appointing . . . a committee for revising the rules, and it is under that action as a precedent that similar action is hoped for this year."[5]

But Harvard undercut that approach also. Adee wrote Camp that per advice from a member of the UAC, "Harvard will not join in a Football Convention," and that "probably covers Pennsylvania's attitude also." Adee had been trying to help, but he now was exhausted and giving up: "I have done all I can in the matter."[6]

Even before the rule-making snafu, other unpleasant matters had led Camp to some uncharacteristic actions. Grantland Rice called Camp kind and gentle with "friends from one coast to another," but Camp also did not want to be taken advantage of, especially when it came to money. By 1894 Camp had grown unhappy with his payments from *Harper's*. No longer receiving regular monthly payments, he was being paid only for special articles and material actually used in Whitney's column. Sorting out what material had been used and giving it a value was not straightforward, and Camp thought *Harper's* fall 1893 payment inadequate. Camp had tried unsuccessfully to arrange a meeting with Whitney in New York in early 1894, before Whitney left for England to gather information for a book. By July Whitney had been back for months, and still there had been no discussion.[7]

Camp responded to the delay with a short note, including an emotional burst that stunned Whitney: "You are avoiding . . . me. I want to know if you yourself have really become as hard as . . . your friend [from] Outing . . . [expecting to get] something for nothing?"[8]

Camp's note brought the matter front and center, and Whitney responded in a six-page June 12, 1894, letter, defensive in the face of Camp's out-of-character belligerence:

> I presume you must have been jesting, but I must tell you that I don't like your comparison, even in fun. . . . I don't think you ought to send me a slip such as this. Is there any time in your connection with *Harper's Weekly* that you have given us anything for nothing? . . . I tell you candidly, a great deal that you have sent me . . . has really had very little body to it. . . . [H]ad it come from any one else, I should have thrown it out. I am only telling you this to show you that it has always been my desire to have you make as much money out of your work as possible.[9]

Camp typed his reply: "If I have done you an injustice, I sincerely beg your pardon. . . . [U]p to a short time ago . . . no man stood higher in my opinion for squareness than you. . . . Perhaps of late you have been misrepresented to me. . . . I counted upon a personal interview. . . . When do you expect to go to New London? Let me know whether you cannot stop off to see me then." In handwriting he added, "Meantime let's suspend judgment and start out anew."[10]

Whitney made no delay in answering, scrawling directly on Camp's letter in large handwriting and sending it back: "What in hades are you talking about. . . . No one ever had cause or assumption to talk to me in such a way. . . . I thought your grievance merely a business one. . . . But when you come to question my 'squareness'—that's a different matter. . . . You will be grey-haired before I would deign to explain any impressions that were taken without giving me a hearing or the benefit of the doubt." He finished abruptly, "Send in your claim against HOB."[11]

Within a week, passions had cooled and an adjustment made. Apparently, Camp sent another letter, suggesting that Whitney was misunderstanding him, but further stating his case and arguing he should be paid more than *Harper's Weekly*'s "average football correspondent." On July 19, Whitney wrote back. If there's been a misunderstanding, Whitney said, the fault "lies more with you than myself." But the bottom line was that Whitney agreed to go over "the amount we paid you for football in '93 and have an additional fifty percent of that amount credited to your account and a check sent to you."[12]

Camp was always the business manager and never hesitated to prompt Whitney if payments or editorial action were late. But now Camp may have had added financial pressure. The New Haven Clock Company was in peril, as finances worsened in one of the United States' most severe financial crises ever, the panic of 1893 in which banks and important railroad systems failed, agriculture declined, and unemployment rose significantly. The clock company was still not profitable, and Camp had additional responsibility because in January 1894 he had been elected to the company's board of directors. In March 1894, three months before Camp's letter to Whitney, the board had voted to issue bonds for fifty thousand dollars (roughly a million dollars in today's currency), with the condition that if those funds were exhausted and a new loan required, the affairs of the company would be placed "in the hands of a receiver, to be wound up as soon as possible." Camp could wonder how long he would have his job.[13]

Camp's dispute with Whitney and the clock company's March 1894 borrowing were unhappy preliminaries to the further distress of the Harvard-Yale 1894 game and the consequent disruption of the football rule committee.

The Harvard-Yale misery was topped off on May 10, 1895, by an amazing letter from Yale's football captain, S. B. Thorne, to Harvard's football captain, A. H. Brewer; Thorne's letter was written in response to an apparently sincere initiative by Harvard for a game with Yale. Thorne imposed conditions: To schedule a game with Yale, he stated, Harvard must first "contradict" the accusations that had been made against Yale's team. "Justice" required such a contradiction. "Should you be unwilling to do us justice in this way we have concluded to arrange no game with you."[14] Thorne said he sent the letter "under advice of coachers and prominent Yale alumni." In fact, the alumni wrote the letter.[15]

How could any responsible member of the Yale community advocate a letter so inflammatory and hopeless? It was impossible that Harvard would provide such a contradiction. The only result of Thorne's letter was to destroy all efforts to regain peace and amity between Harvard and Yale.

Within a week, Camp wrote Thorne that he was resigning as a member of Yale's advisory committee for athletics and football. To newspaper reporters, Camp denied the Harvard-Yale controversy caused his resignation. The only reason Camp said was, "I felt that I had done my share for football and was entitled to be a spectator and rest in peace for awhile."[16] Maybe. But the Thorne letter was one more self-inflicted wound by supposed colleagues preventing a peaceful and unified administration of American football. Thorne's letter was the final straw. Let someone else have their chance at managing Yale's athletics. That fall Camp left town early, in mid-October, to spend a month coaching Stanford, gone a full month smack in the middle of Yale's football schedule, "primarily," he said, "for his health."[17]

While stiff-arming Yale during the winter and spring of 1895, Harvard had been building an athletic partnership with another school—Cornell, a rapidly growing school that was something of a kindred spirit with Harvard in expanding the curriculum and academic inquiry. In just their twenty-fifth year, 1892–93, Cornell had seventeen hundred regular students, more than twelve hundred of whom were undergraduates.[18]

Cornell had played its first intercollegiate football game in 1887 and quickly grown stronger. They had played Harvard in 1890, again in 1892, and every year since. In 1894 the football bond was strengthened when Marshall Newell, Harvard's just-graduated four-year All-American, became coach at Cornell.[19]

On June 11, 1895, a month after Yale captain Thorne's aggressive letter further ruptured Harvard-Yale relations, Harvard's Professor Ames announced that Harvard had entered into a broad athletic agreement with Cornell. The proposition had "originated with Harvard" and provided a series of contests, including football, baseball, and rowing. A rowing contest was planned for June 1896—exactly the month Harvard and Yale had rowed for almost twenty years! Harvard had a substitute ready to take Yale's place.[20]

Cornell was also developing a relationship with Pennsylvania. The schools had played their first football game in 1893 and again in 1894, and beginning in 1895 Cornell would become the final game on Pennsylvania's schedule, Thanksgiving Day at Pennsylvania's new Franklin Field on the Pennsylvania campus. Harvard had also continued to partner with Pennsylvania, and Pennsylvania would still be the final game on Harvard's 1895 schedule, played the Saturday before Thanksgiving at the increasingly improved Soldiers' Field. Pennsylvania would defeat Harvard 17–14 and a few days later on Thanksgiving beat Cornell 46–2, completing a 14–0 season for Woodruff's 1895 team, their second undefeated season in a row.

As for Harvard and Yale, it was as if powerful parties on each side had thrown away limits, refusing compromise whatever the consequences. In a vengeful refusal to cooperate, they seemed to almost seek failure, preventing athletic relations and contests between Harvard and Yale to maintain what they perceived as dignity for their school and themselves.

Football rule making was caught in this disruption, despite Camp's various efforts to head it off. No meeting of the UAC rules committee or any other similar rule-making body was held in 1895. Every year since 1878, the stewards of American football, almost with a sense of fiduciary responsibility, had come together to enact a single unified set of rules. Not in 1895.

Instead, two separate groups met and wrote two separate sets of rules. Harvard, Pennsylvania, and Cornell formed one group and met during the summer to write their rules. Princeton and Yale wrote somewhat different rules, which they called the "rules of the Intercollegiate Football Association," justified by their continuing membership in that association. The only apparent cooperation was inclusion of both groups' rules in the 1895 *Spalding's Official Foot Ball Guide*. With Camp as editor, it was decided to give the public both groups' rules in a single publication.

The Princeton-Yale committee, certainly with strong input from Camp on the committee of two, made a dramatic further limitation of momentum plays, replacing the previous prohibition against "more than three men start[ing] before the ball is in play" with a rule that "not more than one man shall start forward before the ball is in play."[21]

As if to spit in the eye of the Harvard-Yale antagonists, Camp was pictured in the guide in a new full-page photo adjacent the title page, jaunty and stylish in a light-colored summer suit, with a rounded shirt collar and tie, a trimmed walrus mustache, straw hat tipped at an angle. But a jaunty photo could not hide the crisis that faced rule makers in the summer of 1895. Camp knew that multiple football rules were intolerable, potentially dividing the country's football into competing games.

35 The Future Foreseen

A Chicago reporter called the January 11, 1895, meeting "probably the most notable gathering of university men ever held in this city," bringing together presidents of large universities of the fast-growing Midwest: Cyrus Northrup, president of the University of Minnesota, with twenty-two hundred students; Charles K. Adams, University of Wisconsin, more than fifteen hundred students; William R. Harper, University of Chicago, fifteen hundred students; Henry Wade Rogers, Northwestern University, twenty-three hundred students (at least half downtown at professional schools); and Andrew S. Draper, University of Illinois, about six hundred students. The presidents had been gathered by James Smart, president of Purdue University, also about six hundred students, to consider a subject they were persuaded could no longer be avoided—greater cooperative oversight of intercollegiate athletics at their schools. Walter Camp and Yale and most of the large eastern universities had resisted such associations, but younger midwestern schools in the early stages of developing athletic programs seemed eager for consultation and cooperation on challenges facing them.[1]

Smart could be enthusiastic about intercollegiate athletics, apt to put a hug on a neighboring spectator when Purdue scored in football. He was currently trying to woo a permanent football coach—D. M. Balliet, who, after graduating from Princeton in the spring of 1894, had coached Purdue's football team the past fall, producing a winning team of "good character." Smart had proposed that Balliet "take a permanent position" at Purdue, where, given his interest in science and electricity, he could "assist in classes or laboratories, and take charge of the athletics."[2]

But Smart could also testify to "evils" in the college football world. He was quite sure, he wrote one fellow president, that men have played "who have never recited or performed a laboratory exercise in the institution" they represented."[3]

Most recently, Smart was disturbed by a disagreement with Butler College in Indianapolis. Butler had scheduled a game in that city with a semiprofessional team, the Indianapolis Light Artillery, on Thanksgiving Day 1894. Smart thought college teams should not play professional teams, but he was most upset at Butler's confrontational choice of date and place for the game. The championship game of the Indiana Athletic Association was already scheduled for Indianapolis on that day; Purdue and Depauw would be the contestants by virtue of their success in the regular season. The Butler-Artillery game, between teams from Indianapolis, would directly conflict with the Purdue-Depauw championship game.[4]

Unsuccessful in dissuading Butler's president from the competitive semiprofessional game, Smart was moved to undertake a larger effort, beginning tentatively with a letter to President Draper, his peer in the neighboring state of Illinois. First asking Draper's cooperation if the semipro Artillery tried to schedule Illinois as a replacement for Butler, Smart added at the end of the letter: "Would it not be wise for the Presidents of leading northwestern colleges including the Universities of Minnesota, Wisconsin, Michigan,

Chicago, Illinois *and possibly Purdue* to have a meeting in Chicago early in December for the purpose of considering questions of interstate athletics?"[5]

In proposing Purdue as only "possibly" included, Smart perhaps was being modest as president of a smaller college suggesting a meeting with officers of some of America's largest universities. However, he said President Northrup of Minnesota had already given some encouragement for a meeting. Draper also encouraged him, and the week before Thanksgiving Smart sent letters of invitation; in addition to the presidents listed above, he included President James Angell at the University of Michigan, who was supportive but could not attend.

The presidents were ready for a meeting. Despite accepting or even welcoming football, the presidents wanted more control. Management of contests "should be left chiefly to the students," Smart wrote, but other issues that "touch the life of the various institutions in a vital way" should be determined by the college authorities. Such vital issues included standards for "qualification of players" (he suggested a one-year-residency requirement as one qualification), the relationship between college teams and professional teams (football, he thought, was in danger of "being diverted to a scheme for money getting"), and "inducing prominent football men in one institution to matriculate to another for a consideration" (happening, he said, but not widespread).[6]

The media were already encouraging college administrators to take action. Caspar Whitney had observed a few months earlier in his *Harper's Weekly* column, "The undergraduate has just about reached the end of his tether in athletic management. Not that he is incapable . . ., but he is too partisan and the gate receipts . . . too alluring. . . . [T]he time has come for the faculties to take such action as the case demands."[7]

Smart's Indiana colleagues were also pushing for increased oversight of football. The Thanksgiving Day Butler-Artillery game had overwhelmed the Depauw-Purdue championship game, and the Indiana Association presidents were unhappy. They scheduled a meeting for December 11, 1894, and drafted regulations to be considered, which Smart forwarded to the college presidents he had invited to Chicago.

Smart could have participated in the Indiana conference, but a geographically broader conference of "leading" midwestern universities was tugging at him. An initiative by leading universities, he suggested in a letter to President Angell at Michigan, might be followed by smaller colleges: "While helping ourselves we could do a larger work in helping smaller institutions to solve some difficult problems which are now confronting them."[8]

Convening at a meeting room of the recently built Chicago Auditorium on Michigan Avenue, Smart had prepared a set of principles for discussion, but he stepped aside at the meeting to allow Adams to preside, with Rogers as secretary. There was little difficulty in reaching agreement. At the end of the meeting, Smart released twelve principles to which the presidents had subscribed, including (paraphrased except where marked with quotation marks) the following:

- A faculty committee shall be appointed at each participating university to take charge of all athletic matters at the university.
- Players on athletic teams at a university must be bona fide students, "doing full work in a regular or special course as defined in the curriculum of his college." Transfer students must wait six months to play, but those transfer rules would not apply to students in a professional or graduate school.
- No player shall be paid for playing on a university team.
- All games shall be played on grounds owned or controlled by one of the universities.
- The faculty committee of a college shall have a right of approval over team managers and captains elected by the students.
- No games shall be played with professional teams or with athletic clubs.[9]

Shades of Harvard's President Eliot. What Eliot may have aimed to accomplish with his conferences in 1882–83, these presidents seemed to be now accomplishing. Assuming faculty acceptance, the existing laissez-faire oversight of college athletics by college administrators would be replaced with a more direct and close oversight.

In contrast with Eliot, most of these presidents liked football, or were comfortable with it. As President Adams of Wisconsin stated, "Antagonism to football . . . is most intense where the person criticizing the sport knows least about it." However, their approval didn't keep them from calling "upon the expert managers of football teams to so revise the rules as to reduce the liability to injury to a minimum."[10]

Like Eliot, the presidents at the Chicago meeting sought a multi-institution control. Their universities would each have an athletic committee ready to cooperate with one another and take mutual action. Though no ongoing multi-university organization was identified, such an organization was implied.

Caspar Whitney had been a noisy whistle-blower on player-eligibility violations for some time, and the presidents' Chicago agreement did not slow him down. Near the end of the first season after the presidents' agreement, Whitney alleged in his November 23, 1895, *Harper's Weekly* column a "rottenness of the whole structure" of amateur athletics in the West, including at "the universities of Michigan, Chicago, Minnesota, Illinois, and Northwestern." As to Minnesota, Whitney contended that during the 1895 season, Minnesota paid money to a Chicago doctor (a Minnesota graduate and former player) to return to Minnesota and play. The doctor, H. A. Parkyn, was to be paid five hundred dollars "under the guise" of payments for delivering medical lectures. Whitney also claimed Minnesota had offered large sums to a former Princeton player (Hoagland) living in Chicago to play for Minnesota.[11]

Minnesota immediately denied Whitney's allegations in a public letter notarized November 29, 1895, and sent to several newspapers. The letter was signed both by Conway MacMillan, a Minnesota botany professor who had been appointed chair of Minnesota's faculty committee on athletics, and by two student officers, including the student manager of the football team, Grant Van Sant. The letter discussed and denied each of Whitney's charges, point by point.[12]

Whitney answered within a month, relying on evidence he had gathered by a quick trip to Chicago. He printed an affidavit by Hoagland avowing he was recruited to go to Minnesota but denying (and thus contradicting Whitney's initial allegation) that money was offered; instead, the Minnesota football manager, Van Sant, had allegedly promised that "we will use our influence" to secure a business position for Hoagland in Minnesota. Copies of telegrams received by Hoagland from Van Sant were attached: one stated, "Come . . . if only to talk over matters will pay expenses"; a second said, "24-0 great team but need you. Come up Sunday night sure will do all we promised."[13]

Whitney contended Parkyn had also agreed to give an affidavit but had reneged under pressure from his medical partners. As something of a substitute, Whitney published a letter from "Pudge" Heffelfinger, who coached at Minnesota during the 1895 season. Heffelfinger acknowledged that Parkyn "was undoubtedly a ringer" and was no longer seen around campus. "I was given to understand that he was a regular student at the Medical School," implying Heffelfinger had been misled by the student managers.[14]

Minnesota's faculty representative, MacMillan, decided he needed help. Two weeks after Whitney's answering article, MacMillan wrote his fellow "athletic committee chairs" to suggest a convention in Chicago. The response was positive, and seven colleges, each of those represented at the January 1895 presidents' meeting plus Michigan, sent a representative to the Palmer House in Chicago for a meeting on February 8, 1896.[15]

Chicago's representative, Alonzo Stagg, arrived at the meeting a bit late; just coincidentally, he had been meeting with the active Caspar Whitney, visiting in Chicago, and he brought an invitation from Whitney to lunch at one o'clock. The conference was having no part of that, and according to the meeting's minutes the delegates "directed the secretary to return thanks for the courtesy of the invitation and to say that brevity of time at the disposal of the conference compelled them to decline the invitation."[16]

As for the business of the meeting, the gathered faculty representatives began by voting that "this conference endorses fully the spirit of the presidents' agreement" made a year earlier. The presidents' rules were then read section by section, and modifications were made, some for clarity, others more significant. The six-month-residency requirement was made to apply to graduate and professional students, which the presidents had not done. The prohibition against play with professional teams and athletic clubs was limited to football (play with professional baseball teams was apparently okay).[17]

Beyond broad principles, the meeting wrote new regulations—practical regulations for use by a faculty committee. To deal with the issue raised by Whitney's assertions against Minnesota, it was agreed that each athlete representing a member university would be required to complete and execute a certificate of eligibility. A model certificate was provided, essentially the same as one that Harvard had begun to require.

Further, a procedure was outlined for one university to challenge another university's players, requiring the challenged university to investigate and respond to the challenging school. The challenging school was to accept in good faith the results of the challenged school's investigation.

However, "It shall be competent," the group also voted, "for the chairman of any athletic committee to lay before its own committee any charges of irregularity against the athletic committee of any other college, and a full investigation, in which both sides are represented, must be made, and the results shall then be laid before the faculty of each institution concerned."

As to another practical detail faced by athletic committees, the meeting listed expenses that the athletic committee could pay: training-table expenses in excess of a player's ordinary expenses (which he must himself pay), traveling expenses, uniforms, medical expenses, and inexpensive souvenirs for team members.

Although no formal organization had been created, a de facto organization was coming into being. The attendees stated their intention to work with one another, and the precedent was set for meetings and joint action. Explicit undertakings of cooperation had been accepted with rules to guide that cooperation.

The representatives were back again for a meeting in November 1896 and thereafter continued at least yearly. Their meetings acquired a name, "The Intercollegiate Conference of Faculty Representatives of the Athletic Committees or Boards of Control." More conveniently, newspapers began to refer to the group of universities as the "Big Seven" and later, as other colleges participated and the arrangement became more formal, the "Big Nine" or the "Western Conference," and still later the "Big Ten." (Indiana University and the State University of Iowa joined in 1899 and Ohio State University in 1912; the University of Michigan withdrew in 1908 and resumed membership in 1917.)[18]

Another multicollege athletic organization was forming in another part of the country. Southern intercollegiate football competition had gotten under way by 1888 at North Carolina, the University of Virginia, and Duke (then called Trinity); in 1890 at Vanderbilt; 1891, Tennessee; 1892, Alabama, Auburn, Georgia, Georgia Tech, and North Carolina State; 1893, Louisiana State, Texas, and Tulane; 1894, Arkansas and New Mexico State; and 1895, Mississippi State, Oklahoma, and Tulsa.[19]

The southern colleges actually beat the "Big Ten" schools by a few weeks in organizing for cooperative athletic management. Faculty members initiated this effort instead of college presidents, probably Professors Charles Herty of Georgia and William Dudley of Vanderbilt, who oversaw athletics at their schools. Faculty representatives from Alabama, Auburn, Georgia, Georgia Tech, North Carolina, Sewanee, and Vanderbilt gathered in Atlanta on December 22, 1894, to form the Southern Intercollegiate Athletic Association (SIAA).[20] Dudley was elected president and Herty treasurer of the association, which declared its object as "the development and purification of college athletics throughout the South." The organization functioned effectively for many years.[21]

No organization similar to that of the Midwest "Big Ten" or the Southern Intercollegiate Athletic Association was formed by the major eastern universities for many years. Even Harvard with Charles Eliot, who had once proposed a cooperative organization, did not push for it. With well-established programs and still dominant teams, the eastern universities seemed reluctant to join a larger organization that might limit their freedom of action. But there was a cost to such a view. Might not such an organization—with a businesslike apparatus and a background of cooperative decision making—have helped keep eastern football on a more stable path during 1894 and 1895, free of the Harvard-Yale controversy that derailed 1895 rule making?

In any event, football was spreading, and new organizations were forming, making the sport less susceptible to the control of eastern universities.

Pax Intercollegiata 36

Diplomat, politician, friend—any and all might apply to Walter Camp in the summer of 1895, as he reached out to Harvard's W. A. Brooks at the same time he struggled to overcome disruptions Brooks had caused in football rule making. Brooks, the accuser of Yale's Hinkey! The man Camp's Yale friends refused to meet.

"Billy" Brooks and Camp had been friends for several years, exchanging letters at least by 1890 and working together both on the IFA's Graduate Advisory Committee and on the UAC's rules committee. Camp was surely involved in the selection of Brooks to referee every Princeton-Yale game since 1887.

Camp got a productive correspondence under way in the summer of 1895, apparently by requesting photos from Brooks to illustrate a book or article. Brooks sent the photos, and Camp wrote a gracious note of thanks.

Brooks then responded with a letter that unburdened some of his feelings. How much he wished that Harvard and Yale men could let bygones be bygones, could get together and make a fresh start, saying nothing about "what had been." "That 'darn' letter"—his published letter accusing Hinkey—"is the one thing I regret in my athletic career." While insisting that everything in the letter was true, he recognized that subsequent events had gotten out of hand, suggesting that sometimes a perceived wrong must be overlooked for a larger good.[1]

Brooks and Camp had made peace, were still friends despite the storm that engulfed Harvard and Yale. But their resumed friendship was overlaid with a practical political fact: Brooks was still a leader in Harvard football. A relationship with Brooks might help Camp reestablish relations with Harvard as a whole, might nudge Harvard into cooperating on football rules and athletic management.

"We cannot go through another season" like last year, the secretary of the new Southern Intercollegiate Athletic Association wrote Caspar Whitney in January 1896. The previous year, rules for each game had to be compromised from the two different sets published in *Spalding's Official Football Guide.* The SIAA secretary told Whitney their association would appoint its own committee to prepare its own playing rules.[2]

Alonzo Stagg wrote Camp similarly, asking whether the eastern factions "will come together for one set" of rules. "If not, we in the west will probably come up with our own list."[3]

Different sets of football playing rules, here and there around the country, would be intolerable. Football would lose its central identity and appeal, with different games developing around different sets of rules. Negotiations would be required each time a team of one rule set wanted to play a team of a different rule set; sometimes there would be no agreement and no game.

But there was still hope. The secretary of the SIAA finished his letter to Whitney by promising that, if the two factions, Harvard-Pennsylvania-Cornell and Princeton-Yale, would "get together before next season and make a uniform set we will agree to adopt that." Stagg's note to Camp said the same.

Whatever part Camp's diplomacy may have played, this year the UAC was ready to help with rule making. At the end of February 1896, a new UAC president, Princeton graduate C. C. Cuyler, sent invitations for a rule-making meeting to the former "Big Four"—Harvard, Pennsylvania, Princeton, and Yale—plus one more, Cornell, from 1895's Harvard-Pennsylvania-Cornell faction.[4]

The invitees convened at the UAC on March 13, 1896, for a harmonious meeting. Initially, Brooks had been identified as Harvard's intended representative, but by meeting time Harvard had decided to send a new delegate, Joseph H. Sears, an 1889 Harvard graduate and former football captain. Cornell's representative was L. M. Dennis, an 1885 Michigan graduate, presently a professor of inorganic and analytical chemistry at Cornell. The remaining representatives were from the 1894 UAC committee: Bell for Pennsylvania, Camp for Yale, Moffat for Princeton.

Moffat, who had angered Harvard as referee in the 1894 game, was not reelected chairman; instead, Camp was unanimously elected both chairman and secretary. Paul Dashiell, the fifth member of the 1894 UAC rules committee, later joined the group, making a six-man committee.[5]

By April 22, the committee announced agreement on a set of rules. They had grappled with some key features:

- Momentum plays were now completely removed, eliminated by a rule that effectively continues today: one man may be in motion when the ball is snapped, but he must be moving toward his own goal.[6]
  The removal of momentum plays had happened in stages, from the 1895 Princeton-Yale rules in which Camp and Moffat installed a limit of one player moving forward before the snap to this year's total removal.
- Mass play, the close relative of momentum play, was restricted with a rule requiring that at least five men be on the line of scrimmage when the ball was put in play. Additionally, in the complicated language of compromise: if six men were behind the line, at least two must be five or more yards behind the line, *except that* if two or more were outside the ends of the rush line, all six could be within five yards of the line of scrimmage.[7]
  In effect, Camp wrote a few months later, mass play was "practically limited to four men, which does not destroy all chance . . . but certainly makes it improbable that they will be so successful as to be frequently used."
- A further attempt was made to protect the man snapping back in a scrimmage; the opponents could not interfere with him, nor could they "touch the ball until it is put in play." Nor could any player along the line interfere with an opponent to delay putting the ball in play. Camp predicted that under the changed rule, "much of the pulling and hauling" between opposing linemen would be eliminated.[8]
- As for officials, there was also a return to the past, with only three officials—referee, umpire, and linesman—as in 1894.[9]

In addition, the whole rule book was substantially reorganized, and for the first time the ball was described, very generally, as a "prolate spheroid." Spalding advertised the 1896 *Spalding's Official Football Guide* with the claim that the 1896 rules would form "the playing rules for every college, school and athletic club in the country." If so, a degree of peace and normalcy would be returning to American football.[10]

Double high and unavoidable, the headline read:

YALE'S AND HARVARD'S
TROUBLES ARE AT AN END.

Thus, the *New York World* introduced its main sports story on Monday, February 15, 1897. Further details came in a subheading: "Walter Camp and Dr. William A. Brooks Have Finally Reached and Signed a Binding Agreement," and in the story's first sentence, "After many failures Dr. Brooks and Mr. Camp have succeeded in arranging a resumption of athletic contests between Yale and Harvard." It had happened! Delayed until 1897, but happened nevertheless. True, Harvard and Yale had cooperated in 1896 to reinstate the UAC committee and produce a unified set of rules. But the school's sports teams still had not competed. Time and time again, negotiations aiming for such contests were interrupted by partisans jumping in with a demand that effectively shut the door. In 1896 Harvard and Yale did not compete in football, baseball, rowing, or dual-meet track and field. Cornell rowed Harvard on June 26, 1896, replacing the Harvard-Yale race of twenty years' duration.

Now an agreement had been written and signed, and the *World* gave Camp primary credit. He had worked for some time to get the agreement and finally got approval at a New York meeting with Yale alumni three days before the announcement.

Caspar Whitney claimed the long fight between Harvard and Yale was a blessing in disguise. As the furor died down, he sensed a broadened perspective among alumni and student leaders: "I believe it all will lessen the frenzy of winning, . . . take some of the importance out of football, and dissolve much of the business atmosphere."[11]

We know better! But in fact, a new era of stability and peace came to American football after Harvard and Yale made their agreement of 1897. In 1897 the UAC-sponsored rule committee was content with the rules of 1896: for the first time in American football's history, a rules committee made no change from the previous year's rules. Camp later recounted that a bit of worry did arise when "two or three other [football] associations . . . organized rule-making bodies and . . . formulated rules independently" of the central UAC-sponsored rules committee. Following this threat, the UAC-sponsored committee made a wholesale revision in the presentation of the 1898 rules, with titles for each rule included and one-word summaries of rule subject matter added in the page margin adjacent each rule to facilitate location of an appropriate rule.

Notes were also added after some 1898 rules with explanations and cross-references to other rules to further ease the referee's task. The first rule-book mention of a fundamental and irreplaceable football fixture was contained in the note after Rule 1: "It is desirable . . . to provide two light poles about six feet in length and connected at the lower ends by a stout cord or chain exactly five yards long." Early after enactment of the five-yard rule, officials marked ball locations on a field with a handkerchief. It is not known how long poles and a chain had been used.[12]

The 1898 revision of the rule book apparently staved off competitive rule-making bodies that could have led to plural, competing rules. Through the rest of the '90s and into the twentieth century, the composition of the rule committee stayed constant and was apparently well respected.

Striving for More 37

For more than eleven years Walter Camp had worked for a company that couldn't make a profit. Still losing money in March 1896, the company again borrowed—fifty thousand dollars, about one million dollars today. Another mortgage was placed on factory and machinery, despite the resolution just two years earlier to put the company in receivership if additional funding were required.[1]

Camp stayed with NHCC, but he increased his efforts at a writing career. One effort was to increase income from his newspaper articles through syndication. Camp apparently had this effort under way by the early 1890s and continued it for thirty or more years with various syndicates. He paid close attention to the success of a syndicate in placing his articles and pushed them to greater efforts, with the underlying threat of moving to a different syndicate.

He continued to write articles for *Century* magazine, *Harper's Weekly*, and *Outing* and in 1897 essentially took over Caspar Whitney's *Harper's Weekly* column through the football season while Whitney was on a long book-preparation trip in Southeast Asia. For a December issue, Camp named an All-America team and as a new initiative increased the number of honored players by naming first, second, and third teams.

In the summer of 1895, he joined the staff of a new monthly college-oriented magazine, *Bachelor of Arts*, in a job that seemed to offer financial and professional potential. Primarily the venture of John Seymour Wood, a graduate of Yale and then Columbia Law School, the magazine listed a creative staff of three: Wood, editor; Camp, associate editor in charge of the athletic department; and Edward S. Martin, associate editor in charge of university news, who at that time also was doing the editorial page of the nineteenth-century *Life* magazine. However, neither the magazine nor Camp's job continued long. The magazine lasted about three years, to 1898, but Camp as well as Martin were dropped from their editorial roles by May 1896. The situation was amiable enough that Camp continued to have articles published in the magazine.[2]

Camp also continued book writing, preparing a major book on football with a surprising Harvard partner, Lorin Deland, originator of Harvard's flying wedge. Deland was married to a well-published authoress, Margaret Deland, and was a capable writer himself, though he worked as a business consultant. The idea for a football book with Camp was probably Deland's; he shepherded the book to publication and undoubtedly took the main initiative in writing; Deland said they worked on it for almost two years with frequent conferences. Titled simply *Football*, the book was published in 1896 with 340 pages of text and 60 pages of diagrams. The rules for 1896 were also included, sprinkled with commentary and annotated with 1895's multiple two-faction rules.[3]

Camp also coauthored two more books. First was the well-used *Yale: Her Campus, Class Rooms and Athletics*, published in 1899 and coauthored with Lewis Sheldon Welch, an 1889 Yale graduate and former editor of the *Hartford Courant* and *New Haven Register*. Camp's name came first on the cover, though Welch wrote the largest part of the book (about 350 pages of text and 85 pages of appendixes), while Camp wrote about Yale athletics (178 pages, of which 87 pages were data—lists of contests, results, and Yale team members). The second was a book on golf, *Drives and Puts*, coauthored with avid golfer Lilian Brooks.[4]

Periodic revision of Camp's first major book, *American Football*, also required Camp's attention: 1893 brought an added chapter on team play; 1894, revisions based on the new rules; and 1896, a "new and revised edition."[5]

In the summer of 1898, Camp undertook his most public and prominent job yet, a weekly sports column in *Collier's Weekly*. A new form of national newsweekly, *Collier's* was "lighter and breezier" than *Harper's Weekly*, with triple *Harper*'s circulation. Camp now had his own column circulated to a much wider readership than he ever had through Caspar Whitney. But the demands on his time and energy, a weekly commitment with nationwide exposure, had to be the most pressing he faced outside his regular job at NHCC.[6]

A few months into his *Collier's* column, on December 24, 1898, Camp experienced a high point, his chance to name an All-America team attributable directly to him. Camp could well be proud of the All-America team, which in nine years had grown in prestige and end-of-year anticipation. By this time, the All-America idea had been copied by others; in 1898 there would be several All-America teams named besides Camp, including one by Whitney in *Harper's Weekly*. But *Collier's* large circulation would give the team even more prominence and attention.[7]

Before naming the honored players, Camp casually, but surely with purpose, set out some history: "Some ten years ago in a weekly publication since suspended, issued in New York, I described what I called, for lack of a better title, 'The All-American Football Team.'" So far as known, this explicit claim by Camp to the first All-America team in the *Week's Sport*—prominently relying on the *I* word he seldom used—was never challenged by Caspar Whitney or any other possible rival (well after the event, in a 1950 memorandum, a private fan named Clarence G. McDavitt did raise questions about Camp's claim but found no authoritative evidence disproving Camp's claim).[8]

As he had done a year earlier in 1897 when he guest-wrote Whitney's *Harper's Weekly* column during Whitney's absence, Camp named first, second, and third All-America teams:

> In selecting an All-America Team last year and this year, I have endeavored to follow out consistently what would be the course of the management if such a team were to be a real one, destined to meet an outside rival, and equipped as well as are our big teams in point of material. Every big university has for its team not eleven men, but a first eleven and a second eleven, and as many more available men as would go to make up a third eleven. . . . We should hardly do less in our selection of a national team.

Naming three teams also contributed to other possible Camp goals—a strengthening of the game by broadening the number of players who could aspire to and work toward recognition and a response to criticisms of parochialism by recognizing more players from outside the East (on the second and third teams).

Whitney named his own 1898 All-America team in *Harper's Weekly*, eleven members plus eleven substitutes. Whitney's first eleven included only seven players named on Camp's first team, and his substitutes included five players from Harvard, none of whom were on any of Camp's teams. Routinely, in the years after 1898, several All-America teams might be named at the end of a season, generally in separate publications and with differences in players named, but Camp's team in *Collier's* came to be the best recognized and most honored.[9]

In the first year of his *Collier's* column, Camp arranged for a number of guest authors to write on special subjects. But beginning in 1899, he wrote most of the columns. Also in 1899, he traveled to Europe to cover an athletic competition between Cambridge and Oxford and Harvard and Yale, and Alice accompanied him.

5 cents a copy
10 cents in Canada

Collier's

JANUARY 4, 1919 VOLUME 63 NO. 1

H. C. Witwer
"Just Like New!" the story of Ed Harmon's adventures in buying a second-hand car

Edna Ferber
"Un Morso Doo Pang," another of Miss Ferber's stories of small-town life

Lucian Cary
"Peace and the Airplane," an article on the future of air transportation

Walter Camp
"The All-America Team," Mr. Camp's annual review of the football season

Edward Mott Woolley
"Winning the War with Motor Vehicles"

Edward Hungerford
"Merchant Mariners"; training the men for America's new merchant fleet

Also in this issue: "Disorderly Conduct," by Arthur Crabb; "This Year's Automobiles," by Lucian Cary; "Lesson Number One," by R. C. Benchley; "Store-Door Delivery," by Joseph Brinker; a poem by Franklin P. Adams; Editorials, etc.

ANNUAL – AUTOMOTIVE – NUMBER

Camp named All-America teams annually in *Collier's Weekly*, from 1898 until he died, a popular attraction sometimes announced on the magazine's front cover. (*Collier's Weekly*, January 4, 1919, University of Minnesota Library)

At the same time he was building his writing career, Camp was doing his part to build the New Haven Clock Company's business. As sales manager, Camp sometimes expressed frustration at the company's business challenges: "When compared with almost any other industry," the clock business lacked the profits "needed to reward an enterprise." Yet the New Haven Clock Company was an important business in New Haven, one of the city's largest employers, with more than eight hundred employees, creating pressure for results. The *New York Times* cited the company's hiring as a barometer of Connecticut's economic performance.[10]

Camp was working on a new alarm clock that it was hoped could become a major product and help turn the company toward profitability. The company had been selling a standard alarm clock, with an alarm that rang ten to fifteen minutes. Even that long alarm did not awaken some sleepers, which prompted a new idea. "It occurred to us," Camp wrote,

> that an alarm clock made with these successive periods of noise and quiet would solve the problem. . . . We proceeded to perfect such a mechanism, and after covering it liberally with patents, we put it on the market. At that time an ordinary nickel alarm clock was sold from 75 cents to $1.00 and this special intermittent

> clock of ours, being made of a higher grade in quality besides being larger and more massive and having a large bell like a fire alarm bell on the back, we purposed selling for nearly twice what we sold the small alarm clock for.
>
> We had at that time some twenty or thirty salesmen and we showed them the clock, which we had named the "Tattoo." They were greatly interested . . . but when told the price rebelled that they did not think the clock could be sold at that price. . . . At the end of a year we were selling the magnificent total of twenty-five a day.
>
> Upon assembling our salesmen . . . they all reported the usual "I-told-you-so" that people would not purchase even the most reliable nickel alarm clock at a price much higher than they were paying for the cheap articles. [I] became rather disgusted at this attitude and determined to sell the clock direct from the factory. . . . We had some cards printed in colors illustrating a drummer boy beating a tattoo on his drum. . . . We sent out something like 50,000 of these cards, and within three weeks we were selling over 300 a day and within six weeks 500 a day.
>
> Soon after our success in stimulating demand with these cards, [I] added a case of [the clocks] to a jobber's order which came in from the South, writing the jobber a personal letter regarding the advantages of this clock. Before waiting for the receipt of these goods, the jobber wrote back that under no circumstances would he accept the case of Tattoo as he did not care to have any addition to his orders. [I] sent him an immediate apology saying that we should be very glad to take the goods back and that we had no intention of forcing them upon him. Then [I] went into [our] advertising department and instructed them on the following Tuesday to send a certain lot of these cards into the territory tributary to this jobber, following them again on Thursday with another lot of cards of a different character, and on the following Tuesday with still another lot. On Wednesday, a week from the time this plan was started, the jobber telegraphed: "Send on your Tattoo and for God's sake let up." The result of the campaign had been a steady stream of men into this jobber's store to see the Tattoo. It is needless to say that the jobber used something like 5000 during the rest of the year.[11]

Despite the success of the "Tattoo" alarm clock and an overall upturn in business at NHCC, Camp continued to look at other jobs, including an enlarged role at *Collier's*. On July 28, 1900, he wrote Condé Nast, a *Collier's* executive, about expanding "the scope of my department" and "broadening the nature of my work for the paper." He referred to previous conversations with "Mr. Collier" about the subject and laid out his understanding that the department was "proving very successful": "But to make a long story short. . . . I have studied over the situation a good deal, and while I do not see my way clear to give up entirely my other interests, it seems that if Mr. Collier and you are well satisfied with the results as you have indicated, and if you find the association as pleasant as I certainly do, an arrangement might be made whereby I should come to New York for a share of the time."[12]

Was Camp ready to leave NHCC? Perhaps not, since he says he was not ready "to give up entirely my other interests"; his goal could have been to squeeze in one more moneymaking activity. But Samuel Galpin was a youthful and well-regarded president of the company, leaving limited opportunity for Camp to advance. And Camp was clearly drawn to the writing and publishing world.

Whether it was this initiative or not, Camp did take on an added assignment for *Collier's* as manager of a new Young Person's Library. Camp's task was as much administrative as creative—selection of an editor, choice of content of the series, oversight of the selections made, ensuring submission of copy on schedule—a myriad of details that placed new demands on his time and energy.

Somehow Camp seemed on top of time demands. With a Yale professor, William Lyon Phelps, he began about 1900 to go to the New Haven Country Club nearly every day from twelve to two o'clock to play eighteen holes of golf. Camp obviously found ways to limit his NHCC job demands, presumably through delegation and focus on executive tasks. And Camp knew, said Phelps, that "it was better for the average man, who had to be in his place of business both morning and afternoon, to spend the midday interval on the links rather than at the lunch table."[13]

Camp seemed to thrive on an exceedingly full and varied life, yet he maintained balance in his life. Phelps, holder of Yale's William Lampson chair in English literature, said he developed an immense respect for Camp, not only about athletics but also "for his opinions about books, and about human nature." In spite of the many demands on Camp's time, Phelps found Camp to be "exceedingly well-read in general literature, and his criticisms of new novels and essays, and of new plays at the theatre, were original, well-founded, and penetrating." Some have concluded that Camp found his greatest fulfillment in writing and wanted to be known as a writer above all else. His writing also paid off financially; according to the *Dictionary of Literary Biography*, he was for a time one of the United States' most highly paid nonfiction writers.[14]

Yet there is another side. In candid pictures, even playing golf or diagramming a football play to a companion, Camp began to routinely have a cigarette or cigar, apparently some kind of comfort or stimulus. Back in his student days, as an advocate for intercollegiate athletics, Camp had often praised the training required of a student athlete as producing important health benefits, including abstinence from smoking and alcohol. Now, without the spur of serious athletic training, Camp's smoking had grown to a major habit, prevalent enough for a cartoonist to identify Camp in a cartoon by dressing him in a dapper striped suit and straw hat with a cigarette dangling from his mouth. In a photo taken after a game at a 1901 Yale bicentennial observance, Camp sits smoking, surrounded by twenty-five uniformed former Yale players he coached, none of whom are smoking. Camp contended that mature adults apparently were not harmed by smoking, but he later changed his mind and wrote quite forcefully and emotionally of an adult individual's need to minimize or stop smoking for good health. However, for an interval extending probably from the mid-1890s past 1910, he smoked extensively, with unknown long-term effects on his health.

During the latter years of the nineteenth century, Walter and Alice made their first house changes. In July 1896, one and a half years after Walter's mother, Ellen, died, sixty-seven-year-old Leverett married Clara Bradley, a fifty-year-old teacher who had taught at Dwight School for many years. A year later, July 26, 1897, thirty-six-year-old Alice and thirty-eight-year-old Walter had their own addition, a daughter, Janet, joining six-year-old Walter Jr.

Cartoon from an early 1900s New Haven newspaper showing Camp talking football with a friend. (Reprinted from Walter Camp, *The Book of Football*, 336)

With two children, the house on Gill Street, where they had entertained and met with Yale football players and out-of-town visitors, was becoming too small. Soon after Janet was born, Walter, Alice, and the children moved to a different home in a western suburb of New Haven, the Savin Rock area of West Haven, to a house owned by F. E. Morgan, past secretary of the New Haven Clock Company. Morgan was the son-in-law of the deceased Edward J. Stevens and held some of Stevens's stock in the company; he also seemed to be following in Stevens's footsteps, with numerous real estate investments.

The Camps apparently rented from Morgan, an exploration of a new life, exciting and romantic, in a home directly facing the Long Island Sound. It was a larger house than their Gill Street house, with room for guests, and soon after they moved Professor Sumner's wife, Jeannie, stayed with them while Sumner was away. When Alice was a youngster writing to her older professor half brother, she had used the term *Sister Jeannie* as a way to talk about Sumner's wife, and now in a letter to Sumner about Jeannie's visit Camp used the term also. He expressed their appreciation for the larger house and told of their pleasure in entertaining Jeannie. New Haven was visible across the bay, and across the street was a wide shoreline of grass-tufted sand on which six-year-old Walter Jr. could run and play, joined by Walter Sr.—if he had the time.[15]

But in little more than a year, February 1899, the home rented from Morgan was destroyed by fire. The fire occurred during the afternoon when "Mrs. Camp and . . . servants" were in the house, presumably also with at least one-and-a-half-year-old Janet. "Someone," the *New Haven Register* reported, was trying to thaw out a frozen pipe with an oil lamp and the woodwork caught on fire. A strong wind was blowing in from the sound, and within a half hour the house had been reduced to ashes. Camp lost the nearly completed manuscript of a new book plus clippings he had accumulated for use in writing. But he consoled himself with the thought that if the fire had occurred at night, it might have been difficult for everyone in the household to get out of the house safely.[16] The Camps then lived temporarily in Woodmont (another shoreline community but farther from New Haven), and in 1900 they moved to a new development in New Haven, 30 Everitt Street, a few blocks from the home of Professor and Jeannie Sumner.

In 1899 Walter Camp's father, Leverett, moved to New York City, and in 1900 Walter's uncle and aunt Henry and Elizabeth Peck moved to Woodmont, thereby completely emptying the mini family compound that had been Walter and Alice's first home place after their marriage.[17]

More than a Game 38

In his inaugural *Collier's* column, August 13, 1898, Walter Camp preached a mild sermon, starting from an observation about American character: "The American people worship success and reward it with an extravagance beyond that exhibited by other nations. That worship extends to sport, and it is reflected in every contest in which Americans are engaged." Camp wanted it understood he wasn't criticizing winning: "This column will never preach the doctrine of 'not caring which wins,' for such a belief . . . [would bring] . . . farewell to the best part of our indomitable spirit—our good Yankee pluck! . . . Let us hope we never outgrow the determination to win, to make the most of every opportunity, to strive until the very end, never giving up, never despairing, but looking to the goal." Yet Camp wanted change, a new attitude toward athletic contests, "a little more praise for the performance itself, a little more love of the play, a little less flaunting of . . . victory."[1]

As Camp grew older, he developed a philosophy about sports competition and became increasingly public about it. At student banquets, he recited lines from a poem that he now made the opening lines of his *Collier's* column:

> Who misses or who wins the prize,
> Go lose or conquer as you can;
> But if you fail or if you rise
> Be each, pray God, a gentleman!

"Gentleman" had clear meanings for Camp: "A gentleman always plays to win. There is a tacit agreement between [contestants] that each shall do his best, and the best man shall win." "Gentlemen do not cheat nor do they deceive themselves as to what cheating is." A gentleman was courteous and did not cheer an error by opponents. After winning a race or match, "healthy young men should do plenty of cheering but not at the expense of insulting the loser."[2]

The lines of the Thackeray poem and Camp's elaboration were quite high-sounding, but contemporaries believed they represented true conviction. After reporting Camp's use of the poem's lines, Caspar Whitney wrote in *Harper's Weekly*, "As player Walter Camp followed this precept [and] as coach he insisted on its observance." For Camp, the poem's words went beyond manners to the heart of what athletic competition was all about. Pure athletic competition had been primary for Camp from the start, the athletic performance and experience, the determined competition, the mental challenge of tactics and strategy, the physical contact, the bond with fellow teammates, all to be conducted according to principles of sportsmanship, without a thought otherwise.[3]

Camp loved and was motivated by athletic competition, but he also advocated its use for educational purposes that served the public good. Particularly he thought football would lead to improved habits and traits of character in student players: "Nature has provided in the boy's love of personal physical combat and competition the real suggestion as to how [to instill desired habits and character traits]. . . . [S]chool and college championships . . . act as incentives to physical culture. . . . Training means restraint and temperance and ultimate perfect physical condition. Without the game there would be little interest and without the rivalry there would be no training."[4]

But now in the late 1890s, the availability of pure athletic competition and its educational benefits were in jeopardy because American football was changing. Change had come as the games became more important, were attended by larger numbers of people, and were taken more seriously by ever-larger numbers of students, alumni, and others having a school or geographic loyalty. As far back as 1891, Camp had called spectators a major problem threatening amateur athletics. In a magazine article in *Outing*, he illustrated first with gate receipts: in 1890 Princeton and Yale had each received about $180,000 in today's dollars from the Thanksgiving Day game. Such sums of money worried Camp, that somehow they might compromise the amateur ideal. Already he knew some teams anxious for success were offering financial inducements in their effort to recruit players.[5]

Spectators were also a concern, Camp wrote, because they sometimes placed harmful pressure on players, referees, administrators, and rule makers. Sometimes, he said, they aimed abuse at an official who had disqualified a player rather than at the player whose actions caused the disqualification. And spectators encouraged players and captains to overlook eligibility questions about a particular player who would help the team win. Players soon learned that spectators considered "victory . . . more [important] than methods," whereupon the players became "more apt to forget small deceits . . . [with a] feeling that the end justifies even somewhat shady means."[6]

Another change in American football, having both pluses and minuses, was the deepening involvement of coaches. By 1898, when Camp began his *Collier's* column, coaching was becoming a full-time career. John Heisman, an

1891 graduate from the University of Pennsylvania Law School, coached part-time at Oberlin and Akron in 1892–94 and then gradually became full-time at Auburn from 1895 to 1900; he moved to Clemson in 1900 and to Georgia Tech in 1905. Glenn Warner, a Cornell player and graduate, in 1895–96 began coaching at Iowa State for a few late-summer weeks and at Georgia the rest of the season; he was at Cornell in 1897–98 and beginning in 1899 at Carlisle Indian Industrial School (a vocational school that aimed to assimilate Native American youth into Western-style culture); at the end of his first season at Carlisle, he became the school's full-time sports teacher and coach. Fielding Yost graduated from the University of West Virginia Law School in 1897 and then coached a year each at Ohio Wesleyan, Nebraska, Kansas, and Stanford, before moving to Michigan in 1901 for a long and prominent career. Yale graduate Henry (Harry) Williams began coaching at the University of Minnesota in 1900 and achieved a long era of successful teams.

With increased coaching came increased expectations, accompanied by increased perils for coaches. Winning became more important, and a brief lull in winning forced George Woodruff out as coach at Pennsylvania, the first such coaching casualty. Woodruff had coached Pennsylvania to a record sixty-seven wins out of sixty-nine games in 1894 through 1898, but there was grumbling in 1899 when Pennsylvania faltered to an 8-3-2 record, losing to Harvard as well as Carlisle and Lafayette. Then, after Pennsylvania recovered to 12-1-0 in 1900, the next year followed at 10-5-0. Most significantly, in all four years, 1898–1901, Pennsylvania lost to Harvard. Philadelphians and Pennsylvanians had grown accustomed to better results, and Woodruff stepped aside after the 1901 season and gave full time to practicing law.[7]

Other changes occurring around football made the whole game event more enjoyable and popular but also bigger, with greater attendance and greater spectacle. Music and cheering became more organized, and bands began to appear. A University of Minnesota band that had been formed in the 1870s to assist and enliven military drill received new life when football came along. By the mid-1890s, the band was parading the streets before games and playing from the sidelines during the games.[8]

In 1898 an informal band of about twenty Michigan students traveled to Chicago for a Michigan-Chicago game and saw a spectacular Michigan win. After the game, an inspired Michigan student, Louis Elbel, from a musical family in South Bend, Indiana, walked to his sister's house, and "a band got to singing in my head, a sort of victory sound." The refrain of a song came to him, not only the music but some words, "Hail to the Victors, Valiant!" and "Hail to the conquering heroes!" At his sister's house, he wrote the notes down and over the next few days thought the piece through to a full-scale march. "The Victors" was the prototype for a new genre, a "fight song" to inspire the best from college teams. Singing at games had been important at Yale and other colleges from early in intercollegiate football competition, but now Elbel had created a new song that was at another level, more creative, memorable, and stirring.[9]

Two years after Michigan's "Victors," Yale got its own fight song, credited to a Yale student from Richmond, Virginia, Allan M. (Pop) Hirsch; Hirsch was a sort of song and cheerleader at football games. Sometime, probably the summer of 1900, a strain of music came to Hirsch, and together with friends he wrote it out in musical notation and words and called it the "Boola" song. The song came in verse and chorus, and it was the chorus especially that set a crowd swinging and dancing, with Hirsch waving a baseball bat as a baton. In 1900, the year "Boola" was written, Yale defeated Harvard at Yale Field, 28–0, completing a twelve-win season with no losses or ties. When the game ended, Yale students surged over the railings and across the field, lifting Yale players and carrying them on their shoulders. With the Yale band leading the way and Camp perhaps watching from the sidelines, they marched around the field, "swinging from side to side like a great snake, while a thousand voices sang the 'Boola Chorus.'"[10]

A different feature of the growing spectacle was illustrated a day or two after the game when a Boston newspaper printed a cartoon that dramatized Yale's vigorous triumph. It featured a bulldog named "Handsome Dan" bounding in flying leaps, carrying in his mouth John, the Harvard orange peddler. Unable to resist, John and his peddler wagon were being carried away to the "Yale camp."[11]

The Handsome Dan of the cartoon had a real-life model, the pet of a Yale student, Andrew Graves. Graves had named him Handsome Dan and took him everywhere, including 1889 football games, where Dan endeared himself to Yale fans by barking whenever Yale scored. He continued to appear—by at least 1891 he was parading on the sideline, and by at least 1892 Yale's team was referred to as the "bulldogs." A bulldog was prominent in a *New York World* headline of November 25, 1892, with a banner around the neck identifying him as "Handsome Dan." The headline also referred to Princeton as the Tigers, a name that had been developing for the orange-and-black-striped team since the 1880s.[12]

The largest spectacle in American football in the 1890s undoubtedly was the annual Thanksgiving Day game in New York City between Princeton and Yale. Despite the game's popularity, many college officers and observers began to see it as presenting too many challenges. In January 1897, the University Athletic Club, surely with Camp's involvement, recommended a move to the campus and gave reasons essentially as follows:

- The game is becoming a public spectacle, no longer seen as a game between college students, but a public exhibition offered to obtain large gate receipts, which is injurious to the interests of amateur sport.
- The excitement created over the game leads the press to publish sensational articles that greatly exaggerate after-game events attributed to students.
- Management of the game by students is preferred, but the distance between New York and the students' campus residences makes such management difficult.
- Tickets are in too much demand and subject to speculation.
- The best available playing ground in New York—Manhattan Field—is designed for baseball, making a large proportion of seats too far from the football playing surface. Also, less than half the stands are covered (of course, none of the stands would be covered at most college grounds).

A more specific Camp involvement came one month later, in the February 1897 agreement he and Dr. Brooks negotiated to reinstate athletic competition between Harvard and Yale. That agreement specified that all contests between Harvard and Yale, except boat races, would be played on college grounds.[13]

For Camp, the lover of pure athletic competition, American football was attracting too many spectators, too much partisanship, too much spectacle—he actually called the game "overpopular" in the February 1894 *Century*. But there is a contradiction. Camp continued with the newspaper, magazine, and book writing that helped build that popularity. And he wasn't about to stop writing. The income was important—at times his syndicated newspaper column produced a thousand dollars or more in monthly income. Camp might fume at incidents of "overpopularity," but he made little effort to limit the surging media attention that contributed to American football's problematic excesses.[14]

Whatever the contradictions, amateur play and sportsmanship were still prominent in his thinking. The first major subject Camp wrote about in his nationally distributed *Collier's* column was sportsmanship—seeking greater appreciation for the play and less flaunting of victory. And he continued to open essentially every one of his *Collier's* columns with the "Be a gentleman" poetic lines. Camp could seem moralistic and potentially hypocritical, but at the same time competitors asked him to referee their games and wanted him as a football rule maker for life. A Princeton professor later looked back and said that Camp's "influence crossed borders, drawing colleges closer in friendly competition, joining sportsmen in a common devotion to the idealism of sport."[15]

39 Officially a Yale Official

Sports-related work for Yale had long appealed to Camp, and others had pushed him for it. Professor Richards unsuccessfully agitated in *Popular Science* magazine in 1884 for Yale to hire Camp as an athletic supervisor, and in an 1895 speech Richards got more specific, advocating an "Athletic Directorship in the Yale faculty" and naming Camp as "the man he wanted for this important place."[1]

Nothing happened until fall 1899, when Arthur T. Hadley was elevated from a Yale professorship to become the new university president. Camp met with Hadley, who soon reported that the subject of a position for Camp at Yale

> was considered in a meeting of the Prudential Committee of the Corporation three weeks ago. The feeling was expressed in that Committee that you could do a great deal of service to the College as athletic advisor and a sort of assistant dean to the various faculties; but assistant dean did not seem exactly the right title. . . . The Corporation would probably be ready to give any name to your position which should dignify it to the utmost, provided it really described the work you were doing; but that we ought not to appoint you for one purpose and call it by [an inaccurate] name.[2]

Hadley in fact did hire Camp soon after taking office in 1899 into a paid position he called "treasurer of the Yale Field and graduate adviser in athletics"; Hadley said he considered the job equivalent to "head of a department . . . and analogous to that of an independent dean." Camp continued his work at NHCC and his writing for *Collier's* and others, but found time to advise and carry out special assignments for Hadley on athletic matters. Hadley took a western trip to meet Yale alumni groups soon after appointing Camp and confided in a January 23, 1900, letter to Camp, "There was nothing in all that I said in the West which awakened more enthusiasm than the mention of your name and its closer connection with organized Yale athletics."[3]

Camp had worked on athletic matters for Yale for many years, but this new assignment for Hadley in effect made Camp Yale's "athletics director," probably the first job of its kind and further recognition of the growth of college athletics. In 1902, when Hadley created a University Council as a main university administrative organ, he placed Camp on it, listing him first under the heading "treasurer of the Yale Field," and in 1904 more regularly on the roster of faculty members on the council with responsibility for "Athletic Organizations." In support of his work at a faculty-level position, Camp was awarded in 1908 an honorary master of arts degree from Yale.[4]

One of the first matters Hadley assigned to Camp was a request from Professor Munro of Brown College that Camp represent Yale at a New York conference of colleges aiming to develop competition standards. This conference appeared to be an outgrowth of an 1898 Brown conference that Yale had not attended. Camp was skeptical of the value of such conferences; the 1898 conference, Camp wrote Hadley, had been convened when Brown found itself legitimately charged with professionalism and called the conference an "experience meeting" that would rid an institution of its confessed "sin." The reason for the presence of other delegates was "chiefly to make the university which has sinned feel less chagrined over confession." The Brown conference came to nothing in Camp's view and died after a year or so. Now in 1900, it had apparently come to life again, this time with Columbia (coached by Yale graduate George Foster Sanford) "as the storm center" and subject, Camp said, to "public disgrace." At least four players were not bona fide students and were paid to play.[5]

Camp reported to Hadley that he consulted with Munro on the issues to be raised at the New York conference, giving "him my assistance in commenting upon the various rule proposals and approving or disapproving of them in the light of my past experience." But Camp did not attend the conference, writing Hadley that he considered it "merely a repetition of the old story of insatiable appetite for convention and legislation."[6]

In addition to work for Hadley, Camp in 1900 continued an active advisory role in football coaching at Yale, part of a system in which he was said to "coach the coaches." The captain typically selected a new head coach at

Yale (often the previous year's captain), and in most years that head coach and the captain consulted with Camp. Camp's involvement had been less in 1895–99 (mostly by Camp's choice), but in a majority of other years the captain and coach chose to have Camp involved.

Camp's friend and coauthor Lorin Deland described in *Atlantic Monthly* how the system typically worked. During the winter months, Camp analyzed the previous season's results both at Yale and around the country. He and the captain and new coach then discussed and developed strategies and ideas on team personnel for the next season. Through Camp's analysis of play by a number of teams, Deland said, Yale always had the latest development. Once the season began, the captain and head coach often came to Camp's home in the evenings, where they discussed the day's practice, points in dispute, and matters of development and policy, with Camp "advising, supplying data, giving reasons for every proposed action."[7]

One part of the system, reflecting Camp's penchant for studied analysis and preparation, was to keep a book in which the captain or coach kept a record of daily practices and the work done, including improvement or regression and the apparent reasons. This book had been kept for many years, and each year the former year's record was studied and additions made. Although the system was voluntary, past coaches, students, and alumni applied pressure to use it. "To know how the Yale team is doing," a previous captain reported, they found out whether "the coaches . . . are going up to Walter's every night." If they were, "then we know the team is going to be a good one."[8]

Camp's involvement in 1900 was an especially happy one that he wrote about more than once. In a semianonymous style that left his role apparent and admirable, he told of "a graduate advisor" who during the winter of 1899–1900 persuaded the upcoming Yale football captain and field coach to try a new method of play developed by the graduate adviser (Camp). Although not mentioned by Camp, his development apparently started from a "tackle-back tandem" play developed by Yale graduate "Harry" Williams at William Penn Charter School in Philadelphia, which Williams taught Army in 1899 to help them upset Navy in the newly reinstated Army-Navy game.[9]

In the basic tackle-back tandem play, a tackle moves out of the line and takes a position in the backfield behind the other tackle, thus forming a tandem of blocking power. Essentially, the tackle-back play was a kind of mass play, but Camp added refinements and built a new system—for example, adding plays that seemed to begin with the tackle-back movements but then veered into a different play or attacked a different point in the line. Camp's system also included perhaps American football's first "mousetrap" play, with the Yale lineman at the point of attack allowing his opponent to charge through and then diverting him to the side, leaving a spot for the ball carrier to run through.[10]

Adding drama to the story, Camp wrote that in describing the new system to the captain and field coach, the "graduate adviser" warned that the new system's movement of heavy players into the Yale backfield would slow up the offense's attack, causing difficulty in early games of the season until the system was perfected through practice and games. The warning proved correct, with Yale winning only after close challenges in some games, and the captain and field coach grew worried that the new system would not succeed in the upcoming big Harvard and Princeton games. They wanted to quit the system, but the graduate adviser managed to persuade them to continue. In a glorious end to the season and story, Yale achieved dominant wins over a strong Carlisle team (35–0), Princeton (29–5), and Harvard (28–0).

The advances beyond a typical tackle-back tandem play were evident in reports of the Harvard game, which speak of the exhaustion of the Harvard players and the "severe strain across the loins which came from frequent 'pocketing' ["trapping"?] cleverly contrived in the shifting point of attack." Yale continued to use the system in subsequent years, as did other teams in the East; according to Deland, though, there were enough subtleties in Camp's development and teaching that other teams had difficulty in duplicating the Yale system or defending against it.[11]

Yale's coaching was respected and studied by others. When Harvard hired a recent graduate, Bill Reid, as its head football coach in 1905, Reid made it a point to study Yale's coaching methods and playing techniques. He prepared written reports, summarizing techniques and strategies learned from Yale and listing reasons for studying Yale: "In the past fifteen years Yale coaches have taught Yale football to most of the smaller Eastern colleges, notably Dartmouth, Amherst, Bates, Williams, Andover, Exeter, Worcester, etc. Most of the best coaching on the Pacific coast has arisen from work done by men teaching Yale methods and Yale style." In his diary, Reid worried about a contemplated rule change, because Yale, "with Camp's inventiveness, would very likely take the lead." Yale continued to have a dominant football record. During Camp's first head coaching stint in 1888 through 1892, Yale's football record was 67-2. From 1892 through 1906, as the "coach of coaches" system developed, Yale's football record was 152 wins, 9 losses, and 7 ties. Yale continued to be recognized as the country's leader in football and athletic sports generally.[12]

The huge athletic success contributed to an outsize Yale image: F. Scott Fitzgerald created a Yale-athlete character in one of his short stories and described him as "handsome, successful at everything he tried, a living symbol of the splendid, glamorous world of Yale." And Yale's athletic dominance undoubtedly encouraged sports fiction's first big American success, the adventures of the amazingly heroic Frank Merriwell. Merriwell was several times larger than life, what the author, Gilbert Patten, writing under the pen name Burt L. Standish, claimed was "every boy's ideal picture of himself": incomparably athletic, brave, honest, intelligent, humane, and compassionate.[13]

Merriwell's adventures were usually set at Yale, and he never seemed to lose. Heroic deeds filled every issue—Frank might be captured by opponents before an important game but would escape just in time to pull Yale through. Each week beginning April 18, 1896, and continuing for seventeen years, the magazine *Tip Top Weekly* carried a Frank Merriwell story—twenty thousand words about Frank and his exploits; later issues centered on Frank's brother, Dick, and son, Frank Jr. Cumulatively, the stories would fill 204 books of eighty thousand words each. The stories were extremely unrealistic but found a large audience, and many Yale students reported being drawn to the school by the images they developed as young boys reading the Frank Merriwell stories.[14] As the most visible figure in Yale's athletic program, Camp may have appreciated the Merriwell stories and the promotion they offered Yale, though he surely smiled and perhaps occasionally winced at the extravagance common to the stories.

40 Not Done Yet

Without warning on Friday or Saturday, August 1 or 2, 1902, the New Haven Clock Company received alarming news. The company's president, Samuel Galpin, a widower touring London with his son Harry just graduated from Yale, had been brought to a hospital suffering from typhoid fever.[1]

Sunday was quiet, and better news came on Monday: Galpin had improved; his chances of recovery were good. But early Tuesday, there was another cablegram; Galpin had worsened on Monday and died about nine at night, London time, with son Harry and the company's English representative, Frank Stevens, standing by helplessly.[2]

Death of the fifty-six-year-old president was a shock in New Haven and at the clock company. Beginning in the late 1890s, the company had begun to turn around, finally moving toward profitability. Galpin was credited for much of the improvement, "the man who saved the company," preserving one of New Haven's major businesses and employers. Who would take his place? Could the improvement and good results continue without him?[3]

The next-ranking executive at the company was Walter Camp, certainly a potential successor. And Camp was soon named to serve as general manager. But Camp was famed for outside interests—football, books, a regular column in *Collier's,* other newspaper and magazine writing. Some might doubt he had time to be the chief executive of a worldwide business.[4]

Weeks passed with no successor to Galpin named. The two dominant shareholders, Pierce Welch and Henry English, as well as others outside the company, were rumored as candidates. Weeks stretched to months—September and October, no announcement; November, December, no announcement. At year's end, almost five months after Galpin's death, the company still had no president.[5]

Behind the scenes, moves were being made and people being convinced. The delay likely was as much Camp's doing as the company's. Camp wanted further capital invested to prepare for future growth, and he was working to get further investment from Messers. English and Welch. It took some doing and was accompanied by replacing all existing shares in the company with new shares and a newly valued capitalization. A. O. Jennings, a company director, later wrote Camp, "I had no idea that either Mr. Welch or Mr. English could be brought in so deep."[6]

The first hint of a break came at the beginning of January 1903, when *Collier's* announced that Camp's column would be replaced with a new column by a new writer. This probably was Camp's decision, recognizing a need to reduce his outside workload, or perhaps it was a requirement by company directors. But then January also passed without any company announcement and most of February.

The waiting and maneuvering ended February 26, 1903, with a public announcement: Walter Camp would in fact be the new president of the New Haven Clock Company. At age forty-three, he was now in charge of one of New Haven's largest employers and a leader in America's clock industry.[7]

Some things would not change despite his new role at the clock company. About a month after being named NHCC president, Camp joined the rest of the football rules committee in Atlantic City to enact rule amendments for the 1903 season. He had been working on football rules since 1878, nearly twenty-five years, and he was not done yet.[8]

The New Haven Clock Company quickly experienced a number of important developments during Camp's first years as president—increased company profitability sufficient to restore dividends, the first since 1885; purchase of the company's English subsidiary, providing greater control and freedom of operation; and major expansion of the company's watchmaking facilities to help build a business in pocket watches. At the same time, Camp accepted new roles outside NHCC. President Hadley's appointment of Camp to the Yale University Council came the year before his appointment as NHCC president. Uniquely, Camp was now president of a worldwide clock company as well as a paid university administrator responsible for a significant part of university life. That was all in addition to his many roles in football—rule maker, coach, frequent writer in newspapers and magazines and of books, altogether the best-known figure in American football.[9]

In addition, there was community service. In 1903 he was named to the board of trustees and elected secretary-treasurer of Hopkins Grammar School, the private preparatory high school he had attended. The school was impoverished, having difficulty paying teachers' salaries and lagging in educational efforts. Camp got busy, sending the board detailed financial reports, calling on a number of sources for small donations to meet immediate needs, pushing for an increased endowment. "Stimulated by the activity of Walter Camp," the school's historian reports, the trustees undertook other changes—"revised courses to meet new college entrance requirements, rewrote catalogues and composed new advertising" as well as "increase[d] the teachers' salary budget." The school survived this difficult period, and Camp was credited as important to that result. Camp would continue as secretary-treasurer until 1917.[10]

All in all, Camp must have seemed at the pinnacle of worldly success. But there's that old saying, "Pride goeth before . . ."

PART VI

The New Game

"The Game I Have Worked So Hard For" 41

"If in four consecutive downs a team shall not have advanced the ball ten yards, it shall go to the opponents." Except for stylistic word changes, the above rule has been fundamental in American football for more than one hundred years, well proved and routinely accepted without question. But getting to that rule involved the most trying episode in Walter Camp's rule-making life.

The episode didn't seem so troubling when it began in the late 1880s, arising from an increasing reliance on "mass play" in which players on offense gathered in wedges or other concentrations (usually by moving linemen into the backfield) to pound forward with pointed force against a spot in the defensive line. Scattered criticism began to be heard as mass play became more common: it promoted injury, hid action in a pile of players, and displaced "open play," such as end runs, cross-field laterals, and kicks that allowed spectators to easily follow the ball and better see and appreciate athletic performance.

Camp responded to mass-play criticism early, in the January 21, 1893, *Harper's Weekly* article discussed earlier, "A Plea for the Wedge in Football," where he argued that mass play should be limited but not totally abolished; a team should have a variety of plays to choose from, and the creation of such plays and the decision of when to use them was "a chief charm of the game." Still, mass play needed to be limited, and Camp contemplated ways to get teams to voluntarily reduce it. In late 1893, in a newspaper symposium conducted by the *Boston Herald*, he proposed among different ideas that the distance to be gained in three downs be doubled from five yards to ten yards, drawing some notice and favorable comments in the press.[1]

A 1903 mass play from tackle-back tandem formation. (Reprinted from Alexander M. Weyand, *The Saga of American Football*, facing page 112)

Initially, Camp presented the idea as a subject for discussion, proposing that coaches meet to consider his and others' suggestions, but he claimed that by 1896 he was trying to persuade the rules committee to pass the ten-yards-in-three-downs rule. That 1896 effort was unsuccessful, possibly because of distractions arising from efforts to reunite the rule-making committee and eliminate momentum plays (see chapter 36).[2]

Camp said he tried again in 1902, 1903, and 1905, and again was unsuccessful, in part because now significant opposition had developed within

A mass play with hurdling. (*Century* 71 [November 1905]: 103, University of Minnesota Library)

the rules committee. Some committee members were convinced that new playing methodology had to accompany the ten-yard rule to assist the longer advances the rule would require. One commonly mentioned idea was to intentionally weaken the defense by requiring that defensive ends position themselves at least five yards behind the line of scrimmage at the time of snapback, thereby making it harder for the defense to stop an end run aiming at a longer yardage gain. A different suggestion was to spread players apart by marking the field with quadrangles, each four yards by five yards, and require that at snapback, "only one player on the same team shall be standing in any one of the quadrangles." Without some such new method, it was argued, games would degenerate into kicking games: unable to gain ten yards in their first two downs, teams would be forced to kick on the third down, thus creating another boredom—repeated, mind-numbing failure to advance, followed by another kick.[3]

Camp's answer was that the ten-yards rule would force captains and coaches to innovate. And he believed they would do it. It seemed like an article of faith to him—creative Americans would find a way in the face of demonstrated need. Perhaps they would devise new plays. Or through extra effort, they might improve execution of more complicated plays using double handoffs, reverses, misdirection long laterals, or the like to make longer gains. Camp personally perhaps visualized new variations of his basic tackle-back plays. But rules-committee dissenters resisted, and having served on the rules committee for several years they were sufficiently confident to prevent the unanimous agreement the committee had long required—in fact, they revealed stubborn conviction, at least as stubborn and sure of themselves as Camp soon showed himself to be.[4]

Public unhappiness grew as year after year, the rules committee failed to act while mass play continued unabated. Instead of enacting the ten-yard rule that Camp thought would directly limit mass play, the committee grasped at what Camp called experiments, one of which in 1903 made America's football fields into checkerboards instead of gridirons. Under a new rule, the quarterback was allowed to run with the snapbacked ball, if he first ran laterally five yards before turning upfield (thus preventing a quick mass-play plunge into the line). To assist in judging the required five-yard lateral movement, the field was to be marked with lines parallel to the sideline, five yards apart and combining with the existing "gridiron" lines (parallel to the goal line) to form checkerboard squares.[5]

Weary of the rules-committee impasse, experiments, and public criticism, in January 1905 Camp wrote Benjamin I. Wheeler, former professor of Greek at Cornell and now president of the University of California. Camp and Wheeler had become friendly, and Camp let his hair down, "as if you were sitting here and we could talk it over." He wrote of "amateur rule makers" who were making unrealistic suggestions intended to "save" the game. Reflecting unusual frustration, Camp uncharacteristically suggested—"in strict confidence"—that the amateurs included fellow rules-committee members such as Dr. L. M. Dennis, chair of the rules committee who had been Wheeler's colleague at Cornell.[6]

Camp said he admired Dennis "most highly" and had always "cared for him greatly." But in Camp's opinion, Dennis had been suggesting ideas that were unworkable and arose because Dennis no longer followed the sport "closely" to see "what the effect of the rules would be." Men like Dennis seemed to have a fascination for changing rules, "just for the sake of seeing what would happen" and without "seriously caring what does happen anyway." The result was that he would take "bigger chances than you or I who care for the sport and want to see it perpetuated." Camp wanted "the game which I have worked so hard for [to] keep its general characteristics." When legislators suggested "fool[ing] with the defense" and specifying with rules the positions that defensive players were required to occupy, "it makes me feel like throwing up my hands at the hopeless entanglement that will ensue."

Despite his frustration and the public's unhappiness, Camp was dismissive of other new proposals—for example, suggestions for a "forward pass." But what was that? Forget today's forward pass. In 1905 the term *forward pass* had no single commonly accepted meaning. John Heisman had seen a forward pass used accidentally in an 1895 game in Georgia—what seems to have been a short forward lateral in the backfield—and decided it could be beneficial. Writing in 1908, he recalled:

> in 1901, 1902 and 1903 . . . the cry for a more open style of play began to become prolonged and insistent. All sorts of suggestions to open up the game appeared in print, some good, some bad. In 1903 after the season I wrote Mr. Walter Camp of the Rules Committee and suggested that . . . no easier or more certain way of [opening up the game] could be devised than by allowing forward passing. This opinion I also confided at the time to several of my friends and other football experts.
>
> Nothing came of it that year and the "howl" grew louder. In December, 1904, I wrote Mr. Camp again and to the same effect.[7]

Camp and other veteran football proponents had well-established ideas about the essential nature of American football, and forward passing did not fit in such a game. In a disparaging put-down, longtime coach Glenn Warner wrote that "basketball techniques" had no part in American football, which was a game of "rushing or kicking." Camp, Warner, and others had built successful games based on running and kicking, learning to advance with runs supported by well-executed, coordinated blocking schemes.[8]

Passing would cause a huge reconstruction of the game, and who could predict the consequences? Moreover, it would bring more experimentation, more trial and error, requiring endless working out in detail of rules that would be only tentative. Camp saw his own suggested ten-yard rule as simple and direct, not such a step into the unknown. Before experimenting with a forward pass and risking destruction of the existing game, Camp was convinced the rules committee should give the ten-yard rule a chance.

Others on the 1905 rules committee tried to work out a compromise. As a rule-making meeting approached in June 1905, Pennsylvania's longtime representative, John C. Bell, publicly stated that in a spirit of compromise, he would allow forward passes if the passes did not cross the line of scrimmage. He cautioned that he would not accept passes beyond the line of scrimmage, because then the "entire fabric of the game would be altered and the present sport would pass out of existence." When the committee met on June 12, 1905, they talked until "long after midnight" on forward passes and open play, but it was only talk, with no agreement. The committee still required unanimity on rule changes, and that did not exist for either the ten-yard rule or for changes in playing methodology such as weakening the defense or allowing forward passes. In the end, the committee agreed on only a few small changes.[9]

The committee now had tried for at least three years to deal effectively with the issues of mass play but without success. Had the old system broken down, incapable of dealing with the mass-play issue?

The paralyzed committee not only left Camp and other committee members frustrated, but it also excited public agitators. A few months after the ineffective June 1905 rule-making meeting, a trustee of Columbia University wrote to Columbia's president, Nicholas Butler, complaining of football's "abominable" deficiencies and attributing them to the football rules committee, which he angrily described as "self-perpetuating, non-representative, pig-headed, oblivious to public opinion and obstinate." He argued the existing committee should be replaced by a new rules committee appointed by presidents of specified eastern universities.[10]

Butler forwarded his trustee's idea to President Eliot of Harvard, who responded with his own attack: "I should not care to join in appointing a committee on rules for football in the manner proposed. . . . Mr. Camp . . . seems to be as powerful today as he ever was at Yale and elsewhere, and would undoubtedly be appointed the Yale member of a new committee. I should never have any faith in his superintendence of football reform, inasmuch as he is directly responsible for the degradation and ruin of the game."[11]

The seventy-one-year-old Eliot's antagonisms against football and Camp were as pronounced as ever; now in an atmosphere of expanding criticism, he may have sensed an opening for his desired (undefined) makeover of the game. His annual report released in February 1905 contained several pages under the heading "The Evils of Football": "The game of football has become seriously injurious to rational academic life in American schools and colleges. . . . [I]t is time the public, especially the educated public, should understand and take into earnest consideration the objections to this game." Eliot said his "main objection" lay in the "moral quality" of football. It had "become a game in which the actions of the individual players can often be entirely concealed" from spectators as well as umpires because mass play hid foul play. Uniform enforcement of the rules became impossible, and "violations of the rules are in many respects highly profitable toward victory." As examples of such violations, he listed illegal holding of players, disabling opponents by kicking and kneeing, and heavy blows around the head. Some players were never guilty of such violations, he acknowledged, some only when they lost their tempers, but some were habitually guilty of them.[12]

More than reforming, Eliot wanted American football replaced, and that idea also resonated within the Harvard Corporation and Board of Overseers. Rumors of a possible ban on football at Harvard—another ban!—reached Herbert White, Harvard's graduate manager of football, and he promptly called Bill Reid, the new Harvard football coach. (Ironically, in view of Eliot's strong opposition, other Harvard constituencies were pushing for greater Harvard commitment to football. Eager to improve Harvard's success, they had hired Reid with a stupendous effective salary of seven thousand dollars per year [half from the school and half from alumni], compared to the highest Harvard professor's salary of six thousand dollars and Eliot's effective salary of eight thousand.) Together, White and Reid sounded an alarm and gathered Harvard assistant coaches Bertram Waters and William H. Lewis as well as W. D. Sullivan of the *Boston Globe* to discuss some preventative action.[13]

Creatively, the assembled group contrived an artifice. Reid was to write an open letter to the Harvard Graduates Athletic Association criticizing football in terms such as Eliot might use and requesting that the association form a committee to recommend radical changes in the game. Deliberations by such a Harvard committee to change the game, it was hoped, would forestall the Harvard governing bodies from finalizing an abolition of football.[14]

The Harvard Graduates Association accepted Reid's proposal and in early December 1905 appointed a "special" committee comprising Harvard's respected dean of men, Le Baron R. Briggs, plus experienced students of football: Robert Wrenn, a former member of the official football rules committee who was a dissenter from Camp's desired ten-yards-only change; Lorin Deland, sometime Harvard football coach and coauthor with Camp of the 1896 book *Football*; William H. Lewis, a former Harvard and Amherst football player and one of America's first African American football players, now a Boston lawyer helping coach the Harvard team (in 1896 Lewis had written a kind of instruction book for football); Dr. E. H. Nichols, the doctor in charge of the medical needs of the Harvard team; and Reid.[15]

Potentially, this was the most organized effort yet to propose rules for American football apart from the existing football rules committee. Was it simply an artifice, soon to pass away? Or too partisan, centered on one school? Or a serious rival to the existing, supposedly Camp-dominated, rules committee, a way to conduct an end run around the existing committee? Reid revealed some of his thinking in his diary, expressing the hope that the Harvard special committee would put Harvard "on the front seat of the band wagon" for reform and steal "some of Yale's fire."[16]

A President Involved 42

In itself Endicott Peabody's idea for injecting change into American football in the summer of 1905 wasn't so important. But it led to something important. Engulfed in the public outcry against football and having his own complaint, Peabody called for help from his longtime friend, who happened to be the football-loving U.S. president, Theodore Roosevelt.

Peabody's personal complaint, à la President Eliot at Harvard, was about football's "moral climate." As headmaster of Groton School, Peabody watched

Groton players being taught by Harvard graduate coaches to hold an opponent in a way that the referee would not see it. "You and I believe in the game," Peabody wrote Roosevelt, "and in its beneficial effects upon boys and young men when it is carried on fairly." But if young men learned to cheat in games, they would "later cheat in business life."[1]

With the progressive Roosevelt already having intervened dramatically and successfully in major U.S. economic and political matters, Peabody visualized Roosevelt could intervene in football and generate tangible change. Specifically, Peabody suggested Roosevelt get "the coaches of Harvard and Yale and Princeton together" and persuade them to agree to teach their players to play honestly.[2]

Roosevelt accepted Peabody's suggestion and invited leaders and coaches from the named "Big Three" schools to lunch with him on October 9, 1905, at the White House—Edward Nichols and Bill Reid for Harvard, John Fine and Arthur Hildebrand for Princeton, and Walter Camp and John Owsley for Yale. Roosevelt had the U.S. secretary of state at the lunch also, the newly appointed Elihu Root.[3]

Camp and Roosevelt were on friendly terms—Yale and Harvard graduates of 1880 who had kept in touch. After Camp sent Roosevelt a copy of his *Football Facts and Figures* book, Roosevelt responded in March 1895 with a complimentary letter ("All Americans are under [obligation] to you for your championship of athletics"). Later, Roosevelt asked Camp's help in arranging a visit of Harvard representatives to New Haven to explore improving relations between Harvard and Yale. And after being elected vice president, Roosevelt invited Camp to visit him on September 27, 1901, at Roosevelt's summer home in Oyster Bay, New York (canceled when President McKinley died on September 14 and Roosevelt was sworn in the next day as president).[4]

Beyond friendship, Camp and Roosevelt shared an enthusiasm for football. In the March 1895 letter, Roosevelt told Camp, "I personally like football best, and I would rather see my boys play it than see them play any other." As for football's alleged brutality: "I have no patience with the people who disclaim against it because it necessitates rough play and occasional injuries. The rough play, if confined within manly and honorable limits, is an advantage. It is a good thing to have the personal contact about which the *New York Evening Post* snarls so much." Roosevelt's impatience extended to his own alma mater: "I am utterly disgusted with the attitude of President Eliot and the Harvard faculty about football, though I must also say I feel very strongly in favor of altering the rules, so far as practicable, to do away with needless roughness in playing. . . . However, . . . I would a hundredfold rather keep the game as it is now, with the brutality, than give it up."[5]

So the Big Three leaders and coaches had a sympathetic listener when they sat down with Roosevelt at the White House. Harvard's Bill Reid, twenty-six years old and in his initial year as a paid coach trying to rejuvenate Harvard's program, was keeping a diary and recorded his recollection of the meeting.

> Walter Camp sat at the President's right and Mr. Fine at his left, while I sat opposite Mr. Fine and Mr. Root's right and Mr. Nichols sat on his left. The President discussed the question of football in general and made a few remarks . . . [about specific examples of unfair or dishonest play].
>
> Camp made some considerable talk but was very slippery and did not allow himself to be pinned down to anything. [Roosevelt] finally asked the three older men to draw up some kind of agreement on the matter while on their way home on the train together.

Camp ended up in charge of the statement that the group worked out and, after having it reviewed by Roosevelt, released it to the media: "At a meeting with the President of the United States, it was agreed that we consider an honorable obligation exists to carry out in letter and spirit the rules of the game of football relating to roughness, holding and foul play, and the active coaches of our Universities, being present with us pledge themselves to so regard it, and do their utmost to carry out these obligations." It was brief and general, a goal more than a program. But Roosevelt accepted it graciously and wrote Camp, "I cannot tell you how pleased I am at the way you have taken hold. Now that the matter is in your hands I am more than content to abide by whatever you do."[6] That was the initial inside story; the world at large, however, saw something else (perhaps, as it turns out, more insightful), with the progressive Roosevelt having taken charge of football like one more affair of state.

The effectiveness of the pledge made by Camp and the others was soon in question. In a game on November 11, Harvard's starting center, Parker, was ejected for slugging Pennsylvania's center. Parker didn't deny the slugging but insisted it was in retaliation for repeated offenses by the Pennsylvania player, whom the referee refused to penalize.

Within nine days, on November 20, a leader of Pennsylvania athletics was summoned to lunch at the White House. J. William White, professor of surgery, founder of Pennsylvania's Department of Physical Education, and a defender of football, was circumspect after the meeting, simply reporting,

In the cartoonist's mind, football (symbolized by the front figure on the left) took its place in 1905 under the control and direction of President Theodore Roosevelt. (*Harper's Weekly*, October 28, 1905, cover, University of Minnesota Library)

"The President has permitted me to say that we are in complete accord as to the need of the permanent abolition of brutality and foul play, of the increase in the power of officials and of a simple eligibility code for all American colleges and universities." Not much in the way of specific information, but one overall fact seemed clear: Roosevelt was keeping his eye on football and perhaps informing himself of actions that might be needed.[7]

Two weeks later, Roosevelt got involved again, when violations of the pledge were alleged against Yale during its November 25 Cambridge game with Harvard. A particular Yale punt was short and high, and by the time Harvard's Burr received it, he was surrounded by two Yale players—Shevlin, who tackled Burr, and Quill, who reached across Shevlin and pushed Burr in the face, allegedly with open hands but forcefully enough to draw blood. Harvard fans were sure Burr had signaled for a fair catch (the referee disagreed) and were incensed by the rough treatment they believed Burr had received.[8]

President Eliot wrote Roosevelt a few days after the game, contending the incident "perfectly illustrates the fundamental difficulty with the present game of football. Brutality is . . . so very profitable that rules and penalties cannot prevent it. . . . [T]he chance of high profit outweighs altogether the chance of any probable penalty." Eliot attached a letter from a Harvard supporter alleging that Paul Dashiell, the game's umpire and chair of the official football rules committee, was at fault in not penalizing Quill and Yale.[9]

On December 5, Roosevelt wrote Dashiell, a Naval Academy professor ultimately subject to Roosevelt's authority, and severely condemned him: "I have always regarded you as one of the best umpires on the field and if football is to be saved it must be saved by the umpires and referees acting with proper decision. . . . To my mind this kind of brutality ought to be covered by a penalty which would take the man off for the season. . . . It seems to me you had . . . a great opportunity . . . [of which] you failed to take advantage and this duty you failed to perform." Dashiell responded immediately, December 7, expressing "regret more than I can say" but firmly defending his decision.

> I was very close to the spot and was looking directly at the men in question for all possibilities. . . . The facts are as follows: The Yale forwards . . . stood around, and very close to, Burr, as he caught the ball. The nearest man at once tackled him and another pushed him in the face with both hands. There was no blow nor even "straight arm," and the hands were open. . . . It was a case of a player's reaching over another whose body was between him and the man with the ball, and pushing the most available point for upsetting his opponent. . . . The first thought I had of unnecessary roughness was when time was called by Burr and it was seen that his nose was bleeding somewhat and swollen. [Harvard's] trainer, McMasters, told me at the time that his nose had been hurt earlier in the game. . . .
>
> Between halves I chanced to meet Bertram Waters, one of Harvard's coaches, and I spoke to him of the play. He made very light of it and said it amounted to nothing.

Dashiell also wrote, "I am frank to say that I thought that a fair catch should have been allowed, and I asked the referee, who has sole charge of that point, if he were not going to give it. . . . It is simply impossible under the rules for the umpire [Dashiell] to take that decision into his own hands." Dashiell then added that the football rules committee was having a meeting on December 9 and asked whether Roosevelt could see him before that meeting.[10]

Two days later, Roosevelt answered, "It looks to me as if you had made out a very strong case." He wanted to see Dashiell but could not arrange it before the rules-committee meeting. Instead, he asked Dashiell to lunch the following week, on Tuesday, December 12.[11]

Roosevelt was corresponding with Camp at the same time he was interacting with Pennsylvania, Harvard, and Dashiell. Earlier Roosevelt had forwarded a letter from a Mr. Borden, who favored the ten-yard rule but also had other suggestions, including forward passing. Camp immediately replied to Roosevelt, appreciating Borden's advocacy of the ten-yard rule but noting problems with other Borden suggestions: "I am, as you probably know, an advocate of the ten-yard rule. . . . But those who wish to open the game must not allow two facts to escape their attention. One is that if they fritter away any of their energies in manifold suggestions, forward passing, placing men in prescribed squares and a dozen other things, they will never accomplish their purpose. They must unite on direct legislation whether it is a ten yard advance, an eight yard advance or a twelve yard advance." Again, Camp characterized the ten-yards-in-three-downs rule as "direct." No complicated alteration was being made in the game. Forward passing and arbitrary placing of defenders would alter the basic structure of American football and require years of testing and adjustment: What kind of forward passing? What other changes must accompany forward passing? At what point in a play may a player leave his prescribed square? Camp was open to small variations—ten yards, eight yards, twelve yards, all in three downs. The important point was, let's get on with a *direct* change that simply increases the distance to be gained in three downs and give that a try.[12]

Roosevelt never responded to Camp on the specifics of rule change, but a correspondence continued on other matters. On November 24, Roosevelt wrote concerning Roosevelt's son Ted, who was playing on Harvard's freshman football team. Ted was small (taking after his father as a boy) and had been hurt in the Harvard-Yale freshman game; some newspaper reports suggested Yale players had deliberately sought to hurt him. Roosevelt sent Camp a copy of a letter from Ted that said, "All the talk about the Yale boys laying for me was a lie. They played a clean, straight game and played no favorites. . . . They beat us by simply and plainly outplaying us." Roosevelt closed with a compliment. Reporting that a Princeton alumnus had told him that the recent Princeton-Yale game was played cleanly, Roosevelt concluded, "I believe your efforts [under the October 9 pledge to Roosevelt] have borne real fruit for good." Roosevelt might have some unhappiness with football, but he was still confident Camp would help improve the game.[13]

43 Tipping Point

Saturday, November 25, 1905, was a day of tragedy in American football and a day that would lead to fundamental changes in the game and its oversight.

With Union College at New York University (NYU) to play the last game of the year for both schools, Union's right halfback, Harold Moore, a mainstay of the team, ended a run on the bottom of a pile. When the players were cleared away, "Moore was lying flat on his face on the field unconscious. Several doctors ran out from the crowd and examined the player . . . [and one concluded] that Moore was suffering from cerebral hemorrhage and in a very critical condition. . . . [The doctor] applied heroic treatment . . . inject[ing] strychnine over the heart, but Moore did not recover consciousness. He was [taken] to the hospital where he died at 9 o'clock." As if that were not enough, an Indiana high school student also died in a November 25 game, succumbing to a broken "rib piercing his heart."[1]

The deaths were shaded in meaning—Moore had been warned by his doctor not to play football because of existing health issues, and according to the *New York Times* the Indiana school boy was not physically ready for the collisions of football. Still, the horrifying deaths brought further urgency to the rising football controversy.[2]

Confronted with the tragedy of Moore's death on New York University's field, the NYU chancellor, Henry M. MacCracken, telegraphed Harvard's president, Eliot, suggesting a conference of presidents to abolish or reform football. Eliot promptly declined MacCracken's suggestion with some interesting observations: "I do not think it expedient to call a meeting of college Presidents about football. They certainly cannot reform football, and I doubt if by themselves they can abolish it." Then Eliot went on to say, "I should not favor a meeting now. There should be an interval of cooling down. Deaths and injuries are not the strongest arguments against football. That cheating and brutality are profitable is the main evil."[3]

The action-oriented MacCracken—he had managed NYU since 1884 and was credited with reversing NYU's fortunes and building a viable, healthy institution—didn't let the matter drop, but proceeded with steps that would change the course of college athletics. NYU, he decided, would call its own conference. Nineteen institutions were invited, all the schools NYU had played since 1895, for a conference on December 8, 1905, less than two weeks away. The invitation allowed two delegates from each institution, one from the faculty and one from the school's athletic organization, and proposed wide-ranging discussion questions: Should the game be abolished? If not, what steps should be taken to secure its thorough reform? If abolished, what game or games may take its place?[4]

The *Chicago Tribune* kept the spotlight on President Roosevelt with a telegram the night of November 25, published the next day on their front page: "The 1905 football season practically closed today with two dead on the field of battle. Today's fatalities bring the total of slain to nineteen, and the injured (record only being made of accidents out of the ordinary) to 137. This year's record of deaths is more than double that of the yearly average for the last five years, the total for that period being forty-five." Here was a new call for President Roosevelt to intervene, and the *Tribune* was expecting results: Roosevelt, they said, was "the man to whom the safe and sane devotees of college sport are looking to lead the way out of the bloody shambles of football as played at present." Roosevelt was a reformer by nature, a politician with antennae raised in a country agitated about football, himself a lover of the game. Would he act, and how?[5]

Deaths, a president challenged to intervene, conferences of major universities to abolish the game—it was all further grist for those who were upset by or even hated American football. Two days after the deaths, the *New York Tribune* headlined a major article, "MOVE TO OUST CAMP," and below that, "NEW COMMITTEE ASKED." The paper contended that men representing leading universities had met and "practically decided upon" a program involving "abolition of the present rules committee, bag and baggage." It was an emotional article with no facts given and simply a claim that the present committee "is responsible all and severally for the roughness of college football. . . . Who are these fellows anyway? Who appointed them and to whom are they responsible?"[6]

Camp wrote President Roosevelt on November 28, 1905, in the midst of the attacks and unrest, ostensibly to acknowledge and thank him for his letter four days earlier about Yale's treatment of his son Ted. But he took the opportunity to do a bit of politicking by suggesting that Harvard's coach Reid could help the rules committee: "I believe if Reid would join me in fighting for the ten-yard rule we could carry the thing through."[7]

Whether Camp knew it, an opportunity was coming for Roosevelt to influence Reid. At Roosevelt's invitation, Reid and Herbert White, Harvard's graduate manager of football, were visiting the White House on December 4 to "talk over the football season" (the November 30, 1905, *New York Times* reported that Reid had received the invitation through a friend on Saturday, November 25, so it is possible Camp knew of the invitation when he wrote Roosevelt on November 28). Several matters could have been on Roosevelt's agenda—Reid's perceptions on fulfillment of the October 9 pledge, both as to the ejection of Harvard's Parker in the Pennsylvania game and as to the Harvard-Yale Burr incident; the work of the Harvard special committee drafting new football rule ideas, which Roosevelt had likely heard of; and possibly Camp's plea for Reid's help on the ten-yard rule.[8]

Again there was no account after the meeting of the subjects discussed, but a letter Roosevelt sent the day after the meeting (December 5, 1905) to H. S. White, a Harvard professor and chair of the Harvard Athletic Committee (not the Herbert White who had visited the White House with Reid), suggests some possibilities. By coincidence the very night of the Reid-Roosevelt meeting, H. S. White had released a press statement committing Harvard in opposition to Camp and the existing rules committee: "Our committee [the Harvard Athletic Committee] will probably take some action within the next two weeks which shows where Harvard stands regarding the game." "Unless the National Football Rules Committee takes some radical step in modifying the gridiron game, Harvard is going it alone." While speaking on behalf of the Harvard Athletic Committee, White said they were relying on expert advice, including suggestions from the Harvard special committee.[9]

It is not known whether Roosevelt read White's press statement, but Roosevelt wrote to White the same day the statement was published (December 5). After cautioning that he could "not commit myself to any specific program" and that all his "statements have been of a very general kind," Roosevelt added, "I wish you would see Reid and have him repeat some of our conversation" during Reid's December 4 visit to the White House. Apparently, Roosevelt kept his statements "of a very general kind" for the public, but for select persons in position to take action he had something else to say. Something Roosevelt had said to Reid would be of interest to persons like White who were actively seeking rule change.[10]

Camp and the existing football rules committee tried to fight back. Instead of waiting for its normal springtime rule-making meeting, Camp persuaded the committee to meet December 9, a day after the conference that NYU's chancellor, MacCracken, had called.[11]

Camp still had a supporter in Yale's president, Hadley, and a helper in the steadfast and outspoken Alice Camp. With Walter in Chicago as December 9 approached, Alice stepped in and (in possibly more aggressive words than Walter would have used) supplied the inquiring Hadley with Camp's plans for the meeting, which Hadley approvingly summarized in a memorandum. According to Hadley's memo, Alice first explained as background: Despite Camp's efforts, he had "not been able to secure from the Rules Committee the sanction [for] changes which he desired and which would have met some of the criticisms" now being asserted against the game. Camp should now go before the scheduled meeting, Alice said, "with a definite programme of changes which he wants and which Yale wants." This program would principally comprise Camp's proposal of ten yards in three downs as well as a requirement to limit tackling to above the knees. (Camp apparently favored a bar to tackling below the knees, because, if more open play was achieved through enactment of the ten-yard rule, tackling below the knees in the open field would raise a greater "risk of broken legs, arms, and collar bones." Many thought open play at least as dangerous as mass play. Limiting tackling might also ease longer gains required by the ten-yard rule.)[12]

Alice also anticipated possible political moves during the meeting with a rather dramatic plan. "Yale should go into the Rules Conference prepared to secede from it if . . . [the ten-yard rule and other Camp proposals] are not adopted. After such secession Yale would make her own rules, play with those who were prepared to play under those rules, and let others stay out." Alice, and presumably Walter, thought the public would respond to such a Yale position (Yale was the recognized leader and best team in American football). "Yale has unjustly been held responsible for failure to make those changes, and cannot longer be asked to bear this unjust responsibility." In

Walter Camp about 1905. (Images of Yale individuals, ca. 1750–2001 [inclusive], Manuscripts and Archives, Yale University)

Alice Camp about 1905. (Walter Chauncey Camp Papers, 1870–1983 [inclusive], 1870–1925 [bulk], Manuscripts and Archives, Yale University)

a further wifely plea: "Let Mr. Camp go into the conference . . . in the full belief that it is a desirable thing for Yale that the Conference should refuse to accept his suggestion in order that we may go before the public with this as our programme instead of that of the Conference."

Beneath these words, one can sense the pain Walter and Alice were feeling: once respected and deferred to, now resisted, even castigated and pushed aside. Hadley took it all down without indicating disagreement or doubt.

The MacCracken conference would come first on December 8, but the next day the official football rules committee would meet. If Camp could help it, they would take effective action, rule making centered on the ten-yard rule to accomplish open play, and thus demonstrate legislative maturity and capability to maintain their guidance of American football.

Democracy in Action 44

West Point Military Academy proved to be the most crucial participant in the December 8 MacCracken conference—better prepared than other invitees and asserting itself in decisive leadership. Why such readiness and leadership? For one reason, West Point's leaders supported football for both its educational value and its promotion of academy loyalty: West Point graduates around the world followed academy football and sent money to support it.[1]

But consider this also: President Roosevelt, an enthusiastic and outspoken defender of football who had been publicly called upon to help reform football, had a close relationship with the two officers leading West Point—Colonel A. L. Mills, superintendent, and Lieutenant Colonel Robert L. Howze, commandant of cadets. As regular officers, Mills and Howze had been in combat with Roosevelt during key parts of the Spanish-American War, earning generous praise in Roosevelt's autobiography. After the war, Mills and Howze each wrote letters seeking a Congressional Medal of Honor for Roosevelt. In addition, Howze served as military aide at the Roosevelt White House immediately prior to his West Point assignment, and Roosevelt was influential in Mills's promotion to brigadier general, effective shortly after the MacCracken conference.[2]

By coincidence, Mills was one of Roosevelt's escorts at the Army-Navy game on December 2, 1905, just days after West Point received its publicly reported invitation to the football-on-trial MacCracken conference. Such a coincidence would seem hard for either Mills or Roosevelt to ignore. Though Roosevelt might have no direct guidance for Mills, a single word or expression in the right context, especially when Mills already had a good idea what Roosevelt would want, might encourage West Point activity at the conference.[3]

On December 4, two days after Roosevelt and Mills were together at the Army-Navy game, West Point's "Army Athletic Council" (with Roosevelt's friend Howze a member) met to consider the MacCracken invitation. In good bureaucratic methodology, they recommended attendance (represented by Captain Palmer Pierce, a chemistry teacher who was the West Point faculty member in charge of football, and Howze) and approved resolutions detailing West Point's position:

> 1st—That the present game of football should not be abolished, but should be reformed;
>
> 2nd—That we believe the game can be reformed only by the representatives of *colleges* prominent in football *annually electing a* responsible Rules Committee of *9 members* who shall formulate the rules under which the game shall be played;
>
> 3rd—That the lines of reform should be as follows:
>
> (a) To make the game less dangerous to the player and more interesting to the spectator;

(b) To make changes which will result in the certain detection of foul or brutal play;
(c) With these ends in view that mass plays be limited.

Such resolutions obviously aimed to preserve football. But what about the existing football rules committee on which Walter Camp served as senior member? The resolutions called for electing a new committee that, on the face of it, would replace the existing rules committee, including Camp, satisfying the demands of disgruntled critics.[4]

December 8, four days after the Army Athletic Council meeting, West Point's representatives were present as the white-bearded Chancellor MacCracken opened his conference, hoping for a vote to abolish football and replace it with some other sport. Columbia and Union each would vote for abolition, as would three of the other four university presidents at the conference besides MacCracken.[5]

But according to the *New York Times*, football also had quite effective defenders: "Lieut. Col. Howze and Capt. Pierce, who represented the Military Academy, dominated the proceedings . . . [and after] a hard battle [managed to obtain a] two-third vote to continue the game and make such changes as were recommended by the Athletic Association at West Point." The conference required only one change, that the new rules committee have eleven members instead of West Point's recommended nine.[6]

Ready for action, the conference voted to convene again in less than three weeks (December 28 in New York City). At that meeting, they would elect the new rules committee and, more than that, plan a new ongoing organization in which colleges would cooperate to oversee college athletics. Essentially, all U.S. colleges and universities were invited to send delegates.

The presumed goal when Walter Camp called the existing football rules committee to a December 9 meeting was rule making—enactment of rules to effectively limit mass play, thereby exposing whatever action the MacCracken conference might take as unneeded and redundant. But Camp had planned for a possible internal political battle, and that's what he got, as he explained to President Hadley of Yale in a hurried, handwritten memo after the meeting. "It was quite a fight," he began, "and rendered far more complicated by . . . Reid who . . . stated he was not empowered to take any action until [Harvard's Special] Committee . . . could advise him." Given Reid's refusal to vote and the rules committee's practice of making decisions unanimously, the December 9 meeting could not conclude in its intended and desired

Captain Palmer Pierce, chemistry instructor at West Point and faculty member overseeing West Point football. (From West Point's *1904 Howitzer Yearbook*, courtesy of the U.S. Military Academy Library)

manner with a decision on rule amendments. Camp wrote Hadley that he responded to Reid's move by stating that he

> had come prepared to take some immediate action and if the Committee was not prepared to act that night I should not be able to remain on the Committee. That brought matters to a head and the Committee passed a resolution committing themselves to a certain line of policy the details to be determined at a later meeting to be held next Friday. Then I asked that all members commit themselves upon

Lieutenant Colonel Robert L. Howze, commandant of West Point, 1905–9. (From *1906 USMA Class Album*, Special Collections, U.S. Military Academy Library.)

> what plans toward the policy they were prepared to offer. . . . [There was some] friction over this proposition but as Bell of Penn and I had stated our positions and proposed to give those statements to the press it forced the others to do the same Reid alone being unable to do this.[7]

Previously, only final decisions of the whole rules committee had been announced, but the committee went along with Camp's insistence on laying out for the public the individual members' positions to show exactly where responsibility for an impasse lay. The December 12 *Yale News* published point-by-point summaries of individual members' positions (except for Reid, who said he was unprepared), with Camp's position described as follows:

1. Increase of distance to be gained to ten yards
2. Increase of penalties for unnecessary roughness and brutality and the addition of distance penalties for these offenses
3. The appointment of competent and efficient game officials by a central body
4. Forbidding tackling below the knees and also hurdling, in order to decrease the liability to accident
5. More specific definition of holding or how the linemen should hold their arms

Other committee members partially overlapped Camp's position. Five supported an increase in the yardage to be gained in the downs-and-distance rule. But important differences also appeared. Four favored arbitrary positioning of players to weaken the defense, and two (Bell and Dashiell) favored "forward passing behind the line of scrimmage."

In the days after the December 9 meeting, Camp must have sensed hopelessness in his position. Whether originally planned or not, the Harvard special committee offered Harvard and Reid a mechanism to undermine any Yale attempt to get the rules committee to act. Harvard could and apparently would block the football rules committee from making a decision until circumstances were more favorable, such as a desired action by the second MacCracken conference or a climate on the rules committee likely to support rules proposed by the Harvard special committee. Whatever the reason, after consulting with President Hadley, Camp prepared a letter of resignation from the rules committee. Certainly, he had reasons to resign—he had been vigorously castigated and called names and criticized as incompetent, perhaps evil.[8]

But resigning seems unlike Camp. American football was like a child to Camp, for which he had cared since the game was born. He had strong opinions about what the game should be and wanted to preserve it rather than let it be destroyed by harmful rule changes. Also, Camp was functioning on behalf of others besides himself. Charles Baird, the "graduate director" of football at the University of Michigan, had written to Camp to encourage him in his battle against President Eliot and "Harvard's tirades against the game" ("All western football enthusiasts would be pleased beyond expression" if Yale would tell Harvard to stop "whining and complaining" or Yale would stop playing them). Camp had received many similar letters of support and encouragement. He was a fighter who valued and taught determination; he had held to his rule positions in the face of public as well as private disagreement.[9]

Camp could have intended his resignation letter as a political effort, trying to demonstrate how serious he was about the ten-yard rule. Or he may have visualized building public support for Yale by explaining Yale's positions, though his drafts of those positions, suggesting Yale alone understood the need for a decisive rule change, were shallow and patently self-serving. Still another possibility is that writing the letter helped him sort through his position.

The letter was dated December 12 and was signed, but in fact it was never sent. Perhaps Camp changed his mind, realized he truly didn't want to resign or even threaten to resign. Or perhaps he realized the letter would not accomplish its intended purpose.

Instead of resigning, Camp did almost the opposite—granting newspaper interviews to advocate his rule positions. He included new reasons supporting his position, such as "the public demands direct legislation that they can understand," an argument against the artificial schemes being proposed to weaken the defense. As for forward passing, it was "too late after a year of criticism," when ideas might have been examined and tested, to now include untested ideas in the rule book.[10]

His friends were relieved. Julian Curtiss, his friend from Yale and Hopkins Grammar School and now an officer at Spalding, wrote on December 15, "President Hadley told me about a letter of resignation that you expected to send in this week. I have not seen it and am glad of it." The next day, Curtiss wrote again, complimenting Camp on the interviews published the previous day and encouraging that if

> the next meeting of the Rules Committee . . . [enacts] any rules that you do not approve . . . your resignation at that time, together with a statement of what you believe to be for the best interests of the game, will nullify any action they may take.

> . . . [A]ny movement you take, provided it is aggressive and along the lines you have laid out, will meet with the approval of the country. You occupy a position today in football that is stronger than all the rest of the Rules Committee put together.[11]

More positively, Camp worked to gather support. He sent copies of his rule proposals as published in the December 12 *Yale News* to various parties, including West Point's Palmer Pierce, who had taken an active role defending football at the initial MacCracken conference and would surely be involved in the upcoming second conference. Camp and Pierce had met a few years earlier as part of Pierce's faculty oversight of academy football.

Pierce first responded to Camp with a telegram, noncommittal on the changes (they "are undoubtedly good") but encouraging Camp and Yale to participate in the next MacCracken conference. In a follow-up letter, he noted, "The paramount question is one of getting an authorized standing for the Rules Committee and thus stopping the clamor about a self-constituted, self-perpetuating, irresponsible body of men who will not heed the wishes of the public." Pierce called attention to West Point's efforts at the December 8 MacCracken conference "to secure conservative and sane action and I think we succeeded fairly well." Then he urged "you larger institutions" to heed the call to the second, December 28, MacCracken conference. "I feel sure the old rules committee could be elected . . . with the addition, perhaps, of two members from the other colleges. . . . It would be worth your while to try this. No harm could result from your attendance."[12]

Camp answered with a short letter, "most emphatically" thanking Pierce "for your efforts on behalf of the sport." However, "as you have probably seen our authorities will not be represented, but I should hope with your efforts and those of some others . . . helpful action will be taken." Neither Harvard nor Princeton was attending either, suggesting a general caution among the larger schools in getting involved in an unpredictable conference in which they would be so outnumbered. However, Pierce's words might have been encouraging for Camp, certainly not the words of someone seeking to do away with the rules committee on which Camp had sat as a leading member for more than twenty-five years.[13]

Camp did continue to try to move the rules committee along, but Reid stopped that. The committee had planned to meet December 15, but Reid telegraphed Dashiell that he would not have instructions by that date, whereupon, as Camp reported to the committee with open exasperation and sarcasm, never using Dashiell's name, "our chairman" rescheduled the meeting for December 22. That too was not enough for Reid, who wrote again to ask postponement to December 29. Except for Reid, nearly everyone on the existing rules committee was ready for a December 22 meeting and would be disappointed in its cancellation. But majority wishes made no difference, and Dashiell wrote Camp, "If Reid cannot be ready I think we had best put it off."[14]

Camp and the rest of the committee might have been facing something bigger than manipulation by Reid and the Harvard committee, namely, an effective encouragement of Reid's actions by President Roosevelt. Though Roosevelt was trying to keep his involvement quiet, Dashiell got hints he passed along to Camp in a December 17 letter. Dashiell had had his lunch with Roosevelt on December 12, and "things [presumably Roosevelt's criticism of Dashiell's refereeing] seemed to have been largely straightened out all right." More than that, Roosevelt had gone so far as to show Dashiell *confidentially* a *letter from Reid*. Dashiell wrote to Camp, "I received (between ourselves entirely) from the President a letter to him from Reid in which the latter told of how they were getting on with the Harvard committee and while no word was said still I fancy the President would rather, if the thing is possible."[15] To Dashiell it was clear: Roosevelt was supporting the work of the Harvard committee. Such support must also have been clear to Reid, perhaps even made somewhat explicit when Reid visited the White House on December 4. And when Roosevelt wrote to H. S. White, chair of Harvard's athletic committee, asking him to meet with Reid as discussed above, that presumably was one fact he expected White to learn from Reid. To Camp, it must also have seemed clear: Roosevelt sympathized with rule revision beyond the ten-yards-only approach Camp had been trying so hard for.

Roosevelt nevertheless sought secrecy for his role. In a December 19 letter to Dashiell (Dashiell had apparently asked for further guidance from Roosevelt), Roosevelt declined to give advice and added, "I do not want to appear to take too much part in the football business for several reasons."[16]

With the reality of the situation becoming evident, Camp seemed to drastically change course. On Monday, December 18, he telegraphed the rules committee that he had heard nothing from Reid on his request that Reid participate in a December 22 meeting and therefore presumed the committee had to postpone the meeting scheduled for the twenty-second. Most tellingly, he added that "personally" he would consent to a meeting on the twenty-ninth.[17]

A delay to the twenty-ninth would of course allow the second, December 28, MacCracken conference to occur ahead of a rules-committee meeting. A primary purpose of the MacCracken conference was to elect a new rules committee that according to earlier reports would rival and threaten the existing committee. Camp now seemed to accept that. Or had he received some assurances supporting Pierce's predictions that Yale and other existing rules committee members could remain on the committee? In any event, rather than resign, he was staying involved, ready to attempt to influence any change in the rules that might be proposed.

In fact, the second MacCracken conference on December 28 did offer conciliation and compromise, led again by West Point. Instead of a new rules committee to replace the existing committee, West Point now advocated *combining* a new rules committee of five members elected by the MacCracken conference with the existing committee. Upon election the new MacCracken rules committee was to communicate with the existing committee and "propose that the committees be amalgamated into one." Only if the existing committee refused to amalgamate would the new conference committee formulate rules on its own.[18]

West Point's amalgamation proposal was the first business brought forward when the conference convened on December 28, 1906, with sixty-two colleges and universities represented. The West Point proposal produced "a stormy session" lasting nearly nine hours. After the "hardest kind" of a battle, said the *New York Times*, "the practical men of the conference" managed to convince the others that the existing football rules committee had to be recognized and included to achieve progress and effective reforms.[19]

West Point's representative, Palmer Pierce, had one concession he could readily make (and perhaps had planned): he agreed that the new MacCracken conference rules committee would have seven members instead of five, as originally proposed. The seven elected were intentionally chosen to represent districts distributed across the country in contrast to the strong eastern flavor of the old rules committee (New England, E. K. Hall of Dartmouth; New York, Charley Daly of West Point; other middle states, J. A. Babbitt of Haverford; Ohio, C. W. Savage of Oberlin; Midwest, H. L. Williams of Minnesota; Far West, J. T. Lees of Nebraska; Southwest, F. H. Curtis of Texas). This new committee was instructed to go to Philadelphia the next day, December 29, and seek amalgamation with the old committee, which just coincidentally under Reid and Harvard's influence would be meeting there that day.[20]

The large attendance at the convention likely was drawn in part by a plan not only to elect a new rules committee but also to establish a permanent ongoing organization. The conference did establish such an organization, with Pierce elected president; also elected were a vice president, secretary, and four additional persons who would complete an executive committee. When the conference ended on December 28, 1905, it was adjourned to meet a year thence in New York. By then a constitution had been written, establishing the organization as the Intercollegiate Athletic Association, which within five years would change its name to the National Collegiate Athletic Association (NCAA).[21]

The old football rules committee wasn't ready to amalgamate on December 29—they said they needed instructions from their schools—but they must have understood there was no real choice but to amalgamate. President Roosevelt continued his campaign with letters to both General Mills at West Point and Dashiell at Annapolis, noting, "It is very important that Annapolis and West Point should have the same rules"; he asked Dashiell to "do all you can to secure the amalgamation of your old rules committee and of this new rules committee." Both committees soon scheduled meetings in New York on January 12, 1906. Meanwhile, the Harvard special committee managed a "timely" conclusion and on January 9, three days before the expected January 12 amalgamation, announced their recommended new football rules. Among the suggested rules were a ten-yard rule (allowable, they added, only if the defense was weakened or the offense materially strengthened), approval of forward passes for plays begun between the twenty-five-yard lines, creation of a neutral zone between the opposing forward lines of players (with a width equal to the length of the ball), and recodification of the rules and illustration of the rules by means of pictures.[22]

The day after announcing its recommended rules, Harvard sprang another surprise, revealing that Reid would leave the old football rules committee to become a member of the new conference committee. The delays accepted by the old committee in response to Reid's pleas now seemed unnecessary—courtesies and customs rendered meaningless by Reid and Harvard's actions. Upon amalgamation, of course, Reid would have become a member of the amalgamated committee, but his action signified a switching of loyalties and a new distribution of political forces within the amalgamated committee.[23]

Further eye-opening came on January 12 when the two committees assembled and it was proposed that the combined committee should organize with a chairman from the old committee (L. M. Dennis was chosen) and a secretary from the new (J. A. Babbitt was chosen). But once amalgamation had been formally accepted, Babbitt resigned as secretary, and Reid was chosen to replace him. Walter Camp, longtime secretary of the old football rules committee and its predecessors, had been deposed, replaced by Harvard's Bill Reid. However, Camp was requested "to edit the New Rules Book" and thus would continue to be responsible for getting the rules ready for publication in *Spalding's Official Football Guide* (Curtiss and Spalding would have allowed no choice but Camp anyway).[24]

Along with a new rule-making regime and a new role for Camp, new committee procedures were established. Decisions would be by majority vote, so a requirement for unanimity would no longer paralyze the committee. Also, rules would at least initially be developed through working groups. Camp was made a member of a three-man group on "open play," which was to begin work immediately; others on that committee were Reid and E. K. Hall, an 1892 Dartmouth graduate and football player who had coached football at Illinois and now was practicing law in Boston. Having been stymied by the old committee, could Camp obtain a ten-yard rule through the new three-man working group and full committee?[25]

Other working groups were a committee for eliminating brutality and foul play, a committee to consider formation of a central agency to appoint game officials, and a committee for planning a field laboratory to test rule proposals under playing conditions. The full amalgamated committee, which took the name "American Intercollegiate Football Rules Committee," was to meet again in two weeks, at which time the working groups were to report on their deliberations.[26]

Football-reform sentiment was also alive elsewhere in the country. Led by Michigan's president, James B. Angell, representatives from schools of the "Big Ten" (as that conference is known today) met in January and March 1906 and agreed on radical changes in their conference rules—seasons cut in half to five games, no training table or training quarters permitted, coaches to be appointed by university bodies "in the regular way and at moderate salaries," and a three-year limit on an individual student's competition and no graduate students allowed. The changes were relaxed within two years, but not before the regents of Michigan, football enthusiasts who rejected their president's emphases, forced the school to withdraw from the Big Ten; Michigan did not return until 1917; in the meantime, Ohio State, growing rapidly, was admitted to the conference in 1912.[27]

In the Far West, a reform impetus was led by Presidents David Starr Jordan of Stanford, where Camp had coached, and Benjamin I. Wheeler of California, Camp's friend. In 1906 both California and Stanford and a few other schools reverted to playing rugby rather than American football and continued in that play for ten or so years before returning to the American game.[28]

45 Starting from Scratch

When the new amalgamated rules committee held its first substantive meeting, January 27, 1906, forward passing was front and center on the agenda. Here's what the Camp-Hall-Reid working group on open play presented to the full committee after a week of work: "Forward passing of the ball was very thoroughly discussed. It seemed possible to reach an agreement . . . so long as the passing did not go beyond the line of scrimmage, or even a yard or two beyond that line. But when it came to throwing the ball . . . [into a position where] more than one man . . . should be endeavoring to catch this ball, it feared that disagreeable accidents would surely take place." Apparently persuaded, the full committee on January 27 formally approved forward passing if the ball did not cross the line of scrimmage.[1]

Such a limited definition might be acceptable to Camp, but what about Reid and Hall—representatives from Harvard and the MacCracken conference, advertised as activists seeking "radical" rule changes to open the game? Perhaps they were showing respect for Camp, the long-serving dean of rule making. More likely, they were uncertain: How should this running-based game derived from rugby be changed? What was possible without causing serious bodily injury or without undermining the game and turning it into a laughable mess? In fact, just eight months earlier, May 8, 1905, Reid had written a Princeton professor indicating his opposition to forward passing; now the Harvard special committee on which Reid had participated had shown an openness to a limited use of the forward pass (between the twenty-five-yard lines). Attitudes were obviously in flux, and even though Reid and Hall were in the majority, they subscribed to a pass that was more like a backfield lateral; the only game-opening variation was to allow the "lateral" to be thrown forward.[2]

However, the situation had changed by the time of the next committee meeting, February 10. During the intervening two weeks, a majority of the full amalgamated committee had decided a backfield pass was not enough, and that included E. K. Hall from the open-play working group. As a whole, the open-play working group offered no proposal at the February 10 meeting; apparently, neither Camp nor Reid was ready to offer more than he already had. However, as an individual Hall made a three-part proposal, two parts of which Camp would approve: install the ten-yards-in-three-downs rule advocated by Camp, and add a new play called an onside kick (which allowed kicking-team players to recover a kick downfield, thereby keeping ball possession and advancing the length of the kick).[3]

The third part of Hall's proposal went further, allowing forward passes beyond the line of scrimmage, "so long as the pass does not go higher than the passer's head" (apparently an effort to limit the length of the pass). As a further limitation, if the pass touched the ground without being touched by a player of either side, it would *go to the opponents* at the spot from which the pass was thrown; such a turnover risk was sure to discourage pass attempts at least when play was in the passing team's half of the field, where a turnover could place the opponents near the passing team's goal line.[4]

Other individuals also made forward-passing proposals, including Bell (pass could not travel more than ten yards beyond the line of scrimmage, and only players of the passing team behind the passer when the pass was made could receive the pass) and Williams (no height or length limitation but loss of possession if the pass touched ground without being touched by any player).[5]

After discussion of all rule proposals, the ten-yard and onside-kick parts of Hall's proposal were approved, but discussion on the forward pass was postponed until after lunch. Forward passing occupied the rest of the day, and the discussion led to removal of any limitation on the length or height of the pass. By the end of the day, the committee had developed and voted in favor of forward passing as follows (outlining added):

> [1] One forward pass shall be allowed on a play
>
> > [a] provided the ball does not touch the ground before being touched by a player of either side [and]
> >
> > [b] the pass is made by any man who was behind the line of scrimmage when the ball was put in play.
>
> [2] If the ball touches the ground before being touched by a player of either side, it shall go to the opponents on the spot where the pass was made.
>
> [3] The pass shall not be received by a man who was on the line of scrimmage when the ball was put in play, except for the two men playing on the ends of the line.

[4] A direct lob over the line within the space of five yards on each side of the center shall be unlawful.[6]

Three additional meetings were held by the amalgamated rules committee in 1906 before the rules were finally approved, but the rule on forward passing remained as decided at the February 10 meeting. Forward passing had arrived in American football but in a limited form, the primary limitation being the risk of losing possession, either automatically if the pass was not at least touched by a player of either side before striking the ground, through recovery by opponents of a ball that was touched by a player but fell to the ground uncaught (thus being treated as if it were a fumble), or interception of the pass.[7]

Other important 1906 changes by the amalgamated committee included the following:

- Establishing a "neutral zone" at the start of a scrimmage, according to which opposing linemen of the contesting teams were separated a distance equal to the length of the ball (as suggested by the Harvard special committee and more practical than the apparently wider neutral zone proposed by Camp many years before).
- Adding language to establish that a running play ended when any portion of a runner, except his hands or feet, touched the ground
- Further defining "foul play" by naming specific prohibited actions[8]

Camp welcomed the above changes as well as at least two other decisions. First was the creation of a "Central Board of Officials," as Camp and others had been advocating. Comprising five members of the rules committee, the board was to "instruct in the proper interpretation of the rules, enlarge where possible the group of desirable officials, and, if requested by universities and colleges, assist in the selection and appointment of officials." J. A. Babbitt of Haverford College was named chair. Despite Babbitt's complicity in deposing Camp as rules-committee secretary in favor of Reid, Camp agreed to serve on the board with Babbitt, together with Cornell's L. M. Dennis and Princeton's J. H. Fine from the old committee and Oberlin's C. V. Savage from the new.[9]

Second was a steadfast refusal by the amalgamated committee to give in to any of several proposals to arbitrarily weaken the defense (as by requiring the defense to have only five defensive players on the line of scrimmage with other defensive players required at least five yards back of the line). At times such proposals had been favored by a majority of the old rules committee, bringing Camp to the point of despair, and they had also been advocated to the amalgamated committee. But now, finally, Camp and other opponents had succeeded in disposing of any such rule or idea.

In 1906 at least one football coach quickly grasped big possibilities with the newly enacted forward pass. Edward Cochems, a twenty-nine-year-old 1902 Wisconsin graduate and player who had coached at various schools after graduation, had been hired by St. Louis University in 1906 as football coach and professor of physical culture. In the summer of 1906, Cochems took his St. Louis team to practice at Lake Beulah, Wisconsin, and set about studying and experimenting with the forward pass.[10]

The "acme of forward passing methods," he decided, was an overhand spiral, which was quite different from the underhand or round-arm lateral techniques then being used in American football. An overhead spiral was a challenge because it required a large hand to grasp the large melon-size ball then in use—"nearly nine inches from thumb to second finger," Cochems said, along "the contour of the hand." But some players could do it. Bradbury Robinson, who had played end for St. Louis the previous year, was made St. Louis's primary quarterback, and in a practice game between St. Louis and Carroll College on September 5, 1906, in Waukesha, Wisconsin, he threw perhaps the first overhand spiral forward pass in a game under the new rules.[11]

While the possession-loss risk if a 1906 forward pass went awry forced caution, Cochems still made significant use of the forward pass once the regular season began. Against Kansas University, with the game well in hand, Robinson completed a stupendous pass from his forty-yard line to a St. Louis player at the Kansas goal line. On Thanksgiving Day against Iowa, which had defeated St. Louis the previous year 31–0, Cochem's team turned the tables for a 39–0 win, with important use of the pass. St. Louis threw ten times, completed eight, and had an average "flight distance" of twenty yards. Iowa threw only two forward passes—"basketball style," with the ball held over the head with both hands and thrown a short distance. Four of St. Louis's touchdowns were made directly by forward passes. Cochems later wrote of the last play of the game, "Saint Louis was on Iowa's 35-yard line, with but a few seconds to play. The time keeper was walking on the field to call time, when the ball was shot like a projectile in spiral motion 25 yards to a player on the full run who secured a touchdown. The play was so sudden and unexpected that the whole Iowa team stood gaping at the remarkable performance." Overall, St. Louis won eleven games without a loss or tie, scoring 407 points to 11 for the opposition.[12]

Having learned of St. Louis's notable success with the forward pass, Walter Camp requested Cochems to write an article for the 1907 edition of Spalding Library's *How to Play Football.* Using photos of Robinson to demonstrate, Cochems described various throwing techniques but focused on the overhand spiral because of the distance, speed, and accuracy possible with that throw.

Cochems wrote again in 1908 for a new magazine, the *Baseball Magazine*, with a broader theme and title, "Needed: A New Ball and Widened Field." He contended that "if the forward pass is to continue, it ought to be possible for any ordinary hand" to throw an accurate forward pass. Cochems said he had already suggested to Amos Alonzo Stagg of the rules committee that the ball be made "slimmer—narrower through its short diameter and longer through its long." Also, he would add two extra stitches to the lacing to further assist in gripping the ball and would make the ball heavier, presumably to make passes more straight and accurate. As a further advantage, he noted that a slimmer ball would be less susceptible to fumbling.[13]

In the same article, Cochems also advocated widening the field, to allow even greater and more effective use of the forward pass and onside kick. Cochems obviously envisioned and wished for a wide-open game.

As questioning of the forward pass as Camp had been, he nevertheless used it in 1906 and to Yale's huge benefit. Yale had practiced forward passes during the season, but Camp wrote that "nothing had come of it save the simple forward pass over the corner of the line which all teams were using, and which the defense was solving better and better every day." Then, with language undoubtedly pointing to himself but avoiding the first person, Camp wrote:

> One night while studying over the problem of how to get men down the field in a position to take a longer forward pass, the thought suggested itself, "Why not let the fullback take up a position as if to kick, and then, as soon as the ball was passed to him, let him run directly back toward his own goal, say five or even ten yards, and turn and throw the ball?" . . . In trying the play out, it became at once apparent that the mere sight of the fullback . . . running back[ward] . . . would put the defense on its guard at once. . . . This was solved by the pretense of a try-at-goal from a drop-kick or kick from placement. Such a move was sure to draw the line of the opponents, but the time thus taken up was half as long as necessary. Hence a second "fake" so-called was added to this first movement. As soon as the

> ball came back, Veeder, the Yale back and drop-kicker, who had been apparently preparing for a drop-kick and getting his line, started on a wide-swinging end run, as if the whole affair had been a deception to draw the end rusher in [to allow an end run]. . . . Then when Veeder had run a considerable distance out, he passed a long, high throw down the field to Alcott.

Yale waited to use the play until its last game of the year, the Harvard game that could make the year worthwhile. Yale also had to wait during the game until near enough the Harvard goal to make a field-goal try seem reasonable. But "the opportunity came, the signal was given, and all went as planned"—touchdown made, point-after scored, Yale winning, 6–0.[14]

Yale and Camp had continued their mastery over Harvard—since 1883 Yale had won 13 times against 3 losses and 2 ties. Ironically, Coach Camp also had defeated Coach Reid, using the forward pass forced on him by Reid and Harvard's actions. Reid had written in his diary before the 1905 Harvard-Yale game, "Hardly anything is more important than beating Yale." Overall, Reid's record at Harvard in 1905 and 1906 was 18-3-1, but he had lost twice to Yale, a major disappointment. After the 1906 loss, Reid decided to give up coaching.[15]

Few changes were made in forward-passing rules in the years immediately following the 1906 introduction. That was not surprising in view of the rules committee's standard modus operandi—fearing unforeseen consequences with large changes, the committee proceeded cautiously. They also may have been influenced by the dean of rule making, Walter Camp, who continued to advocate against passing. And they were undoubtedly encouraged by the fact that football injuries and deaths had declined after passage of the 1906 rules, from the nineteen deaths listed by the *Chicago Tribune* in 1905 to eleven each in 1906 and 1907 (college deaths remained the same, three in 1905 and 1906 and two in 1907).[16]

When the rules committee met to make 1907's rules, they relaxed one rule, lessening adverse effects on the passing team if a forward pass struck the ground before touching a player. Instead of such an event causing a transfer of possession from the passing team to the opponents, as in 1906, the passing team retained possession in 1907 but was penalized fifteen yards—still serious but not as game changing as loss of possession would be. A year later, in 1908, rule makers actually added a restriction on forward passing: under the 1908 rule, only a player of the passing team who had touched an uncaught forward pass could recover the ball on the ground until an opposing player had touched it, thus making a forward pass riskier for the offense.[17]

No changes were made in the forward-passing rules in 1909, but *other* significant changes were made, introducing two rules still in force today:

- The value of a field goal, which had been reduced from five points to four in 1904, was again reduced, from four points to three.
- A team that had taken a touchback in their goal, which previously required a rugby-style kick-out, was now allowed the option of placing the ball on their twenty-five-yard line and proceeding with a regular three-down scrimmage series.[18]

Perhaps encouraged by Cochem's St. Louis team, the Midwest was a leader in the early years of forward passing. Writing after the 1908 season, Alonzo Stagg reported that although 1906 had largely been a year of experiment, with only limited and isolated uses of a forward pass, in 1907 there was greater use and even more in 1908. Stagg said forward passing in 1908 became a regular tool of many midwestern teams, with the ball thrown "hard and direct and low like a baseball": in 1908 Minnesota made nine successful passes against Carlisle; Chicago, eleven against Minnesota; and Wisconsin, ten against Chicago. Even more passes were used in one-sided games: in 1908 Chicago completed twenty-one against Purdue.[19]

46 Football as We Know It

The future of forward passing in American football was still uncertain as the twentieth century's first decade came to a close—liked and much used in some parts of the country, not much used in others. A new surge in football injuries and deaths further confused the situation—thirteen deaths at all levels in 1908, with six college deaths, and then suddenly in 1909 twenty-six deaths, ten of which were college deaths with major colleges involved: quarterback Earl Wilson of Navy fatally injured on October 16 in a game against Villanova; tackle Eugene Byrne of Army, October 30, against Harvard; and halfback Archer Christian of Virginia, November 13, against Georgetown.[1]

Again there were diametrically opposed ideas about how to respond to the new crisis. Camp happened to be writing his last major football treatise, and a passage in the book illustrates his view. He took note of those who wanted to see the game banned and in response inserted letters from friends of football, explaining why it should be continued. Camp, of course, agreed with the continuation but added: "At the same time I should be glad to see changes made in the rules that would prevent, or at least limit, mass plays and other rough features of the game." How should that be done? For Camp, not with a forward pass, and in his book he again asserted an argument he had already made many times: "The taking away of the defensive half from [the defensive] tackle by the forward pass has worked toward a renewal of the old heavy plays against [the tackle] position." Camp seemed to fasten on the danger to tackles as a compelling reason to limit or prevent forward passing. But others wanted to expand passing, and it would take a long time to decide whose view would prevail—four meetings totaling seven days spread from February to May.[2]

The first meeting on February 10 exposed serious doubts about the forward pass. Of five rule proposals made, only one of them—from Chicago's Alonzo Stagg—proposed removing restrictions from forward passing. Stagg's writing partner from Minnesota, Henry L. (Harry) Williams, would allow a forward pass beyond the line of scrimmage but require that the receiver of the pass "touch the ball to the ground before taking more than two steps, if he wants to run with it." Parke Davis, in his second year as the Princeton representative, and Lieutenant H. B. Hackett, representing West Point, would both limit forward passes to completion behind the line of scrimmage.[3]

The fifth proposal was strange—presented by Harvard's delegate, Crawford Blagden, "at the request of Mr. Foster Sanford," a former Yale player and Yale Law School graduate. Many Yale football leaders and alumni did not like Sanford or want him involved at Yale, but he also had admirers and was presently assisting at Yale. Sanford was described as an advocate and good teacher of line play and of a running attack based on plunges through the line. Consistent with that, the "Sanford-Blagden" proposal opposed forward passes beyond the line of scrimmage and proposed a downs-and-distance rule of seven yards in four downs—a great incentive to line-plunging mass play, quite opposite from the ten-yards-in-three-downs rule in place since 1906 and fought for so vigorously by Camp.[4]

The rules committee waited almost seven weeks to meet again, March 25 and 26, but by then, with apparent soul-searching, some committee members had changed positions. Princeton's Davis now favored forward passes to ends and backfield men without other restrictions. Stagg basically maintained his previous proposal for unrestricted forward passing. But Hackett of Army remained steadfast, limiting forward passes to completions behind the line of scrimmage, and on the second day Camp joined in Hackett's proposal.[5]

Numerous other proposals besides forward passes were also made, causing the committee to postpone a decision on forward passing and instead discuss and approve six noncontroversial but important rule changes:

1. Removal of restrictions on running by the quarterback (previously, the quarterback was required to run laterally five yards before turning upfield). The checkerboard pattern on football fields would be coming to an end.
2. At snapback the offensive team must have seven men on the line of scrimmage. Moving extra players into the backfield, generally heavy linemen for mass plays, was also ending.
3. Game divided into four periods of fifteen minutes each.
4. No pushing or pulling the runner by the offensive team and no "locked interference."
5. No diving tackles (tackler must have at least one foot on the ground).
6. Onside kick must travel twenty yards or more before it can be downed by the kicking team.

As for forward passing, it was agreed to conduct "further study and experiment" on two alternative rule changes—one that allowed a forward pass beyond the line of scrimmage and one that did not. Thereupon, the rule makers adjourned for a month.[6]

The next meeting (on April 29 and 30) proceeded smoothly at first but came to an abrupt and dramatic end. Forward-passing advocates spoke first, with Crawford Blagden of Harvard, now separated from Yale's Sanford, proposing an alteration of the downs-and-distance rule to require eight yards in three downs and further proposing that forward passes be allowed beyond the line of scrimmage to a length of sixteen yards. John Bell of Pennsylvania offered a rule to protect pass catchers, either receivers on offense or interceptors on defense: no player was to "tackle or throw, push, pull, shoulder or straight-arm an opponent on either the offense or defense [who was] attempting to catch . . . a forward pass," but any player was "at liberty to try to catch or intercept the ball."[7]

With momentum now building for forward passing, a motion passed to "devise" a game that included "a forward pass across the line of scrimmage." Further, it was decided that players eligible to receive a forward pass should not be interfered with, "until they have gone down the field" twenty yards, and that Bell's proposal (described in the previous paragraph) be used to define the protection a pass receiver was to have during the act of catching.

Agreement seemed near when "considerable discussion" broke out whether pass receivers were sufficiently protected and whether the rules adopted on that issue had become "so intricate and complex" as to cause "an almost interminable tangle . . . in undertaking to either play or officiate the game." Although Camp is not identified with any statement in the meeting minutes, the latter statement sounds like one he could have made, and his views were perhaps influential enough to cause the drastic shift in discussion momentum that quickly developed; a new vote was taken, and in a sudden reversal a majority voted "to *rescind all legislation of the present session* and to adopt a rule in which a *forward pass would be allowed only behind the line of scrimmage*" (Camp later wrote that despite Parke Davis's earlier approval of a forward pass, Princeton at this point supported the decision to rescind and made the motion to adjourn). A subcommittee was named to work out the details of such a game.[8]

It was a strange moment. Camp believed, and said for publication in the *New York Times*, that the committee had decided that it was impossible to have a forward pass beyond the line of scrimmage while at the same time protecting defensive tackles from severe pounding (because the threat of long forward passing across the line of scrimmage would force defensive backs away from a position supporting the tackles). But Stagg did not take the committee's action so seriously; when he reached Chicago and was questioned by reporters, he "threw up his hands and said the committee was going to the bow wows." He also predicted a short life for the just-enacted rules.[9]

By the next meeting (May 13), forward-passing advocates had reorganized, and the matter had essentially been decided outside the meeting room. Princeton had again changed its position. A new delegate would attend for Princeton, Bill Roper, the Princeton coach, and Camp had been told Roper would vote in favor of unrestricted forward passing.[10]

At the meeting, Harvard's Percy Haughton, an 1899 Harvard graduate now coaching the Harvard team, made detailed arguments against the enacted rules, asserting, for example, that the idea of a forward pass behind the line was theoretical only; it wouldn't be used. The practical effect of a rule preventing forward passing across the line of scrimmage would be no forward passing. After discussion the committee voted eight to six to approve forward passes with two significant limitations: the forward passer must be five yards behind the line of scrimmage at the time of throwing the ball, and the pass must be caught no more than twenty yards beyond the line.[11]

Surprisingly, only three of the eight votes for expanded forward passing came from MacCracken conference schools, while five came from schools of the "old rules committee"—Chicago, Harvard, Navy, Pennsylvania, and Princeton. Barring forward passing beyond the line of scrimmage was favored by only two of the old-committee schools, Cornell, represented by Dennis (the chair of the committee), and Yale, represented by Camp.[12]

Whatever the lineup of votes, Camp had been defeated. He had been so sure he was correct, but now he had been outvoted—forward passing was here to stay in American football. In his youth, he had been a pioneer, suggesting fundamentally new playing methods; now, in his midforties, he seemed out of touch with a majority sentiment building among younger coaches and observers.

The whole 1906 and 1910 rule-making proceedings had produced several unpleasant and unhappy experiences for Camp—roughly and deceptively pushed aside during the initial amalgamation process, displaced as committee secretary, outvoted several times in his resistance to forward passing. Yet through both 1906 and 1910, Camp had continued on the committee and worked with those who had defeated him to get the committee-approved rules into form for inclusion in the rule book. E. K. Hall, secretary of the rules committee in 1910, later wrote of Camp: "More than once I have seen him face the bitterest disappointment with a smile on his face that was a joy to see and with a fortitude that was literally inspiring. Time and again I have watched him and marveled as he held his temper under conditions that would have tested the temper of a saint. His fairness toward those whose views he opposed and his consideration for the feelings of others was never failing." When Camp announced in a few years that he was resigning from the rules committee, Paul Dashiell wrote that what the committee would miss most was "the man that he is."[13]

Camp had a way of reaching out to his rivals. During the 1906 football season, a few months after Reid had displaced Camp as committee secretary, they traveled together to watch a Princeton game, likely at Camp's initiative and in any event an example of Camp working with someone who had caused him pain. Similarly, even though Roper switched Princeton's position for the last, decisive, committee meeting, voting against Camp on forward passing and severely condemning Camp in a letter to President Wilson of Princeton, Roper and Camp ultimately worked together on the rules committee. And when Camp did not appear for the second day of the 1925 rules committee, it was Roper who went to look for him.[14]

American football had turned a corner, but Camp was not enthusiastic. In an article in *Outing*, he gently disparaged "the new football" of 1910 as "more than . . . officials can possibly handle." Of course, game officials routinely make complex observations and judgments today, though with twice as many officials. But even if Camp was correct in his criticism, the rest of the committee was ready to move on. When the rules committee met in 1911 after a year of play, no effort was made to ease the officials' jobs.[15]

For 1911 the major change in the rules, a step toward today's passing rules, was to limit lawful forward passes to those actually caught in the air without striking the ground. Another significant occurrence in 1911 was a change in the composition and organization of the rules committee. L. M. Dennis, chair of the committee, retired, and E. K. Hall, who had been serving as committee secretary, was elected chairman in Dennis's place. To take Hall's place, Camp was elected secretary, still respected and appreciated, despite his continued resistance to forward passing, and now restored to the combined role of secretary and editor he had served on the old football rules committee.[16]

Rule changes in 1912 gave American football the fundamental form it has today. Motivation for these changes came mainly from within the football profession—coaches, writers, and members of the rules committee who were convinced the offense needed strengthening. Even Camp seemed to have been converted, as indicated in an article he wrote about the "unsatisfactory" scoreless 1911 Harvard-Yale game. Each team, he said, "wanted to win or nothing," but the offenses of both teams had difficulty in advancing the ball, making it difficult for the better team to score and distinguish itself. Too many games, Camp acknowledged, were being decided by flukes—a lucky break—while a well-planned and -executed effort went without reward. It wasn't "a true sporting proposition unless [the] better team can win."[17]

Thus, when the rules committee met in 1912, they were motivated to strengthen the offense, and also to simplify—even the officials didn't understand all the rules, as Camp had contended for a couple of years.[18]

The committee needed only one two-day meeting (February 2 and 3, 1912) to accomplish the desired changes. After a first day of organization, brainstorming, and listening to ideas from outsiders (Sanford, Cochems, Adee, and Warner), the second day brought major decisions of lasting importance:

- The number of downs for advancing ten yards was increased from three to four, a clear strengthening of the offense. (Camp said he suggested the change to four downs, which presumably was true at the meeting, but Camp and others had been talking about such a change for a number of years.)[19]

- Forward passes could be completed across the goal line (previously, if a forward pass crossed the goal line, it was a touchback for the defenders).
- Field dimensions were altered to accommodate cross-the-goal-line passing, thereby essentially producing today's dimensions. Specifically, the playing field was shortened to one hundred yards, with a space of ten yards left beyond each goal line, an "end zone" in which forward passes could be received.
- A touchdown's value was increased from five points to six.
- The twenty-yard length limitation on forward passes was removed. (The requirement that a forward pass be thrown from a point five yards back of the line of scrimmage was retained, and a forward pass that went out-of-bounds still resulted in a turnover to the defense.)[20]

The 1912 rules also contained the first numerical specifications for an acceptable game ball, including a weight of fourteen to fifteen ounces (the same as today) and a short-axis circumference of 22 1/2 to 23 inches (today's rules specify 20 3/4 to 21 1/4 inches). By contrast, the rugby ball originally used in American football had a short-axis circumference of about 27 inches and apparently weighed twelve to thirteen ounces. Specifying the ball dimensions ensured that games would be played with regulation balls that, incidentally, had a shape, size, and weight more conducive to forward passing.[21]

After the 1912 rules had been tested during the 1912 season, Camp seemed as pleased and excited as he had ever been by new rules. "If ever there was a complete justification for rule-making in football," he wrote in the 1913 *Spalding Guide*, "it was certainly demonstrated during . . . 1912." And he was not shy in suggesting that he had a role: "When the writer advocated the rule calling for four tries in which to gain ten yards," critics worried it was an attempt to revive mass play and "hammering" features (because an added down increased the possibility of accumulating a ten-yard gain with line plunges). But the results, Camp said, were far different: "The casualty list is small, the interest was never greater, . . . and not for years has there been so little criticism."[22]

47 Besides Rule Making

When Walter Camp became president of the New Haven Clock Company in 1903, he and other company officers decided to focus on the watch business, particularly on pocket watches of an inexpensive, nonjeweled variety that might be sold for a dollar. The company's work on such so-called cheap watches was well under way by the time the rule-making crisis of 1905 exploded, keeping Camp busy and well occupied apart from the rule-making controversy. On April 4, 1905 (three months before the no-action rule-making meeting of June 12 and one month after his father died), Camp wrote to E. P. Root, the next-in-line NHCC officer who was out of town, to discuss major business issues. Camp had been tracking watch sales—not at desired levels, he said, but improving—and after thinking through the risk-gain equation of further investment, he was reaching a decision point: "I think I will give instructions to close the contracts" on the new building needed for the watchmaking effort. He also reported that he would be proceeding with a planned trip to England in a few days to attempt to "get things started right over there." If "I could in any way get the cheap watch started . . . so that we could have a small outlet over there, it would be a good thing."[1]

Significant investment by a company struggling to move away from years of financial losses was a bit perilous, but the decision proved correct: sales of the cheap watch soon became a significant part of NHCC's business. By 1909 the company built another watch-manufacturing building, five stories high and eighty feet long, and in 1911 they built one more, thereby completing a building quadrangle called Clock Square. By 1910 the company had accumulated a surplus of more than five hundred thousand dollars and declared an extra dividend of 8 percent.[2]

In 1915 NHCC took another step in the watchmaking business by introducing a wristwatch. Wristwatches had developed little sales interest in the 1800s—few men wore bracelets. But now military needs were spurring

Headquarters and factory of the New Haven Clock Company, as pictured in a 1920s company booklet. (Courtesy of the New Haven Museum, New Haven, Conn.)

the use of wristwatches, reflecting the increasing importance of timing in military actions and a wristwatch's ease of access.[3]

Despite Camp's many activities outside NHCC, the company was satisfied with his performance as president. His leadership and judgment had proved sound, leading the company into a successful and prosperous watch business. And in preparation for the watch-expansion initiative, even before accepting the company presidency, he had successfully persuaded further investments from Welch and English to provide sound financing for the effort.

Camp's health and vigor helped his performance. He was up early and on his way to work by seven thirty, walking more than a mile. One neighbor who often saw him on his way to work said he carried his overcoat over his arm and walked briskly, "as if out to break a record." Once there he handled NHCC issues as well as other matters; his NHCC secretary assisted him both with NHCC work and with work outside the clock business.[4]

Root saw NHCC as foremost in Camp's mind: "Though he was known all over the nation as an expert in matters pertaining to athletics, . . . his basic thought and interest were here in the Clock Company, where his business career began." Root also noted benefits from Camp's fame: "Walter Camp was a nationally known man. In any situation where a difficult piece of negotiation was necessary, Camp's prominence made him invaluable. He could represent us before any committee, or at any meeting, and do us unusual credit."[5]

In 1908, with the football rule-making crisis of 1905 past and NHCC business moving on nicely, the opportunistic and writing-oriented Camp was ready for a new venture, fictional sports books for boys. One friend called ventures like these Camp's "hobbies," but another observer thought writing was Camp's primary vocational urge. Income was also important, and Camp routinely and persistently negotiated about royalties and the effectiveness of publishers' marketing efforts. Camp was fairly early in recognizing an opportunity in juvenile sports books. Frank Merriwell stories had been published in huge volume, but they were the stuff of pulp magazines, fantastic and sensationalized. The real models for Camp's efforts probably were the clothbound hardback boys sports books of a young professional writer, Ralph Henry Barbour, who began in 1899 with *The Half-Back* and had continued so far with two or three more. Camp had tried fiction on a few occasions and gotten some reactions and advice from publishers, but this would be his first actual publication of a fictional work. His athletic background supplied realistic issues and playing specifics, and an editor at D. Appleton advised him several times on story-enhancing ideas, such as lengthening particular episodes to increase suspense.

His first book, *The Substitute*, published in 1908, was about a boy named Richard Goddard who graduates from a fictional private college-preparatory high school (Chesterfield), attends Yale, and lands a place as a substitute tackle on Yale's football team. An opportunity to increase his playing time arises when one of the regular varsity tackles is hurt, but first Goddard must overcome several hurdles. For example, he is demoted after a practice game in which he has difficulty blocking the other varsity tackle, Warner. The evening of the demotion, another player comes by to encourage Goddard and explain that he has an idea what is wrong: "You don't think about the game enough. [You don't think about] why Warner beats you [and] then study some way to stop it." He illustrates by discussing a playing tendency he has noticed in Warner: when Warner's side is on offense and the runner is to come his way, Warner tends to stand back a bit, and then, when the ball is snapped, he ducks down and tries to bowl his man over. Knowing this, Goddard should dodge quickly about the time Warner gets his head down and press his hand on the back of Warner's neck. If Goddard does that, the friend tells him, "instead of butting you over, Warner will go past you altogether, and perhaps fall on his nose."[6]

This item of Goddard's football "education" was reminiscent of a conviction Camp taught in his first book (*How to Coach a Team*, published in 1886), that "brains will beat brute force every time." And it was further evidence, already shown by the earlier 1889–90 instructional series in the youth magazine *St. Nicholas*, of Camp's interest in teaching youthful readers.

A second book published the next year, *Jack Hall at Yale*, was about the same group of boys as in *The Substitute* but focused on a different boy, Jack Hall, who is from a low-income family and needs to work to put himself through college. The work limits his participation in sports and forces him to juggle his schedule to participate in football. Yet Hall gradually wins a place on the varsity team and learns that he has a natural aptitude for placekicking. When he is pressed into kicking a goal in a critical situation near the end of the season, he makes the kick to win the game.[7]

In 1911 Camp published *Old Ryerson*, about still another friend from the Goddard group at Yale. Thomas Eugene Ryerson is a slow-moving, physically awkward student but is fascinated by football and, as it turns out, has an aptitude for devising football plays. The story line again involves a development

Camp's first three fiction books for boys.

struggle, as Ryerson first makes an effort to compete in wrestling, which a friend perceives is the sport to which he is best adapted. Through the friend's teaching, Ryerson manages a win. On a different level, Ryerson is able to help Yale's football team by contributing a game-changing play for the final championship game.[8]

Old Ryerson was delayed a year because Camp thought the time was right for a new technical book on football. His boys-book publisher, Appleton's, didn't agree but Century did, and *The Book of Football* was published in 1910, Camp's longest book yet and more comprehensive than his previous books on the history and technical details of the game.[9]

In one more revelation, Camp found time in 1909 to make an offering in a quite different book genre, bridge advice. Bridge was apparently a joint activity with Alice because the book, *Condensed Bridge for the Busy Man*, was dedicated to "A. S. C., My Best Partner." Consisting of thirty-two pages, the pamphlet contained a list of don'ts—"Don't forget that doubling is dependent upon score." "Don't double just to show your 'sand.'" "Don't forget that doubling locates strong hand for your opponents." Camp would go on to write two similar pamphlets of bridge advice in later years.[10]

Camp's 1910 treatise on American football.

He also continued with fictional books under an agreement with a different publisher, Hurst and Company, who apparently convinced him of a sales opportunity in a series of low-priced boys books. He was to provide three books by April 1, 1911, and another three by April 1, 1912. The books would be published under a pen name presumably chosen by Camp, Matthew M. Colton, and would sell for 60 cents, versus the $1.50 for books such as Camp's first set of three for Appleton's. Very early, probably after Camp had written one of the books, Camp hired a ghostwriter, Everard Thompson, an assistant editor at the *Yale Alumni Weekly* with whom Camp had worked (Camp was associate editor of the weekly until resigning in January 1905; Thompson was still at *Yale Alumni Weekly*, though since September 1906 he had also managed all Yale athletic ticket sales). As the deadline for submission of the first manuscript came and passed, Hurst wrote Camp, trying to hurry him along; Camp responded on October 24, 1910, "I have done considerable work on one book." The manuscript was finally delivered on January 4, 1911. Two additional books were published in 1911 and the last three in 1912, 1913, and 1914, respectively. All the books centered around a student named Frank Armstrong. A difference in writing style between the first and remaining books suggests Camp wrote the first one and Thompson the others. Camp worked with Thompson even on the books Thompson was writing, supplying ideas and information, reviewing, and revising, and Thompson respected and depended on such input. The books were later reissued in a slightly different format by A. L. Burt Company.[11]

In 1913 Camp began another set of books for boys for Appleton's under his own name, much like the Goddard series but featuring a new boy, Danny Phipps. Red-haired Danny is hotheaded and struggles to live in peace and harmony with some of those around him. Camp possibly wrote the first book in the series, *Danny Fists*, published in 1913, but another ghostwriter, William Heyliger, who had already published such books under his own name, was needed to complete the series; given a stylistic similarity between all three books, it is likely Heyliger wrote all three. Correspondence with Heyliger in the Camp Papers begins by March 1914 and refers to articles to be sent to Camp for review. It appears that Heyliger's Danny books were written as a series of installments or "articles" sent to Camp for review and possible modification before being published; apparently, the articles were published through a syndicate and then compiled into a book by Appleton's. *Captain Danny* was published in 1914 and *Danny the Freshman* in 1915 (the last included paintings by a young Norman Rockwell).[12]

Camp's books for boys were just one small part in a larger culture growing around the game of American football. Football made it to Broadway in 1904 with the play *The College Widow*, by George Ade, a comedy that was a hit from the rise of the opening curtain. The genre of fight songs continued to grow with "The Eyes of Texas" (the University of Texas, 1903), "Down the Field" (Yale, 1904), "Cannon Song" (Princeton, 1906), "Gridiron King" (Harvard, 1906), and "Anchors Aweigh" (Naval Academy, 1907, a patriotic song, but composed by the Naval Academy music director specifically "for the 'Midshipmen'"). In 1908, following a Michigan–Notre Dame game, brothers Michael and John Shea from Notre Dame composed a college fight song regarded by many as one of the best:

> Cheer, cheer for old Notre Dame,
> Wake up the echoes cheering her name,
> Send a volley cheer on high,
> Shake down the thunder from the sky.

Organized college homecoming festivities began about 1910, when two Illinois seniors planned an event around the Chicago-Illinois game, anxious to jog the team out of a losing pattern; the student body, faculty, and local businesses took an interest and promoted a successful event, with the campus decorated and a full crowd attending the game. The University of Missouri and Baylor introduced homecoming-type activities to their campuses about the same time. In 1902 the eleven-year-old Tournament of Roses in Pasadena California decided to add football to its well-attended flower parade. They persuaded Michigan to come west, where it defeated Stanford 49–0; subsequent tournament administrations dropped football, but it was reintroduced in 1916 and has been present ever since.[13]

Meanwhile, Palmer Pierce was working diligently to build up the Intercollegiate Athletic Association. He continued to approach the Big Three about membership, and in 1909 Harvard broke ranks and joined; by that year, membership had grown to sixty-seven, and Pierce was credited with

An early football cheerleader. (*Century* 71 [November 1905]: 99, University of Minnesota Library)

forming a stable and smooth-running organization. Expanded membership made the association more national, and in 1910 its name was changed to the National Collegiate Athletic Association, which also distinguished it from other "intercollegiate" organizations. (Pierce resigned the presidency in 1912 when assigned to military duty in China, and Dean Le Baron R. Briggs of Harvard replaced him, but when Pierce returned to duty in the United States before the 1916 convention, Briggs resigned and Pierce was again elected president and served until 1930.)[14]

The Central Board of Officials appointed by the amalgamated rules committee in 1906 proved quite effective, appointing more than eight hundred officials in its first year and helping provide interpretations of rules. In September 1908, the board arranged a meeting in which "nearly eighty of the most prominent football men of the country [coaches and officials]" gathered to discuss rule interpretations. Babbitt opened the meeting but then turned it over for Camp to chair and lead an informal discussion of questions such as the protection to be afforded a player who had signaled for a fair catch and then juggled the ball while running to catch it. Such interpretation meetings continued for many years.[15]

The Camps changed residences often in these years. They lived at two different houses on Everitt Street from 1900 to 1907 (two years at number 30 and five years at number 58), before renting rooms for two years at the New Haven House, a hotel located near the Yale campus. In 1909 they moved to 215 Bishop Street, nearly back-to-back with the home of Professor Sumner and Jeannie; likely, they were there to be of help, because Professor Sumner had suffered increasingly severe strokes in 1908 and 1909 and would die in April 1910. Jeannie continued to live in the longtime Sumner house until her death in June 1917.[16]

Later in 1910, the Camps moved a few blocks to 34 Hillhouse Avenue. A few blocks from the Yale campus, Hillhouse was the grand street of New Haven, wide, lined with large arching elms, and populated by mansion-size houses having large setbacks; it reportedly had been called "the most beautiful street in America" by Charles Dickens during a visit in March 1868. Henry English, a principal stockholder and board member of the New Haven Clock Company, lived next to the Camps. Walter Jr. was twenty years old and a student at Yale and Janet was fourteen when the Camps moved to Hillhouse. At least at times, a domestic staff of six young Irishwomen lived in the house with the family.[17]

Home of the Walter Camp family from about 1910 to 1922. (Courtesy of the New Haven Museum, New Haven, Conn.)

Alice Camp with her and Walter's daughter, Janet. (Walter Chauncey Camp Papers, 1870–1983 [inclusive], 1870–1925 [bulk], Manuscripts and Archives, Yale University)

The wedding party of Walter Camp Jr. and Frances English. Janet Camp is in the back row, second from right. W. Averell Harriman, Walter Jr.'s Yale classmate, is in the front row, far right. (*New Haven Saturday Chronicle*, October 24, 1914, courtesy of the New Haven Museum, New Haven, Conn.)

Major family events occurred during the family's years in the house: About four years after moving into the house, Walter Jr. married Frances English, an actress in local theater productions and a granddaughter of the English family that had been the Camps' backyard neighbors. In a perhaps shaky marriage, Frances was living in the house with the Camps at the time of the 1920 census, while Walter Jr. worked and lived in New York City. Janet made her debut from the house after school in New York City and Switzerland, and in about 1920 she married (Francis) Thayer Hobson, who was employed as an English teacher at a preparatory school as well as at Yale.[18]

48 Away with the Old

Walter Camp was "advisory football coach" at Yale from 1888 through 1906 with only a few gaps. But by 1907, he knew he was falling out of favor.[1]

Camp was unhappy about being pushed aside, unhappy personally and worried about how the Yale team would fare, and he expressed some of those thoughts in his second novel, *Jack Hall at Yale*, published in 1909. Although a boys book, *Jack Hall* was written also for adult readers, such as Yale students or alumni who might potentially make changes in response to the book's warnings. One warning came in a conversation between two fictitious newspaper staffers—"Stanley," a member of the *Harvard Crimson* newspaper staff, and "Harry," a friend of Jack Hall and a member of the *Yale News* staff. Stanley speaks of athletic relations between Harvard and Yale:

> You [Yale] have often had the best of us. . . . But this sort of thing is not going to go on forever. Our turn is coming. . . . I can already see it beginning to come. Everybody used to be so loyal down here [at Yale] to the management . . ., but I can see in the last two years that there are more divergent views and you are not so ready to follow the leader as you were before. Oh, we went through it all up at Cambridge. . . . [But] last year we actually let our football coaches alone and let them really run things and did not criticize everything they did. It worked out well.

A Yale upperclassman listening in interjects: "You may be half right on the fact that [respect for management] is not as strong as it was . . . but I think it is only a few kickers, and I do not believe it has touched, or ever will touch, the main body of men." The *Crimson* man disagrees: "You just wait and see. It begins a little at a time, and pretty soon it gets bigger. . . . [B]efore you know it you have got a mess, and the bigger the university and the more it is growing the more separate interests the men have and the less they are willing to get together or listen to the opinions of others."[2]

Camp's coaching participation had always depended on the captain, but there had been pressure within the larger Yale community and from old captains to involve him. Now it was different. In a letter to a friend some years later, Alice wrote of Walter's experience as he began to be pushed aside. Walter was "asked to 'prove it' to the most inexperienced coaches or critics," men who had been taught that Walter "is only an older man trying to force his opinion and methods on up-to-date players." Yet, Alice said, Camp still tried to help, sacrificing "every personal feeling on the chance of saving a team here from disaster."[3]

Besides age-based skepticism, Camp's critics might also have felt reinforced by another 1905–6 storm, arising from an "exposé" of college athletics in *McClure's* magazine. In the first of two installments (June 1905), allegations were made against eight colleges, including Yale—partly factual but also relying on innuendo and omission to create a sense of scandal fitting with then popular "muckraking" fashions.[4]

The allegations against Yale specified a just-graduated student, James J. Hogan, described in the article as a good student but financially impoverished and thus well qualified for scholarships granted on the basis of "indigence and good promise." Hogan, we are told, also had jobs: in his freshman year, he began and operated an eating club for fellow students; in subsequent years, he and two other athletes had the "scorecard privilege," giving them the proceeds from scorecard advertising and sales; and still later, the American Tobacco Company hired him to distribute cigarettes around New Haven, where, the company said, he achieved good success.

What likely most excited the *McClure's* author and readers was the story of a December 1903 trip for Yale's highly regarded trainer, Mike Murphy, who was ill and sent to Cuba for a ten-day rest. Murphy took Hogan along as a traveling companion, an undoubted privilege and unusual benefit for a student, raising questions of favoritism and over-the-top largesse for athletes. But Murphy had mentored Hogan, and Hogan would be a good traveling companion—twenty-eight years old because of work-related delays and well liked: "His manly demeanor," one Yale student wrote, "made him one of the . . . most lovable of Yale men"; at graduation Hogan was second in the vote for "the man most to be admired." Hogan was a Yale star not only as an athlete but also as a student and citizen.[5]

No Camp involvement in the Cuba trip was shown—the best evidence suggests Hogan's trip was the work of student managers—but the trip was financed by athletic receipts that ultimately came under Camp's jurisdiction as graduate adviser. An associated issue was the partial secrecy of accounts of the Yale Financial Union under Camp's direct control: Yale's athletic income and expenses were managed and accounted for by student athletic associations, but the surplus of income over expenses was paid into the YFU fund. The total of accumulated surpluses in the YFU fund was not reported, nor were any gains or losses on investment of the fund or disbursements from the fund. Camp explained the secrecy as supporting one of the fund's purposes, namely, to limit extravagant expenditures (not always successfully!) by not advertising the significant funds Yale was accumulating, which were intended for major down-the-road athletic costs and support of minor non-self-sustaining sports.[6]

After the Hogan story appeared in *McClure's*, Yale graduate Clarence Deming published more information about Yale's athletic accounts, including the YFU fund. Camp agreed to be interviewed by Deming and "freely disclosed" the facts and figures of the fund. Deming reported that the surpluses had been accumulated "to meet future athletic emergencies," and there was not the "slightest hint or suspicion of 'graft.'" The accumulated funds had been overseen and handled by responsible and competent New Haven leaders and investors, whom Deming interviewed.[7]

To Deming, the problem was the size of an "athletic revenue so large that it has to be disguised." Deming was upset by the growth and commercial implications of athletics at eastern universities, creating an "atmosphere of wealth," "lavishness and luxury," and "greater and greater expansions," and he apparently saw the secrecy of the accumulated fund as an effort to camouflage the size of Yale's athletic program.

Among Deming's questions and Camp's answers in the *New York Evening Post*:

> Q: Is it true that athletes at Yale have had expenses to make up scholarship for private tutoring paid for from athletic funds?
> A: It is true.
> Q: And under what head do such tutorial payments appear in the athletic accounts?
> A: I think under the head of "maintenance."
> Q: Under what head have been entered the expenses of Hogan and Murphy on the trip to Cuba for the health of the latter?
> A: Under the head of "miscellaneous."[8]

Camp's admission in Deming's report of tutoring and Cuba-trip payments has led some historians to erroneously regard the YFU fund as a giant "$100,000 slush" fund used to bolster Yale's competitiveness. The statement is erroneous: First, Deming himself reports that no withdrawals had been made from the fund over its life (and the records were made available to Deming), the fund being intended to preserve receipts for major expenditures. Second, Deming reports that the tutoring and Cuba-trip payments were accounted for in *published* accounts (though camouflaged under the head of "maintenance" or "miscellaneous"). "Published" accounts means student accounts because YFU accounts were not published. The tutoring and Cuba-trip expenditures came from the regular receipts of the student associations, not the YFU fund.

The editors of the *Harvard Crimson* didn't see the YFU fund as a slush fund when they wrote in praise of Camp:

> In the early days the problem of athletic deficits seemed an insoluble one and wholly irreconcilable with the necessity of maintaining diversified sports. As treasurer of the Financial Union at Yale, Camp worked out the first satisfactory solution of the difficulty. By pooling the finance of all sports and placing them under a unified control, he showed that taken altogether they could be made to pay for themselves. Since that time centralized finance for athletics has been adopted by the leading colleges of the country, with the result that minor sports which were once thought impossible without private subventions, now flourish in American colleges.[9]

Setting aside the issue of the YFU fund, Camp likely knew of Murphy's rest trip to Cuba, given that Camp was athletic director and closely involved in Yale football. But knowledge that Hogan was accompanying him is not so clear. Camp had not closely monitored student accounts for several years. No evidence was offered that Camp had knowledge of the Hogan-related expenses, and the Yale officials familiar with his work, President Hadley and Anson Stokes, secretary of Yale, corresponded and acted as if he had not.[10]

The students' camouflage of tutoring and Cuba-trip payments in "maintenance" and "miscellaneous" accounts does suggest a desire to keep those payments quiet. But camouflage of tutoring payments could have been for expediency rather than hiding ethical violations. Tutoring-type assistance was being offered by other colleges (see an entry in the 1905 diary of Harvard's coach Bill Reid, who, as part of an effort to get a former Harvard player, LeMoyne, to return to Harvard and play, went to "Nolen, the tutor," who promised "to tutor LeMoyne through his staff of men, and in every way do what he could to help put him through," without cost to LeMoyne). More than tutoring, some schools were officially instituting what they called "athletic scholarships" for players identified by the school's athletic advisory committee. Tutoring payments to assist a student-athlete's studies were growing to be an accepted practice.[11]

But some influential persons disagreed with tutoring payments, and that was undoubtedly the reason for camouflage. In fact, a Yale faculty member included tutoring payments in his request for an investigation of Yale's athletic program discussed below, and the faculty report after the investigation also criticized tutoring payments. It was more convenient and safe for Yale's student managers to not publicly disclose such payments.

The Cuba-trip payments are in a different category. Camp undoubtedly understood he had not been sufficiently attentive, and Yale officials asked him to be more involved. Yale had begun a period of financial retrenchment even before the *McClure's* and Deming articles, initiated with a June 1, 1905, memorandum from Yale secretary Anson Stokes, describing a looming "Yale crisis" in financial resources. Mainly stating a need for increased endowment, the memorandum also asked for more restraint in internal Yale spending to give donors confidence in the safety of their endowment gifts.[12]

As efforts for financial restraint proceeded into October 1905, Stokes wrote to Camp, "I feel sure there is opportunity for a considerable increase in economy," in athletic expenditures and "all that is needed to bring about these improvements is a frank and serious talk by you to the athletic managers." Nothing was said about the Hogan affair, but Stokes suggested that the United States had "been living in a period of extravagance," and it was now necessary to limit spending: "You are the man to emphasize it, as you are the only person connected with athletics at Yale who has the entire confidence of all concerned." Stokes was undoubtedly trying to cajole Camp into a desired course of action, but his suggestion that Camp had the "entire confidence of all concerned" was a strong endorsement.[13]

However, Camp did have more severe critics, respectful but definitely agitated. In a long September 1905 letter to President Hadley, Yale faculty member William Beebe asked for an investigation and reconsideration of Yale's athletic procedures and policies. Hadley brought the matter to the University Council, and a three-person faculty investigatory committee was named. The investigation included vigorous faculty debates, at one of which Camp appeared by request. Prior to that appearance, Beebe wrote Camp with a list of subjects he wanted to discuss: athletic "expenses, training tables, graduate coaches, secret practices, out-of-town games," plus Camp's "status as a member of the Faculty." Beebe realized that "a majority of the Faculty will be ready to take your point of view on any matter connected with athletics," but Beebe still wanted to discuss and challenge some existing practices.[14]

The designated three-person investigating committee wrote an eighteen-page report with several recommendations and also wrote Camp a shorter letter that concluded with restrained recommendations for Camp's "consideration," including that there be a "more complete itemizing of accounts with some degree of publicity." The purposes of the YFU fund and Camp's superintendence of it were unchanged. Camp continued as the effective "athletics director" and a member of the University Council for many years, and Hadley relied on and supported Camp throughout the rule-making battles of the early 1900s.[15]

It appears President Hadley had little sympathy with Beebe's complaints, but a letter Camp sent Hadley on March 6, 1906, raises added questions. The letter outlined subcommittees Camp had formed to establish cost controls in athletics and included at the end, "Now about a small personal matter. I should like very much to bear some share in retrenchment and would ask that the arrangement made between you and me at the time when my salary was reduced from $5000 to $3750 be further altered by the reduction of another $500." It is not known when or why Camp's salary had been reduced from $5,000 to $3,750, but that number matched the $3,750 standard pay of Yale faculty members. The change seemed to have Camp's acquiescence ("arrangement made between you and me"), and many reasons for it can be imagined—perhaps the most likely is Camp's recognition or acceptance that he was no longer performing all the tasks he originally did, such as giving close oversight to student accounts. Also, since his new salary matched that of an average professor, it may have been intended to soothe disgruntled Yale professors like Beebe about Camp's status "on the Faculty," or to counter public attacks on the higher pay of athletic personnel over scholarly professors who did the main work of a college.[16]

From a personal perspective, Camp got in a last word on the Hogan affair. In his second book, *Jack Hall at Yale*, published in 1909, the admired main character, Jack Hall, has the same initials as James Hogan, is poor like Hogan, works like Hogan, and like Hogan achieves athletic success in spite of that work. To reinforce the correlation, a trainer in the book who mentors Hall is named Matt Manning, matching the initials of Mike Murphy, who mentored Hogan and took him to Cuba. Camp published *Jack Hall* only after first asking Stokes's opinion on Hogan; Stokes replied positively, confirming Camp in his view that the *McClure's* criticism was unjustified. McClure's had untruthfully blackened Yale's name and that of its students and administrators, but to those in the know, there was a different and positive reality: Hogan (like Hall) had persevered, overcoming some major financial disadvantages through striving and achievement. Far from feeling resentment, Hogan's classmates liked and admired him, and Camp did also.[17]

There is another subject on which Camp could have seemed insensitive and out-of-date to some Yale players, coaches, or officials, namely, the subject of head injuries and protection against them. Through football's early years, there had been little head protection, but in the mid- to late 1890s a few players began to wear protective helmets of their own design. Spalding entered the business in 1898 with helmets that comprised a crown made of "sole leather . . ., filled with air holes and lined with lamb's wool padding," and by 1902 the business had advanced sufficiently for helmeted players to be pictured on the *Spalding Guide* cover. A temporary setback occurred in 1903 when Paul Dashiell, concerned about the danger of hard helmets, persuaded the rules committee to outlaw helmets made from "sole leather, papier mache, or any other hard or unyielding material." Spalding responded by offering a helmet "made with soft black leather . . . padded with felt and well ventilated" and the next year added a "pneumatic head harness" having an "inflated crown."[18]

Helmet use achieved a new status in 1907 when Harvard began requiring their players to wear "a properly fitted headguard." Use was also growing elsewhere; the photo of a 1907 game between Cornell and Princeton seems to show all players of both teams wearing helmets.[19]

But Yale players played those years without a helmet. In the 1908 Harvard-Yale game, all Yale players were bareheaded, in contrast to the uniformly helmeted Harvard players. Camp likely was influential in the Yale practice. His 1910 *Book of Football* has eight pages on a football player's "costume," but there is not a word about helmets. Caps such as Camp had worn in his playing days, including sun-shielding visors, were discussed approvingly but not helmets. For Camp, helmets were apparently not worth discussing.[20]

Medical knowledge at the time, at least as understood in the football community, was that concussions caused "no permanent injury." After more than twenty-five years of coaching, Glenn Warner wrote in 1912 that he had "never seen an accident to the head which was serious," even though he had seen players who "lost their memory for a time and had to be taken out of the game." He did not encourage the general use of helmets, saying they interfered with hearing, were warm, and added weight. But Warner also did not object to their use and thought "men who carry the ball would do well to wear light head protectors."[21]

1908 Harvard-Yale football game. (Reprinted from Walter Camp, *The Book of Football*, 28)

One can imagine Camp, the studious coach and data-driven business manager, wanting real proof on the value of helmets. From today's perspective, the thinly padded helmets of the 1900s, covering part of the head in an almost pasted-on, close-fitting style, must have had limited effectiveness. Camp could reasonably have believed there was no important health reason for wearing them and that they were a distraction and hampered good play. He had played American football without helmets and had watched many others play without them for more than thirty years. "Pudge" Heffelfinger of Yale's 1888–91 teams led running plays into the opposition, helmetless and sometimes bent over and leading head first, without apparent harm.

Yet with younger coaches and other schools willing to give helmets a try, to be open to the possible danger and seek to limit it, Camp's refusal to present the subject in his 1910 book seems another example of slowness to adapt. No document has been found in which Camp disparages the wearing of helmets, but such silence would be typical—he had his view, and others could do as they liked; he would not judge them. Nevertheless, Yale players

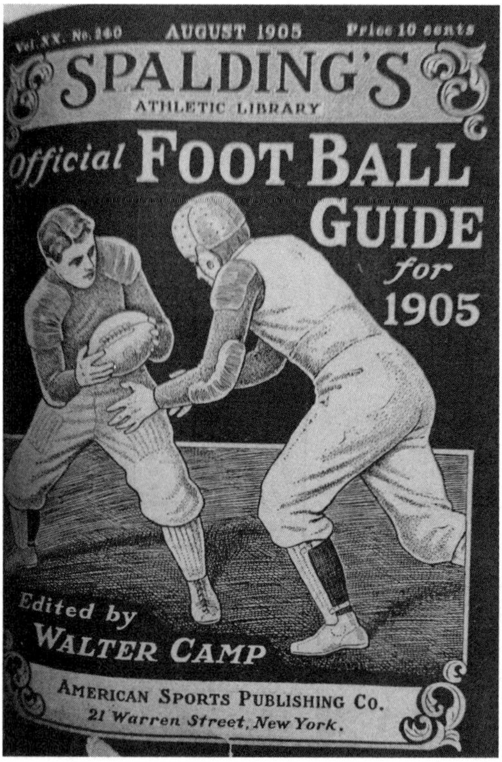

Cover of the 1905 *Spalding's Official Foot Ball Guide*, illustrating an early football helmet. (University of Minnesota Library)

seemed to agree with Camp's view well into the first decade of the twentieth century. Gradually, that changed, and by at least 1913 some Yale players were wearing helmets, apparently by individual choice more than team-wide rule. Those who did not wear helmets were not alone. Even in 1934, a consensus All-American at the University of Minnesota, Bill Bevan, did not wear a helmet, and the rules committee did not require them until 1939.

Camp was again involved in coaching the Yale football team in 1908 and 1909, but 1910 brought an even more pronounced change from the past. The 1910 captain, Fred Daly, chose the last year's captain as head coach but also gave a large role to George Foster Sanford, the erstwhile Columbia coach unwelcome to many at Yale. Sanford was with the team before the season started, had responsibility for coaching the line all year, and after Yale lost to Army and was tied by Vanderbilt was put in charge of the whole team as they prepared to play Brown.[22]

Camp went west early in the 1910 season, presumably on business, but on the way he stopped to visit Tom Shevlin, a former star end for Yale who was now working for his father's lumber business in Minnesota and was helping Harry Williams coach the Minnesota team. Shevlin had learned another new play from Williams, a shift play involving player movements just before snapback to change the point of attack. Camp and Shevlin discussed the Williams shift during Camp's visit and concluded that it would be a desirable improvement at Yale.[23]

Camp was back in New Haven by midseason, but, as he wrote Ray Tompkins, an old Yale friend and football player, the Yale captain and coaches did not show any interest in him: "The coaches never darkened my doors and on Thursday night before the Brown game I went to two of them, who told me they could win the Brown and also the Princeton and Harvard games with straight line-plunging plays [a favorite of Sanford's] and turned down the shift plays which Shevlin and I [had discussed]." But the Brown game proved an even bigger Yale loss, 21–0, whereupon according to Camp, "Immediately after the Brown game Daly came to see me and confessed the error they had all been under and asked me to take hold." Camp wrote that he "telephoned to Shevlin [who was then in New York] and sent a car up for him and in my office we three [presumably Camp, Daly, and Shevlin] laid out a definite plan for the next two weeks. At that meeting, besides the offense of the Minnesota [shift] plays, I proposed a reorganization of their defense and laid it out on paper. We agreed upon it and put it into effect."

The biggest two games of the year were left, Princeton and Harvard. Whether it was the result of Camp's efforts or not, the team did regroup, defeating Princeton 5–3 and playing favored Harvard to a scoreless tie.[24]

A year later, in 1911, with a new captain and head coach, Camp was again out of favor. In response to Tompkins's inquiries, Camp said, "The Yale captain never came inside my door in spite of requests, being kept away by the head coach, I presume." Tompkins had asked Camp what he would like to see done, and Camp continued, "I don't propose to do anything but keep my mouth shut, grin, bear the stories that 'Haughton has at last beaten Camp, etc.,' but I do want our captains who were so strongly with me in times past to know what the situation is." The season's results were mediocre, with a loss to each of Army and Princeton and a tie with Harvard.[25]

The situation was similar in 1912, with Camp essentially not involved in coaching, and a season's record of 7-1-1, with a loss to Harvard, 20–0, and a tie with Princeton.

In 1913 a new Yale captain, Henry Ketcham, tried to rebuild Yale's football program. After meetings and consultations, he named a "coaching committee" of five persons, with Camp as committee chair. With input from the coaching committee, Ketcham announced on February 16, 1913, that Howard Jones, a 1908 Yale graduate who had coached Yale to a perfect season in 1909, would be head coach. While previous Yale coaches had generally received only expenses, Jones would be paid a salary. Unfortunately, the changes didn't help, and Yale's 1913 record declined even further, to 5 wins, 2 losses, and 3 ties, tying Princeton and losing to Harvard.[26]

At the same time their football fortunes were in decline, the Yale community came to believe they needed a new place to play, a permanent cement stadium to replace their existing wood grandstand. Actually, they were somewhat late in facing up to this issue. A permanent concrete football stadium had already been built ten years earlier, incredibly at Harvard University, administered by football's implacable foe, President Charles W. Eliot.

Eliot and Harvard, as well now as Yale, were caught in an irony. Eliot had long advocated that intercollegiate competition take place on college grounds, and in 1897 the UAC suggested moving the Princeton-Yale game from New York to college grounds, and Harvard and Yale also moved their game to college grounds. The consequences of such moves—large numbers of viewers coming to campuses to watch games—must have been somewhat anticipated, but perhaps not fully. At the time of the move, did Harvard authorities expect their wood stands at the Henry Higginson–gifted Soldiers' Field would need to hold thirty-six thousand for the 1899 Harvard-Yale game and forty thousand for the 1901 game and even then refuse many ticket applicants?

Wood stands' deficiencies had been cataloged by I. N. Hollis, an engineering professor who was the current chair of Harvard's athletic committee: unsightliness, risk of fire, danger of collapse, high cost of maintenance. Intrigued by the engineering challenge of replacing the wood stands, Hollis considered concrete-slab seats supported on steel stands. When more money became available, Hollis and Harvard decided on a more pioneering effort—building the stadium of steel-reinforced concrete, apparently the first steel-reinforced concrete stadium in America. A prominent New York architect gave the stadium the classical form of an ancient European coliseum, with a surrounding arcade of side-by-side arches forming the stadium's exterior base and providing entrances and a second tier of surrounding arches directly above the first. Permanent concrete seats would accommodate twenty-one to twenty-three thousand spectators, while temporary wood seats for twelve thousand could be added onto a promenade around the top of the stands; an additional five thousand seats could be placed across the open end. It was by far the largest building on Harvard's campus but less prominent because Soldiers' Field was across the Charles River, a few blocks from the main campus.[27]

Yale had delayed building a concrete stadium, allegedly because Yale did not have Harvard's roster of wealthy supporters. But one wonders: Was Walter Camp, the chief athletics officer at Yale, enthusiastically in support of such a stadium? He seemed ambivalent about the spectacle and large number of spectators at some of the big games.

Yet replacement of Yale's wood stands was inevitable. Repairs were made every year, but at some point the wood stands and support structure would need replacement. Occasional letters published in the *Yale Alumni Weekly* indicated sentiment was rising for a new stadium, and by 1911 a consensus was reached to proceed. Alumni formed a "Committee of Twenty-One" to solicit financial contributions. The stadium was to be built near the existing Yale Field, but added land would be needed both for the stadium and for additional playing fields for other sports. Camp negotiated and completed purchase of needed property, and fifty of the ninety thousand dollars' total land cost came from the Yale Financial Union. Beyond purchase of the land,

Camp had little if any direct involvement in planning the new stadium or raising money for it. He had remained active as Yale "athletics director" while the fund-raising and construction continued, but funds were raised and construction managed by the Committee of Twenty-One.[28]

The design selected for the stadium had been suggested by Yale graduate Charles Ferry, a New Haven civil engineer working in the field of filtration plants, not stadiums, who proposed a stadium half-embedded in the ground like a reservoir. Dirt excavated for the embedded half would be piled in a landscaped slope around the aboveground portion of the stadium walls, leaving little of the stadium structure to show from outside. Yale was still close enough to its glory years, and ticket demand continued to so far exceed existing capacity at Yale Field that the planners were persuaded to build large and grand. A huge elliptical, dish-shaped seating structure was built, having the largest capacity of any stadium so far built in the United States, regularly seating seventy thousand and capable with temporary additions of eighty thousand. Entrances were at ground level, tunneled through the sloping bank of excavated dirt, allowing patrons to walk into the stadium at midheight. Lying as an open geometrical cavity in the ground, the term *bowl* was quite descriptive, and "Yale Bowl" became its accepted name.[29]

Princeton built a new stadium at the same time as Yale, a gift from Edgar Palmer in memory of his father. Princeton's Palmer Stadium was scheduled to be opened and dedicated on November 14, 1914, with Princeton hosting Yale; one week later, on November 21, the Yale Bowl was to be opened and dedicated, with Yale hosting Harvard. In each case, the home team proved quite hospitable: Yale defeated Princeton on November 14 at the Princeton dedication, and Harvard defeated Yale November 21 at the Yale dedication, 36–0. The Haughton-coached Harvard team was reaching its acme, and Yale's football dominance had ended. The next year, Yale played Harvard in Cambridge and lost 41–0.[30]

49 "I Will Give It Up"

Before the Yale Bowl was opened and dedicated in the fall of 1914, Walter Camp resigned from his Yale "athletics director" job, including his work for President Hadley and his position on the University Council. He had worked with Hadley for fifteen years and been central to Yale athletics for decades, but now he was retiring.[1]

War had broken out among European nations in the preceding weeks, and Camp gave that as a reason—clock-company issues brought on by "the present disturbed condition of the country" required his attention. Such issues were undoubtedly real, but Camp's unhappiness with Yale football and his inability to do anything in response must have been involved also. Besides, Alice was pushing him to get away.

A few months after his Yale resignation, Camp also advised he would retire from the national football rules committee. To mark the event, he arranged to host a farewell dinner at the committee's February 1915 rule-making meeting. As might be expected, committee members used the occasion to offer him tributes for his long and influential service. But almost all added another message—a request that he change his mind or at least continue as an emeritus member, welcome to attend meetings. The committee proceeded to elect him an "emeritus member for life."[2]

Camp seemed equivocal about continuing, perhaps desirous of some assurances: Did Yale still want him to represent them? Did all rules-committee members welcome him? That's one likely explanation for the out-of-the-blue publication in the *Yale News* of "Appreciation of Walter Camp" on December 16, 1915, ten months after his retirement dinner but only two months before the next rules-committee meeting. Three individuals contributed to it—Professor Corwin, having effectively succeeded Camp as athletics manager at Yale several months earlier, and two members of the football rules committee, Parke Davis, who had written the longest tribute to Camp at Camp's February dinner and had proposed Camp's election as an emeritus member, and Paul Dashiell, who had offered a tribute at the dinner but had not requested that Camp continue on the committee. Dashiell had served on the rules committee with Camp for twenty years, and their relationship had seemed quite warm, but they were often on opposite sides during the 1905–10 rule-making controversies.[3]

If Camp was looking for a clear invitation from Dashiell, the latter's statement in the *Yale News* seemed somewhat ambiguous. The last paragraph read, "As the only member left of the original committee I am sure I voice the feeling of every single man who has served with him in that body. Let us hope that his considered retirement is only from the official connection and that the game at large may still have the benefit of his experience and judgment." "Retirement from official connection" sounds like separation from the rules committee. He could provide "the benefit of his experience" as a consultant or through articles in newspapers or magazines. But perhaps what Dashiell was really saying was: "Walter, it's up to you to decide; if you want to retire, retire; if you want to continue on the committee, you and your contributions will be welcome."[4]

Whatever. Camp did change his mind, and when the committee gathered on February 27, 1916, he was at the meeting with no apparent change in his role: he was secretary before his resignation, and, whether he was officially an emeritus member or a regular member, he continued as secretary in 1916 and for the rest of his life.[5]

One more notable change occurred in 1915—Yale joined the National Collegiate Athletic Association, the last of the Big Three to do so. Had Camp's withdrawal as chief athletic official at Yale opened the way? Perhaps, but it was Camp who explained Yale's change of mind. Yale's original decision to stay out of the NCAA, Camp wrote in the *Yale News*, had "rested principally upon two beliefs—first, that [becoming a member] would take control of Yale athletics out of the hands of the University," and second, legislation in such a body would be unduly influenced by the "unusual excitement" attending the formative years of such a body. To illustrate, Camp quoted a speaker at the NCAA's first meeting who contended that saving college athletics would require placing them "under complete faculty control," thus threatening Yale's tradition of student management.[6]

But now, Camp said, over its several years of existence, the NCAA had in fact "judiciously avoided enacting impractical legislation that would impose rules across the spectrum of universities that differ so widely in their conditions and environments." The NCAA had become "a body for the interchange of ideas and its actions are binding on members only to the extent the *members* think it wise or advisable *in their institution*." Camp had attended last year's (1914) meeting of the NCAA, with one hundred representatives, and found it quite interesting, demonstrating the value of information exchange from across the country while leaving members free to control and solve their own athletic problems. Camp had been sent to the meeting to evaluate whether Yale should join the NCAA, and he wrote in his *Yale News* article that he was now recommending that Yale join, which it proceeded to do.[7]

After Yale's 1914 and 1915 losses to Harvard by unheard-of margins, the Yale University Athletic Association (YUAA) established an ad hoc committee to recommend a new coach and to reorganize the football system at Yale. The committee chair was Vance McCormick, captain and quarterback of Yale's undefeated and unscored-upon 1892 football team and a longtime friend of Camp, who was also named to the committee. McCormick was from a wealthy Pennsylvania family and had joined the family's coal mining business after graduation. He also entered the newspaper business and then politics, becoming mayor of Harrisburg and in 1914 the unsuccessful Democratic candidate for governor of Pennsylvania.[8]

During the years Camp was being pushed aside by Yale student leaders, McCormick had written Camp, expressing his willingness to "join . . . in any effort" to get the old system reestablished with Camp again involved. But now, in 1915 and 1916, circumstances were different. With increased enrollment at Yale and with growing interest in football, there were many more candidates for the team—two or three hundred—requiring, said McCormick, "a head [coach] with assistants in the field daily." A perfectly organized system was needed to cover the smallest details, as regards not only the coaching but also the physical and mental training of the men. Now McCormick wanted a professional coach on a long-term basis to establish the needed system.[9]

With that background, the committee recommended (and the YUAA voted to accept) T. A. Dwight (Tad) Jones as head coach for 1916. Jones was a 1908 graduate of the Sheffield School at Yale and brother of Howard Jones, who had coached Yale in 1909 and 1913; Tad had quarterbacked Yale in 1906 and 1907 and captained it in 1907; and Camp credited Tad's generalship and leadership with obtaining wins against both Princeton and Harvard. Since graduation Jones had coached at Exeter.[10]

Following completion of the work of the ad hoc committee, the Yale University Athletic Association on February 2, 1916, decided to appoint an ongoing Committee on Football to have full charge of all matters pertaining to football and to be responsible only to the Athletic Association and university authorities. McCormick was again chosen to chair the committee.[11]

Camp was named a member of the new committee, but Alice was not happy and wrote McCormick sometime in March 1916, saying things Walter would not say:

> I have finally convinced Walter to give up the position on the committee. . . . For several years Walter has been asked to "prove it" to the most inexperienced coaches or critics. . . . [T]hese men have been taught that Walter's advice is of no consequence, that he is only an older man trying to force his opinion and methods on up-to-date players. . . . I will not have Walter in the position now from which he was forced when he was the real head, when he was in his prime, when no one

> defended him. . . . I've seen him sacrifice every personal feeling on the chance of saving a team here from disaster.
>
> . . . Walter . . . will of course be happy to help always, if his help is sought, but his days of anxiety and worry over the situation must be over.

Camp also wrote to McCormick a few days later, affirming his agreement with Alice but with a different perspective and tone:

> I am sure you and the others will understand how I feel when I tell you I have telegraphed Alice that I will give it up. I know of no more ideal Committee and staff of coaches we will have and to work with all would be the real thing once more. But Alice feels very strongly . . . and . . . this year will be one of great work and worry. Besides, my directors are especially sensitive to my becoming officially . . . [involved in] football again after once getting clear of it.
>
> You . . . must all come out and have your meetings at my house where, if you will, we can build up in a really congenial atmosphere the old time spirit and plans, I am sure. And you can count on my most loyal support and all the time I can possibly give.
>
> Do let me work with you just the same.[12]

Camp had promised "loyal support and all the time I can possibly give," and he followed through. By mid-June 1916, McCormick had accepted election as chairman of the Democratic National Committee, and later in the month he was chosen by President Wilson as manager of Wilson's 1916 reelection campaign; both commitments would prevent McCormick from deep involvement in Yale's athletic affairs. Also, all other committee members lived away from New Haven; Camp was the only one on site, able to routinely observe practice, consult with the coaches, observe their performance, and even negotiate agreements (Camp negotiated an employment agreement with at least Jones's choice for assistant coach).[13]

The whole idea of a Committee on Football with which a head coach had to work was dubious, and difficulties quickly arose, with Jones concerned he didn't have the operating freedom he expected and needed. Camp addressed the matter in at least two April 1916 letters to McCormick, besides participating in a meeting of the committee ("our" committee, Camp called it) and having a long talk with Jones, attempting to smooth out the dispute.[14]

When Yale's 1916 spring football practice started, Camp gave even more time, attending every day of the three-week practice. In the fall, though he initially wrote McCormick, "It is going to be impossible for me to give the time I had hoped to the Foot Ball interests" because of "illness in my family" (Alice seemed to suffer from neurasthenia during these and subsequent years) and "very confused business conditions," in fact he could not stay away. On October 18, he reported that he had "given up the afternoon for every day of the scrimmage this fall—the two to three weeks preliminary and ever since." Also, "I have had Tad to luncheon with me every noon and occasionally we have gotten Brides and Alcott together in the evening."[15]

The season results were good, an 8-1-0 record, the best in seven years, with a loss only to Brown and victories over both Princeton and Harvard. It was Yale's first defeat of Harvard after four years of losses, a close 6–3 victory but a vast improvement over last year's 41–0 loss. After the Harvard game, Camp received a surprising letter:

> Dear Walter:
>
> For the past few years it has been my privilege to receive from you congratulations upon a Harvard victory over Yale. Times have changed and as I have been told that you had a great deal to do with Yale's splendid victory over us this year, I want in turn to give you personally my heartiest congratulations. I have always maintained that Harvard's victories in recent years were due to a great measure to Yale's unsound methods. But this year it was Greek meeting Greek—and the "Big Fellow" won.
>
> Sincerely yours,
> Percy D. Haughton

It was a letter he could cherish, a reminder of past days. The 1916 season had been encouraging and likely rekindled the hopes of Camp and many other Yale supporters. But it was a futile hope. War soon turned the United States' world upside down. Football was set aside at Yale, and by the time the war ended Camp had acquired new interests and activities. After 1916 he truly did "give up" any close involvement in Yale football and athletics.[16]

PART VII

Keeping the Nation Fit

50 Alternative Service

On April 6, 1917, when the U.S. Congress formally voted to enter the war in Europe, Walter Camp was three days from his fifty-eighth birthday. Notwithstanding his age, Camp wanted to support the war effort, and he had an idea what he could do. He knew that U.S. leaders, both in government and in private industry, would face demanding tasks and work schedules that placed them under a physical strain, and from his experience in physical training he was convinced that exercise and time outdoors would help those leaders stay healthy and effective. He was also sure they would need some organization to remain in such an exercise program, and he set out to establish such an organization.

His plan was to gather local groups of men to jointly exercise one hour a day, three days a week. He got the idea into effect in New Haven the first week after the congressional declaration of war: a squad of fifty formed quickly and doubled in size within two weeks, perhaps reflecting the public's readiness for a war effort and Camp's persuasiveness and credibility. The squad drilled in a gymnasium and hiked on the streets in business attire. Camp began to call them the "Senior Service Corps" and believed their public exercise would inspire patriotism.[1]

Camp wrote an article, "Patriotic Service by Men over 45," and got it published in the June 1917 *Rotarian*, describing his idea and its initial response. The article invited groups to organize in other communities and to request a weekly work schedule prepared under the care of a Yale medical doctor. Camp unabashedly pushed the formation of local Senior Service Corps in letters to friends or business associates, attaching relevant information and materials with a request that it be distributed to other likely groups.

Camp also envisioned bringing the Senior Service Corps idea to Washington, and Vance McCormick arranged for him to meet with the secretary of the army, who supported his plan. By mid-July 1917, a Washington group had been organized that on any given day might include the attorney general and secretaries of the interior, labor, and treasury—about twenty-four men exercising out of the home of a Yale graduate who was a member of the U.S. Tariff Commission (1925 F Street, N.W.). Franklin Delano Roosevelt, assistant secretary of the navy, was part of the group and an active supporter of the project who had written Camp asking him to also "come down here and help me . . . maintain [my staff's] physical condition."[2]

Camp sometimes went to Washington, leading an initial group exercise at seven thirty in the morning, followed by a group walk. Toward the end of one walk, a *New York Times* reporter saw Camp challenge the group to a gentle race up a hill; six joined him, including Roosevelt, still a few years from a bout with polio. After exercise the executives could shower in a bathhouse built on the property and have a rubdown and breakfast.[3]

Camp believed his exercise program could also have value for active military personnel. In a full display of entrepreneurial conviction and persistence,

Camp's Washington exercise group. Franklin D. Roosevelt, assistant secretary of the navy, often participated and is reportedly in the pictured group, back row, eighth from the left. (Walter Chauncey Camp Papers, 1870–1983 [inclusive], 1870–1925 [bulk], Manuscripts and Archives, Yale University)

he set about to pitch it to the secretary of the navy, Josephus Daniels. On May 3, 1917, he sent Daniels a description of the methods of his Senior Service Corps and claimed it had already improved the health and efficiency of the participants. Three weeks later, he wrote again, reporting that the YMCA's general secretary suggested that the Senior Service Corps program "should be in all the [U.S. military] training camps." He likely also enlisted help from Assistant Navy Secretary Roosevelt.[4]

The military was already developing a program to better care for military personnel, including providing alternative forms of recreation through army and navy commissions on training-camp activities. Athletics were included as one part of the commission's activities, which it was believed could "promote and maintain military efficiency and morale" as well as provide wholesome recreational opportunities.[5]

Daniels responded favorably to Camp's initiative and in July asked Camp to be on the navy commission, where he served as director of athletics. A wide diversity of activities were included, from football to physical exercise. A military reviewer considered football important to the program—"of great disciplinary value," "spectacular" enough to interest the men, and "enjoyable to play." Camp reported that at some naval stations, as many as "fifteen football teams [were] running through the fall of 1917."[6]

Camp sought to make a military contribution and seemed happy in uniform. (Images of Yale individuals, ca. 1750–2001 [inclusive], Manuscripts and Archives, Yale University)

Besides supervising competitive sports, Camp also taught and promoted individual physical training, paralleling his Senior Service Corps effort. He came to the task with a disregard for strenuous exercises designed to build muscle; instead, his aim was supple and quick actions, which he illustrated with golf. It is the "supple youth," he said, in contrast to the big, powerful, muscular man, who "turns his body at the waist" as he swings and drives "the ball . . . 250 yards."[7]

Camp first developed six simple exercises for the navy and later added six more, all of them "largely stretching" or "breathing exercises . . . [plus exercises that] strengthen the muscles of the neck, shoulders and back, for the purposes of attaining proper poise and carriage." An aim of the exercises was to "so strengthen and make supple the vital muscles, the muscles of the trunk, that the men taking them will, after a while, stand erect habitually . . . and take full breaths." Selection of an even dozen undoubtedly set the stage for salesmanship, which he accentuated by organizing them in four groups with alliterative titles—hands, hips, head; grind, grate, grasp; crawl, curl, crouch; and wave, weave, wing. The complete twelve-exercise program he called the "Daily Dozen Set-Up."[8]

When World War I ended in November 1918, Camp shifted aim. He and the country's leaders had been shocked at the nearly 30 percent of men rejected by draft authorities for lack of physical fitness, a health crisis to which Camp wanted to respond. In a December 1918 article in the *Independent* magazine, "Keeping the Nation Fit," Camp said many of America's health experts were urging legislation "to improve materially the physical condition of our citizens," including legislation to make physical training compulsory for school-age youth.[9]

Camp's personal interest was a voluntary program for adults that would be willingly performed by the average person and achieve measurable improvement. "In the last half dozen years," Camp said, "I have had a lot of experience with men and women and I know what they will do and will not do. . . . What they have to have, therefore, is something that can be done with daily routine, that will take little time and will effect the result." No specific exercises were described in the *Independent* article, but within three months, in a March 1919 article in *American Magazine*, Camp presented the twelve specific exercises he had developed for the navy, described in words and drawings under the heading "Walter Camp's 'Daily Dozen' Set-Up." The origin of the name is not known, though Camp used it in the navy and later in a number of different magazines and books, suggesting he had title or freedom to use it.[10]

Daily Dozen setup exercises as developed by Camp for the navy. (*Outing*, November 1918, 98, University of Minnesota Library)

The *Independent* and *American Magazine* articles were the beginning of an extended fitness campaign by Camp. Friends saw Camp as rejuvenated by his new mission, having a cause that ignored Yale's football decline and his own separation from Yale football and athletics. Once more he was at the forefront, pioneering a new program and campaign. He seemed genuinely motivated to get the general population to exercise: the greatest need in this country, he contended, was for proper standards and programs of physical training and exercise that a man may carry through his life (Camp regularly spoke in masculine terms, consistent with the times, but he also taught physical training for women). Two more magazine articles appeared in 1919; three in 1920; four in 1921, including two particularly for women and published in *Women's Home Companion*; three in 1922; and so on. The Daily Dozen exercises were the main subject of three of the articles. Camp also wrote books directed to fitness (some of which may have been ghostwritten for him)—two in 1919 (*Keeping Fit All the Way: How to Obtain and Maintain Health, Strength and Efficiency* and *Athletes All: Training, Organization and Play*), one in 1920 (*Handbook on Health and How to Stay Fit*), and two in 1921 (*The Daily Dozen for Men and Women* and *Training for Sport*).[11]

A 1923 article in the *World's Work*, "What I Am Trying to Do," brought a kind of summary, with helpings of marketing inspiration and cracker-barrel philosophy. Asserting that a person's "best possession in the world is health,"

Camp's 1921 booklet teaching the Daily Dozen exercises.

Camp argued for a look at nature to help retain that health: "Nature meant man to earn his bread by the sweat of his brow, and just so far as he departs from that, Nature demands some compensation." More colorfully, Camp stated that he developed his exercises after he suddenly got the idea that we humans are "all wild animals in a state of captivity." "So I went to see what other wild animals in captivity did. I went to the Bronx zoo and watched the lions and tigers." He saw them "stretch their great body muscles a hundred times." They took "hold of the bars of their cage and then stretched their great back." From this study of wild animals, Camp said he worked out his exercises—one to "lift up the shoulders and give the lungs room to expand," another "to strengthen the abdominal muscles . . . [to give] suppleness and muscular power to the trunk, and so on."[12]

The "wild animal in captivity" story was used to provide an attractive marketing symbol. In 1922, when the Reynolds Publishing Company published an attractive manual for the Daily Dozen exercises, they prominently displayed on the front cover an artfully drawn tiger in side view, on all fours, head and haunches up, with back in a concave curve and enviable stretch. By May 1924, Reynolds had sold almost five hundred thousand copies of the manual. In addition, movie and phonograph versions were under way. The exercises became so popular and widespread that "Daily Dozen" became a household word, a generic term in America's vocabulary and still today a routine dictionary entry. Camp went to work on a more extensive book to go on sale in 1925—more than one hundred pages of text with personal-improvement advice beyond physical exercise, including ideas on how to lose weight and on "getting what you want," whatever the reader considered "success."[13]

There was a preachiness to Camp's fitness articles, perhaps a sharing of his own experience. At an earlier time, Camp had smoked a great deal, but in later years he apparently managed to get smoking under control. A biographer who knew him personally in the postwar years said Camp "was a smoker" but one "who smoked very little" and "had a great scorn" for the chain-smoker. In one of his fitness articles, Camp wrote of a smoker who received "three warnings from Nature." First was when he smoked as a boy and became ill. Second was when he graduated to chain-smoking, lighting one from another, and one day felt "a jiggle in his heart," which caused him to again quit. And third was after he was feeling well again and said, I will smoke but not in the heavy amount I smoked before, and then in fact returns to chain-smoking until one night as he sleeps, his heart is missing some beats and "he is really frightened" and promises God, "don't kill me tonight and I will never smoke again." But when morning comes and he is feeling well, he does light up another cigar. Not long after, "Nature comes, taps him on the shoulder," and takes him away.[14]

Preachy as he might have been, his convictions were sincere and intended to improve the physical condition and health of the country individually and as a whole. He wanted to open to all his readers the possibility of the rich and healthy life he was enjoying and perceived would continue, and he believed such a life depended on physical fitness. It may have been about this time that Camp filled out a personal questionnaire that included the question, "If you had your life to live over what profession would you choose?" His answer: "Corrective and preventative medicine or the science that will develop from this in the long run"—still interested in medicine and public service and seemingly having forgotten the torture of Anatomy.[15]

Related to Camp's encouragement of exercise was support for public playgrounds. He had long supported municipal playgrounds; in January 1890, he wrote to New Haven's mayor, who happened to be his uncle through marriage (Henry Peck), advocating that a part of grounds recently acquired for use as a public park be set aside for athletic games. At the time, grounds for playing baseball or other sports in New Haven were available only by payment of a rental fee. The result was to deny many young persons outdoor exercise that was their "rightful enjoyment" and would be "thoroughly beneficial."[16]

Camp's interest in playgrounds continued into his later years. He was elected chairman of the Connecticut Chamber of Commerce's Committee on General Welfare and in that role in 1920 sent out questionnaires to officials of Connecticut communities, asking about the availability of playgrounds and industrial athletic facilities in their communities. The gathered information was used in developing a program to ensure adequate availability of playing fields and grounds.[17]

Still focusing on fitness in 1923, Camp began to write more often about golf. Although golf didn't provide the best exercise for younger people—persons younger than forty should take more vigorous exercise, he said—golf was a useful exercise for older ages. Men and women who had been active in sport and exercise in their youth needed to continue in later life: "It is essential that they secure . . . [at least] a modicum of athletic exercise out-of-doors a day or two a week."[18]

He wanted to broaden participation in golf and became an advocate for municipal golf courses to make golf available to more than country club members. He was quite harsh on municipal leaders, noting that in 1923 there were only eighty-five municipal golf courses in the United States, a "disgraceful and inexcusable" number. The following year, he criticized the extravagance of country clubs—experimenting in one way or another with the course layout or making the club larger or more pretentious, all of which raised the cost of membership and limited those who could participate.[19]

The Frankenstein of College Athletics 51

American football extended across the nation long before World War I, but it grew even faster after the war, inspiring added commentary by Walter Camp in the 1921 and 1922 *Spalding's Official Football Guides*. Camp was "astonished" that on any given Saturday during the 1921 season, the game played by only a handful of colleges in his playing days now was played by more than ten thousand players. And some college grandstands were filled over the course of the season by a quarter of a million people, with many more "turned away unable to secure seats."[1]

With more seats needed, Camp reported in 1922, "Almost every college is now building or contemplating building for increased capacity." And they were building permanent concrete stadiums, some with very large seating capacities, prominent on the college campus in line with colleges' acceptance of football as a major commercial venture. In a phenomenon of the age, more than fifty concrete stadiums were built on college campuses in the 1920s, including the following:[2]

College	Year built	Capacity when built
University of Washington	1920	46,000
Stanford	1921	60,000
Ohio State	1922	63,000
Nebraska	1923	31,000
Illinois	1923	55,000
Purdue	1924	13,500
Minnesota	1924	53,000
Texas A&M	1925	33,400
Missouri	1926	25,000
Northwestern	1926	25,000
Michigan	1927	72,000
Alabama	1929	12,000
Iowa	1929	53,000

Other sports were also growing in popularity, making the 1920s a "Golden Age of Sport," but football was the leader. By the early 1920s, football received the most column inches of any sport covered in the *Chicago Tribune* sports page. New media forms were also covering and publicizing the game: movie newsreels regularly displayed football games by 1915, and radio broadcasts began not long after that. Magazines with sports coverage were growing more numerous and enlarging their circulations.[3]

Camp had been one of the pioneers of "sportswriting" beginning in the late 1880s, but sportswriting was now becoming an established and large profession. During the 1920s, Camp had been writing a few articles for *Collier's* in addition to his annual All-America selections, and in November 1923 he was asked to begin a new weekly department called the "Walter Camp Sports Page." In each issue of the magazine, on a single page, Camp included in a folksy blend of commentary, anecdote, or information a dozen or so tidbits about a variety of sports. Items of information not routinely known were reported (how Robert Tyre "Bobby" Jones became "Junior," though it was his grandfather, not his father, with whom he shared the name). Many of the items also involved exhortation, attempts to encourage or push readers

Watching football games and gathering information on teams and possible candidates for an All-America team were common Camp activities. (Walter Chauncey Camp Papers, 1870–1983 [inclusive], 1870–1925 [bulk], Manuscripts and Archives, Yale University)

into better habits and perhaps a bit of scorn for those who don't manage the discipline (one typical issue had a piece about a baseball player who stays in shape and succeeds in big-league competition in contrast with another player who arrives at spring camp overweight and short of breath; on that same page, another piece claimed "most of us receive shining gifts" at birth, and what is "depressing" is the way "those gifts are subsequently mishandled").[4]

The "Walter Camp Sports Page" lasted about a year, ending in November 1924 when Camp was sixty-five years old; at that time, Grantland Rice began a regular weekly column. There was some turbulence at the magazine, and in March 1924 Camp received a letter from the editor of *Collier's*, Richard Walsh: "I am through as Editor of Collier's. . . . You will understand I cannot write you more fully now. But I do want to tell you how deeply I have appreciated working with you." Handwritten below Walsh's signature, he wrote, "God bless you for your kindness to me."[5]

Although excited about the growth and spread of American football, Camp continued to be disturbed by distortions from what he considered the game's ideal usage. In a 1923 magazine article titled to grab attention, "The Frankenstein of College Athletics," he contended, "Athletics has come into college and 'taken charge.' This Frankenstein has shouldered his way in, and his bulk is now sprawled out over all the college life outside the line of the strict curricular work." Camp called what was happening "over-organization," with large sums of money spent to develop football teams. "Hundreds of thousands of dollars are spent" to produce "a few score athletes trained to the last notch" and who are displayed "before a frenzied public a few times every year." He saw the problem as arising from an undue focus on big games and pressure to take all possible steps to win those games. The supporters of one team argue that the "other team has so many individual coaches, so many special facilities, so many this, that, and the other that they will surely win if we do not expend an equal amount along those lines."[6]

Camp wanted to spread receipts from athletic contests over a greater proportion of the student body. He wanted the experience he had enjoyed as a youth to be more widely enjoyed by today's college students: "Every boy ought to have his chance to put his last ounce of disciplined strength and his last blow of great-hearted courage into some competitive game. And this chance is lost . . . [because of] the enormous sums spent on college athletics . . . unwisely and wrongly spent on over-organization." He recognized with disappointment that "unnumbered thousands of college students are satisfied with the second hand glory in the skill of 'our team' and for the most part do not realize their own failure to . . . share in the athletic benefit." Camp seemed to have a vision that colleges could encourage, perhaps even require, athletic participation by a larger part of the student body. He wanted enlarged campus athletic facilities to allow and attract participation in athletics and exercise by the larger student body. "How much better in every way—financially, morally, physically—it would be if athletics were . . . brought into the life of every [student] and if all of them got its benefits personally instead of . . . second hand" as spectators."[7]

Such a vision, of course, would fit into Camp's dominant 1923 athletic interest—the physical welfare of the American people as a whole. He wanted young people (as well as adults) to use their bodies in athletic effort, and he believed it was vital to the health of both individuals and the country.

52 Unrecognized Legacy

Business had been good at the New Haven Clock Company during World War I—one and a half million watches shipped in 1917, with total sales well over $3 million, the company's best year ever to that point. Good business continued after the war. When reporting 1920 results at the annual stockholder meeting on January 26, 1921, Walter Camp noted that besides paying regular dividends during the past year, the company had erected two new buildings to relieve congestion, retired $40,000 of preferred stock, and built accumulated surplus to $785,000.[1]

However, a drastic change was coming. Camp followed the good 1920 report with a warning that "business of the country, including ours, took a sudden drop" at the beginning of 1921. Company sales for January and February 1921 were one-fifth the volume of the previous year. Sales stayed bad through the year, and at the beginning of 1922 the company temporarily restricted manufacture to watches and automobile clocks and required a 10 percent salary and wage reduction from every member of the organization.[2]

At this time, NHCC requested George H. Burr and Company, their brokerage firm for several years, to conduct a careful analysis of the company's financial situation. Burr arranged with a second company to conduct the analysis together with a Burr employee named Richard H. Whitehead, an engineer who had been employed by Burr for less than a year.[3]

One wonders about Burr's hiring of Whitehead because within three months after the review began, Whitehead was engaged as general manager of NHCC. Camp knew George Burr personally and likely had played golf and attended sporting events with him, where he could have discussed upcoming personnel needs at NHCC. An officer of NHCC soon reported that the thirty-five-year-old Whitehead's "policies appeared economical and constructive and were bringing about good results in our factories." Progress continued, and at a later annual meeting Camp reported that the "betterment of our position" had been "largely due to internal economies worked out . . . by our general manager and his corps of loyal and capable assistants."[4]

Conditions were now right for Camp to make a change, revealed at a special meeting of the board of directors on February 19, 1923. Camp left the company's presidency and became chairman of the board (salary, twenty-five hundred dollars per year). Edwin Root, previously in charge of manufacturing, would be the new president (salary ten thousand dollars). And Richard Whitehead would be vice president and general manager (salary twenty-four thousand dollars). Youth was in place, and the sixty-four-year-old Camp was stepping back, though not completely away.[5]

In a related lifestyle change, the empty-nester Camps sold their Hillhouse mansion and moved a few blocks to a smaller house at 460 Humphrey Street.[6]

However unhappy Camp might have been about the "over-organization" of American college football, he continued to write about it for publication and to participate in football rule making. He still looked forward to the rules-committee meetings, which had been central in his life for nearly fifty years and allowed him to exchange information, stories, and opinions with fellow football leaders. Rule-making issues had become of less importance in recent years, which Camp considered important and good. The rules had "crystallized," he said, becoming stable from year to year, so players, coaches, and especially viewers didn't have to learn new rules but could play and watch a game they understood.

As the date for the 1925 rule-making meeting approached in March, newspapers listed likely subjects for rule amendment—minor matters such as options for winner and loser of the opening coin toss. Yet the discussion list was still long enough that when the committee met for its first session on Friday evening, March 13, at the Hotel Pennsylvania in New York City, it was nearly midnight when the group said their good-byes, planning to reconvene the next day at nine. The committee was surprised on gathering the next morning that the normally prompt Camp was not present; when he still had not arrived at ten, Ed Hall, the committee chairman, asked Princeton's Bill Roper and Trinity's William Langford to go to Camp's hotel and learn what was the matter. Receiving no answer at Camp's room, Roper and Langford persuaded the assistant manager to let them in, where they found Camp in bed, having apparently died peacefully about five that morning of a heart attack.[7]

Camp's death was shocking news on front pages across the country, stunning in the sudden departure of American football's "father" and leading personality, ironic in the coincidence that death came while he was making football rules—"Died in Harness," "Busy to the End with Game He Loved," the headlines read. Even more ironic was death's caveat to Camp's physical fitness teachings. He had so clearly been proud of his physical condition and seemed confident that exercise was a prescription for good health and long life. Now he was dead at age sixty-five. To crown the irony, even after his death *Collier's* published three Camp fitness articles already in the publishing queue, "It's Easy to Keep Fit," "Make Your Sport Fit Your Age," and "Getting the Most Out of Life." Also, his most extensive Daily Dozen book, nearly ready for publication when he died, was published later in 1925.[8]

Of course, his manner of death could be envied, apparently painless and quick. But for family and friends, so suddenly left alone, it was a stunning loss. Alice chose a quiet, private funeral with just family and a few close friends present, Monday, March 16, two days after he died. The service was conducted in the Camps' home by the pastor of the Church of the Redeemer, a church within blocks of their former Everitt Street homes.[9]

Possibly posthumous 1925 painting of Walter Camp by Herman Sodersten, probably prepared from a photograph. It now hangs at the entrance to the Walter Camp Athletic Center at Hopkins School, successor to the Hopkins Grammar School. (Courtesy of the Hopkins School)

Three months later, on June 15, during Yale's Commencement Week, a memorial service was held at Yale's Battell Chapel. The current Yale president, James R. Angell, opened the service, and Bishop Sidney C. Partridge from Camp's Yale '80 class gave a closing benediction. In between were four tributes, one each from Harvard and Princeton and two from Yale. Harvard's representative was Le Baron R. Briggs, dean at Harvard for thirty-four years while concurrently serving many years as president of Radcliffe College. As dean he had overseen Harvard athletics and worked with Camp, and he had been president of the NCAA in 1913–16. Briggs spoke of Camp's "preeminence in athletics" and of the fact that "from ocean to ocean . . . [Camp was] known as the father of American football." But Briggs's main emphasis was Camp's native kindness, and he described an occasion when he felt extraordinary friendliness and sensitivity from Camp.[10]

Yale's first speaker was Professor William Lyon Phelps, whose theme was Camp "as my friend." They had often played golf together and had lived near one another for the past ten or twelve years. Phelps noted that, "as we both had the habit of early rising, I used to see him every morning about half-past seven on his way to business."

> But he always had time in those early mornings to stop for a moment and talk. To see him and to speak with him freshened me up for the whole day. . . . There was something about him so clean, so wholesome, so inspiring. . . .
>
> In all the years I knew Walter Camp, and in all the conversations I had with him, I never heard him use bad language, I never heard him say anything querulous, petulant or jealous. I never saw him overexcited, and I never heard him complain of the unfair treatment that had more than once been shown him.

President-emeritus Arthur T. Hadley was Yale's last speaker, telling of his work with Camp on Yale athletics. As they worked on such matters,

> Walter Camp laid aside his habitual reserve, and let me see what manner of man he was, and how he made himself what he was. In all the matters that came before us, he showed himself not only clear headed but clean minded—anxious to avoid prejudice and unwilling to listen to the idle talk which lies at the root of so many unnecessary quarrels. . . . He neither repeated nor entertained idle gossip. When a suspicion was unproved he simply said, "I don't believe it."[11]

For Princeton the speaker was Professor Charles Kennedy, a student of athletics who would soon write a book, *Sport and Sportsmanship*, and who spoke of Camp "as a great and generous sportsman." He asserted Camp's responsibility—"almost single-handed"—for development of "the game of modern American football" from the "formless" rugby of the 1870s. But broader than that, he saw Camp as "endowed with a natural love of athletic games, an ability to play them surpassingly well," a man who had "labored without ceasing to weave the love of athletic games into the fabric of our national life."[12]

A few months after Camp died, the sportswriting word-artist Grantland Rice, who was succeeding Camp in selecting and presenting *Collier's* annual All-America team, wrote about Camp's All-America teams and the approximately three hundred different players Camp had chosen for those teams. Rice assumed Camp still remembered those players and that he occasionally thought about them, imagined them as they marched "along the skyline of memory."

> As they marched by how often must have come to him the memory of the great battles which brought them fame, battles in rain and snow, in sun and shadow—the flying tackle and the savage line thrust—the forward wall braced for the shock—the graceful spiral careening against a sky of blue and gray—the long run down the field—the goal-line stand—the forward pass—the singing and cheering of great crowds—young and old America gathered together on a golden afternoon, with bands playing and banners flying—
>
> It may have been in the midst of such a dream that the Call to Quarters came, and Taps was sounded as the great knight came down the field.[13]

Camp's friends and admirers considered how to provide an appropriate memorial for him. Suggestions that the Yale Bowl be renamed the Walter Camp Bowl were soon set aside in favor of a memorial that would recognize Camp's support for all athletics, not just football, and for his encouragement to widespread student participation. It was decided that Yale Field, which accommodated many sports—not only the Yale Bowl for football but also baseball diamonds, a running track, tennis courts, intramural, and other fields—would be renamed Walter Camp Field. A monumental gateway, four or five stories high and even greater in width, as big as the wall of a major building, would be built as a colonnaded entrance to the field.[14]

A Yale committee was appointed to raise funds, and the NCAA decided to participate by promoting and facilitating donations from individual member schools. Cost for the contemplated monument was estimated at three hundred thousand dollars—a major sum, as large as the cost of some football stadiums then being built; Yale was to raise half and the NCAA the other half. The NCAA's effort drew a massive response—224 colleges and 279 preparatory and high schools, an outpouring that E. K. Hall called an endorsement of Camp's high standards and sportsmanship. Schools large and small across nearly the whole country understood the contributions Camp had made and were ready to honor him.[15]

The monument was ready for dedication on November 3, 1928, and still stands, well kept, wide, and tall—four cylindrical cement pillars between two rectangular side pillars supporting a central span, with "Walter Camp Field" sculpted across the top. The two rectangular side pillars are faced in brick and are flanked by shorter brick walls in which marble panels are embedded front and back; each of the four panels is engraved with the names of contributing colleges from a different section of the country, in total a large majority of American colleges. One wonders how many other monuments there are like this, large stand-alone structures built by donations from around the country to honor a single person, not from government but a private citizen?

As impressive as the gateway and other memorials are, another way Camp could be honored is through American football itself. Yes, a multitude of

Memorial gateway to Walter Camp Field. (Yale University buildings and grounds photographs, 1716–2004 [inclusive], Manuscripts and Archives, Yale University)

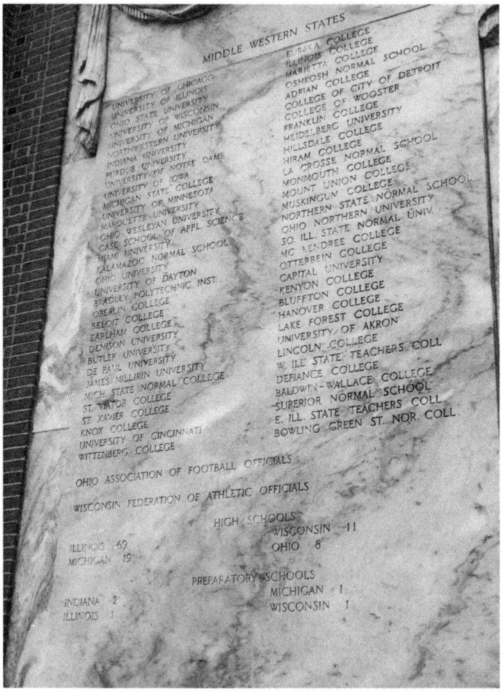

One of four panels embedded in the sidewalls of the memorial gateway to Walter Camp Field, listing contributing schools from across the country.

others were involved in creating, developing, and sustaining American football through the years. And important parts of today's game were initially resisted by Camp.

Yet Camp remains the father of American football. Through football's foundational years, when the game's continued existence was in doubt and the basic mechanism of the game was being developed, Camp was tireless in constant effort, the main impetus for development as well as the inventor of major features that still define the game.

High on a list of Camp's contributions—what he himself considered his most important rule contribution—is the downs-and-distance rule, four downs to gain ten yards. That rule shapes and energizes American football, crucial to almost every play of every game. When the teams come to the scrimmage line and players, coaches, and crowd catch their breath in suspense, anxious whether needed yardage will be achieved or denied, Camp's rule is at work. When the ball is snapped and players whirl into action both on offense and on defense, each moving in roles that have been carefully designed and practiced for yardage situations like those now faced, Camp's rule is at work. When a fresh down immediately succeeds a previous one, presenting a new opportunity to reverse previous failures or build on previous successes, Camp's rule is at work. When downs expire and chances end, confirming defeat or victory, Camp's rule is at work. Without Camp's contributions, without the downs-and-distance rule that was a turning point in the game's faltering beginning, the game we know as American football would not exist.

Today's players and spectators are mostly unaware of Camp's role. Immediate events are what is important, this year's players and teams and the outcome of today's contests. But in a spare moment now and then, we might remember Camp. American football lives because of him, a gift hardly ever recognized or acknowledged, an ongoing legacy to be enjoyed by all those who play, watch, and love the game.

Appendix

Chronology of Major Rule Changes That Transformed Rugby into American Football, 1876–1924

1876 At the founding convention of the American Intercollegiate Football Association, November 23, 1876, English rugby rules are adopted, except that:

A referee is included to oversee the game (thus beginning a new regime of decision making that will obsolete predecessor rugby procedures in which umpires, one appointed by each team, or team captains, decided disputes).[1]

A game shall be decided by touchdowns instead of kicked goals, as in rugby. But each kicked goal shall count four touchdowns.[2]

1879 If a player purposefully fouls an opponent to gain ground for his side, the referee can award ball possession to the offended side.[3]

1880 A new scrimmage procedure is defined: "A scrimmage takes place when the holder of the ball . . . puts it down on the ground in front of him and puts it in play . . . by kicking the ball or snapping it back with the foot."[4]

1882 Basic new game methodology is added: if in three consecutive downs a team has not advanced the ball five yards or lost ten, it must give up the ball to the opposite side at the spot where the ball was last downed.[5]

1883 Point system of scoring introduced: a safety counts one point for the opponents, a touchdown counts two points, a goal-after-touchdown counts an additional four points, and a goal from the field counts five points.[6]

1884 Point values are changed: a safety counts two points instead of one, a touchdown counts four points, and a goal-after-touchdown counts two points.[7]

1885 No delay shall continue more than five minutes. Either side refusing to play after ordered by referee shall forfeit the game.[8]

1887 An "umpire" (a neutral official, not one appointed by each team) is added to judge players' conduct.[9]

1888 Blocking in advance of a runner is legalized; offensive players are barred from using hands or arms during blocking.[10]

"Intentional" tackling below the knees is forbidden (replacing a previous rule that prohibited tackling below the hips).[11]

1889 The referee shall use a stopwatch in timing the game.[12]

Both referee and umpire shall use whistles to indicate cessation of play for fouls or downs.[13]

Game stopwatch shall be stopped while the ball is positioned for a try-at-goal after touchdown or for a kickoff or kick-out (in these early years, after a team took a touchback or safety, play was resumed by that team kicking out onto the playing field). Time shall not be called at the end of a half until the ball is dead.[14]

1890 An injured player who has been replaced shall not later play in the game.[15]

1892 The umpire shall allow no coaching, either by coaches or by anyone else inside the ropes or by substitutes coming on the field.[16]

1894 Linesman added as third game official.[17]

A rule-required kick (for example, a kickoff) must travel at least ten yards unless stopped by opponents.[18]

Momentum-mass plays in which more than three men start moving forward before the ball is snapped are barred.[19]

Player intending fair catch must raise hand and cannot run after catch. Catcher's side awarded fifteen yards for interference with catch.[20]

The offended side in a rule infraction may refuse penalty when to its advantage. If penalty would carry ball across goal line, only half the intervening distance shall be given.[21]

1896 Before the ball is put in play in a scrimmage, all players on offense must come to a full stop, except one may be in motion toward his own goal. At least five players on offense must be on the line of scrimmage at snapback.[22]

1898 A player may be substituted for another at any time at the discretion of the team captain, but a replaced player cannot later return to the game.[23]

Value of touchdown increased to five points, and goal-after-touchdown reduced to one point.[24]

(A note is added at the end of Rule 1, suggesting the usefulness for measuring five yards in three downs of "two light poles . . . connected at the lower ends by a . . . chain.")

1903 Between twenty-five yard lines, at least seven offensive players must be on the line of scrimmage at snapback. Person receiving the snapback may run forward only after first running five or more yards to the side of the snapback position.[25]

Portion of field between twenty-five-yard lines shall be marked with lines five yards apart and parallel to the sidelines, creating a checkerboard rather than gridiron appearance.[26]

Side scored upon given option to kick off or have opponents kick off.[27]

No shoe leather, papier-mâché, or other hard material may be used in head protector; other protective devices must be padded, so as, in discretion of umpire, not to endanger other players.[28]

1904 Value of field goal reduced from five points to four.[29]

If the winner of the toss at the start of the game selects the goal, the loser must take the kickoff.[30]

1905 Referee is to blow whistle to stop play as soon as forward progress of the ball is stopped.[31]

A substitute entering the game must report to the referee.[32]

1906 The distance to be gained in three downs to retain ball possession is increased to ten yards.[33]

A pass may be thrown forward once per scrimmage provided that if the ball touches the ground before being touched by a player of either side, the opponent shall be awarded the ball at the point the pass was thrown.[34]

In the case of a kick from scrimmage by a player other than the snapper-back, all players of the kicking team are onside as soon as the ball touches the ground (meaning they can down the ball and thus gain possession).[35]

Neutral zone established by making the line of scrimmage for each side an imaginary line parallel to the goal line and passing through that point of the ball nearest the side's own goal line.[36]

Hurdling another player is prohibited.[37]

1907 The penalty if a forward pass touches the ground before touching a player of either side is changed to fifteen yards instead of loss of possession.[38]

Fourth official, called a field judge, is added to assist the referee in decisions downfield.[39]

1908 When a forward pass is legally touched by a player of the passing side but falls to the ground uncaught, any player of the team on defense may recover the ball (and receive possession), but only the player of the passing team who touched the ball may recover it until it is touched by an opponent.[40]

1909 The value of a field goal is reduced from four points to three points.[41]

A side entitled to a kick-out (for example, having taken a touchback) may instead place the ball on its twenty-five-yard line for a scrimmage from first down.[42]

1910 A forward pass may be completed only within twenty yards of the line of scrimmage, and the pass must have been thrown from at least five yards behind the line of scrimmage.[43]

Over the whole field of play, seven players of the team on offense must be on the line of scrimmage at snapback.[44]

No player on offense shall push, pull, or hold on his feet the ball carrier, nor shall there be any interlocked interference.[45]

A player removed from a game for any cause except disqualification or suspension may return to the game once at the beginning of any subsequent period.[46]

The sides shall change goals at the beginning of the second and fourth periods.[47]

1911 A forward pass touched by either side but falling to the ground uncaught shall be considered incomplete, without penalty other than exhaustion of the down.[48]

1912 Downs-and-distance rule changed to allow four downs to gain ten yards.[49]

Field reconfigured to present dimensions—one hundred yards between goal lines with ten-yard end zones behind each goal line. Goal posts positioned on goal line.[50]

Forward pass may be completed at any distance.[51]

Forward pass may be completed in end zone.[52]

Specifications established for a ball: long-axis circumference, 28–$28\frac{1}{2}$ inches; short axis circumference, $22\frac{1}{2}$–23 inches; weight, 14–15 ounces.[53]

1913 A "relic of the old time" eliminated in the definition of snapping back by deleting backward kicking by "the foot."[54]

Wording clarified to ensure that after a forward pass is made, no player of either side shall "in any means interfere with an opponent until the ball has been touched, except in an actual attempt to catch said pass himself."[55]

1914 Passer shall not intentionally throw ball to the ground to make an incomplete pass.[56]

No "roughing" allowed of player who has made pass.[57]

Receiver of forward pass in the end zone must have both feet down inside the end zone for completed pass.[58]

Side making a touchback or safety shall put the ball in play by a scrimmage from its twenty-yard line.[59]

No one, including coaches, shall walk on the sideline during a game.[60]

1915 Rules committee recommends players be numbered.[61]

Beginning about 1916, a number of years passed without major rule changes. The game was "in a well-balanced condition," Camp wrote, causing the rules committee to believe that "the rules should be allowed to crystallize as nearly as possible in their present form." Both players and the public would be saved from learning new rules, and players and coaches could concentrate on improving play of the game as is. Rule changes in 1916 and 1917 were for purposes of clarification, not for adjusting the play.[62]

World War I drew attention away from college football. In 1918 and 1919, the rules were left essentially unchanged. Even after the war ended, rule changes were less numerous and seldom fundamental.

1920 Game clock is stopped from the moment a forward pass becomes incomplete until play starts again.[63]

A false starting signal intended to draw the defense offside shall be penalized by loss of five yards.[64]

1921 Treatment of safety and touchback differentiated. The side making a safety shall put the ball in play by a scrimmage from the thirty-yard line. The side making a touchback shall continue putting the ball in play by a scrimmage from the twenty-yard line.[65]

1922 A "try-for-point" is introduced in which after a touchdown, the scoring side can attempt to score from any point along or behind the five-yard line by either a placekick, a dropkick, a run, or a forward pass, receiving a single point when successful.[66]

1924 The location of a try-for-point is moved from the five-yard line to the three-yard line.[67]

Notes

Abbreviations

1892 Clipping	Undated, unlabeled newspaper or magazine clipping headed with a picture, "The First Rugby Team at Yale," and imaged with other clippings on a page of reel 41 of the Camp Papers, stamped with the date 1892. Other items on the page are headed "The Poor Man at Harvard," "Yale's Football Record," and "Sporting Gossip."
Advocate	*Harvard Advocate*, student newspaper.
AIFRC 1910	Minutes of the American Intercollegiate Football Rules Committee for the year 1910, found as a fifty-nine-page typescript in box 40, folder 127, of the Camp Papers.
AIFRC Minutes	Minutes of the American Intercollegiate Football Rules Committee for the year 1906, found as a thirty-five-page section of a larger typescript cited as "Football Rules Committee Minutes, 1876–1926, University of Delaware Library," in Nelson, *Anatomy of a Game*, 565; the transcript is presently held in Special Collections at the University of Delaware as MS 328. The thirty-five-page section closes on the last page with the typed words, "Very sincerely, (signed) W. T. Reid, Jr." Although the minutes for individual meetings are numbered 1, 2, 3, etc., page

	numbers 1–35 have been added by the present author for convenience and clarity.
Bailey	Chris H. Bailey, "A Century of Manufacturing: The New Haven Clock Company," in a 1977 reprint of an 1880 catalog of the New Haven Clock Company (Bristol, Conn.: American Clock and Watch Museum, 1977).
BH	*Boston Herald.*
Camp Papers	Collected papers of Walter Camp at YUMA. Most of the papers have been microfilmed, and citations in the following notes are usually to a microfilm reel, sometimes supplemented by citation of the box and folder number in which the cited document is stored.
CCAR	Alumni record of Charles Camp at YUMA.
ChiTrib	*Chicago Tribune.*
Correslog	Six pages containing more than two dozen reproduced items of correspondence between Camp and football rules committee members in December 1905. Camp Papers, reel 26, box 39, folder 115.
Courant	*Yale Courant*, student newspaper.
Crimson	*Harvard Crimson*, student newspaper.
Critic	Student newspaper at Hopkins Grammar School.
DAB	*Dictionary of American Biography* (1946).

Football rules:

1876 AmRugby	*The Rugby Game, Rugby Union Rules* (New Haven, Conn.: Tuttle, Morehouse, and Taylor), found in YUMA, File Yed5, folder 7-1, box "Undated to 1899."
1878 Rules	*Rules of the Rugby Game of Football, as Amended by the Inter-Collegiate Association Nov. 23, 1876 and Oct. 9, 1877* [*sic*]. As discussed in chapter 5 of the text, the second date, October 9, 1877, is incorrect; there was no convention on that date. The convention at which the rules published in this booklet were enacted was held October 9, 1878.
1879 Rules	"Rules of American Football—as Amended by the Inter-Collegiate Association, October 4th, 1879," in *Handbook of Winter Sports*, by Henry Chadwick (New York: Beadle and Adams, 1879), 51–59, reprinted in *Sports in North*

	America, edited by George B. Kirsch (Gulf Breeze, Fla.: Academic International Press, 1995), 4:243–48.
1881 Rules	"Rules of the Rugby Game of Foot Ball," as printed in *Yale Courant*, supp., October 29, 1881.
1882 Rules	*Inter-Collegiate Football Rules, as Amended by the American Inter-Collegiate Association Nov. 23d, 1876; Oct. 9th, 1877* [*sic*]*; Oct. 4th, 1879; Oct. 13th, 1880; Oct. 8th, 1881; April, 1882.* Found in file labeled "Yx 880Cla" at YUMA.
1883 Rules	*Foot-Ball Rules,* Revised by Walter Chauncey Camp. Authorized and Adopted by the American Intercollegiate Association November 1882. For the Season of 1883. Copyright 1883, by Walter C. Camp. Published by Wright and Ditson, Boston. Found in Camp Papers, series II, folder 150, YUMA.
Other years	For the years 1884–89, the rules were printed in a booklet titled *Football Rules and Referees Book*, published in Boston by Wright and Ditson; those booklets are abbreviated herein as [year] *Football Rules*. In 1890 a book titled *Football Rules and Referees Book* was published by A. G. Spalding and Bros. and is called herein 1890 *Football Rules.*

From 1891 until 1925 (the last year covered in this book), the rules were printed in a document titled *Spalding's Official Football Guide*, which was published from 1891 to 1892 by A. G. Spalding and from 1893 to 1925 by Spalding's subsidiary, American Sports Publishing Company. By at least 1921, the front cover of the booklet read *National Collegiate Athletic Association Football Rules*, with added labeling indicating the booklet was published by the American Sports Publishing Company as part of the Spalding Athletic Library; the inside title page still read "Spalding Official Football Guide." For convenience, all the rules-containing booklets from 1891 until 1925 are abbreviated herein as [year] *Spalding Guide.*

Hadley In	Incoming correspondence records of Yale president Arthur T. Hadley, YUMA.
HGM	*Harvard Graduates' Magazine.*
HPrRep	Harvard University. Annual reports of the president and treasurer.

HW	*Harper's Weekly.*
JSH	*Journal of Sports History.*
LCAR	Entry for Leverett Camp in *Record of Association of Alumni*, kept in the archives of Central Connecticut State University in New Britain.
NCAA Proceedings	Proceedings of the annual conventions of the National Collegiate Athletic Association (called Intercollegiate Athletic Association for its first five years). NCAA Proceedings I is for the convention held in December 1906.
NHCC	New Haven Clock Company.
NHCC Minutes	Business minutes of the New Haven Clock Company, generally minutes of stockholder and board of director meetings.
NHReg	*New Haven Register.*
NYEP	*New York Evening Post.*
NYH	*New York Herald*
NYT	*New York Times.*
NYTrib	*New York Tribune.*
NYW	*New York World.*
SFExam	*San Francisco Examiner.*
SLPD	*St. Louis Post-Dispatch*
SQ	Undated questionnaire headed "Select Features Co." with answers in Camp's handwriting. Camp Papers, reel 47, box 66, folder 1.
TR Coll	Papers of Theodore Roosevelt at the Library of Congress.
WCAR	Alumni record of Walter Camp at YUMA.
WGS Papers	Papers of William Graham Sumner at YUMA.
WHAR	Alumni record of Walter (Pudge) Heffelfinger at YUMA.
YAW	*Yale Alumni Weekly.*
YLit	*Yale Literary Magazine.*
YNews	*Yale News*, student newspaper.
YUMA	Manuscripts and Archives Collection at Sterling Memorial Library, Yale University.

Preface

1. Sally Jenkins, *The Real All Americans* (New York: Doubleday, 2007), 1; George Stade, "Game Theory," *Columbia University Forum* 9, no. 4 (1966): 40; Glen Mason quoted in Sid Hartman's column in the *Minneapolis Star Tribune*, November 11, 2011. A new exten-

sively researched and well-crafted biography of Walter Camp was recently published: Julie Des Jardins, *Walter Camp: Football and the Modern Man.* The main focus of the book is America's changing views of manhood and Camp's relation to those views and participation in their formation. While touching on American football's creation, the book does not closely examine the events and circumstances of that creation.

Chapter 1

1. W. E. DeCrow, *Yale and the City of Elms* (Boston: n.p., 1882), 64. See also *Advocate,* November 24, 1876, 53, where the same field is described for a game a year later; and *Courant*, November 20, 1875, 98.

2. Adrian Harvey, *Football: The First Hundred Years*, for soccer 134–49, for rugby 170–71; *Courant*, October 25, 1873, 63; Thomas B. Davis, *Chronicles of Hopkins Grammar School,* 431.

3. Manuscript, Camp Papers, reel 47, box 66, folder 1.

4. *Courant,* October 25, 1873, 63; *Advocate*, October 17, 1873, 41. See also October 11, 1873, letter of Henry K. Grant, captain Harvard football team, reprinted in John A. Blanchard, *The H Book of Harvard Athletics*, 356–57. For a description of Harvard's game, see ibid., 350, 356, 609 ("Appendix A. Rules of the Harvard Game, Rule 8"); James D'Wolf Lovett, *Old Boston Boys and the Games They Played* (Boston: Riverside Press, private printing, 1906), 81–86; and Winthrop S. Scudder, ed., *Gerrit Smith Miller: An Appreciation* (Dedham, Mass.: Noble and Greenough School), 19–25 ("ball-carrying" and "tackling," 20).

5. *Advocate*, April 3, 1874, 58; May 29, 1874, first page.

6. *Advocate*, October 22, 1875; *Crimson*, October 29, 1875; *Yale Record*, October 1875, 69, November 1875, 114. See also Walter Camp, "A Historic Game . . .," *Youth's Companion* (November 20, 1900): 625.

7. Camp, "A Historic Game . . .," 625; CCAR; *Critic*, November 1, 1874; T. Davis, *Chronicles of Hopkins Grammar School*, 426; manuscript, Camp Papers, reel 47, box 66, folder 1.

8. *Spirit of the Times*, November 20, 1875, 364.

9. *Courant*, November 20, 1875, 98; *Yale Record,* November 1875, 69.

10. Harris Poll, in *Entertainment Close-Up*, January 22, 2013 ("Football continues to be America's favorite sport"). Harvard's first rugby game with a U.S. team was against Tufts in June 1875 (see Blanchard, *H Book*, 371), but it was the Harvard-Yale games in November 1875 and 1876 that led to the formation of an intercollegiate football association and development of American football.

Chapter 2

1. LCAR; George Rogers Taylor, *The Transportation Revolution* (New York: Holt, Rinehart, and Winston, 1951), 4:77; Robert Luther Thompson, *Wiring a Continent* (Princeton, N.J.: Princeton University Press, 1947), 8.

2. LCAR. See also David Nelson Camp, *Recollections of a Long and Active Life*. Elah Camp's mother was Phoebe Spencer, a relative of the English family that included Winston Churchill and "Lady Di"; Orit was a direct lineal descendant of Theophilis Eaton, a wealthy London

businessman and an early leader of the New Haven colony. For "Walter Campe," see P. H. Reany, *The Place Names of Essex* (London: Cambridge University Press, 1969), 26; W. Winters, *Memorial of the Pilgrim Fathers* (Essex: n.p., 1882), 26; and Federal Writers' Project of the W.P.A., *Milford, Connecticut* (Bridgeport, Conn.: Braunworth, 1939), 1–7, 11.

3. D. Camp, *Recollections*, 2; LCAR.

4. David N. Camp, *History of New Britain* (New Britain: William B. Thomson, 1889), 239–40; LCAR.

5. LCAR; entry for Ellen (Cornwell) Camp in *Record of Association of Alumni*, archives of Central Connecticut State University, New Britain; Alfred Andrews, *Genealogy and Ecclesiastical History*, 258 (listed as Chauncey Cornw*a*ll).

6. LCAR.

7. WCAR.

8. C. Bancroft Gillespie, comp., *A Century of Meriden* (Meriden: Journal, 1906), 386.

9. LCAR; Rollin G. Osterweis, *Three Centuries of New Haven, 1638–1938*, 227–29, 194.

10. *New Haven Educational Report* for the year 1864.

11. The *New Haven City Directory* lists Leverett Camp as living at 170 Chapel Street, but no real estate record shows his purchase of that property. New Haven Land Records, bk. 217, p. 349; 1880 census; *New Haven Register*, March 14, 1915; *1888 Atlas of the City of New Haven, Connecticut* (Philadelphia: G. M. Hopkins, 1888).

12. 1880 U.S. Census and yearly issues of the *New Haven City Directory*; New Haven Land Records, bk. 215, p. 299; D. Camp, *New Britain*, 365.

13. For relationship, see Andrews, *Genealogy and Ecclesiastical History*, 258; New Haven Land Records, bk. 197, p. 494; *Benham's New Haven City Directory* for 1876.

14. Norris Galpin Osborn, ed., *Men of Mark in Connecticut* (Hartford, Conn.: Johnson-Wynn, 1904). See also Arthur Raymond Mead, *The Development of Free Schools in the United States* (New York: Teachers College, Columbia University, 1918), 16, 59, 215; D. Camp, *Recollections*, 75–77; and CCAR.

15. Andrews, *Genealogy and Ecclesiastical History* 104 (listed as Chauncey Cornwall); *New Haven City Directory* for 1873.

16. 1870 and 1880 U.S. Censuses and *New Haven City Directories*. Walter Camp biography in *DAB*, written by Norris Galpin Osborn, editor of the *New Haven Register*.

17. *New Haven Educational Report* for the year 1870. Map of New Haven in 1868, from the Atlas of New Haven County, compiled by F. W. Beers, New York, 1868; reproduced in Osterweis, *Three Centuries*, facing 344. *New Haven Evening Register*, January 3, 1871.

18. *New Haven Education Report* for the year 1870.

19. For Leverett Camp and female teachers, *New Haven Education Report* for the year 1870; for manufacturing worker, Clarence D. Long, *Wages and Earnings in the United States, 1860–1890* (Princeton, N.J.: Princeton University Press, 1960), table 1, p. 14.

20. David Q. Voight, *The League That Failed* (Lanham, Md.: Scarecrow Press, 1998), 4. *Football Rules* (Rugby: J. B. Crossley, n.d.), title page, describes rules in the booklet as "sanctioned" by a "Levee" at Rugby School on August 28, 1845; copy from the Rugby Museum, Twickenham, England. For a more extensive discussion of the development of rugby at Rugby School, see Eric Dunning and Kenneth Sheard, *Barbarians, Gentlemen and Players*, chap. 4. According to a plaque mounted in the business district of Rugby, railroad service reached the town in 1838.

An 1857 book about life at Rugby School, Thomas Hughes, *Tom Brown's School Days*, has a few descriptions of rugby as it was played presumably in the 1830s when the author, Thomas Hughes, was a Rugby student. In the 1830s, Rugby's game already had an elevated goal—"a sort of gigantic gallows of two poles eighteen feet high, fixed upright in the ground some fourteen feet apart, with a cross-bar . . . at the height of ten feet" (109)—perhaps to allow kicking over masses of younger-age students who defended goals at Rugby. Catching the ball was clearly allowed, as was dribbling by kicking, but running with the ball was more ambiguous. *Tom Brown* does not clearly refer to running, though the 1845 rules do. Perhaps running was introduced after Hughes's stay at the school, but there is disagreement about how such running developed. Rugby School credits one player, William Webb Ellis, with one day disregarding existing rugby rules and running with the ball; the school has erected a stone tablet to commemorate that act. Jennifer Macrory in *Running with the Ball* agrees with Rugby School's credit to Ellis. Dunning and Sheard, *Barbarians, Gentlemen and Players*, chap. 4, and other scholars disagree ("It is just not sociologically plausible that a deeply entrenched traditional game could have been changed fundamentally by a single act" [60–62, 61]).

Additional innovation was also occurring at Rugby School. In 1837, at the same time as Rugby School students were developing the game of rugby, they also established the "hare and hounds run," the earliest known cross-country race. See J. H. Hardwick, *Distance and Cross-Country Running* (London: British Sports, n.d.), 55.

21. Though kicking-only games were older than rugby, the first printed kicking-only rules were apparently published at Eton Public School in 1849. See Dunning and Sheard, *Barbarians, Gentlemen and Players*, 98; and Harvey, *Football*, 134–49, 170–71.

22. Peter Lindsay, "The Impact of the Military Garrisons on the Development of Sport in British North America," *Canadian Journal of History of Sport and Physical Education* 1, no. 1 (1970): 41, citing C. P. Stacey, *Canada and the British Army, 1846–1871* (Toronto: University of Toronto Press, 1963), 122. For development of rugby play in Canada, see also Alan Metcalfe, *Canada Learns to Play* (Toronto: Oxford University Press, 1987), 55; and Don Morrow, *A Concise History of Sport in Canada* (Toronto: Oxford University Press, 1989), 141–43.

23. T. Davis, *Chronicles of Hopkins Grammar School*, 423; John Hays Hammond to Camp, December 2, 1892, Camp Papers, reel 9.

24. Harford Powell Jr., *Walter Camp*, 4.

25. Manuscript, Camp Papers, reel 47, box 66, folder 1.

26. Powell, *Walter Camp*, 4; Samuel T. Wheelwright, *A New System of Instruction in the Indian Club Exercise* (New York: Thomas O'Kane, 1871). The Yale crew practiced with Indian clubs. See Alice J. Hoffman, *Indian Clubs* (New York: Harry N. Abrams, 1996), 6. See also Camp, *The Book of Football*, 139.

27. Powell, *Walter Camp*, 7, 11.

28. *Critic*, November 1, 1874; T. Davis, *Chronicles of Hopkins Grammar School*, 426; Albert G. Spalding, *America's National Game* (New York: American Sports, 1911), 481–85; T. Davis, *Chronicles of Hopkins Grammar School*, 426.

29. *Critic*, April, 1875, lists editorial staff for Camp's senior year at Hopkins. SQ, question 7; *Critic*, October 1875, 2. Printed card describing the class leaving Hopkins Grammar School in 1876 is included on reel 47, Camp Papers; compare Powell, *Walter Camp*, 9.

Chapter 3

1. 1892 Clipping.

2. George W. Pierson, *The Education of American Leaders* (New York: Frederick A. Praeger, 1969); *Advocate*, May 12, 1876, 77; *Crimson*, November 3, 1876; *Advocate*, November 10, 1876; *Courant*, November 11, 1876.

3. *Courant*, September 30, 1876; manuscript, Camp Papers, reel 38, box 58, folder 412.

4. *Yale Banner* 33 (1876–77), list of freshmen and addresses.

5. 1892 Clipping.

6. *Advocate,* November 24, 1876; 1892 Clipping.

7. 1892 Clipping.

8. *Advocate*, November 24, 1876.

9. 1892 Clipping.

10. Letter to the editor, *Forest and Stream*, December 7, 1876: 285; *Advocate*, November 24, 1876.

11. *Courant*, November 25, 1876. See also a Camp manuscript in the Camp Papers, "The First Match under Rugby Rules," reel 29, box 45, folder 210. The plaque is now in Yale's trophy room.

12. 1892 Clipping.

13. Samuel Eliot Morison, *The Founding of Harvard College* (Cambridge, Mass.: Harvard University Press, 1935), 148, 161–70. The listed numbers of colleges are from Donald G. Tewksbury, *The Founding of American Colleges and Universities before the Civil War* (New York: Teachers College, Columbia University, 1932), 16; Tewksbury, *Founding,* 3 (citing speech by Peter Lindsley from LeRoy J. Halsey, ed., *The Works of Peter Lindsley* [1864], 1:404–5); Tewksbury, *Founding of Colleges and Universities*, 3 (citing statement by Henry P. Tappan from his book, *University Education* [1850], 64).

14. David Potter, *Debating in the Colonial Chartered Colleges* (New York: Teacher's College, Columbia University, 1944), 64.

15. James M. Whiton, "The First Harvard-Yale Regatta (1852)," *Outlook*, June 1, 1901, 286–89. For "450" at Yale, see Lewis Sheldon Welch and Walter Camp, *Yale: Her Campus, Class-Rooms and Athletics*, 426. For "350" at Harvard, see Moses King, *Harvard and Its Surroundings* (Cambridge: Moses King, 1884). Other sports: *Williams Quarterly* 7, no. 1 (1859): 95; *Rutger's Targum*, November 1869, 5; and Samuel Crowther and Arthur Ruhl, *Rowing and Track Athletics* (New York: Macmillan, 1905), 268–69.

16. Blanchard, *H Book*, 32. Other sports: soccer, *Courant*, October 25, 1873, 63; track and field, *NYT*, December 5, 1875; Crowther and Ruhl, *Rowing and Track*, 271; baseball, Harold Seymour, *The People's Game* (New York: Oxford University Press, 1990), 143.

17. *Princetonian* (Princeton student newspaper), October 19, 1876.

18. Frank Presbrey and James H. Moffatt, eds., *Athletics at Princeton*, 278–80. See also *Princetonian*, November 11, 1876. "Nine or ten" from analyzing teams and years of playing in Harold Claassen, *Ronald Encyclopedia*. See also *Courant*, November 25, 1876, 67.

19. *Courant*, November 25, 1876, 67.

20. Ibid.; *Spirit of the Times*, December 2, 1876.

21. *Courant*, November 25, 1876, 67.

22. Percy Royds, *The History of the Laws of Rugby Football* (Twickenham, England: n.p., 1949), 60; *Courant*, December 13, 1873, 155. Rowland Bowen, *Cricket* (London: Eyre and Spottiswoode, 1970), 29–30, writes, "One of the peculiarities of cricket is its numbering system, all based on eleven or sub-divisions or multiples of eleven. There is no apparent reason why it should play such a prominent part . . . (though the number has been borrowed by soccer and hockey and no doubt other games). . . . The only possible reason seems to be that there must have been a numbering system in and about the area where cricket arose, itself based on eleven." Bowen then suggests that cricket developed in an area of northern France, "from the Seine on in to Flanders" where there was such a numbering system, with "eleven inches to a foot," and where there is a reference to cricket in 1478.

23. *Springfield Republican*, November 24, 1876.

24. Diana Karter Appelbaum, *Thanksgiving* (New York: Facts on File, 1984), 153, 185–205.

Chapter 4

1. Walter Camp, "The New Idea in Athletics," *Outing*, March 1910, 655–56; *Courant*, November 15, 1873, 101.

2. Henry B. Twombley, *Personal Reminiscences of a Yale Football Player*, 21–23. The dimensions in the drawings are taken from the following: For rugby ball, undated ad, presumably from Peck and Snyder in New York, which lists the no. 5 rugby ball as twenty-seven inches in circumference (the *Springfield [Mass.] Republican*, November 24, 1876, reports that the delegates at the inaugural November 23, 1876, IFA convention agreed to play with a no. 5 ball). For soccer ball, *2001 Men's and Women's Soccer Rules* (Indianapolis: National Collegiate Athletic Association, June 2001), 16. For today's U.S. football, *The National Collegiate Athletic Association Football Rules and Interpretations* (Indianapolis: National Collegiate Athletic Association, 2001), FR-24.

3. *Spalding's Official Football Guide for 1894*, 33.

4. *Courant*, February 24, 1877, 134; *Yale Banner* 34 (1877–78), list of sophomore class with addresses; Cornelius H. Patton and Walter T. Field, *Eight O'Clock Chapel*, 199.

5. Lyman H. Bagg, *Four Years at Yale*, 551, 550; *YLit* 43 (October 1877); Bagg, *Four Years at Yale*, 552.

6. Angela Sorby, *Schoolroom Poets* (Durham: University of New Hampshire Press, 2005), xi. For aphorisms, Camp Papers, reel 38, folders 416–27.

7. *YLit* 43 (1877–78): table of contents, 224. Camp is listed as the contributor in the table of contents, though in the text the poem is followed only by the initial "s." Walter Camp, *The Substitute*, 3.

8. Diary of a student, 6, Camp Papers, reel 47; Samuel W. Lambert, introduction to *The Daily Dozen*, by Walter Camp (New York: Reynolds, 1925), xi.

9. Welch and Camp, *Yale*, 539.

10. Ibid., 518.

11. Presbrey and Moffatt, *Athletics at Princeton*, 287; *Courant*, November 10, 1877; *Princetonian*, December 13, 1877.

12. Presbrey and Moffatt, *Athletics at Princeton*, 287.

13. Welch and Camp, *Yale*, 578–79.

14. Ibid. The silver pitcher is now in the Yale trophy room.

Chapter 5

1. The *Week's Sport*, probably published January 1, 1890, found in Camp Papers, reel 41 (page stamped "1890"). Extensive quotations from the article also appear in *Crimson*, January 7, 1890.

2. Ibid.

3. Hughes, *Tom Brown's School Days*, 118.

4. Walter Camp, "Methods and Development in Tactics and Play," *Outing*, November 1900, 172.

5. Alumni record of Eugene Baker, YUMA; *NYT*, November 29, 1878. It should be noted that Thompson was already captain of the Yale crew, the big sport on the Yale campus. Welch and Camp, *Yale*, 505.

6. *Yale Banner* 35 (1878–79), list of juniors.

7. Parke H. Davis, *Football: The American Intercollegiate Game*, 467; *Princetonian*, October 1878, 94; *Crimson*, October 11, 1878.

8. *Courant*, October 19, 1878. See Welch and Camp, *Yale*, 536, where Yale is said not to be an IFA member only in 1876 and 1877; that statement is not made for 1878 and thereafter.

9. 1878 Rules, Rule 15 (which appears to be a modification of Rule 14 of the 1876 rules) (emphasis added). Instead of offense and defense, the original American rule patterned after English rugby rules suggested equality in a scrimmage: "The holder of the ball . . . puts it down on the ground in front of him and *all* who have closed round on their respective sides endeavor . . . by kicking . . . to drive [the ball] in the direction of the opposite goal" (emphasis added).

The hinted-at concepts of "ball possession" and offensive and defensive roles were incidental in the rule; the real intention of the rule change, Camp later wrote, was to put an end to another experimental technique that the new-to-rugby Americans were trying out in parallel with the kicking-back method; in that technique, the man with the ball placed it on the ground and then immediately picked it up to run with it. To twenty-first-century observers, the choice seems obvious, but Camp regarded the amendment to Rule 15 as a real and significant choice that eventually directed American football into quarterback play. *Week's Sport*, January 1, 1890; *Advocate*, May 12, 1876, 78.

Chapter 6

1. Twombley, *Personal Reminiscences*, 23.

2. Ibid.

3. *Courant*, November 2, 1878, 40.

4. Walter Camp, *The Book of Football*, 10.

5. Ibid., 32.

6. Manuscript, Camp Papers, reel 22, box 31, folder 29.

7. *The Football Annual* for 1882 (published in England by John Lillywhite), 6, where A. G. Guillemard states, "At Rugby, years ago" . . . 'quarter-back' was used as a term of reproach."

8. Walter Camp, "Methods and Development in Tactics and Play," *Outing*, November 1900, 173–74.

9. Robert Watson, quoted in *YAW* 26 (January 14, 1916): 508; Camp, *The Substitute*, 3; George Santayana, "A Glimpse of Yale," in *George Santayana's America*, edited by James Bal-

lowe (Urbana: University of Illinois Press, 1967), 48–56. Santayana explained the Yale spirit, which he saw as unique, as a consequence of a number of factors, including a student body that had come to the school with a long-held dream of attending there and in the isolation of life on the school campus took up the school's traditions and causes. Yale's vigorous disciplines brought further unity: everybody "must be at chapel at ten minutes to eight; at half past eight everybody has a recitation." "The habit of doing things together is thus formed at Yale and concerted action of all kinds is easy for them." Arthur T. Hadley, section on Yale University in *Four American Universities* (New York: Harper and Brothers, 1895), 90.

10. Baker to Camp, November 25, 1893, Camp Papers, reel 2.

11. Twombley, *Personal Reminiscences*, 20; manuscript, Camp Papers, reel 47, box 66, folder 1.

12. Camp, *How to Coach*, 6; *St. Nicholas* 17 (November 1889–October 1890): 167.

13. *Crimson*, November 12, 1875; the quoted poem is taken from Edmund Morris, *The Rise of Theodore Roosevelt* (New York: Coward, McCann, and Geoghegan,1979), 83. See also *NYTrib*, November 9, 1878; Allen L. Sack, "Yale 29. Harvard 4: The Professionalization of College Football," *Quest* 19 (Winter 1973): 26; and Endicott Peabody, "The Ideals of Sport in England and America," *American Physical Education Review* (1914): 277–83.

14. See Sack, "The Professionalization of College Football."

15. *NYT*, November 24, 1878, 1; *NYW*, November 24, 1878, 2.

16. Twombley, *Personal Reminiscences*, 6. Manuscript, reel 29, box 45, folder 210, Camp Papers.

Chapter 7

1. *NYW*, November 29, 1878: 1.

2. Geoffrey W. Clark, *History of Stevens Institute of Technology* (Jersey City, N.J.: Jensen/Daniels, 2000), 15–16, 147–48.

3. Harold Seymour, *Baseball: The Early Years* (New York: Oxford University Press, 1960), 18.

4. *NYW*, November 29, 1878, 1; *Princetonian*, December 5, 1878.

5. *NYW*, December 1, 1876; *NYT*, December 9, 1877; *NYW*, November 29, 1878.

6. HPrRep, 1881–82, 19.

7. Arthur S. Link, ed., *The Papers of Woodrow Wilson*, 1:405–6 (editorial of September 26, 1878).

8. Princeton enrollment, Varnum L. Collins, *Princeton* (New York: Oxford University Press, 1914), 410; Yale enrollment, Welch and Camp, *Yale*, 427 (combining Yale's undergraduate college, fine arts college, and Sheffield Science School). Welch and Camp, in the table on p. 536, state that Yale was not a member of the IFA in 1876 and 1877; that statement is not made for 1878 or the years thereafter, implying Yale had joined by 1878.

9. *NYW*, November 29, 1878.

10. *NYT*, November 29, 1878, 8.

11. Twombley, *Personal Reminiscences*, 6.

12. *YNews*, February 5, 1879; Walter Camp, "Junior Promenade at Yale," *HW*, February 18, 1893, 159 (paraphrased in parts).

13. *New Haven Journal-Courier*, February 5, 1879.

14. Camp, "Junior Promenade," 159.

15. *Courant*, September 13, 1879, 7.

16. Walter Camp, "Senior Society Elections at Yale," *Bachelor of Arts* 3 (June 1896): 75–79.

17. Ibid.

Chapter 8

1. *Courant*, September 13, 1879, 7.

2. *Century*, o.s., 47 (February 1894): 633.

3. *Princetonian*, October 10, 1879; 1879 Rules.

4. *Princetonian*, October 10, 1879.

5. Morris A. Bealle, *The History of Football at Harvard* (Washington, D.C.: Columbia, 1948), 37–38; Poultney Bigelow, *Seventy Summers* (London: Edward Arnold, 1925), 302.

6. *Advocate*, November 14, 1879; *YLit* 45 (1878–79): 82–83.

7. *NYT*, November 28, 1879, 1.

8. Welch and Camp, *Yale*, 539; *NYW*, November 28, 1879.

9. William H. Edwards, *Football Days*, 73–74.

10. *NYW*, November 28, 1879, 1. So far Americans had kept rugby's umpires, one appointed by each team; in England the umpires resolved disputed points, but Americans had added a neutral referee, leaving umpires to advocate (and get in the way) but not decide. With Yale's umpire directing cheers, the *Princetonian* complained that Yale's "canine chorus" came with too "painful regularity." *Princetonian*, November 1879, 129.

11. *NYW*, November 28, 1879.

12. *NYT*, November 28, 1879.

13. *NYW*, November 28, 1879, 8.

14. *Courant*, September 13, 1879, 78.

15. Ibid., 74–75.

16. Bagg, *Four Years at Yale*, 484.

17. *YLit* 45 (1879–80), table of contents. (The poems are printed in the magazine at 8 ["Only"], 164 ["Bubbles"], 201 ["Jim"].) Document entitled "Data Taken from Biographical Notes of the Biographical Cyclopaedia," found on biographical reel 47 of Camp Papers. Some verses of the latter poem are as follows:

JIM

You remember Jim Tregarvan,
    The fellow who used to row,
Who was such a splendid boxer,
    Could hit such a straight left blow?

Well, I was shut in the office,
    Conversing over a fee,
When the boy brought in the message,
    "A gentleman asking for me."

. . .

I remembered him then in a moment,
    And, as soon as we'd shaken hands,

I asked him over to dinner
With me at Hildebrand's.

The poem continues with college recollections and a brief rehashing of Jim's experiences, including his young wife's death, which had overwhelmed him, leading to a downward spiral and dramatic turn developed in a few concluding stanzas:

Then, turning to me, half hiding
With a cough what seemed a sob,
He said, "Good-bye, old fellow,
Remember me to Bob."

And before I could move a finger,
He lay at my feet stone-dead!
In his hand a small revolver,
The muzzle touching his head.

18. Bagg, *Four Years at Yale*, 484.
19. *YLit* 45 (1879–80): 41.
20. *YNews*, June 30, 1880. The poem is in a booklet for Presentation Day, June 29, 1880, and the last verse reads:

O song birds, cease your merry notes,
To chant a mournful lay;
Dear whisp'ring elms soft farewell breathe
In minor strains today.
For 'tis to 'Eighty and to Yale;
With saddened hearts we cry;
"God give and grant forevermore
All blessings and 'Good-by.'"

Questionnaire headed, "From Cyclopaedic Biography," Camp Papers, reel 47.
21. *NHReg*, July 1, 1880.
22. *NYT*, July 2, 1880. Other awards given were the next higher "first colloquy," then "first or second dispute," "dissertation," "oration," "high oration," until "philosophical oration," the highest honor. George W. Pierson, *Yale College: An Educational History*, 1:320.

Chapter 9

1. *YNews*, October 15, 1880.
2. Ibid.
3. Ibid.
4. *Crimson*, October 15, 1880.
5. Ibid.
6. Camp, *The Book of Football*, 32.
7. Rule 18, 1879 Rules.
8. *YLit* (October 1880); *President's Book* kept by president of the Yale University Foot Ball Club Association, Record Unit 507, YUMA; *Crimson*, October 15, 1880.

9. *Week's Sport*, January 1, 1890; Camp, *The Book of Football*, 31–32.

10. *Toronto Mail*, November 3, 1879.

11. *NYT*, November 28, 1879.

12. Testimonial by Parke Davis at February 5, 1915, rules committee dinner, Camp Papers, reel 48, box 68, folder 34.

13. *Courant*, September 25, 1880, 1–2.

14. SQ. "Surgeon" implied from answer for question 8. "Statistics of the Class of '80," Yale College. Thirty-nine were reported as entering law, seventeen in medicine, six in theology, and four in teaching.

15. SQ, question 8.

16. *NHReg*, March 7, 1881. See also *Courant*, April 3, 1880; *NYT*, October 2, 1879; and *YNews*, October 3, 1879.

17. *NHReg*, March 7, 1881.

18. Booklet, 3⅝ by 5¾ inches, twenty pages, bound in a blue cover with a printed title on the front, "FOOT BALL RULES," and on the back cover a penciled notation, "Yed5, F7, 1"; found in File No. Yed5, folder 7, YUMA.

19. The date 1880 for the rule book is suggested by both a penciled notation of that date on the rule book and a comparison of the words in the 1879 and 1881 Rules and the October 15, 1880, *Crimson* report of the 1880 convention; for example, the term *quarterback*, first introduced at the 1880 convention, is present (Rule 17), but not the provision for added play in case a game is tied at the end of regulation play, first introduced at the 1881 convention.

20. "Hints for Practice" begins on page 10 of the booklet identified in note 18; the quotation is from pages 10–11.

21. Ibid., 15.

22. Ibid., 16.

23. Ibid., 18.

Chapter 10

1. *NYT*, November 26, 1880; *NYW*, November 26, 1880.

2. Stew Thornley, *Land of the Giants* (Philadelphia: Temple University Press, 2000), 8.

3. P. Davis, *Football*, 77.

4. *NYW*, November 26, 1880; Welch and Camp, *Yale*, 536.

5. *Sexennial Record of the Class of '80* (New Haven, Conn.: Stafford, 1887); *NHReg*, April 8, 1881.

6. Welch and Camp, *Yale*, 574, lists Camp as one of the nine regular players on the Yale varsity baseball team.

7. *YNews*, October 11, 1881.

8. Ibid.; *Princetonian*, October 21, 1881.

9. Presbrey and Moffatt, *Athletics at Princeton*, 300; *Week's Sport*, January 1, 1890.

10. *Princetonian*, October 21, 1881.

11. *NYH* October [16?], 1880, reports the 1880 convention "voted not to count 'safety touchdowns.'"

12. *Week's Sport*, January 1, 1890, which states, "From the wording of the rule it can be seen how difficult it was to get this point through."

13. *NYT*, November 25, 1881.
14. *NYW*, November 25, 1881; Presbrey and Moffatt, *Athletics at Princeton*, 304.
15. Percy D. Haughton, *Football and How to Watch It*, 62.
16. Presbrey and Moffatt, *Athletics at Princeton*, 305.
17. *NYH*, November 26, 1881.
18. Walter Camp and Lorin F. Deland, *Football*, 66.

Chapter 11

1. *NYW*, April 30, 1882.
2. *Courant*, supp., December 17, 1881, 2.
3. *NYW*, April 30, 1882.
4. 1894 *Spalding Guide* 35; Twombley, *Personal Reminiscences*, 22; *Outing*, November 1900, 173 ("no adherents except the man who proposed it"); Cohane, *Yale Football Story*, 36–38.
5. *Princetonian*, May 12, 1882; manuscript, Camp Papers, reel 21, folder 5; *Princetonian*, May 12, 1882, 27.
6. *Princetonian*, December 2, 1881, 115. The four-down proposal appeared in an editorial comment. A letter published in the same December 2 *Princetonian* at pages 117–18 makes a similar proposal but states three downs as the limit for possession. For Camp's warning, see *Courant*, supp., December 17, 1881, 2.
7. *Princetonian*, May 12, 1882, 17.
8. *Crimson*, April 12, 1882.
9. During Camp's young adult years, his handwriting varied between the Palmer style taught in schools to a more casual, slightly left-leaning style that eventually became his uniform style. He seemed to use the Palmer style in formal situations such as when he registered as a student in medical school or when he prepared a document that might be preserved or used in some way as a reference document. One such document was an April 1882 rules document he annotated with historical information, which became a collector's item (discussed in note 4 of chapter 12). In the note collection pictured on page 59 of the text, the "Decisions," "Interpretations," and "Unfair tactics" papers each contain useful information that might desirably be preserved and consulted as a reference document. On the other hand, the rule proposals and draft constitution were only working documents that would be modified and replaced with a printed document.
10. *Boston Post*, October 1, 1889; Powell, *Walter Camp*, 148. Many of Camp's notes are in the Camp Papers, reel 26, box 39, folder 111.
11. *SFExam*, December 4, 1892 ("preacher"); Twombley, *Personal Reminiscences*, 23 ("eyes").
12. Manuscript labeled 1914, Camp Papers, reel 29, box 45, folder 210.
13. *Princetonian*, May 12, 1882, 17.
14. Lottie G. Bishop, memo from the Office of the Dean of the Yale University School of Medicine, October 9, 1950, copy in Walter Camp alumni folder at YUMA.
15. Twombley, *Personal Reminiscences*, 20.
16. Ibid., 21.
17. Ibid., 22, 26–29.
18. Ibid., 31–32.
19. *Princetonian*, December 8, 1882, 149.

Chapter 12

1. 1894 *Spalding Guide* 35; Walter Camp, "A Plea for the Wedge," *HW*, January 21, 1893, 67.

2. *Crimson*, December 1, 1882.

3. *Spirit of the Times*, December 23, 1882; *New York Clipper*, December 16, 1882. Some historians have mistakenly assigned some of the December 1882 convention actions—such as a point system—to the convention of October 1883, but the just-cited newspaper reports, outlining the agreed point system, disprove that contention. Game reports in the fall of 1883 before the October convention also give game scores in points.

4. Camp's handwritten draft of revised rules is in the Camp Papers, reel 26, box 39, folder 111. Camp's annotated April 1882 rule book is filed in YUMA, File No. Yx 880 Cla, having been purchased from a collector by Yale benefactors.

5. 1883 Rules, Camp Papers, series II, folder 150.

6. *Princetonian*, October 27, 1882, 107. A copy of the constitution in Camp's handwriting is in the Camp Papers, reel 1, box 1, folder 23. See also *Courant*, November 29, 1882 ("constitution which Yale drew up was adopted").

7. *Princetonian*, October 27, 1882, 107.

8. *Courant*, November 29, 1882.

9. Guy Stanton Ford, "International Expositions," in *Encyclopedia of the Social Sciences*, edited by Edwin F.A. Seligman and Alvin Johnson (New York: Macmillan, 1951), 6:26 (emphasis in the original).

Chapter 13

1. *NYW*, November 26, 1883.

2. Harvard numbers from Moses King, *Harvard and Its Surroundings* (Cambridge: Moses King, 1884), 15, combining "College" and "Scientific School" numbers; Yale numbers, also combining college ("Academic Department") and "Sheffield Scientific School" from Welch and Camp, *Yale*, 427.

3. Henry James, *Charles W. Eliot*, 1:12–13.

4. *DAB*, vol. 3, pt. 2, 71; James, *Charles W. Eliot*, 1:79–81.

5. James, *Charles W. Eliot*, 1:285, 303.

6. HPrRep, 1881–82, 19.

7. Ibid., 18.

8. Ronald A. Smith, "Preludes to the NCAA: Early Failures of Faculty Intercollegiate Athletic Control," *Research Quarterly for Exercise and Sport* 54, no. 4 (1883): 375, citing Luther W. Warren, "The Charles W. Eliot Centennial," *Journal of Physical Education* 5 (March 1934): 24; HPrRep, 1873–74, 23, as quoted in Alar Lipping, "Charles W. Eliot's Views on Education, Physical Education, and Intercollegiate Athletics" (Ph.D. diss., Ohio State University, 1980), 247.

9. *Harvard College Report of the Committee Appointed to Consider the Subject of College Athletics, and to Report Thereon to the Faculty* (Cambridge: John Wilson and Son, 1888), 11.

10. Louise L. Stevenson, *Scholarly Means to Evangelical Ends*, 2; Reuben A. Holden, *Profiles and Portraits of Yale University Presidents* (New Haven, Conn.: Bond Wheelwright, 1968), 84.

11. Pierson, *Yale College*, 58. See also Noah Porter, *The American Colleges and the American Public* (New Haven, Conn.: Charles C. Chatfield, 1870), 40–52.

12. Stevenson, *Scholarly Means*, 51, 60, 118–19; Noah Porter, *American Colleges*, epigraph.

13. John S. Brubacher and Willis Rudy, *Higher Education in Transition* (New York: Harper and Row, 1958), 365; Brooks Mather Kelley, *Yale: A History*, 271–72.

14. *YLit* 48 (Fall 1882): 22–23.

15. David Q. Voight, *American Baseball* (University Park: Pennsylvania State University Press, 1983), 1:205–6, citing *St. Louis Globe-Democrat,* April 12, 1884; James, *Charles W. Eliot*, 2:69.

16. *NYW*, November 26, 1883.

17. HPrRep, 1881–82, 17. Harvard ended its ban against play with professional teams in 1889. See Blanchard, *H Book*, 196.

Chapter 14

1. Patton and Field, *Eight O'Clock Chapel*, 117; *DAB*, vol. 9, pt. 2, 218; A. G. Keller, *Reminiscences (Mainly Personal) of William Graham Sumner* (New Haven, Conn.: Yale University Press, 1933), 3.

2. Harris E. Starr, *William Graham Sumner* (New York: Henry Holt, 1925), 2–3, 12–15.

3. Ibid., 15–16.

4. WGS Papers, box 22, folders 622–27.

5. Starr, *Sumner*, quoting from an essay, "The Challenge of Facts"; 1880 U.S. Census.

6. SQ, question 5.

7. Letters from Alice to "Dear Brother Will" in WGS Papers, box 22, folders 622–27.

8. *New Haven Educational Directory* for 1884, 1885.

9. William M. Sloane, *The Life of James McCosh* (Edinburgh: T. and T. Clark, 1896), 172; *DAB*, vol. 6, pt. 1, 615. He was Princeton's second Scottish pastor-president, the first being John Witherspoon, the highly regarded academic and American Revolutionary leader. Thomas J. Wertenbaker, *Princeton* (Princeton, N.J.: Princeton University Press, 1946), 290.

10. J. David Hoeveler Jr., *James McCosh and the Scottish Intellectual Tradition* (Princeton, N.J.: Princeton University Press, 1981), 329; Varnum L. Collins, *Princeton* (New York: Oxford University Press, 1914), 410; Henry Wilkinson Bragdon, *Woodrow Wilson: The Academic Years*, 19.

11. Pierson, *Yale College*, 60; Hoeveler, *James McCosh*, 252.

12. Frank L. Mott, *A History of American Magazines*, 2:359, 362; Edmund M. Norris, *The Story of Princeton* (Boston: Little, Brown, 1917), 216; *New York Ledger*, April 7, 1883.

13. Each of the quotations is from the *New York Ledger*, April 7, 1883.

14. Bragdon, *Woodrow Wilson*, 20. As an example of a condescending comment, Camp satirized the use McCosh made of parental statements to demonstrate an alleged overemphasis on competitive college games: "I sent my son to college that he might become a scholar and assist me in my law office, I find that you have made him a tumbler." Camp responded, "If the venerable Dr. McCosh were a tumbler, he would know that tumblers learn and work under a roof and on mattresses or sawdust," that is, in the gymnasium McCosh says he supports.

15. T. Barton Brune to Camp, November 24, 1883, Camp Papers, correspondence files; Presbrey and Moffatt, *Athletics at Princeton*, 141. Presbrey notes that the faculty were

influenced also by Princeton's baseball captain, who appeared before them with a copy of the rules adopted by the professional league forbidding swearing, card playing, gambling, and boisterous conduct.

Chapter 15

1. The first lawn tennis play in the United States is not certain but apparently happened about 1874. See Max Robertson, ed., *The Encyclopedia of Tennis* (New York: Rainbird Reference Books, Viking Press, 1974), 26; and *YNews*, November 1, 1882.

2. *YNews*, June 11, 1883; Lawrence B. Goodheart, *Mad Yankees* (Amherst: University of Massachusetts Press, 2003), 9, 159–60; *YNews*, March 31, 1884.

3. Bill Talbert with Pete Axthelm, *Tennis Observed* (Barre, Mass.: n.p., 1967), 14.

4. E. Digby Baltzell, *Sporting Gentlemen* (New York: Free Press, 1995), 47; *Crimson*, June 8, 1883.

5. Quotation is from Paul Johnson, *Darwin* (New York: Viking-Penguin Group, 2012), 20. Darwin failed Anatomy.

6. SQ, question 8; Powell, *Walter Camp*, 30.

7. SQ, question 9.

8. Lottie G. Bishop, memo from the Office of the Dean of the Yale University School of Medicine, October 9, 1950, copy in Walter Camp alumni folder at YUMA.

9. Michael C. Harrold, "Manhattan Watch Company," *Watch and Clock Bulletin* (NAWCC) (April 2010): 149; Manhattan Watch Company incorporation papers (Articles of Incorporation and Certificate to increase capital stock), available from Corporations Division of the Vermont Office of the Secretary of State. See also William Henry Jennings, *A Genealogical History of the Jennings Families* (Columbus, Ohio: n.p., 1899), showing on 2:432, 433, and 435 that the fathers of Arthur O. Jennings and Walter Jennings were both sons of Abraham Gould and Anna (Burr) Jennings. Powell, *Walter Camp*, 30.

10. A July 8, 1883, Camp letter is implied by Adee's letter to Camp, July 18, 1883, Camp Papers, reel 1; Welch and Camp, *Yale*, 480–81.

11. July 20, 1883, letter from Adee to Camp, Camp Papers, reel 1.

12. *YNews*, October 12, 16, 1883.

13. *YNews*, October 2, 12, 1883.

14. First letter undated and second dated November 21, 1883, both on the letterhead of the National League of Professional Baseball Clubs and signed by A. E. Young, secretary. Camp Papers, reel 13, correspondence files, National League.

Chapter 16

1. *YNews*, November 23, 1883; Linda Dowling, *Charles Eliot Norton: The Art of Reform in Nineteenth-Century America* (Hanover, N.H.: University Press of New England, 2007), ix.

2. *YNews*, November 23, 1883; *Herald-Crimson*, November 27, 1883.

3. *YNews*, November 26, 1883.

4. *YNews*, December 3, 1883; *NYT*, November 30, 1883; *NYW*, November 30, 1883.

5. *YNews*, December 6, 1883; *Crimson*, December 8, 1883. Accounts of the convention in the *YNews* and *Crimson* were identical, meaning, perhaps, that secretary Camp notified them both of the convention results.

6. Ronald A. Smith, *Sports and Freedom*, 136.

7. Laurence R. Veysey, *The Emergence of the American University*, 50, quoting March 9, 1880, letter of Eliot to D.C. Gilman in the Daniel Coit Gilman Collection, Sidney Lanier Room at Johns Hopkins University; *YNews*, January 10, 1884.

8. *YNews*, February 14, 1884.

9. *YNews*, February 15, 1884.

10. HPrRep, 1882–83, 23.

11. *New Haven Journal-Courier*, August 6, 1912.

12. *Popular Science Monthly*, March–April 1884, 446–53, 587–97.

13. *Outing*, April 1884, 66.

14. Ibid., 72.

15. Ibid.

16. HPrRep, 1883–84, 58.

17. *YNews*, March 5, 1884.

18. *YNews*, March 13, 1884.

Chapter 17

1. *YNews*, October 18, 1883.

2. The Library of Congress's copy of the booklet is stamped in "January, 1884."

3. *YNews*, December 6, 1883.

4. Library of Congress copy stamped in "May, 1884."

5. One person who took notice was Henry Chadwick, the leading American baseball writer at the time, who, for example, wrote annual reviews of professional baseball seasons in a baseball guide published by the sporting-goods company A. G. Spalding and Brothers. On March 29, 1884, Chadwick wrote to Camp and suggested that he and Camp cooperate in preparing and publishing a "College Baseball Guide," which Chadwick thought would be "profitable in a pecuniary point of view." Camp's response is not known, but nothing came of Chadwick's suggestion. Henry Chadwick to Camp, March 29, 1884, Camp Papers, reel 3.

6. *YNews,* February 12, 1884; David B. Potts, *Wesleyan University, 1831–1910* (New Haven, Conn.: Yale University Press, 1992), 183.

7. A. M. Wheeler to Camp, December 21, 1893, Camp Papers, reel 18 (emphasis added).

8. Walter Camp, *Athletes All* (New York: Charles Scribner's Sons, 1919), 25; *Courant*, December 15, 1883.

9. *NYT*, May 31, 1884, 2.

10. *Advocate*, October 1883; *YNews*, October 23, 1883.

11. *Popular Science Monthly*, April 1884, 593.

12. Dudley Allen Sargent, *An Autobiography* (Philadelphia: Lea and Febiger, 1927), 143.

13. Welch and Camp, *Yale*, 563, 540–41; *NHReg*, June 27, 1884.

Chapter 18

1. *Sexennial Record of the Class of '80* (New Haven, Conn.: Stafford, 1887).

2. Bailey, 77; Osterweis, *Three Centuries*, 354. As for "breakthrough" machining technology, see David A. Hounshell, *From the American System to Mass Production, 1800–1932* (Baltimore: Johns Hopkins University Press, 1984), 16–19.

3. *Sexennial Record for the Class of '80*; *NYT*, September 26, 1884, March 6, 1887, 2 ("waiting in vain"); *NHReg*, September 29, 1884.

4. New York City directory for 1886–87, 1887–88; 1880 U.S. Census for Louis Mealia family.

5. *NYT*, January 27, 1886, 3.

6. *NYT*, March 6, March 7, 1887, 2; correspondence of Alice Camp in Camp Papers, reel 47, box 66, folder 6.

7. William Warren Vaughn, *Northeast Harbor Reminiscences* (n.p.: White and Horne, 1930), 30.

8. *New Englander and Yale Review* 44 (January 1885): 138–40.

9. *YNews*, February 5, 1885.

10. *YNews*, December 3, 1884.

11. *NYEP*, November 30, 1886.

12. HPrRep, 1884–85, 71.

13. *YNews*, December 3, 1884.

14. Ibid.

15. *Crimson*, January 7, 1885.

16. *YNews*, February 9, 1885.

17. David B. Potts, *Wesleyan University, 1831–1910* (New Haven, Conn.: Yale University Press, 1992), 239.

18. Edwin E. Slosson, *Great American Universities*, 372, reports a total "college" enrollment at Pennsylvania in 1888–89 of 407 (plus more than 800 in professional schools and graduate school), and enrollment in 1885 was less. Edward Potts Cheyney, *History of the University of Pennsylvania* (Philadelphia: University of Pennsylvania Press, 1940), 342–45; George W. Orton, *A History of Athletics at Pennsylvania* (Philadelphia: Athletic Association of the University of Pennsylvania, n.d.), 102ff.

19. 1885 *Football Rules*, Rules 16, 17, 4, and 26. See also *YNews* and *Princetonian* for February 9, 1885.

20. *Princetonian*, February 13, 1885. The *Princetonian* stated that the separation proposed was for five yards, which, if true (doubtful), could explain why the delegates did not approve the idea.

21. HPrRep, 1885–86, 10.

22. Ibid., 35.

23. Samuel Eliot Morison, *Three Centuries of Harvard*, 359.

Chapter 19

1. *Outing*, April 1886, 99 (emphasis added).

2. Mott, *American Magazines*, 4:634; Poultney Bigelow, *Seventy Summers* (London: Edward Arnold, 1925), 300–301.

3. Andrew J. Stott, *Indiana Football: College, Athletic Club and High School*, 29, 33.

4. Number and named colleges compiled from Harold Claassen and Steve Boda Jr., eds., *Ronald Encyclopedia of Football*.

5. *Outing*, January 1887, 391–92.

6. Camp, *How to Coach*.

7. Ibid., 4, 27–28.

8. Camp to Sumner, August 30, 1886, WGS Papers, box 3, folder 73.

9. Alice Sumner to W. G. Sumner, Aug, 31, 1886, WGS Papers, box 22, folder 623.

10. Eliza Hotchkiss to Camp, September 7, 1886, Camp Papers, reel 10.

11. *NYT*, March 6, 1887, 2. Essentially, all the facts of the incident set forth in the text are taken from this newspaper report. For further background, see *NYT*, March 4, 1887, 1; March 5, 1887, 5; and March 7, 1887, 2.

12. *NYT*, November 28, 1887 (under "All Sorts of Paragraphs"); job title listed in the *New Haven City Directory* for 1888; letter of June 23, 1925, from Edwin P. Root of the NHCC to Miss Marian L. Phillips at Yale in WCAR; NHCC Stock Ledger, August 6, 1887, 24.

13. Minutes, January 25, 1889, stockholders' meeting, NHCC.

Chapter 20

1. Disputes about the game's scheduling were discussed after the game in *NYT*, November 27, 1886; see especially the statement of Cuyler.

2. Yale's agreement to play is discussed in *NYT*, November 24, 1886, 5. The impasse had continued until two days before Thanksgiving, when Yale's football management sent an S.O.S. to Camp. He and George Adee quickly met with two Princeton graduates and after exploring further options did what the Yale undergraduates seemed unable to do—agreed that the game would be played in Princeton on Thanksgiving Day. At that point, Yale's undergraduates also capitulated. The play of the game is discussed in *NYT*, November 26, 1886, 5.

3. *NYEP*, November 30, 1886; *YNews*, December 8, 1886.

4. *Princetonian*, May 18, 1887; *YNews*, June 13, 1887.

5. *Crimson*, June 21, 1887; *Princetonian*, September 21, 1887.

6. *NYT*, June 12, 1887; *YNews*, June 13, October 11, 1887.

7. Article III, Sec. 2, of the 1887 Constitution of the American Intercollegiate Football Association as printed in the 1887 *Football Rules*; *Crimson*, October 11, 1887; *YNews*, October 11, 1887. The final, approved constitution had important differences from Camp's committee-approved June draft, which retained some power for students. Sometime before the October ratification of the new constitution, the student powers of Camp's June draft had been removed and the graduate members reduced in number.

8. 1887 Constitution, Article III, Sec. 3.

9. 1887 Constitution, Article III, Sec. 6 and 7. Section 6 specified different responsibilities for the referee (judge game action) and new umpire (judge players' actions); in the latter connection, see also Camp's letter in *Outing*, January 1888, 380; Article IV, Sec. 1–2; and Article VIII.

10. For the prior "below the hips" bar, see the 1878 *Football Rules*, Rule 59. For the new "down to the knees" rule, see the 1888 *Football Rules*, Rule 27; *Princetonian*, March 7, 1888; and *YNews*, March 5, 1888. The new Graduate Advisory Committee had organized, with R. M Hodge, an 1886 Princeton graduate then in Princeton seminary, elected president and Camp secretary. Other members were W. A. Brooks, a just-graduated Harvard player now in Harvard Medical School; W. S. Harvey, Pennsylvania; and F. L. Beattys, Wesleyan.

11. 1878 Rules, Rules 24 and 25; 1887 *Football Rules*, Rule 14.

12. *Outing*, January 1888, 380.

13. 1888 *Football Rules*, Rules 10, 24, and 25. See also *Princetonian*, March 7, 1888.

14. Camp, *The Book of Football*, 51–52; *Outing*, December 1888, 266–67.

15. Powell, *Walter Camp*, 177–79.

16. Walter Camp, "Methods and Development in Tactics and Play," *Outing*, November 1900, 173.

17. *Outing*, October 1887, 68–86.

18. *HW*, November 10, 1888, 858.

19. Number of colleges playing intercollegiate football compiled from Claassen and Boda, *Ronald's Encyclopedia of Football*.

20. *St. Nicholas* 17 (November 1889–October 1890).

Chapter 21

1. *NHReg*, June 30, 1888.

2. Harris E. Starr, *William Graham Sumner* (New York: Henry Holt, 1925), 542; CCAR.

3. *New Haven City Directory* for 1889; *YAW* 44 (January 11, 1935): 365 with photo; New Haven real estate records, vol. 404, p. 221.

4. *YAW* 44 (January 11, 1935): 365.

5. *YAW* 25 (January 14, 1916): 509; Corbin to Camp, June 11, 1888, Camp Papers, reel 6.

6. Walter Camp, "A Day's Football Practice at Yale," *HW*, November 24, 1888, 890. The description of the trip to the field follows closely after George Santayana, "A Glimpse of Yale," *Harvard Monthly* 15 (December 1882): 89–97.

7. *HW*, November 24, 1888, 890.

8. William H. Corbin as quoted in Edwards, *Football Days*, 110; *YAW* 44:365.

9. *YAW* 44:365; Stagg testimonial to Camp at 1915 rule meeting; Camp Papers, reel 2, box 2, folder 35.

10. *HW*, November 19, 1892, 1115.

11. Edwards, *Football Days*, 93.

12. *Minnesota Alumni Weekly*, November 9, 1914, 10; Peg Meier, *Too Hot, Went to Lake* (Minneapolis: Neighbors, 1993), 120, shows photo with Heffelfinger on the team. Without documentation, this book states Heffelfinger attended the University of Minnesota (alumni record of Walter [Pudge] Heffelfinger at YUMA). The recent graduate was Harlow S. Gale, who became a professor at the University of Minnesota.

13. Betsey Beeler Creekmore, *Knoxville* (Knoxville: University of Tennessee Press, 1967), 49.

14. *Exonian*, Jan 9, 1915.

15. Amos Alonzo Stagg, *Touchdown! "As Told by Coach Amos Alonzo Stagg to Wesley Winans Stout,"* 45–52.

16. Ibid., 116; *NYH*, February 2, 1888.

Chapter 22

1. *Princetonian*, January 16, 1889.

2. Presbrey and Moffatt, *Athletics at Princeton*, 577, reprint of official statement sent by Harvard's Athletic Committee, sec. 1; Alexander M. Weyand, *Football Immortals* (New York: Macmillan, 1962), 44–45.

3. Eugene J. Richards Jr. to Camp, November 14, 1889, Camp Papers, reel 15; Edwards, *Football Days*, 188; Presbrey and Moffatt, *Athletics at Princeton*, 577–78; Weyand, *Football Immortals*, 45.

4. Letter from H. Leeds to Cumnock, 1889, Harvard University Archives.

5. *NYT*, November 1, 1889.

6. Gerald R. Gems, ed., *Sports in North America* (Gulf Breeze, Fla.: Academic International Press, 1996), 5:26; *NYT*, November 16, 1889, 3, slightly paraphrased.

7. Presbrey and Moffatt, *Athletics at Princeton*, 338, 586, reprinting "The Answer Made by Princeton," sent to Harvard on February 24, 1890, and published in *Princetonian*, supp., March 7, 1890.

8. Ibid., 585.

9. Ibid., 587.

10. Ibid., 586.

11. Ibid.

12. Ibid., 584.

13. *NYEP*, November 13, 1889.

14. A report of the meeting appears in *NYEP*, November 14, 1889. See also Presbrey and Moffatt, *Athletics at Princeton*, 586; and Richards Jr. to Camp, November 14, 1889, Camp Papers, reel 15.

15. *NYW*, November 15, 1889: 3.

16. Presbrey and Moffatt, *Athletics at Princeton*, 585; Richards Jr. to Camp, November 14, 1889, Camp Papers, reel 15.

17. Richards Jr. to Camp, November 14, 1889, Camp Papers, reel 15.

18. Presbrey and Moffatt, *Athletics at Princeton*, 586; Beattys to Camp, November 14, 1889, Camp Papers, reel 2.

19. *NYW*, November 17, 1889. Five Princeton players were named later that year to Camp's first All-America team—Ames, Channing, Cowan, George, and Poe—in *Week's Sport*, December 18, 1889.

20. *NYEP*, November 21, 1889.

21. *NYEP*, November 27, 1889.

22. A manuscript in Camp's handwriting early in reel 34 of the Camp Papers discusses Yale's position during the negotiations.

23. *HGM* 28 (March 1920): 375; Bliss Perry, *Life and Letters of Henry Lee Higginson* (Boston: Atlantic Monthly Press, 1921), especially chap. 9 and the appendix.

24. Perry, *Life and Letters*, 292.

25. *HGM* 28 (March 1920): 385.

26. Perry, *Life and Letters*, 531, 535.

27. Ibid., 536.

Chapter 23

1. *NYW*, November 29, 1889, 3.

2. George Juergens, *Joseph Pulitzer and the "New York World"* (Princeton, N.J.: Princeton University Press, 1966), vii–xv; *NYW*, masthead, October 18, 1889.

3. Juergens, *Joseph Pulitzer*, 119–20; *NYW*, May 4, 1884, 4, as quoted in ibid., 121.

4. Juergens, *Joseph Pulitzer*, 119–20.

5. *NYW*, November 29, 1889, 3.

6. Ibid.

7. Ibid.

8. John K. Winkler, *William Randolph Hearst* (New York: Hastings House, 1955), 62; William H. Nugent, "The Sports Section," *American Mercury* 16 (March 1929): 329–38.

9. Manuscript, Camp Papers, reel 22, folder 22, p. 1.

10. *HW*, January 21, 1893, 67.

11. Davis's tribute to Camp at February 1915 rules committee "retirement" dinner is in Camp Papers, reel 2, box 2, folder 35.

12. George Stade, "Game Theory," *Columbia University Forum* 9, no. 4 (1966): 40. As to military campaigns, see Michael R. Real, "Super Bowl Football versus World Cup Soccer: A Cultural-Structural Comparison," in *Media, Sports, and Society*, edited by Lawrence A. Wenner (Newbury Park, Calif.: Sage, 1989), 196.

13. Francis A. Walker, "College Athletics," *HGM* 2 (September 1893): 13; Paul Gallico, *The Golden People* (Garden City, N.Y.: Doubleday, 1964), 139.

14. Brenda Harper Mattson, "George Petrie: The Early Years, 1862–1892" (master's thesis, Auburn University, 1983), 134, 135, 145–53; John F. Stegeman, *The Ghosts of Herty Field* (Athens: University of Georgia Press, 1966), 2, 3, 8; Wiley Lee Umphlett, *Creating the Big Game* (Westport, Conn.: Greenwood Press, 1992), 48ff; University of Georgia's 1895 *Pandora* graduation annual, 123.

15. Dates of intercollegiate football play at the listed schools are taken from Claassen and Boda, *Ronald Encyclopedia of Football.*

Chapter 24

1. Charles E. Clay (editor of *Week's Sport)* to Camp, December 23, 1889, Camp Papers, reel 18; *NYT*, July 31, 1931.

2. Clay to Camp, December 23, 1889, Camp Papers, reel 18.

3. Starting date calculated from issue of October 16, 1889, identified as vol. 1, no. 9 (clipping in series 3 of Camp Papers).

4. Whitney to Camp, September 11, 1890, Camp Papers, reel 18.

5. *Week's Sport,* December 18, 1889.

6. Stephen Hardy, "Entrepreneurs, Organizations, and the Sport Marketplace," *JSH* 13 (Spring 1986): 21.

7. *HW*, December 12, 1891, 1003; a copy of the *Week's Sport*'s 1890 All-America article is in the Camp Papers, reel 48, box 72, as part of the Janet Camp Troxell Papers.

8. Whitney to Camp, September 11, 1890, Camp Papers, reel 18.

9. Camp to Whitney, November 11, 1890, Camp Papers, reel 18.

10. Whitney to Camp, December 26, 1890, Camp Papers, reel 18. A few fragments of issues are in series 3 of the Camp Papers. The magazine was sold and modified and in a convoluted line was ultimately succeeded as *Vanity Fair*. See note in Mott, *American Magazines*, 4:47.

11. Whitney to Camp, December 26, 1890, Camp Papers, reel 18.

12. Arthur Lubow, *The Reporter Who Would Be King* (New York: Charles Scribner's Sons), 74–77. Davis needed no convincing that sports reporting would have appeal; he had played

football at Lafayette College and occasionally wrote about it, including for the *Week's Sport* (ibid., 77). Whitney had proven in the *Week's Sport* that he could help *Harper's Weekly*.

13. *Nation*, January 30, 1929, 121.

14. Whitney (for Harper Bros.) to Camp, February 23, September 16, 1891, Camp Papers, reel 9.

15. Camp to Whitney, December 2, 1891, Camp Papers, reel 9.

16. Ibid.

Chapter 25

1. Whitney (for Harper Bros.) to Camp, August 17, 1891, Camp Papers, reel 9.

2. Whitney to Camp, September 10, 1891, Camp Papers, reel 9.

3. Camp to Whitney, October 12, 1891, Camp Papers, reel 9; *YNews*, November 2, 1891.

4. Walter Camp, *American Football*, 25–37.

5. For "tackle" name, Camp, "Intercollegiate Football in America," *St. Nicholas* 17 (February 1890): 322; Camp, *American Football*, 41–52 ("line halfback," 42).

6. Camp, *American Football*, 49.

7. Ibid., 117–29.

8. Ibid., 83–85.

9. Ibid., 133–64.

10. Camp, "Intercollegiate Football in America," 241–45. Additional descriptions of Thanksgiving Day events accompanying the Princeton-Yale game appear in Richard Harding Davis, "The Thanksgiving Day Game," *HW*, December 9, 1893, 1170–71; and Edwards, *Football Days*, 1–3.

11. Camp, "Intercollegiate Football in America," 242–43.

12. Camp, "American Game . . . ," *HW*, November 10, 1888, 858.

13. *HW*, March 5, 1892, 226.

Chapter 26

1. *YAW* 1, special number (March 1, 1892): 2.

2. A drawing of the cup is printed in *HW*, March 5, 1892, 227.

3. *YAW* 1, special number (March 1, 1892): 2.

4. *National Cyclopedia of American Biography*, s.v. "Camp, Hiram."

5. Bailey, 78.

6. *NHReg*, May 28, 1889; minutes, NHCC shareholder meeting, January 29, 1890.

7. *NHReg*, March 3, 1890, 1; minutes, NHCC board of directors meeting, April 18, 1890; minutes, NHCC board of directors meeting, May 3, 1890. Edward J. Stevens was the son-in-law of Chauncey Jerome, the $1.50-clock pioneer, and had been the third-largest stockholder in NHCC. Hiram Camp would soon retire, so with the deaths of Stevens, Welch, and English the major owners and upper management of the company almost completely changed in the few years after Camp joined the company. Bailey, 77.

8. Minutes of May 30, 1890, adjourned meeting of NHCC board of directors.

9. Letter June 23, 1925, from Edwin P. Root, president of New Haven Clock Company, to Marion L. Phillips, alumni registrar at Yale University, copy in WCAR. Gertrude Atherton, *Patience Sparhawk and Her Times* (1895), as quoted in Lubow, *Reporter Who Would Be King*, 76.

10. Minutes, NHCC directors meeting, June 9, 1891; Yale college class of 1870 biographical record published in 1904.

11. Bailey, 77; minutes, NHCC board of directors, January 28, 1892.

12. *YNews*, April 28, 1892.

13. *NYT*, June 21, 1892, 3; November 24, 1893, 3.

14. Welch and Camp, *Yale*, 454–56.

15. *HW*, March 5, 1892, 226.

16. Richard Harding Davis, "A Day with the Yale Team," *HW*, November 18, 1893, 1110.

Chapter 27

1. Stagg, *Touchdown!*, 130.

2. Ibid., 131; Harvey Green, *Fit for America* (New York: Pantheon Books, 1986), 182.

3. James Naismith, *Basketball* (Lincoln: University of Nebraska Press, 1996), ix; minutes of the Ahikamin Circle for November 27 and December 11, 1890, Babson Library, Archives and Special Collections, Springfield College, Springfield, Mass.

4. Stagg, *Touchdown!*, 132. See also William Henry Ball, "Stagg and the Madison Square Garden Game," 5–9, typed manuscript dated 1941, Babson Library.

5. Stagg, *Touchdown!*, 143–44; *Ball Manuscript*, 11–12.

6. Thomas Wakefield Goodspeed, *William Rainey Harper* (Chicago: University of Chicago Press, 1928), 26, 70ff; *DAB*, vol. 4, pt. 2, 287, 288; Allan Nevins, *John D. Rockefeller* (New York: Charles Scribner's Sons, 1941), 2:230–34.

7. Stagg, *Touchdown!*, 143.

8. Ibid.

9. Letter dated January 20, 1891, in "Extracts from Letters Written by A. A. Stagg to His Family," Amos Alonzo Stagg Papers, Special Collections at Joseph Regenstein Library, University of Chicago.

10. Veysey, *Emergence of the American University*, 326, citing H. P. Judson, *The Higher Education as a Training for Business* (Chicago: n.p., 1911), originally published in 1896.

11. *Daily Palo Alto*, November 10, 1892.

12. Ibid.

13. *SFExam*, December 1, 1892.

14. *Daily Palo Alto*, December 1, 1892; *HW*, February 25, 1893, 191.

15. *SFExam*, December 2, 1892 (almost daily reports followed and the December 11, 1892, issue shows a drawing of Camp); *Daily Palo Alto*, December 1, 1892, 1.

16. *SFExam*, December 11, 1892.

17. *SFExam*, December 18, 1892.

18. Edward Potts Cheney, *History of the University of Pennsylvania* (Philadelphia: University of Pennsylvania Press, 1940), 315–16, 342–43; Dan Rottenberg, *Fight on, Pennsylvania*, 27.

19. Alexander M. Weyand, *The Saga of American Football*, 43.

20. Ibid., 43.

21. Ellen Axson Wilson to Anna Harris, November 22, 1892, in Link, *Papers of Wilson*, 8:47–48.

Chapter 28

1. Weyand, *Saga of American Football*, 44–45.

2. Deland also had a mass-momentum play from scrimmage in the 1892 Harvard-Yale game. Ibid., 45–46.

3. Walter Camp, "A Plea for the Wedge in Football," *HW*, January 21, 1893, 67 (emphasis added).

4. Walter Camp, "Team Play in Football," *HW*, October 31, 1891, 845–46.

5. 1891 *Spalding Guide*, 7; Walter Camp, "Football of 1891," *Outing*, November 1891, 155.

6. 1891 *Spalding Guide*, 7.

Chapter 29

1. Spalding is first identified as the publisher of the annual *Football Rules and Referee's Book* in 1890, perhaps without calling it *Spalding's Official Football Guide* (it is not clear whether the copy of the 1890 rule book in YUMA is missing a cover that could have labeled it *Spalding's Official Football Guide*). The first rule book found in YUMA with a *Spalding's Official Football Guide* cover was published in 1891. The publisher of the rule books in 1888 and 1889 was Wright and Ditson, though the 1888 book also has a cover identifying it as part of the Spalding Athletic Library. Spalding was apparently in the process of developing a silent partnership with Wright and Ditson. See Peter Levine, *A. G. Spalding and the Rise of Baseball*, 80.

2. 1890 *Football Rules*, 8.

3. *HW*, March 5, 1892, 226.

4. McCormick to Camp, December 5, 1892, Camp Papers, reel 12.

5. Walter Camp, "Undergraduate Limitation in College Sports," *HW*, February 11, 1893, 143.

6. *NYT*, January 15, 1893.

7. *NYT*, January 21, 22, 1893.

8. *YNews*, February 4, 1893.

9. *YNews*, February 1, 1893. Camp later wrote that he believed he was the first to suggest barring varsity play by "first year men."

10. *NYT*, February 2, 1893. On February 10, 1893, another vote was held, which reversed the first vote, 689–502 (see *YNews*, February 11, 1893), but the divided votes still kept the undergraduate limitation under a cloud.

11. *NYT*, October 14, 1893, 2.

12. *Crimson*, May 1, 1893.

13. The new Harvard-Pennsylvania rules provided, in summary, with emphasis added:

- No student shall be eligible who either before or since entering the university has been paid, beyond legitimate expenses, for engaging in any athletic competition.
- To play a student must be, and intend to be throughout the college year, a bona fide member of the university, taking a full year's work.
- No student transferring into the "*college or scientific school*" of the university who has ever played on an intercollegiate team of another college shall play for the university until he has resided at the university one academic year.

- No student shall play in intercollegiate contests for more than four years.
- Players shall be announced to the opposing team at least twenty-five days before their contest. Objection to any player shall be considered waived unless taken at least twenty days before the contest.

The limitation to "*college or scientific school*" in the third rule above exempted graduate and professional school students; "college" meant the undergraduate college; "scientific" school meant undergraduate scientific school, so graduate or professional school students were not included in a one-year residency requirement.

14. *NYT*, October 22, 1893.

15. Ibid.; *Princetonian*, October 23, 1893.

16. *NYT*, October 22, 1893.

17. *NYT*, October 28, 1893.

18. Ibid.

19. Ibid.

20. *NYW*, October 31, 1893.

21. *Princetonian*, November 8, 1893. Pennsylvania also withdrew from a Pennsylvania state debating society about the same time because the society refused to allow Pennsylvania's law students to participate.

22. *NYW*, November 5, 1893.

Chapter 30

1. *NYT*, May 1, 1892. *HW*, December 2, 1893, 1113.

2. *NYT*, December 21, 1893.

3. Adee to Camp, January 15, February 7, 1894, Camp Papers, reel 1.

4. For biographical information about Dashiell, see J. C. Gray, "Paul Joseph Dashiell, Ph.D.," *U.S. Naval Institute Proceedings* (August 1938): 1143–47; and *NYT*, July 7, 1937, 23.

5. Dashiell to Camp, April 30, 1893, Camp Papers.

6. *NYT*, May 9, 1894, 2; *Outing*, October 1897, 29. The quoted rule language, "As soon as a runner attempting to go through . . .," is from Rule 30(a), 1894 *Spalding Guide*.

7. The number of colleges playing was compiled from Claassen and Boda, *Ronald Encyclopedia of Football*.

8. 1894 *Spalding Guide*, 23.

Chapter 31

1. J. Kenneth Doherty, *Modern Track and Field* (Englewood Cliffs, N.J.: Prentice Hall, 1953), 110; Joseph E. Dineen, *The Illustrated History of the U.S. Military Academy* (Norfolk and Virginia Beach: Donning,1988), 20; *Outing*, October 1892, 58.

2. *YAW* (November 20, 1931).

3. *Ahikamin Circle Letter*, no. 6 (copy in Springfield College Archives).

4. Williams to Camp, October 11, 1893, Camp Papers, reel 18.

5. Ibid.

6. *Publisher's Weekly* (December 23, 1893): 1023.

7. James R. Church, ed., *University Football* (New York: Charles Scribner's Sons, 1893).

8. *Walter Camp's Book of College Sports* (New York: Century, 1893).

9. *Nation*, November 23, 1893, 395–96.

10. *NYT*, October 27, 1894; Sullivan to Camp, July 27, 1894, Camp Papers, reel 16. (Camp already had written a pamphlet on college baseball for the Spalding Athletic Library in 1893.)

11. Grantland Rice quote from Allison Danzig, *The History of American Football: Its Great Teams, Players and Coaches*, 124.

Chapter 32

1. *NYEP*, November 18, 1893, 4.

2. *NYEP*, November 23, 1893, 7.

3. Walter Chauncey Camp, "Youth the Time for Physical Development," *New Englander and Yale Review* 34 (January 1885): 140; Eugene L. Richards, "The Football Situation," *Popular Science Monthly*, October 1894, 730; Camp, *The Book of Football*, 140.

4. *HW*, December 16, 1893, 1212.

5. *Boston Medical and Surgical Journal* 131 (October 18, 1894): 381–86. In this article, Conant wrote, "No one can, I think, contend that it [American football] is not a rough game, but very few who know anything about the game believe it to be brutal."

6. *NYT*, December 2, 1893, 2.

7. Walter Camp, *Football Facts and Figures*, v; James Brown Scott, *Robert Bacon: Life and Letters* (New York: Doubleday, Page, 1923), 73ff.

8. Camp, *Football Facts and Figures*, v–vi.

9. *NYT*, March 9, 1894, 6; Camp, *Football Facts and Figures*, 59.

10. Camp, *Football Facts and Figures*, 59–60.

11. Ibid., 60–63.

12. Ibid., 63.

13. Ibid., 15ff.

14. Ibid., 233–37.

15. Samuel C. Prescott, *When M.I.T. Was "Boston Tech"* (Cambridge, Mass.: Technology Press, 1954), 129ff.

16. *HGM* 2 (September 1893): 1–18. All quotations in the paragraph come from p. 1.

17. Ibid., 5, 6, 7.

18. Ibid., 13.

19. Ibid., 14.

Chapter 33

1. Camp, "College Football," *HW*, November 20, 1897, 1162; *NYT*, November 25, 1894, 1; *NYW*, November 25, 1894, 12.

2. Blanchard, *H Book*, 403.

3. The game details in this and following paragraphs are derived from *NYW*, November 25, 1894, 10. See also *NYT*, November 25, 1894, 1.

4. See May 18, 1895, letter of J. B. Ames to the "Athletic Authorities of Yale University" reprinted in *HGM* 4 (September 1895): 119–20; Brooks to Camp, September 1, 1895, Camp Papers, reel 3; *NYTrib*, November 27, 1894, 3; and *NYW*, November 27, 1894, 6.

5. *Crimson*, November 26, 1894.

6. *NYTrib*, November 27, 1894, 3.

7. *Crimson*, December 17, 1894.

8. Adee to Camp, January 15, 1895, Camp Papers, reel 1.

9. Rottenberg, *Fight on, Pennsylvania*, 9.

10. Weyand, *Saga of American Football*, 50, 51.

11. Ibid., 51–52.

12. *NYW*, November 11, 1894, 11; Rottenberg, *Fight on, Pennsylvania*, 9–13. Another marker of Pennsylvania's growing athletic strength appeared in the *New York Times* a month after the Princeton game, when it was announced that Pennsylvania was planning a new football field to be called Franklin Field, near the existing campus. Construction had already commenced and an alumni committee appointed to raise funding. *NYT*, December 13, 1894, 7.

13. *Meriden (Conn.) Journal*, January 25, 1895. Ellen was buried in a family plot at the city cemetery of Meriden, Leverett's hometown, where the Camps were still well known. There was more coverage in the Meriden newspaper when Ellen died than in New Haven's.

Chapter 34

1. Adee to Camp, March 3, 1895, Camp Papers, reel 1.

2. Camp to Adee, February 21, 1895, Camp Papers, reel 1.

3. *Crimson*, March 7, 1895; *NYT*, March 17, 1895.

4. Adee to Camp, March 12, 1895, Camp Papers, reel 1. Ames was also battling with the Harvard faculty, which had again voted in mid-February to ban football at Harvard. Ames answered as chair of the athletic committee on February 25, 1895 (see *Crimson*, March 20, 1895), detailing efforts by the committee to achieve improvements in the game, regretting they were not consulted before the faculty's action, and stating the committee's position that football should be maintained and efforts made to improve the game. On April 10, 1895 (see *NYT*, April 11, 1895), the Harvard Board of Overseers upheld the athletic committee's position and rejected a ban on football while efforts were made to improve it.

5. *NYT*, March 19, 1895, 6.

6. Adee to Camp, April 22, 1895, Camp Papers, reel 1.

7. Grantland Rice quote from Danzig, *History of American Football*, 124.

8. A copy of Camp's note is attached to Whitney's June 12, 1894, reply (see below), Camp Papers, reel 9.

9. Whitney to Camp, June 12, 1894, Camp Papers, reel 9 (Harper and Brothers correspondence file).

10. Camp to Whitney, June 14, 1894, Camp Papers, reel 9.

11. Whitney's response is on Camp's June 14, 1894, letter.

12. Whitney to Camp, July 19, 1894, Camp Papers, reel 9.

13. Ernst L. Bogart, *The Economic History of the United States* (New York: Longmans, Green, 1917), 399; Bailey, 77.

14. Thorne to Brewer, May 11,1895, *HGM* 4 (September 1895): 119.

15. *NYT*, May 17, 1895, 6; *HW*, October19, 1895, 1003.

16. *YNews*, May 18, 1895.

17. *NYT*, October 9, 1895, 6.

18. Slosson, *Great American Universities*, 343.
19. Waterman Thomas Hewett, *Cornell University* (New York: University Publishing Society, 1905), 3:301; Claassen and Boda, *Ronald Encyclopedia of Football*, 4–59.
20. *Crimson*, June 12, 1895.
21. 1895 *Spalding Guide*, Rule 30.

Chapter 35

1. *Chicago Record*, January 12, 1895.
2. Robert W. Topping, *A Century and Beyond* (West Lafayette, Ind.: Purdue University Press, 1988), 142; W. E. Stoue (?) to D. M. Balliet, November 27, 1894, James H. Smart Papers, Purdue University Archives and Special Collections, West Lafayette, Ind.
3. Smart to Northrup, November 26, 1894, Letterbooks of 1894–1895, Smart Papers.
4. Stott, *Indiana Football*, 38; Smart to P. D. John, president of Depauw, November 30, 1894, Smart Papers.
5. Page 2 of a letter apparently to Draper in mid-November, Smart Papers (emphasis added).
6. Smart to President Adams of Wisconsin, November 22, 1894, Letterbooks of 1894–1895, Smart Papers.
7. *HW*, October 29, 1894, 1029.
8. Smart to Angell, December 13, 1894, Letterbooks of 1894–1895, Smart Papers.
9. *Chicago Record*, January 12, 1895; *Michigan Daily* (University of Michigan student newspaper), January 14, 1895, 1. See also Carl D. Voltmer, *A Brief History of the Intercollegiate Conference of Faculty Representatives*, 6–7.
10. *Michigan Daily*, January 14, 1895, 1.
11. *HW*, November 23, 1895, 1123.
12. *HW*, December 28, 1895, 1251.
13. Ibid.
14. Ibid.
15. MacMillan to Stagg, January 10, 1896, box 90, folder 1, Stagg Papers.
16. "Minutes of the First Intercollegiate Conference of Faculty Representatives," in *Proceedings of the Intercollegiate Conference of Faculty Representatives* (Minneapolis: University of Minnesota Press, 1901), 5–6. See also *ChiTrib*, February 8, 1896.
17. "Minutes of the First Intercollegiate Conference," 5–9.
18. Ibid.; *ChiTrib*, November 26, 1898, 7.
19. The listed colleges and their date of entry into intercollegiate football competition compiled from Claassen and Boda, *Ronald Encyclopedia of Football*.
20. *Atlanta Constitution*, December 23, 1894.
21. 1903 Constitution of the SIAA, prefatory note.

Chapter 36

1. Brooks to Camp, September 1, 1895, Camp Papers, reel 3.
2. *HW*, January 18, 1896, 70.
3. Stagg to Camp, January 11, 1896, Camp Papers, reel 16.
4. *Princetonian*, March 3, 1896.
5. *Princetonian*, March 16, 1896.

6. 1896 *Spalding Guide*, Rule 22(a).
7. Ibid., Rule 22 (b) and (c).
8. Ibid., Rule 21(b).
9. Ibid., Rule 13(a).
10. Although no mention is made in the rule book, according to Spalding's ads, their "Official 'Intercollegiate' Foot Ball" was "officially adopted by the [IFA] for 1896, marking the fifth year of its adoption."
11. *HW*, January 4, 1896, 19–21.
12. 1898 *Spalding Guide*, 126–28.

Chapter 37

1. Bailey, 78.
2. *Bachelor of Arts* 1 (May 1895). *Bachelor of Arts* was well designed and attractive, aimed more at a popular than a scholarly readership. Camp was responsible for about twenty pages each month (first issue, May 1895), written himself or parceled out to other writers. Sometimes he left athletics aside, with articles on such signature Yale topics as Mory's (Mrs. Moriarity's Ale House) and Yale's Senior Society elections (the tensions and disappointments of tapping night).
3. Camp and Deland, *Football.*
4. See Welch and Camp, *Yale.*
5. *HW*, January 28, 1893, 95, ad at bottom of page.
6. *Collier's Weekly*, August 13, 1898, 19.
7. *Collier's Weekly*, December 24, 1898, 20.
8. Many years after the naming of the first All-America team, a private citizen, Clarence G. McDavitt, studied and wrote a memorandum on the issues of who had conceived the first All-America teams, selected the players, and written the article naming those selected. Tim Cohane, in *The Yale Story* (New York: G. P. Putnam's Sons, 1951), 67–70, joined McDavitt in the questions. After some investigation, both took the view (with Cohane relying largely on McDavitt) that probably Caspar Whitney had suggested the idea of an All-America team and that Camp may have chosen the players. Neither McDavitt nor Cohane presented contemporaneous evidence supporting their claim. Both apparently were unaware of a December 2, 1891, letter in which Camp sent Whitney the 1891 All-America team plus an accompanying text; the context and sending of the letter suggest Camp was doing what he had done in 1889 and 1890, that is, naming the All-America team and writing the accompanying text and sending it to Whitney for publication. The only change was that Camp sent the 1891 team intending it to be a separate article in *Harper's Weekly*; Whitney objected, wanting the team to appear in his column, though he had not written the article. McDavitt reports that when questioned, Whitney said he did not remember who had originated the idea of the All-America team. Camp repeated his claim several times with explicit language that he originated and chose the first All-America team, and at least to this writer McDavitt and Cohane offer no persuasive evidence to disprove Camp's claim.
9. *HW*, December 24, 1898, 1248.
10. Manuscript, Camp Papers, reel 37, box 58, folder 405; *NYT*, January 18, 1894, 1.
11. Manuscript, Camp Papers, reel 37, box 58, folder 405.
12. Camp to Nast, July 28, 1900, Camp Papers, reel 4.

13. Phelps eulogy of Camp reprinted in Powell, *Walter Camp*, 192.
14. Ibid.; *Dictionary of Literary Biography* (2001), 241:53.
15. *New Haven City Directory* for 1898.
16. *NHReg*, February 9, 1899, 1.
17. *New Haven City Directories* for 1899 and 1900.

Chapter 38

1. *Collier's Weekly*, August 13, 1898, 19.
2. Camp, *The Book of Football*, xii–xiii.
3. *HW*, March 5, 1892, 226.
4. Walter Camp, "What Are Athletics Good For?," *Outing*, December 1913, 266.
5. Walter Camp, "The Two Problems of Amateur Athletics," *Outing*, December 1891, 197–200.
6. Ibid., 198–99.
7. Rottenberg, *Fight on, Pennsylvania*, 30. Early in considering what to do after leaving coaching, Woodruff wrote Camp, proposing that Camp might want him to work at Yale in an assistant financial leadership role. That didn't happen, but in December 1903 Woodruff's Yale classmate Gifford Pinchot, who had become U.S. forester in Theodore Roosevelt's administration, asked Woodruff to be the chief legal officer of the Bureau of Forestry. There he became an important part of Pinchot and Roosevelt's expanding conservation efforts. Eleven times he argued cases before the U.S. Supreme Court, and Roosevelt credited him with formulating and giving practical effect to the "idea that the Executive is the steward of the public welfare." Roosevelt, *Theodore Roosevelt: An Autobiography*, 420.
8. *Minnesota Hats Off to Thee* (Dallas: Taylor, 1992), 9–12.
9. Louis Elbel, "Michigan Inspired 'The Victors,'" *Michigan Alumnus* (October 19, 1957): 24–25.
10. *NHReg*, October 8, 1936; *YAW* 10 (November 28, 1900): 84.
11. *YAW* 11 (November 27, 1901): 75.
12. Sam Rubin, *Yale Football* (Charleston, S.C.: Arcadia, 2006), 22; Alexander Leitch, *A Princeton Companion*, 470.
13. *NYT*, January 15, 1897, 4; *NYW*, February 15, 1897, 8.
14. Walter Camp, "The Current Criticism of Football," Open Letters, *Century* (February 1894): 633; Camp to McClean at Consolidated Press Association, September 23, 1920, Camp Papers, reel 6.
15. Statement of Charles Kennedy, *YAW* 34 (July 3, 1925).

Chapter 39

1. *YAW* (February 13, 1895): 4.
2. Hadley to Camp, August 21, 1899, Camp Papers, reel 9.
3. Hadley to Camp, January 23, 1900, Camp Papers, reel 9. At least some of Camp's compensation for his work for Hadley and Yale apparently was paid by outside benefactors; see Hadley to Bertron, June 29, 1900, Camp Papers, reel 9.
4. 1902 and 1904 Yale Banner; Yale Corporate Minutes, February 1908, 335.
5. Camp to Hadley, March 19, 1900, Camp Papers, reel 9.

6. Ibid.

7. Lorin Deland, "Football at Harvard and Yale," *Atlantic Monthly*, November 1910, 704.

8. Ibid., 710.

9. Camp told the story in "American Sports," *Century*, o.s., 79 (November 1909): 61–63; and in Camp, *The Book of Football*, 184–91. For the Army-Williams story and Camp's role, see Weyand, *Saga of American Football*, 68–72.

10. As to Camp and the "mousetrap" play, see Danzig, *History of American Football*, 100.

11. Camp, *The Book of Football*, 191–92; Weyand, *Saga of American Football*, 71. The quotation "some strain across the loins" is a statement of Lorin Deland, knowledgeable of the facts as a Harvard insider, in his article "Football at Harvard and Yale," 713.

12. Ronald A. Smith, ed., *Big-Time Football at Harvard, 1905: The Diary of Coach Bill Reid*, includes various references to Yale methods (30–31, 32, 42–51); William Reid, "Two Styles of Defense," Harvard University Archives, file HUD 10906.76, pp. 555–66; Smith, *Big-Time Football*, 34.

13. "The Captured Shadow," in *The Stories of F. Scott Fitzgerald* (New York: Scribner's, 1950), 356, as cited in Robert J. Higgs, "Yale and the Heroic Ideal," in *Manliness and Morality*, edited by J. A. Mangan and James Walvin, 161; "The Man Merriwell," *Saturday Evening Post*, June 11, 1927, 127, as quoted in John Levi Cutler, "Gilbert Patten and His Merriwell Saga," *Maine Bulletin* 36 (May 1934): 99.

14. Cutler, "Gilbert Patten," 31; Robert H. Boyle, "Frank Merriwell," *Sports Illustrated*, December 24, 1962, 88.

Chapter 40

1. Messages received August 1 or 2 surmised from *NHReg*, August 5, 1902.

2. *NHReg*, August 5, 1902.

3. Bailey, 78.

4. Minutes, special meeting of the NHCC directors, October 22, 1902.

5. A. O. Jennings to Camp, February 28, 1903, Camp Papers, reel 11.

6. Ibid.

7. *NHReg*, February 27, 1903, 1.

8. *NYT*, March 30, 1903, 5.

9. 1902 *Yale Banner.*

10. T. Davis, *Chronicles of Hopkins Grammar School*, 478, 481–82, 483.

Chapter 41

1. *HW*, January 21, 1893, 67; *BH*, November 30, 1893, 7; *Outing* 23, January 1824, Monthly Record, 66: Camp's ten-yard proposal appears to be "the aptest."

2. Undated manuscript of speech by Camp, Camp Papers, reel 27, box 40, folder 142.

3. *NYT*, March 13, 1905, 8; December 6, 1905 ("Woodruff suggests . . ."); December 11, 1905, 9; December 14, 1905, 11; December 14, 1905, 11 (statement of Wrenn); *BH*, November 29, 1904, reprinted in *YAW* 14 (December 7, 1904): 188–90 (spreading by quadrangles).

4. A requirement for rule-committee unanimity was enacted at least by 1894; see the May 8, 1894, letter of Alexander Moffat, as chair of the new UAC rules committee, to the

athletic committee of the UAC, reprinted in the 1894 *Spalding Guide*, 37–41; the rule was again enacted in 1896, with Moffat moving and Sears seconding, when the UAC committee was reconstituted; see the 1896 rules-committee meeting minutes, Camp Papers, reel 26, folder 113.

5. *NYT*, June 9, 1903, 10.

6. Camp to Wheeler, January 17, 1905, Camp Papers, reel 18. Although friendly, Camp and Wheeler did have differences that gradually grew and eventuated in Wheeler presiding over adoption of rugby at the University of California. See Roberta J. Park, "From Football to Rugby and Back, 1906–1919," *JSH* 11 (Winter 1984): 5–40.

7. For the 1895 Georgia game, see Wiley Lee Umphlett, *Creating the Big Game* (Westport, Conn.: Greenwood Press, 1992), 51–52. For Heisman quote, see *Baseball Magazine* 1 (October 1908). The Camp Papers do not appear to include the letters Heisman says he sent.

8. The quotation is from Glen Scobey Warner, *Football for Coaches and Players* (Stanford University: self-published, 1927), 62–63. Even in 1927 Warner was convinced legalizing forward passing in American football had been a mistake. Alexander Weyand (a player at Army from 1911 to 1915) wrote in his book *The Saga of American Football* that players also liked the game as it was being played in the mid-1900s. According to Weyand, the push for change came primarily from the public. Some coaching rivals contended Camp wanted to maintain the existing mid-1900s playing style because he and Yale were having success with it (see note 10 in chapter 46).

9. *NYT*, April 30, 1905, 10; June 13, 1905, 7. The no-action June 1905 rules-committee meeting was the first rules meeting attended by Bill Reid, who became Harvard's football coach in 1905, and Reid reported on the meeting in his diary (Smith, *Big-Time Football*, 33–35). He noted absolute positions taken during the meeting that understandably could interfere with agreement: "Camp, Stagg and Bell would not hear of" artificially limiting the offense and defense (for example, by requiring defensive players to line up in artificial positions that handicapped their play). They had heard that idea more than once and were adamant and fixed in opposition. Rather than accepting such an idea, Camp was feeling "pretty well satisfied with things as they are." On the other hand, when Camp made his ten-yard proposal, "no one was willing to consider that for a moment," suggesting that that idea also must have been discussed and rejected at a previous meeting, making it a futile subject for discussion. Camp's presentation of the idea was sufficient, however, that Reid recorded in his diary, "I believe now, as I think of it, that that is really a good scheme."

Hints of tension within the rules committee began to appear in public media reports after the June 1905 meeting. Letters from three committee members (Dennis, Dashiell, and Camp) were published in the October 1905 issue of *Outing* (p. 232), responding to an invitation from the editor (Caspar Whitney) for comments on the inaction at the June 1905 rules-committee meeting. Dennis refused to comment on the details of rule discussions, but brought up the issue of possible "changes in the organization or personnel of the committee"; however, he said comment on that issue would "more properly emanate from outside sources." Dashiell, among other things, expressed resentment that *Outing* had named "certain members of the committee [as] urging changes," thus implying that others on the committee were "in opposition to modifying the game. *Outing* was misinformed," Dashiell said, "or else guessed wrong." Camp's letter simply continued to argue for his ten-yard rule.

Ironically, in contrast to the refusal to adopt a ten-yard rule in the United States, such a rule did appear in a Canadian hybrid of rugby and American football, beginning around 1899. At that time, a University of Toronto student, Thrift Burnside, together with some associates, persuaded fellow intramural players to alter their traditional rugby game by incorporating an American-style snapback scrimmage, but with differences, including the ten-yards-in-three-downs rule and a prohibition on American-style interference (see the University of Toronto *Varsity* student newspaper, volume 19, p. 125, December 15, 1899 [pages were numbered consecutively from issue to issue], and volume 21, pp. 55–58, November 12, 1901; and see also the *Toronto Globe*, November 23, 1899:10). In adopting the American scrimmage, Burnside and coworkers necessarily knew of the American five-yard rule, and must also have known of the widely-discussed impact of the relatively short five-yard distance goal in promoting mass play versus a more open game. According to a Burnside associate, in developing their rules they considered five, ten, and fifteen yards for the distance to be gained, but ten yards was chosen as a workable compromise that could make the game more open (*Toronto Globe*, December 15, 1902:10).

After narrow, localized use mainly in intramural University of Toronto play (*Toronto Globe*, Nov. 8, 1901:8 and Dec. 11, 1901:10), the "Burnside" rules were adopted in 1902 by the province-wide Ontario Rugby Football Union (*Toronto Globe*, Dec. 22, 1902:10). Camp included in the 1903 *Spalding Guide* an article by an officer of the Ontario Union listing the Burnside rules and reporting their adoption by the Union (Frank D. Woodworth, "Rugby Football in Canada," 1903 *Spalding Guide*, 163–65).

With a ten-yard rule in use in Canada before it was in use in the United States, some have suggested that the Canadian rule was a model for U.S. rule makers. However, such a suggestion overlooks Camp's proposal of the ten-yard rule in 1893 and his continuing (and finally successful) advocacy during subsequent years for its installation in the United States. It also overlooks the resistance Camp faced in the United States, which a Canadian model would also have faced. The differences between the Burnside and U.S. games (such as the Canadian prohibition on interference) also would have limited a U.S. adoption of the Canadian ten-yard rule. In a December 13, 1904 letter, Woodworth wrote to Camp of the Ontario Union's happiness with the ten-yard rule, under which they managed an open game with needed yardage gains using "combination runs and [lateral] passes." But after Camp visited Canada in 1905 and witnessed Ontario games with the described plays, he contended in a Canadian speech that such plays would not succeed against U.S. defenses, arguing in effect that American interference rules were needed in sophisticated football to make a ten-yard rule effective (*Toronto Globe*, Oct. 23, 1905:10).

Despite acceptance of the Burnside rules by the Ontario Union, other Canadian teams and provinces resisted them (*Toronto Globe*, January 24, 1900: December 11, 1901; December 22, 1902:10), and the resulting diversity of Canadian rugby-centered rules (see 1903 *Spalding Guide*, 163–65) would have further limited their use as a model. Canadian historians note that Canada's football rules situation was in "chaos" until after World War I (T. A. Reed, compiler, *The Blue and White* [Toronto: The University of Toronto Press, 1944] 80–83 and 97–100, 83; and Gordon Currie, *100 Years of Canadian Football* [Toronto: Pagurian Press, 1968] 29–35).

10. Francis S. Bangs to Nicholas Murray Butler, October 28, 1905, Bangs Papers, 1905–10, folder, Columbia University Central Files, as cited in Smith, *Sports and Freedom*, 200.

11. Butler to Bangs, October 30, 1905, ibid.

12. *HGM* 14 (1905–6): 405–6.

13. Reid later recalled some of the events of this time for a *Boston Herald* reporter (*BH*, October 17, 1926, 7). See also Ronald A. Smith, "Harvard and Columbia and a Reconsideration of the 1905–06 Football Crisis," *JSH* 8, no. 3 (1981): 5–19. For Reid's and others' salaries, see note 41 of Smith's article.

14. *BH*, October 17, 1926, 7. See also *HGM* 14 (1905–6): 300.

15. *HGM* 14 (1905–6): 300, with committee members listed at page 488. Lewis's book was *A Primer of College Football* (New York: Harper, 1896).

16. Smith, *Big-Time Football*, 266. The flames of Harvard-Yale rivalry were further fanned by publication in the December 1905 *Harvard Graduate's Monthly* of a piece by a Harvard graduate vigorously attacking Yale as academically deficient and devoted only to winning in athletics; see *HGM* 14 (1905–6): 216–23. Camp and others in the Yale community were very upset and wanted Harvard to officially repudiate the article.

Chapter 42

1. Peabody to Roosevelt, September 16, 1905, TR Coll.

2. Besides well-known studies of Roosevelt's economic and political interventions, there have also been studies of Roosevelt's involvement in football's management. See, for example, Guy M. Lewis, "Theodore Roosevelt's Role in the 1905 Football Controversy," *Research Quarterly* 40 (December 1969): 717–24; Ronald A. Smith, "Harvard and Columbia and a Reconsideration of the 1905–06 Football Crisis," *JSH* 8, no. 3 (1981): 5–19; and John J. Miller, *The Big Scrum* (New York: HarperCollins, 2011).

3. *NYT*, October 10, 1905, 1.

4. Roosevelt to Camp, March 11, 1895, in *The Selected Letters of Theodore Roosevelt*, edited by H. W. Brands (New York: Cooper Square Press, 2001), 99; Roosevelt to Camp, September 17, 1895, Camp Papers, reel 15. Roosevelt's secretary G. B. Courtelyou canceled the invitation in a September 14, 1901, letter to Camp.

5. Brands, *Selected Letters*, 99.

6. Smith, *Big-Time Football*, 193–95; *NYT*, October 12, 1905; Roosevelt to Camp, October 11, 1905, TR Coll and Camp Papers, reel 15.

7. J. William White, "Football and Its Critics," *Outlook*, November 18, 1905, 662; *NYT*, November 21, 1905, 1.

8. *BH*, November 26, 1905; Smith, *Big-Time Football*, 316; Dashiell to Roosevelt, December 7, 1905, TR Coll.

9. Eliot to Roosevelt, undated copy incorporated in December 5, 1905, letter from Roosevelt to Dashiell, TR Coll.

10. Roosevelt to Dashiell, December 5, 1905, and Dashiell to Roosevelt, December 7, 1905, TR Coll.

11. Roosevelt to Dashiell, Dec 9, 1905, TR Coll.

12. Borden letter apparently forwarded to Camp about October 11 by William Loeb Jr., Roosevelt's secretary. Camp to Roosevelt, October 13, 1905, Camp Papers, reel 15.

13. Roosevelt to Camp, November 24, 1905, Camp Papers and TR Coll.

Chapter 43

1. *NYT*, November 26, 1905; *ChiTrib*, November 26, 1905.

2. *NYW*, Nov 26, 1905, 1; *NYT*, December 3, 1905.

3. *NYT*, November 29, 1905.

4. Theodore Francis Jones, *New York University* (New York: New York University Press, 1933), 151–91; *NYT*, November 30, 1905, 6.

5. *ChiTrib*, November 26, 1905.

6. *NYTrib*, November 27, 1905, 10.

7. Camp to Roosevelt, November 28, 1905, Camp Papers, reel 15. Curiously, a copy of this letter typed on the letterhead of the Harvard University Football Association is at the Harvard University Archives. Did Roosevelt show it or give it to Reid when the latter visited Roosevelt on December 4, as discussed in the next paragraph of the text?

8. *NYT*, November 30, December 5, 1905.

9. *NYT*, December 5, 1905.

10. Roosevelt to H. S. White, December 5, 1905, TR Coll.

11. *Princetonian*, December 7, 1905; Dashiell to Camp, December 4, Correslog.

12. Telegram Alice Camp to Walter, December 1, 1905, Camp Papers, reel 47, box 66, folders 6–9; Hadley memo, December 2, 1905, Hadley In. Hadley certainly knew Alice; and Alice and Mrs. Hadley had social contacts, for example, hosting receptions and the like together. See *Saturday Chronicle*, May 11, 18, 1907, for "Our Society" membership lists and events.

Chapter 44

1. Tim Cohane, *Gridiron Grenadiers* (New York: G. P. Putnam's Sons, 1948), 27–28.

2. Roosevelt, *Theodore Roosevelt: An Autobiography*, 245–49, 254, 270–72; Hamilton H. Howze, *A Cavalryman's Story* (Washington, D.C.: Smithsonian Institution Press, 1996), 4. Howze's time as a military aide at the White House was apparently from July 1904 to June 1905; Howze's obituary in the June 13, 1927, annual report of the Association of Graduates of the U.S. Military Academy does not report his service as a military aide but leaves this time period unfilled; Robert Howze's son Hamilton Howze states in his book that Robert Howze was a military aide at the White House during Roosevelt's term as president. Roosevelt, *Theodore Roosevelt: An Autobiography*, 245; Howze, *A Cavalryman's Story*, 4.

3. *NYTrib*, December 3, 1905.

4. Proceedings of the Army Athletic Council, December 5, 1905, West Point Archives, U.S. Military Academy Library, West Point, N.Y. (emphasis added).

5. MacCracken's underlying feelings were further revealed on December 20, 1905, at NYU's annual alumni dinner. MacCracken called the rules committee "Grand Dukes" like Russia's Grand Dukes, a "Committee on Misrule," "high and mighty potentates" who refuse to alter football in the face of an "almost universal verdict" that the game is "dull and deadly." *NYT*, December 21, 1905, 6.

6. *NYT*, December 9, 1905, 10.

7. Camp to Hadley, December 10, 1905, box 15, Hadley In.

8. The draft letter of resignation, dated December 12, 1905, and addressed to Dashiell, who was chairman of the committee, is found among the Dashiell correspondence on reel 7 of the Camp Papers.

9. Baird to Camp, February 7, 1906, copy at Bentley Historical Library, University of Michigan, Ann Arbor.

10. *NYT*, December 15, 16, 1905.

11. Curtiss to Camp on Spalding letterhead, December 15, 16, 1905, Camp Papers, reel 16.

12. Pierce to Camp telegram and letter, December 20, 1905, Camp Papers, reel 14.

13. Camp to Pierce, December 22, 1905, Camp Papers, reel 14.

14. See multiple items of correspondence from December 12 to 20 in Correslog, including particularly Camp's letter to the committee on December 15. Dashiell to Camp, December 17, 1905, Correslog.

15. Ibid. Yale backers were futilely trying to find their own support in Washington for Camp and his position. On December 6, 1905, George Sawyer wrote William Howard Taft, secretary of war in the Roosevelt administration, asking for "a strong word . . . in favor of Camp's [ten-yard] rule." Camp, Sawyer said, had "anticipated the present criticism and was stubbornly resisted in the rules committee." Sawyer to Taft, Camp Papers, reel 16.

16. Roosevelt to Dashiell, December 19, 1905, TR Coll.

17. Camp's telegram partially quoted in December 18 letter from Bell to Camp, Correslog.

18. *NYT*, December 29, 1905, 7.

19. Ibid.

20. Ibid.

21. Ibid.

22. Roosevelt to Dashiell, January 10, 1906, TR Coll. As the new MacCracken rules committee met in on January 6 to develop ideas on rules legislation and a plan for the amalgamated session, they were visited by Lieutenant Colonel Howze from West Point, who later told the press "he was the bearer of a confidential communication," but was "not in a position to state" publicly the nature of the communication or its source (see *NYT*, January 7, 1906, 8). Quite likely, Howze was there on behalf of Roosevelt in a further effort to encourage amalgamation. For Harvard rules, see *NYT*, January 10, 1906, 6; and *HGM* 14 (1905–6): 486–88.

23. *NYT*, January 11, 1906, 10.

24. *NYT*, January 13, 1906, 7; AIFRC Minutes, 3–4 (January 12, 1906, meeting minutes, 2–3).

25. AIFRC Minutes, January 12, 1906, 4.

26. Ibid.

27. Voltmer, *Brief History*, 17–21.

28. Roberta J. Park, "From Football to Rugby and Back, 1906–1919," *JSH* 11 (Winter 1984): 5–40.

Chapter 45

1. AIFRC Minutes, 5, under the heading "Meeting of the Sub-committee on Rules for Opening Play, January 13th and Continuing through the Following Week." AIFRC Minutes, 13 (January 27 minutes, 2).

2. Smith, *Big-Time Football*, 333.

3. AIFRC Minutes, 15. The "onside" kick got its name from its contrast with rugby's offside rules, which had been retained in American football rules. Under these still-held-

over rules, players on the kicking team in front of the kicker, such as players on the kicking team's line, were offside and ineligible to touch the kicked ball until the receiving team had touched it or the kicker had advanced downfield to their position. Hall proposed to change the held-over rugby rule by making all players on the kicking team onside as soon as the kicked ball touched the ground, thus allowing any player on the kicking team (as well as the receiving team) to down the ball as soon as it touched the ground and retain (or gain) possession for their team. With a well-placed kick, members of the kicking team might be closest to the ball when it struck the ground and by downing the ball achieve a significant advance.

4. AIFRC Minutes, 15.

5. Ibid., 16.

6. Ibid., 17.

7. By implication from other rules, either the passing team or the opponents could gain ball possession by recovering a forward passed ball that was touched but fell to the ground uncaught; this was made explicit in the 1907 rules, and a variation was introduced in 1908. See Rule 19, Sec. 5c, 1907 and 1908 *Spalding Guides*.

8. AIFRC Minutes, 13; 1906 *Spalding Guide*, Rule 20, (e); AIFRC Minutes, 12, 17, 18.

9. AIFRC Minutes, 22.

10. Wray's column, *SLPD*, April 12, 1953. See also *SLPD*, September 18, 22, 1906.

11. Edward B. Cochems, "The Forward Pass and On-Side Kick," in *How to Play Football*, edited by Walter Camp (New York: American Sports, 1907), 46; *SLPD*, April 12, 1953.

12. *SLPD*, November 4, 1906, 12; Nelson, *Anatomy of a Game*, 129.

13. *Baseball Magazine* 2 (November 1908): 57–60.

14. Camp, *The Book of Football*, 114–19.

15. Smith, *Big-Time Football*, xiii, 323, xx.

16. John Sayle Watterson, *College Football*, 401.

17. Rule 19, Sec. 4, 1907 *Spalding Guide*; Rule 19, Sec. 5c, 1908 *Spalding Guide*. After the initial amalgamation of 1906, the rules committee was formed for several subsequent years by a pro forma amalgamation of the old rules committee and a committee elected by the Intercollegiate Athletic Association. Reid was still Harvard's representative on the 1907 committee, though he would not coach Harvard in the fall because he was returning to California to be assistant headmaster at his father's preparatory high school; Reid was replaced as secretary by E. K. Hall, with Camp continuing as editor of the *Spalding Guide*.

18. Rule 5, 186, and Rule 15, Sec. 15, both in 1909 *Spalding Guide*.

19. A. A. Stagg, "Foot Ball in the Middle West," in 1909 *Spalding Guide*, 55–57.

Chapter 46

1. Watterson, *College Football*, 401; *NYT*, October 19, 31, November 15, 1909, 4.

2. Camp, *The Book of Football*, 79–82. Camp's concern was borne out and later discussed by Harvard's coach Percy Haughton in the latter's book *Football and How to Watch It*, 201–2. Camp's antagonist, Harvard's President Eliot, had retired in May 1909 at age seventy-five.

3. AIFRC 1910, 13, 15–18.

4. Ibid., 14. For Yale football leaders and alumni who disliked Sanford or opposed his involvement as a coach at Yale, see McCormick to Camp, February 12, 1913, reel 12; Stokes

(as Yale University secretary) to Camp, January 17, 1913, reel 20; and Stokes to Sanford, August 11, 1905, Camp Papers, reel 20.

5. AIFRC 1910, 22–28, esp. 22, 23, 27.

6. Ibid., 29–30.

7. Ibid., 32–33.

8. AIFRC 1910, 43 (emphasis added); Camp to Hadley, May 16, 1910, Camp Papers, reel 9.

9. *NYT*, May 4, 1910, 12; May 9, 1910, 8; May 4, 1910, 12.

10. AIFRC 1910, 54.

11. AIFRC 1910, 54, 57.

12. Ibid., 57. With Princeton having generally sided with Yale and Camp over the whole of the 1905–10 reform battles, Camp wrote Hadley after the vote reporting Princeton's reversal (Camp to Hadley, May 16, 1910, Reel 9, Camp Papers). Roper, who made the vote for Princeton, was a new voter, Princeton's coach in 1906–8 and coach-to-be in 1910–11 and 1919–30. In part, Roper's viewpoint is illustrated by a letter he sent to Princeton's President Wilson in June 1910, contending Camp opposed "the new rules for one simple reason, because Yale's style of play is practically destroyed." A biographical sketch of Roper in David L. Porter, ed., *Biographical Dictionary of American Sports, 1992–1995 Supplement* (Westport Connecticut: Greenwood Press, 1995), 517–19, credits Roper with "participating in the successful revolt against Walter Camp's domination" of the rules committee.

Roper's letter criticizing Camp arose as follows: Troubled by the increased deaths in 1909, the "Big Three" presidents—Hadley (Yale), Abbot Lawrence Lowell (who had succeeded President Eliot at Harvard) and Wilson (Princeton)—early in February 1910 appointed a committee of Camp, Percy Haughton (Harvard coach), and Howard H. Henry (Princeton representative) to advise them on the causes of injury and to suggest rule changes to reduce the danger. Having delayed deliberations until completion of the rule-committee's work, the smaller Camp-Haughton-Henry committee would now be acting, and the Roper/Princeton position would influence the smaller committee's report; perhaps that's the main reason Camp wrote to Hadley reporting the Roper/Princeton vote. On behalf of the smaller committee, Haughton drafted and sent to the three presidents a brief report that was basically a summary of the rules and positions just decided by the rules committee; Princeton's Henry signed Haughton's report but Camp did not. Wilson responded to Haughton about the report, questioning whether the new rules were sufficient but stating his willingness to use the rules for the upcoming season. Haughton informed Roper of Wilson's letter and presumably also of a letter he had received from Hadley criticizing the smaller committee's report, whereupon Roper wrote Wilson, noting Camp's influence on Hadley and Yale, stating the criticism of Camp noted above, and encouraging Wilson to allow play next season under the new rules. Documents related to the Camp-Haughton-Henry committee can be found in the Wilson Papers, Vol. 20 (aspects of the committee's formation are at pp. 11, 12, 54, 72, 88, 118); Camp's refusal to sign is referred to on 487 and 488; Haughton's report is on 539; Wilson's questioning of the sufficiency of the new rules is on 540; and Roper's letter to Wilson condemning Camp is on 547–48. For further discussion of the Hadley-Lowell-Wilson initiative, see John S. Watterson, "The Football Crisis of 1909–1910: The Response of the Eastern Big Three," *JSH* 8 No. 1 (Spring 1981): 33–49.

13. Powell, *Walter Camp*, viii–ix. Dashiell tribute to Camp at Camp's "retirement" dinner in February 1915, Camp Papers, reel 2, box 2, folder 35.

14. On travel of Reid and Camp together, see, for example, Walter Camp, "American Sports," *Century*, o.s., 79 (November 1909): 69.

15. *Outing*, October 1910, 17–25. Camp noted that officials would be required to determine whether:

- the ball was passed from a position at least five yards behind the line of scrimmage
- the pass traveled no more than twenty yards past the line of scrimmage
- backfield players of the passing team were, at the time of snapback, "at least one yard" back of the line of scrimmage
- no player from either side while in the act of catching a pass had been "tackled, thrown, pushed, pulled, shouldered or straight-armed until he had caught the ball and taken one step"
- any interference had merely been incidental to a bona fide attempt to catch or intercept the pass

16. 1911 *Spalding Guide*, Rule 19, Sec. 4, and title page.

17. *NYT*, November 26, 1911.

18. *NYT*, December 29, 1911.

19. 1912 *Spalding Guide*, Rule 21, Sec. 1. Camp's claim to have suggested four downs: 1913 *Spalding Guide*, 11.

20. 1912 *Spalding Guide*, Rule 19, Sec. 5; Rule 1, Sec. 1; Rule 5, Sec. 3.

21. 1912 *Spalding Guide*, Rule 2, Sec. 1.

22. 1913 *Spalding Guide*, 11.

Chapter 47

1. Camp to Root, April 4, 1905, Camp Papers, reel 15.

2. NHCC Minutes, folder D, 53. Further information about the NHCC headquarters and factory can be found in "The Architecture of Clock Square and a Brief for Its Preservation" (copy at Whitney Library, New Haven Museum, catalog no. TS 540 N3 H24).

3. Bailey, 78.

4. Statement at Camp's memorial service by William Lyon Phelps, *YAW* 34 (July 3, 1925).

5. Resolution by NHCC Board of Directors following Camp's death. Statement of E. P. Root quoted in Powell, *Walter Camp*, 149–50.

6. Camp, *The Substitute*, 93–96.

7. Walter Camp, *Jack Hall at Yale*.

8. Walter Camp, *Old Ryerson* ((New York: D. Appleton, 1911).

9. Walter Camp, *The Book of Football*.

10. Walter Camp, *Condensed Bridge for the Busy Man* (New York: P. F. Collier and Son).

11. Contract dated February 14, 1910, Camp Papers, reel 10, under Hurst and Company; *YAW* 11 (November 27, 1901): 76, publisher's box; Stokes to Thompson, September 22, 1906, Camp Papers, reel 20 (Yale University secretary section). No clear evidence has been found as to when Thompson began writing the Frank Armstrong books. The earliest letter

found definitely involving Thompson is dated February 15, 1912, whereas the first Frank Armstrong book was published in 1911.

12. Walter Camp, *Danny Fists* (New York: D. Appleton, 1913). Heyliger to Camp, March 31, 1914, Camp Papers. By 1913 Heyliger had written at least four sports fictions for boys. He reportedly got "his facts about boys from first hand observation." An ad for a Heyliger book in about 1913 reported that each year, Heyliger coaches "some baseball or football team of school boys."

Some significant philosophic views are revealed in the *Danny Fists* book. In Danny's slang name and in the book title, the name "Phipps" is replaced with "Fists" because Danny gets into a lot of fistfights. Danny's father approves of Danny's fighting spirit, and as a possible surprise the principal of the preparatory school Danny attends (Manor Hall) favors boxing for working out disagreements; the school has a boxing ring, boxing gloves, a referee, and a system of rules to govern the fighting. Most of the first forty pages of the book are devoted to fistfighting and include a major match in Manor Hall's boxing ring, where Danny knocks out an upper-class bully. Thirty years earlier, the book's approval of limited fistfighting by preparatory school students might well have raised eyebrows, but now it would be consistent with a positive valuation on physical toughness and fighting spirit, including in football and also with a growing acceptance in American society that a boy's fistfighting can be a sign of developing manly character. See E. Anthony Rotundo, *American Manhood* (New York: Basic Books, 1993), 222–46, esp. 225–26.

13. Fred C. Kelly, *George Ade* (Indianapolis: Bobbs-Merrill, 1947), 187–94; William E. Studwell et al., "College Fight Songs: An Annotated Anthology," *Music Reference Services Quarterly* 7, nos. 1–2 (1998); *College Fight Songs, A Supplementary Anthology* (New York: Haworth Press, 2001). See also *Music Reference Services Quarterly* 3–4 (1996): 34–35; Murray Sperber, *Shake Down the Thunder* (New York: Henry Holt, 1993); Cary Clive Burford, *We're Loyal to You, Illinois* (Danville, Ill.: Interstate, 1952), 161–62; and Joe Hendrickson, *The Tournament of Roses: The First 100 Years* (Los Angeles: Knapp Press, 1988), 11–12.

14. 1912 NCAA Proceedings, list of officers; 1916 NCAA Proceedings, 59. Pierce was born in Savannah, Illinois, October 23, 1865, but grew up in Traer, Iowa, where his father was a grain merchant. He attended Grinnell College for four years but left before graduation when he won appointment to West Point at age twenty-one. Older than most fellow students, he was elected president of his class and held that office through his life. Upon graduation from West Point, he served in various infantry assignments in New York, Puerto Rico, and the Philippines, interspersed with two assignments teaching chemistry at West Point; the last assignment at West Point was from 1901 to 1907, when the MacCracken conferences were held and the NCAA was formed. From 1912 to 1915, he served in China and the Philippines, during which time he resigned from the presidency of the NCAA. Upon returning to the United States, he was reelected NCAA president in 1916 and continued to serve until 1930, though he served in Europe during World War I as commanding general of an infantry brigade. In 1920 he retired from active service in the army and entered the employ of Standard Oil of New Jersey for thirteen years, the last four of which he was assistant to the president. See the *Annual Report of the Association of Graduates of the U.S. Military Academy*, June 10, 1940, U.S. Military Academy Library, 201–9. Camp and Pierce maintained friendly relations even though Yale continued to resist joining the NCAA.

15. 1907 NCAA Proceedings, 22; *NYT*, September 26, 1908, 8.

16. *New Haven City Directories* for the cited years. For a discussion of Professor Sumner's declining health, see A. G. Keller, *Reminiscences of William Graham Sumner* (New Haven, Conn.: Yale University Press, 1933), 107–10; and *NHReg*, June 4, 1917.

17. U.S. Census for 1920.

18. Alumni record of Walter Camp Jr., YUMA. Walter Jr. was divorced by Frances in 1927. He had three additional marriages before dying at age forty-nine of chronic pulmonary tuberculosis in Los Angeles, where he had been associated with the motion picture industry. U.S. Census for 1920. Janet's first marriage ended in 1925. After a short second marriage, she was married to Gilbert Troxell, a Yale curator with whom she shared an interest in languages and collection of original historical literature and related materials. She collected and wrote about manuscripts by and related to Dante Gabriel Rossetti, a mid-1800s English poet, illustrator, painter, and translator, and the larger Rossetti family; her collection was eventually acquired by the Princeton University Library. She also entered into a vigorous correspondence defending her father against questions of whether he originated All-America teams. In her will, she left a bequest of more than one million dollars to Hopkins School, the successor of Hopkins Grammar School, which her father attended and of which he was a longtime trustee, to provide scholarships for Hopkins students who are of "good moral character, proficient in athletics or any program promoting physical fitness, all of which my late father held in high esteem during his life without discrimination as to race, color, sex, nationality or religion." Princeton University Library Finding Aid, retrieved March 10, 2017; correspondence between the author and Thom Peters of the Hopkins School faculty.

Chapter 48

1. "Football Coaching since 1899," *YAW* 25 (January 28, 1916): 561.

2. Camp, *Jack Hall,* 106–10.

3. Alice Camp to Vance McCormick, undated but approximately March 15, 1916, Camp Papers, reel 47, box 66, folders 6–9.

4. Henry Beach Needham, "The College Athlete," *McClure's Magazine*, June 1905, 115–28.

5. *Obituary Record of Graduates of Yale University,* June 1910, 1285. Hogan died of Bright's disease five years after his Yale graduation. Stokes to Camp, January 11, 1908, Camp Papers, reel 20 (Yale University secretary section).

6. Stokes to Camp, October 14, 1905, Camp Papers, reel 20 (Yale University secretary section) ("Details of expenditures have to be left so largely to different undergraduate managers"); and speech of Hadley to New York alumni in *Yale News,* January 20, 1906 ("We . . . give the managers and captains as much freedom as possible [but] they must realize the sums of money coming into their hands are held in trust").

7. Clarence Deming, "Athletics in College Life," *Outlook*, July 1905, 569–72; *NYEP*, January 18, 1906.

8. *NYEP*, January 18, 1906.

9. *Crimson*, March 16, 1925.

10. As to Camp's oversight, see Camp to Frank B. Smith, July 19, 1900, Camp Papers, reel 16.

11. Smith, *Big-Time Football*, 11; minutes of the Executive Committee of Pennsylvania State College, 62 and 63 (July 1900), 3–53 (1901), and 3–128 (1903).

12. The Stokes memorandum is in Camp Papers, reel 38, box 58, folder 409.

13. Stokes to Camp, October 14, 1905, Camp Papers, reel 20 (Yale University secretary section).

14. Beebe to Hadley, September 27, 1905, Hadley In; Beebe to Camp, January 16, 1906, Camp Papers, reel 2. Beebe also noted that Yale College, of which Beebe was a faculty member, was now paying part of Camp's salary, and he wanted a voice with other faculty members in defining Camp's status.

15. The full eighteen-page report, dated January 31, 1906, is in Camp Papers, reel 19, folder 801.

16. Camp to Hadley, March 6, 1906, Camp Papers, reel 9.

17. "Matt Manning" appears in *Jack Hall*, 137; Stokes to Camp, January 11, 1908, Camp Papers, reel 20 (Yale University secretary section).

18. 1898 *Spalding Guide*, advertising page at end of booklet; Dashiell to Camp, November 4, 1902, and Camp to Dashiell, November 6, 1902, Camp Papers, reel 7; 1903 *Spalding Guide*, Rule 27(a) and p. 189.

19. Haughton, *Football and How to Watch It*, 123.

20. Camp, *The Book of Football*, 236–47.

21. Glenn Warner, *Football for Players and Coaches* (Carlisle, Pa.: n.p., 1912), 6.

22. *YAW* 25 (February 4, 1916): 586.

23. Camp to Tompkins, December 10, 1910, Camp Papers, reel 17.

24. Ibid.

25. Camp to Tompkins, November 21, 1912, Camp Papers, reel 17.

26. *YNews*, January 13, 1913, 1.

27. Detailed discussions of the Harvard stadium may be found, for example, in I. N. Hollis, "Origin of the Harvard Stadium," *Harvard Engineering Journal* 3 (June 1904): 92–103; and "The Steel-Concrete Work of the Harvard Stadium," *American Architect and Building News* (August 13, 1904): 85.

28. *YAW* 21 (February 23, 1912): 557, 562–63.

29. Yale alumni record for Charles Ferry.

30. Leitch, *A Princeton Companion*, 351ff.

Chapter 49

1. *YNews*, October 10, 1914, 6. The job from which he resigned was treasurer of the Yale University Athletic Association, a position he assumed in 1912 when the Yale Financial Union was folded into the newly organized YUAA; the Yale Financial Union was replaced by a financial committee of the new association, with a treasurer of the association to be elected annually, and Camp was elected. See *YNews*, March 22, 1912.

In 1914, when Camp resigned as treasurer of the YUAA, the *Yale News* (October 10, 1914) reported he would continue as "Chairman of the Board." But three months later, on January 15, 1915, the *Yale News* reported that Professor Robert Corwin of Yale's Sheffield Scientific School had been elected chairman of the association, thereby completing Camp's withdrawal from active participation and service as a director of Yale athletics. See Corwin to Camp, January 18, 1915, reel 19, folder 802, explaining Corwin would take the job only if he was sure Camp wanted to resign.

2. Copies of the tributes are in Camp Papers, reel 2, box 2, folder 35. Camp's election as emeritus member for life is reported in the *Yale News* of December 16, 1915, 3, in Parke Davis's tribute. The tributes could have been written after the meeting; at the end of the meeting, Camp asked Davis for a summary of the tributes he could show Alice, but Davis asked the individual members to give him their tribute in writing.

3. After noting that Camp had been elected an emeritus member, the December 16, 1915, *Yale News* article reported, "There is a question whether Mr. Camp will attend the Rules Committee meeting next year."

4. Ibid.

5. *YNews*, February 18, 28, 1916; 1916 *Spalding Guide*, title page listing rules committee members, with Camp named as secretary.

6. *YNews*, January 12, 1915, 1.

7. Ibid. (emphasis added); *NYT*, January 30, 1915.

8. Michael Barton, ed., *Citizen Extraordinaire* (Mechanicsburg, Pa.: Stackpole Books, 2004), ix–x.

9. McCormick to Camp, November 27, 1912, Camp Papers, reel 12; McCormick to Camp, January 15, 1916, Camp Papers, reel 12.

10. *YNews*, February 3, 1916.

11. *YNews*, February 3, 1916, 1.

12. Alice Camp to McCormick, Camp Papers, reel 47, box 66, folders 6–9; Camp to McCormick, March 15, 1916, Camp Papers, reel 12.

13. Barton, *Citizen Extraordinaire*, x; Camp to McCormick, telegrams of February 22 and 23 and letter of February 24, Camp Papers, reel 12.

14. Camp to McCormick, April 19, 21, 1916, Camp Papers, reel 12.

15. Camp to McCormick, August 25, September 8, October 18, 1916, Camp Papers, reel 12. "Neurasthenia," or nervous exhaustion, could reveal itself as migraine headaches, poor digestion, fatigue, depression, or pain in various parts of the body. Beginning about this time, Walter and Alice occasionally went to a resort in Maine, where the advertised benefits were rest and relaxation.

16. Haughton to Camp, November, 1916, Camp Papers, reel 9. For Camp's hopes following Yale's 1916 season, see W. H. Morse to Camp, December 3, 1919, Camp Papers, reel 13.

Chapter 50

1. Camp to McCormick, April 10, 1917; *NYT*, June 24, 1917, 60. A preparer by nature, Camp had for some time been encouraging the country to prepare militarily. In September 1914, a month after Europeans began the fighting of World War I, Camp published in his syndicated sports column a poem with the opening lines:

Guard your shores and train your men,
    Teach your growing youth to fight,
Make your plans ere once again
    Ships of foes appear in sight.

During succeeding years, he continued to support a military-readiness movement led in part by General Leonard Wood, a football-loving acquaintance from Camp's mid-1890s Stanford coaching days.

2. *NYT*, July 22, 1917; F. D. Roosevelt to Camp, June 2, 1917, Camp Papers, reel 15; also reprinted in Kathleen D. Valenzi, ed., *Champion of Sport*, 89.

3. *NYT*, July 22, 1917.

4. Camp to Daniels, May 3, 21, 1917, Camp Papers, reel 6.

5. Wanda Ellen Wakefield, *Playing to Win* (Albany: State University of New York Press, 1997), 12.

6. Telegram, Daniels to Camp, July 7, 1917, Camp Papers, reel 6; Joseph E. Raycroft, *Mass Physical Training* (Washington, D.C.: United States Infantry Association, 1920), v; Walter Camp, "Navy Training Camp Activities," *NCAA Proceedings* 12 (1917): 11.

7. Walter Camp, "What I Am Trying to Do," *World's Work* (October 1923): 600–604. One illustration of Camp's belief in the value of an exercise program was his advocacy of physical training for aviators, contending it would improve the coordination of mind over muscle and increase suppleness and quickness of action that might save an aviator or plane in a delicate situation. He believed pilot fatigue resulted in lost aircraft and pilots and that savings in expensive equipment and trained personnel would more than pay the cost of trainers on site. He wanted trainers assigned to each naval aviation station to assist and ensure the training, and he urged colleges to make their trainers available. See Camp's speech in the 1917 NCAA Proceedings, 11–12; Walter Camp, "You Pass Your Physical Zenith between 31 and 35," *American Magazine,* March 1919, 31–33; and Camp, "What I Am Trying to Do," 603.

8. Camp, "What I Am Trying to Do," 603; *Outing,* November 1918, 98. The origin of the name is not known, though Camp used it in the navy and later in a number of different magazines and books, suggesting he had title or freedom to use it. Evidence Camp used the Daily Dozen name in his navy work appears in a July 10, 1918, letter from Colonel L. Williamson to Camp in Camp Papers, reel 17, which thanks Camp for sending "the Daily Dozen Set-Up" in response to Williamson's request. Also, the November 1918 *Outing* article, which necessarily was prepared before the end of World War I, discusses preparation of the Daily Dozen exercises for the navy. How the exercises happened to be presented in *Outing* is not known, but Camp later wrote that his purpose with the Daily Dozen was philanthropic. He may not have had a clear idea how or if he was going to use or distribute the Daily Dozen program. *Outing* was on its last legs (it ceased publication in 1923), so if Camp was uncertain about how he would use the exercises, he could have given *Outing* permission. He does not appear to have written the *Outing* article.

9. Walter Camp, "Keeping the Nation Fit," *Independent* 71 (December 21, 1918): 400–401.

10. Camp, "What I Am Trying to Do," 601; Camp, "You Pass Your Physical Zenith," 33.

11. Walter Camp, *Keeping Fit All the Way: How to Obtain and Maintain Health, Strength and Efficiency* (New York: Harper, 1919), *Athletes All: Training, Organization and Play* (New York: Scribners, 1919), *Handbook on Health and How to Stay Fit* (New York: Appleton, 1920), *The Daily Dozen for Men and Women* (New York: Reynolds, 1921), and *Training for Sport* (New York: Scribners, 1921).

12. Camp, "What I Am Trying to Do," 602.

13. C. H. Smith of Reynolds Publishing Company to Camp, May 14, 1924, Camp Papers, reel 14. Camp received a royalty of one half cent per book. The 1925 book was published after his death: Walter Camp, *The Daily Dozen* (New York: Reynolds, 1925).

14. Powell, *Walter Camp*, 173–75; Camp, "What I Am Trying to Do," 604.

15. SQ, question 9.

16. *New Haven 1889 City Yearbook*, 303–4.

17. Questionnaire, October 12, 1920, Camp Papers, reel 4, box 5, folder 137.

18. Walter Camp, "The Craze for Costliness in Golf," *World's Work* 48 (July 1924): 313–17.

19. Walter Camp, "Are City Golfers Free and Equal?," *Collier's*, July 7, 1923, 9–10; Camp, "Craze for Costliness."

Chapter 51

1. "The Growth of Football," in 1921 *Spalding Guide*, 8–9; "Highlights of the Football Season, 1921," in 1922 *Spalding Guide* 43–45.

2. 1922 *Spalding Guide*, 43. The list of stadiums in the table came from a table in Ronald A. Smith, "Far More than Commercialism: Stadium Building from Harvard's Innovations to Stanford's 'Dirt Bowl,'" *International Journal of the History of Sport* 25 (September 2008): 1460, supplemented from a list of stadiums in Judith S. Baughman, *American Decades, 1920–29* (New York: Gale Research, 1996), 437. For "capacity when built," some information was obtained from *Wikipedia* histories for individual stadiums.

3. Janet Lever, "The *Chicago Tribune* Sports Page, 1900–1975," *Sociology of Sport Journal* 1, no. 4 (1984): 299–313; Michael Oriard, *King Football*, 38–64.

4. *Collier's*, September 6, 1924, 22; September 27, 1924, 24.

5. Walsh to Camp, March 22, 1924, Camp Papers, reel 5, under Collier's correspondence.

6. *World's Work* (November 1923): 101–5, 102.

7. Ibid.

Chapter 52

1. NHCC Minutes, folder E (1917–37), 23; NHCC Minutes, folder E, shareholder meeting, January 26, 1921.

2. NHCC Minutes, folder E, board of directors meeting, February 23, 1921; May 24, 1922.

3. Ibid., June 28, 1922. Whitehead was a graduate of Lewis Institute in Chicago (which became part of the Illinois Institute of Technology), who had worked several years for Consolidated Edison in Chicago and then moved to New York to work in the construction industry before being hired by Burr. See Lockwood Barr, "The New Haven Clock Company," *Bulletin of the National Association of Watch and Clock Collectors, Inc.* 71 (December 1957): 11.

4. NHCC Minutes, folder E, board of directors meeting, August 10, September 27, 1922; NHCC Minutes, folder E, shareholder meeting, January 1923.

5. NHCC Minutes, folder E, special board of directors meeting, February 19, 1923, 92.

6. *New Haven City Directory* for 1923.

7. *NYT*, March 13,1925, 15.

8. *NYW*, March 15, 1925, 1; *Collier's*, March 28, 1925, 17–19; April 25, 1925, 15, 43; September 12, 1925, 18–19.

9. *New Haven Journal-Courier*, March 16, 1925.

10. *YAW* 34 (July 3, 1925); *DAB*, supp. 1:118; NCAA Proceedings 7:1, 11:59.

11. *YAW* 34 (July 3, 1925).

12. Ibid.

13. Grantland Rice, "An All-Time All-American," *Collier's*, May 9, 1925, 10, 46.

14. Yale University News Statement from Secretary's Office, June 9, 1927.

15. NCAA Proceedings, 20:59. Yale University News Statement from Secretary's Office, June 9, 1927, 2. Over the years, Camp has also been honored with other memorials: Hopkins School (Hopkins Grammar School renamed and repurposed as a country day school, with multiple buildings on a 108-acre New Haven campus) named a large and beautiful athletic center—three basketball courts, swimming pool, fitness, wrestling and weight rooms, and administrative space—the Walter Camp Athletic Center. And in 1967, a group of New Haven civic leaders established the Walter Camp Football Foundation. A primary activity is to annually name an All-America team, thus continuing under Camp's name the institution he began in 1889. The team is chosen by coaches and sports information directors of Football Bowl System schools (the most highly rated football conferences) and is feted along with other honorees—player of the year, coach of the year, man of the year, and others—at a major banquet on the Yale campus. The foundation also supports a variety of charitable and youth-centered causes financially and in other ways.

Appendix

1. *Princetonian*, November 30, 1876, 7–8. Rule 59 enacted at the 1876 founding convention called for "a referee" and "two judges"; the same officials had been specified three years earlier in the rules adopted when soccer-playing American colleges formed an association (see *Courant*, October 27, 1873). One "judge," later called an "umpire," was to represent each competing college and to help "reason" out disputes in a gentlemanly way. However, that is not what happened; with the referee in practice exercising decisive power, the judges or umpires became quite partisan and were eventually discarded.

2. Ibid., where the pertinent rule, Rule 7, is quoted; see also *Courant*, November 25, 1876, 67. For comparison, Rule 7 of *The Rugby Game: Rugby Union Rules* (New Haven, Conn.: Tuttle, Morehouse, and Taylor), found in YUMA, file Yed5, folder 7-1, box "Undated to 1899," reads, "A match shall be decided by a majority of goals only."

3. 1879 Rules, Rule 61.

4. *Crimson*, October 15, 1880.

5. 1882 Rules, Rule 33.

6. *Crimson*, December 9, 14, 1882; *Spirit of the Times*, December 23, 1882; 1883 *Football Rules*, Rule 27.

7. *YNews*, December 6, 1883; *Crimson*, December 8, 1883; 1884 *Football Rules*.

8. 1885 *Football Rules*. See also *YNews*, February 9, October 12, 1885; and *Princetonian*, February 13, October 12, 1885.

9. 1887 *Football Rules*, Rule 16; 1887 IFA Constitution, Art. III, Sec. 6.

10. *YNews*, March 5, 1888; *Princetonian*, March 7, 1888; 1888 *Football Rules*, by implication from Rules 10, 24, and 25.

11. *YNews*, March 5, 1888; *Princetonian*, March 7, 1888; 1888 *Football Rules*, Rule 27.

12. 1889 *Football Rules*, Rule 15.

13. Ibid.

14. Ibid., Rule 16.

15. 1890 *Football Rules*, Rule 28.

16. 1892 *Spalding Guide*, Rule 15.

17. 1894 *Spalding Guide*, Rule 14.

18. Ibid., Rule 19.

19. Ibid., Rule 30.

20. Ibid., Rule 8.

21. Ibid., Rule 26.

22. 1896 *Spalding Guide*, Rule 22.

23. 1898 *Spalding Guide*, Rule 27.

24. Ibid., Rule 26.

25. 1903 *Spalding Guide*, Rule 18.

26. Ibid., note following Rule 1.

27. Ibid., Rule 13.

28. Ibid., Rule 27.

29. 1904 *Spalding Guide*, Rule 26.

30. Ibid., Rule 13.

31. 1905 *Spalding Guide*, note following Rule 20.

32. Ibid., note following Rule 27(b).

33. 1906 *Spalding Guide*, Rule 15.

34. Ibid., Rule 14.

35. Ibid., Rule 16, exception (2).

36. Ibid., Rule 5(c).

37. Ibid., Rule 22(c).

38. 1907 *Spalding Guide*, Rule 19, Sec. 4, penalty.

39. Ibid., Rules 27 and 30.

40. 1908 *Spalding Guide*, Rule 19, Sec. 5(c).

41. 1909 *Spalding Guide*, Rule 5.

42. Ibid., Rule 15, Sec. 15.

43. 1910 *Spalding Guide*, Rule 19, Sec. 3.

44. Ibid., Rule 8, Sec. 1.

45. Ibid., Rule 17, Sec. 6.

46. Ibid., Rule 3, Sec. 2.

47. Ibid., Rule 7, Sec. 1(b).

48. 1911 *Spalding Guide*, Rule 19, Sec. 4.

49. 1912 *Spalding Guide*, Rule 21, Sec. 1.

50. Ibid., Rule 1, Sec. 1.

51. Ibid., Rule 19, Sec. 3.

52. Ibid., Rule 19, Sec. 5.

53. Ibid., Rule 2.
54. 1913 *Spalding Guide*, Rule 6, Sec. 2.
55. Ibid., Rule 18, Sec. 3(a) and (b).
56. 1914 *Spalding Guide*, Rule 18, Sec. 9.
57. Ibid., Rule 23, Sec. 2.
58. Ibid., Rule 18, Sec. 6.
59. Ibid., Rule 14, Sec. 14.
60. Ibid., Rule 24, Sec. 4.
61. 1915 *Spalding Guide*, Rule 3, note at end.
62. 1916 *Spalding Guide*, 123; 1917 *Spalding Guide*, 123.
63. 1920 *Spalding Guide*, Rule 15, Sec. 1.
64. Ibid., Rule 14, Sec. 6 and penalty.
65. 1921 *Spalding Guide*, Rule 14, Secs. 13 and 14.
66. 1922 *Spalding Guide*, Rule 10.
67. 1924 *Spalding Guide*, Rule 10.

Selected Bibliography

Andrews, Alfred. *Genealogy and Ecclesiastical History*. Chicago: A. H. Andrews, 1867.

Bagg, Lyman H. *Four Years at Yale*. New Haven, Conn.: Charles C. Chatfield, 1871.

Blanchard, John A. *The H Book of Harvard Athletics*. Cambridge, Mass.: Harvard Varsity Club / Harvard University Press, 1923

Bragdon, Henry Wilkinson. *Woodrow Wilson: The Academic Years*. Cambridge, Mass.: Belknap Press, 1967.

Camp, David Nelson. *Recollections of a Long and Active Life*. Edited by his grandchildren. New Britain, Conn.: Humford Press, 1917).

Camp, Walter. *American Football*. 1891. Reprint, New York: Arno Press, 1974.

———. *The Book of Football*. New York: Century, 1910.

———. *Football: How to Coach a Team*. Boston: Wright and Ditson, 1886. Copy in Babson Library, Archives and Special Collections, Springfield College, Springfield, Mass.

———, comp. *Football Facts and Figures*. New York: Harper and Brothers, 1894.

———. *Jack Hall at Yale*. New York: D. Appleton, 1909.

———. *The Substitute*. New York: New York Book, 1908.

Camp, Walter, and Lorin F. Deland. *Football*. Boston: Houghton Mifflin, 1896.

Claassen, Harold, and Steve Boda Jr., eds. *Ronald Encyclopedia of Football*. 3rd ed. New York: Ronald Press, 1963.

Danzig, Allison. *The History of American Football: Its Great Teams, Players and Coaches*. Englewood Cliffs, N.J.: Prentice Hall, 1956.

Davis, Parke H. *Football: The American Intercollegiate Game*. New York: Charles Scribner's Sons, 1911.

Davis, Thomas B. *Chronicles of Hopkins Grammar School*. New Haven, Conn.: Quinnipiac Press, 1938.

Des Jardins, Julie. *Walter Camp: Football and the Modern Man*. New York: Oxford University Press, 2015.

Dunning, Eric, and Kenneth Sheard. *Barbarians, Gentlemen and Players*. New York: New York University Press, 1979.

Edwards, William H. *Football Days*. New York: Moffat, Yard, 1916.

Guttmann, Allen. *From Ritual to Record*. New York: Columbia University Press, 1978.

Harvey, Adrian. *Football: The First Hundred Years*. London: Routledge, 2005.

Haughton, Percy D. *Football and How to Watch It*. Boston: Little, Brown, 1924.

Hughes, Thomas. *Tom Brown's School Days*. Boston: Ginn, 1918.

James, Henry. *Charles W. Eliot*. 2 vols. Boston: Houghton Mifflin, 1930.

Kelley, Brooks Mather. *Yale: A History*. New Haven, Conn.: Yale University Press, 1974.

Leitch, Alexander. *A Princeton Companion*. Princeton, N.J.: Princeton University Press, 1978.

Levine, Peter. *A. G. Spalding and the Rise of Baseball*. New York: Oxford University Press, 1985.

Link, Arthur S., ed. *The Papers of Woodrow Wilson*. Princeton, N.J.: Princeton University Press, 1966.

Macrory, Jennifer. *Running with the Ball*. London: CollinsWillow, 1991.

Mangan, J. A., and James Walvin, eds. *Manliness and Morality*. New York: St. Martin's Press, 1987.

Morison, Samuel Eliot. *Three Centuries of Harvard*. Cambridge, Mass.: Harvard University Press, 1936.

Mott, Frank L. *A History of American Magazines*. Cambridge, Mass.: Harvard University Press, 1957.

Nelson, David M. *Anatomy of a Game*. Newark: University of Delaware Press, 1994.

Oriard, Michael. *King Football*. Chapel Hill: University of North Carolina Press, 2001.

———. *Reading Football: How the American Press Created an American Spectacle*. Chapel Hill: University of North Carolina Press, 1993.

Osterweis, Rollin G. *Three Centuries of New Haven, 1638–1938*. New Haven, Conn.: Yale University Press, 1953.

Patton, Cornelius H., and Walter T. Field. *Eight O'Clock Chapel*. Boston: Houghton Mifflin, 1927.

Pierson, George W. *Yale College: An Educational History*. New Haven, Conn.: Yale University Press, 1952.

Powell, Harford, Jr. *Walter Camp*. Boston: Little, Brown, 1926.

Presbrey, Frank, and James H. Moffatt, eds. *Athletics at Princeton*. New York: Frank Presbrey, 1901.

Roosevelt, Theodore. *Theodore Roosevelt: An Autobiography*. New York: Macmillan, 1914.

Rottenberg, Dan. *Fight on, Pennsylvania*. Philadelphia: University of Pennsylvania Press, 1985.

Slosson, Edwin E. *Great American Universities*. New York: Macmillan, 1910.

Smith, Ronald A., ed. *Big-Time Football at Harvard, 1905: The Diary of Coach Bill Reid*. Urbana: University of Illinois Press, 1994.

———. *Pay for Play: A History of Big-Time College Athletic Reform*. Urbana: University of Illinois Press, 2011.

———. *Sports and Freedom*. New York: Oxford University Press, 1990.

Stagg, Amos Alonzo. *Touchdown! "As Told by Coach Amos Alonzo Stagg to Wesley Winans Stout."* New York: Longmans, Green, 1927.

Stevenson, Louise L. *Scholarly Means to Evangelical Ends*. Baltimore: Johns Hopkins University Press, 1986.

Stott, Andrew J. *Indiana Football: College, Athletic Club and High School*. Indianapolis: Carlon and Hollenbeck, 1896.

Twombley, Henry B. *Personal Reminiscences of a Yale Football Player*. Private publication.

Valenzi, Kathleen D., ed. *Champion of Sport*. Charlottesville, Va.: Howell Press, 1990.

Veysey, Laurence R. *The Emergence of the American University*. Chicago: University of Chicago Press, 1965.

Voltmer, Carl D. *A Brief History of the Intercollegiate Conference of Faculty Representatives*. New York: n.p., 1935.

Watterson, John Sayle. *College Football*. Baltimore: Johns Hopkins University Press, 2000.

Welch, Lewis Sheldon, and Walter Camp. *Yale: Her Campus, Class-Rooms, and Athletics*. Boston: L. C. Page, 1899.

Weyand, Alexander M. *The Saga of American Football*. New York: Macmillan, 1955.

Index

ROGER R. TAMTE is a patent attorney and scholar of early American football who has studied Camp for many years.

The University of Illinois Press
is a founding member of the
Association of American University Presses.

University of Illinois Press
1325 South Oak Street
Champaign, IL 61820-6903
www.press.uillinois.edu